MEGUMI OSUGA

APPARENTLY MY PERSONAL FATIGUE HIT ITS BREAKING POINT WHILE I WAS DRAWING THE COVER FOR VOLUME 4. I ACTUALLY FELL ASLEEP IN THE MIDDLE OF SPEAKING A SENTENCE. THE MYSTERIES OF THE HUMAN BODY... HANG IN THERE, ME!! IT'S NOT BEDTIME YET. THINGS CAN GET REALLY HARD, BUT IT'S STILL FUN DRAWING MANGA.

MEGUMI OSUGA

BORN DECEMBER 21 IN CHIBA PREFECTURE, MEGUMI OSUGA MADE HER DEBUT WITH *TONPACHI*, WHICH RAN IN *SHONEN SUNDAY R*, AND HAD A SHORT SERIES IN *SHONEN SUNDAY SUPER* CALLED *HONOU NO ANA NO YOMI*. IN 2007, HER SERIALIZATION OF *MAOH: JUVENILE REMIX* STARTED IN *SHONEN SUNDAY*.

KOTARO ISAKA

BORN IN 1971 IN CHIBA PREFECTURE, KOTARO ISAKA IS ONE OF THE MOST POPULAR JAPANESE NOVELISTS AND HAS RECEIVED NUMEROUS AWARDS. HE HAS MANY TITLES UNDER HIS BELT, MOST OF WHICH HAVE BEEN

MAOH: JUVENILE REMIX

Volume 04

Shonen Sunday Edition

Original Story by **KOTARO ISAKA**
Story and Art by **MEGUMI OSUGA**

© 2007 Kotaro ISAKA, Megumi OSUGA/Shogakukan
All rights reserved.
Original Japanese edition "MAOH JUVENILE REMIX" published by SHOGAKUKAN Inc.

Logo and cover design created by Isao YOSHIMURA & Bay Bridge Studio.

Translation/Stephen Paul
Touch-up Art & Lettering/James Dashiell
Design/Sam Elzway
Editor/Alexis Kirsch

Printed in the U.S.A.

Published by VIZ Media, LLC
P.O. Box 77010
San Francisco, CA 94107

10 9 8 7 6 5 4 3 2 1
First printing, February 2011

MAOH
JUVENILE REMIX

ORIGINAL STORY BY
KOTARO ISAKA

STORY AND ART BY
MEGUMI OSUGA

THE STORY UNTIL NOW

Nekota City is roiling under the effects of the New Urban Center Project, an attempt to develop a high-class corporate mega-complex over a poor neighborhood while ignoring the existing socioeconomic issues of the city. Ando, a teenager with a mysterious "ventriloquism" ability, learns of the hidden dark side of Inukai, the charismatic young leader of the vigilante group Grasshopper that has sworn to protect the city. As Inukai's influence and leadership rapidly transform the attitude of the citizenry, Ando feels a stab of fear for the future of his city. When the two met in person, Inukai said that he believed it was his role to change the world. And he tells Ando, "It might be your role to stop me."

Surprisingly, the son of the president of the Anderson Group, the large foreign conglomeration that is working with the mayor to push forward the New Urban Center Project, joins Ando's class at school. Meanwhile, unexplained accidents plague the Anderson Group's construction sites. When President Anderson learns that the accidents are being caused by agents of Grasshopper, he hires a deadly assassin, Suzumebachi, to take them out.

One night, while she is hunting down Grasshoppers, Suzumebachi runs across Ando and Machiko. Now desperate to get Machiko treatment for Suzumebachi's poison, Ando is rescued by a passing police car. But the car suspiciously takes them to a restricted zone. In the instant that Suzumebachi readies her final strike, a large group of masked Grasshopper agents appears. Ando and Machiko are saved, and Suzumebachi is apprehended. Shocked, Ando looks up to see...Inukai.

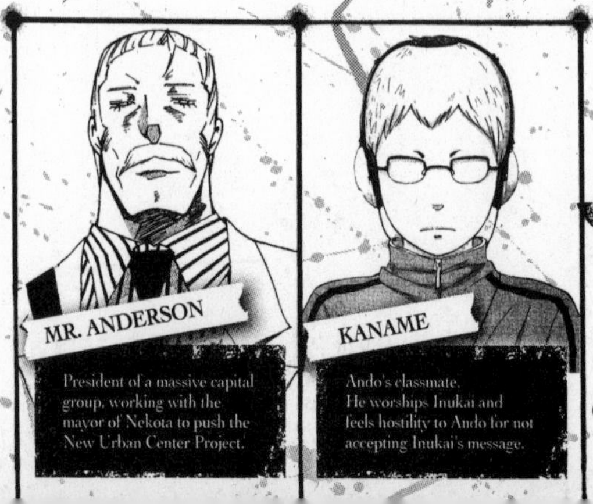
MR. ANDERSON
President of a massive capital group, working with the mayor of Nekota to push the New Urban Center Project.
KANAME
Ando's classmate. He worships Inukai and feels hostility to Ando for not accepting Inukai's message.

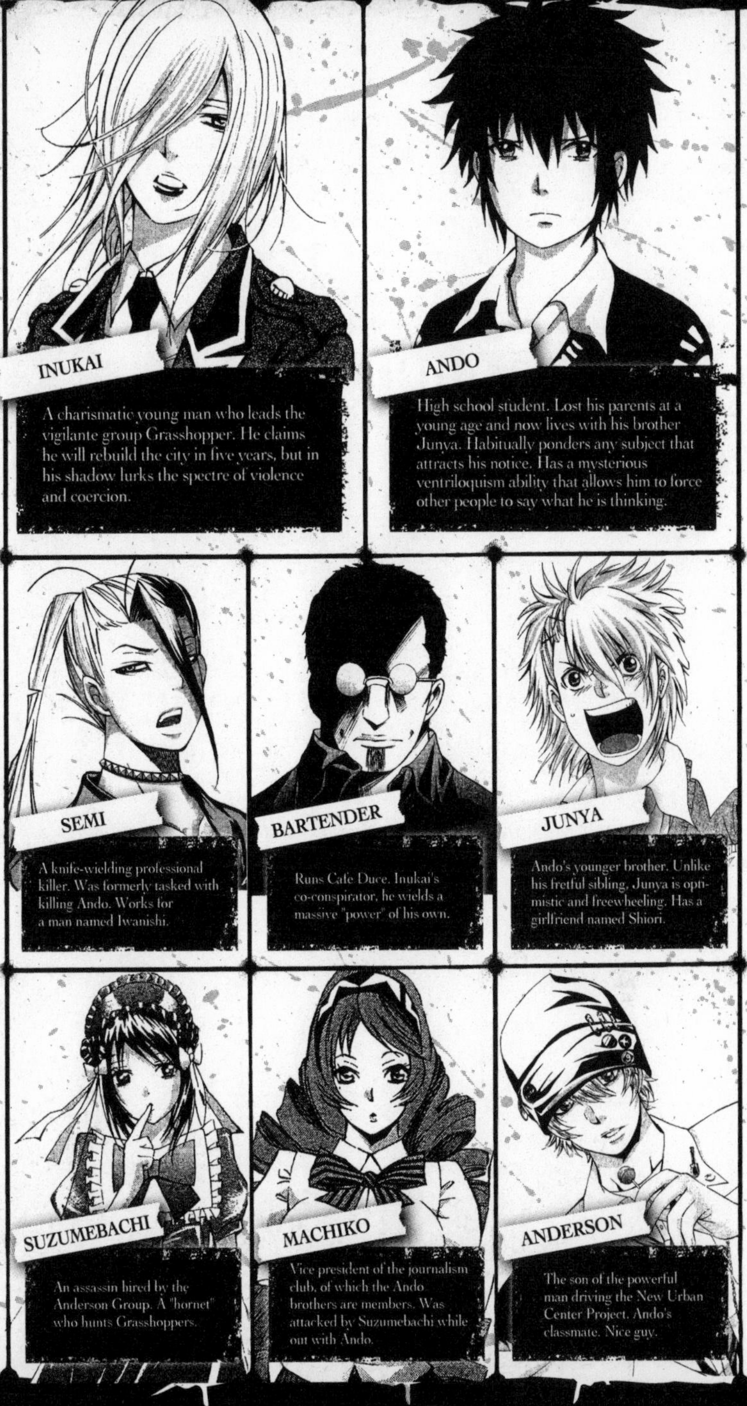
ANDO
High school student. Lost his parents at a young age and now lives with his brother Junya. Habitually ponders any subject that attracts his notice. Has a mysterious ventriloquism ability that allows him to force other people to say what he is thinking.
INUKAI
A charismatic young man who leads the vigilante group Grasshopper. He claims he will rebuild the city in five years, but in his shadow lurks the spectre of violence and coercion.
JUNYA
Ando's younger brother. Unlike his fretful sibling, Junya is optimistic and freewheeling. Has a girlfriend named Shiori.
BARTENDER
Runs Cafe Duce. Inukai's co-conspirator, he wields a massive "power" of his own.
SEMI
A knife-wielding professional killer. Was formerly tasked with killing Ando. Works for a man named Iwanishi.
ANDERSON
The son of the powerful man driving the New Urban Center Project. Ando's classmate. Nice guy.
MACHIKO
Vice president of the journalism club, of which the Ando brothers are members. Was attacked by Suzumebachi while out with Ando.
SUZUMEBACHI
An assassin hired by the Anderson Group. A "hornet" who hunts Grasshoppers.

CONTENTS

Chapter 28 Lights of Solidarity

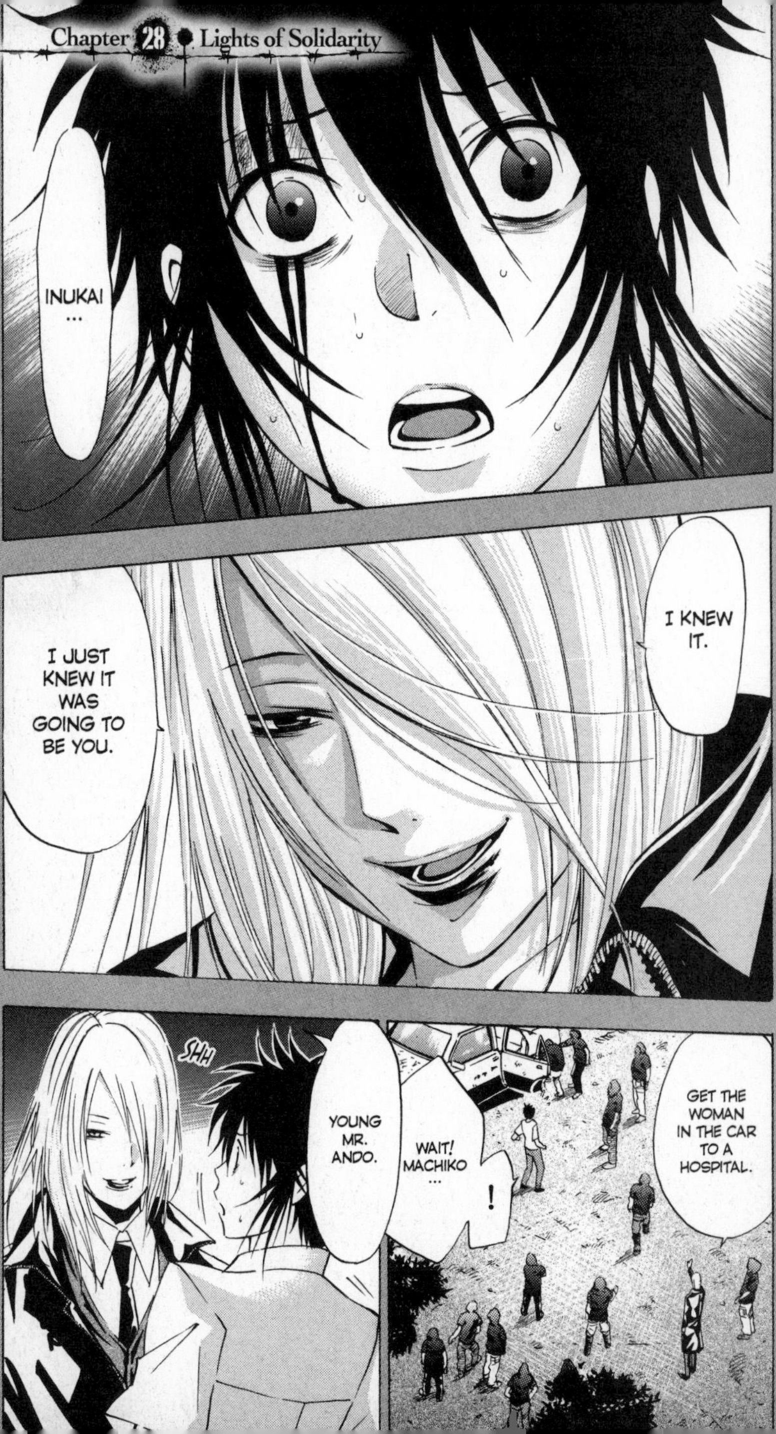
INUKAI ...
I KNEW IT.
I JUST KNEW IT WAS GOING TO BE YOU.
GET THE WOMAN IN THE CAR TO A HOSPITAL.
!
WAIT! MACHIKO ...
YOUNG MR. ANDO.
SHH

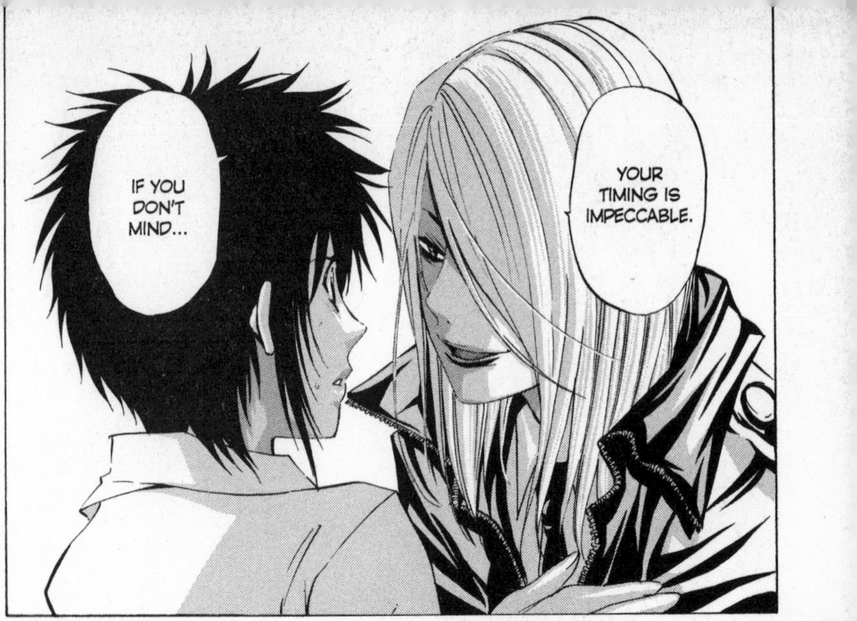
YOUR TIMING IS IMPECCABLE.
IF YOU DON'T MIND...

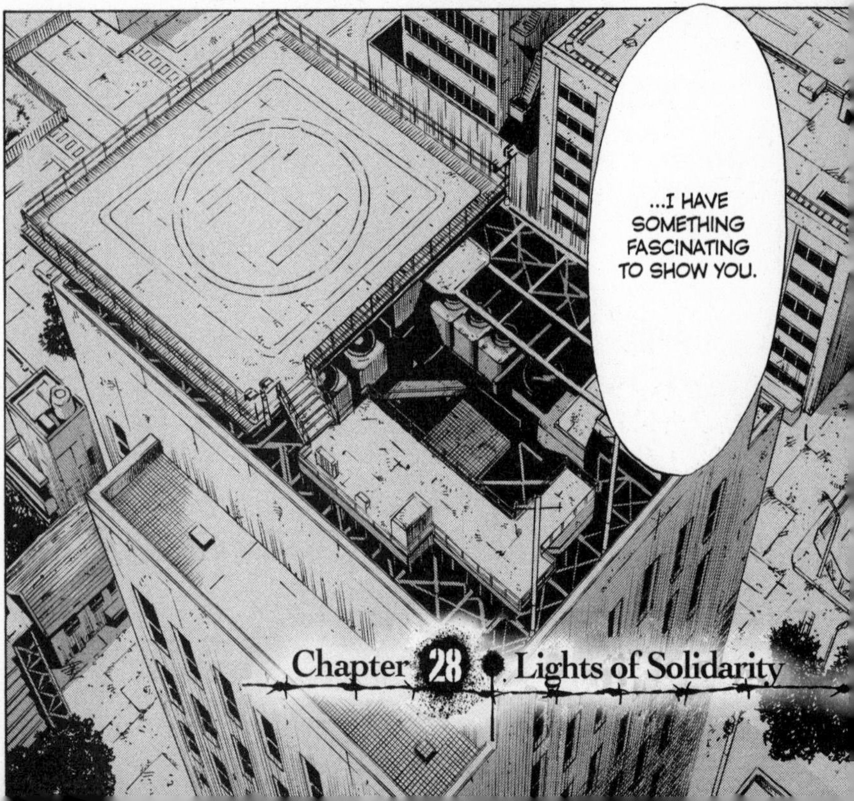
...I HAVE SOMETHING FASCINATING TO SHOW YOU.
Chapter 28 Lights of Solidarity

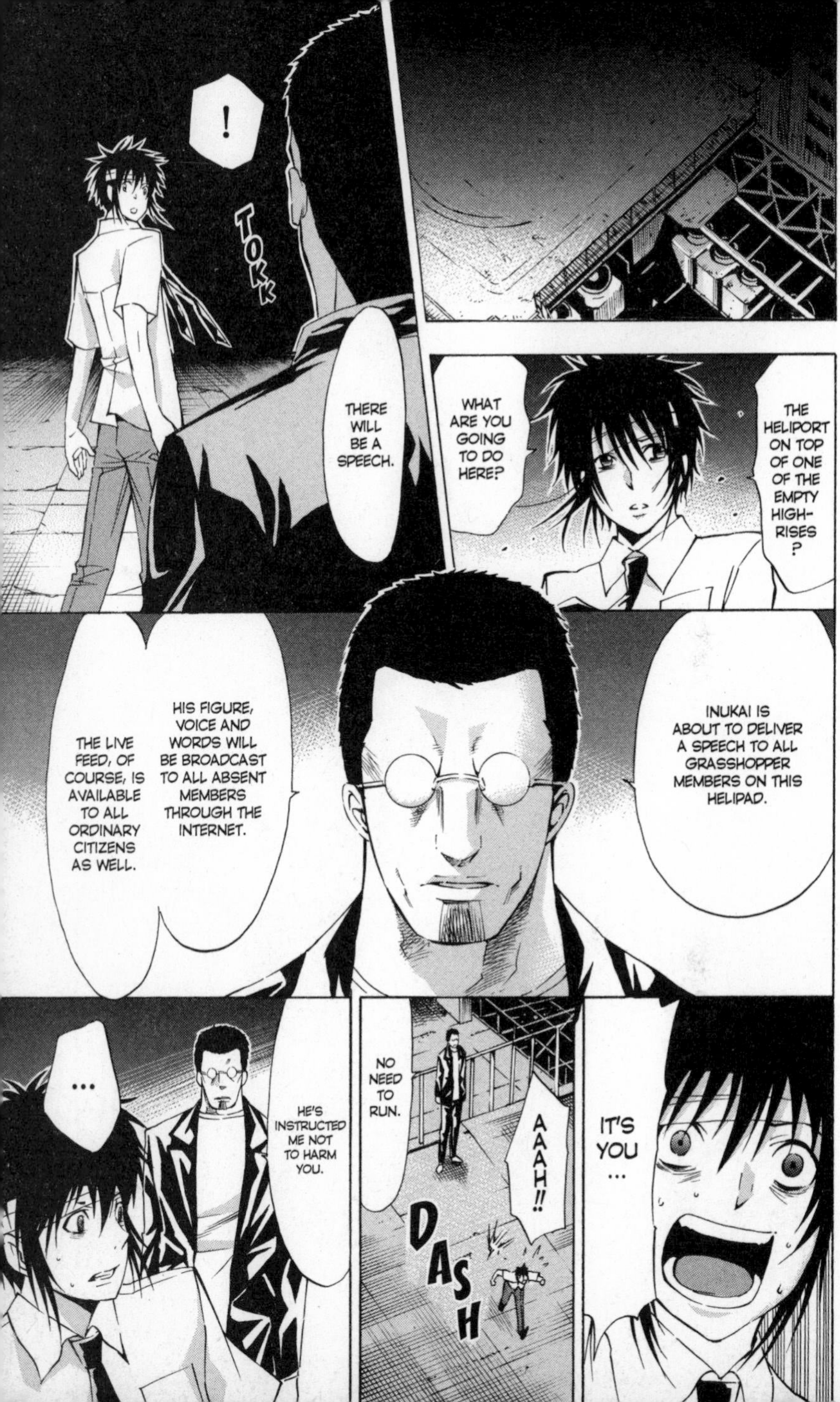
THE HELIPORT ON TOP OF ONE OF THE EMPTY HIGH-RISES?
WHAT ARE YOU GOING TO DO HERE?
!
TOKK
THERE WILL BE A SPEECH.
INUKAI IS ABOUT TO DELIVER A SPEECH TO ALL GRASSHOPPER MEMBERS ON THIS HELIPAD.
HIS FIGURE, VOICE AND WORDS WILL BE BROADCAST TO ALL ABSENT MEMBERS THROUGH THE INTERNET.
THE LIVE FEED, OF COURSE, IS AVAILABLE TO ALL ORDINARY CITIZENS AS WELL.
IT'S YOU...
AAAH!!
DASH
NO NEED TO RUN.
HE'S INSTRUCTED ME NOT TO HARM YOU.
...

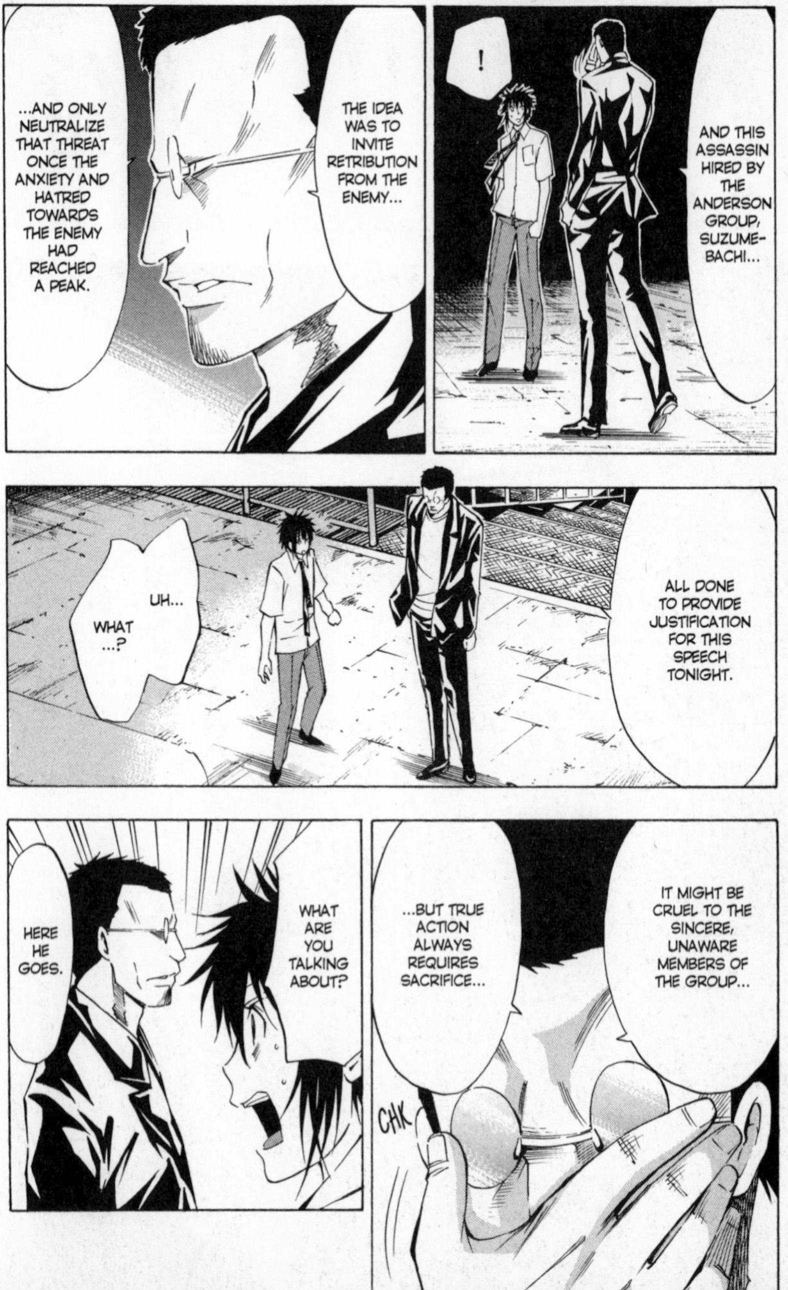
AND THIS ASSASSIN HIRED BY THE ANDERSON GROUP, SUZUME-BACHI...
!
THE IDEA WAS TO INVITE RETRIBUTION FROM THE ENEMY...
...AND ONLY NEUTRALIZE THAT THREAT ONCE THE ANXIETY AND HATRED TOWARDS THE ENEMY HAD REACHED A PEAK.
ALL DONE TO PROVIDE JUSTIFICATION FOR THIS SPEECH TONIGHT.
UH...
WHAT ...?
IT MIGHT BE CRUEL TO THE SINCERE, UNAWARE MEMBERS OF THE GROUP...
...BUT TRUE ACTION ALWAYS REQUIRES SACRIFICE...
CHK
WHAT ARE YOU TALKING ABOUT?
HERE HE GOES.

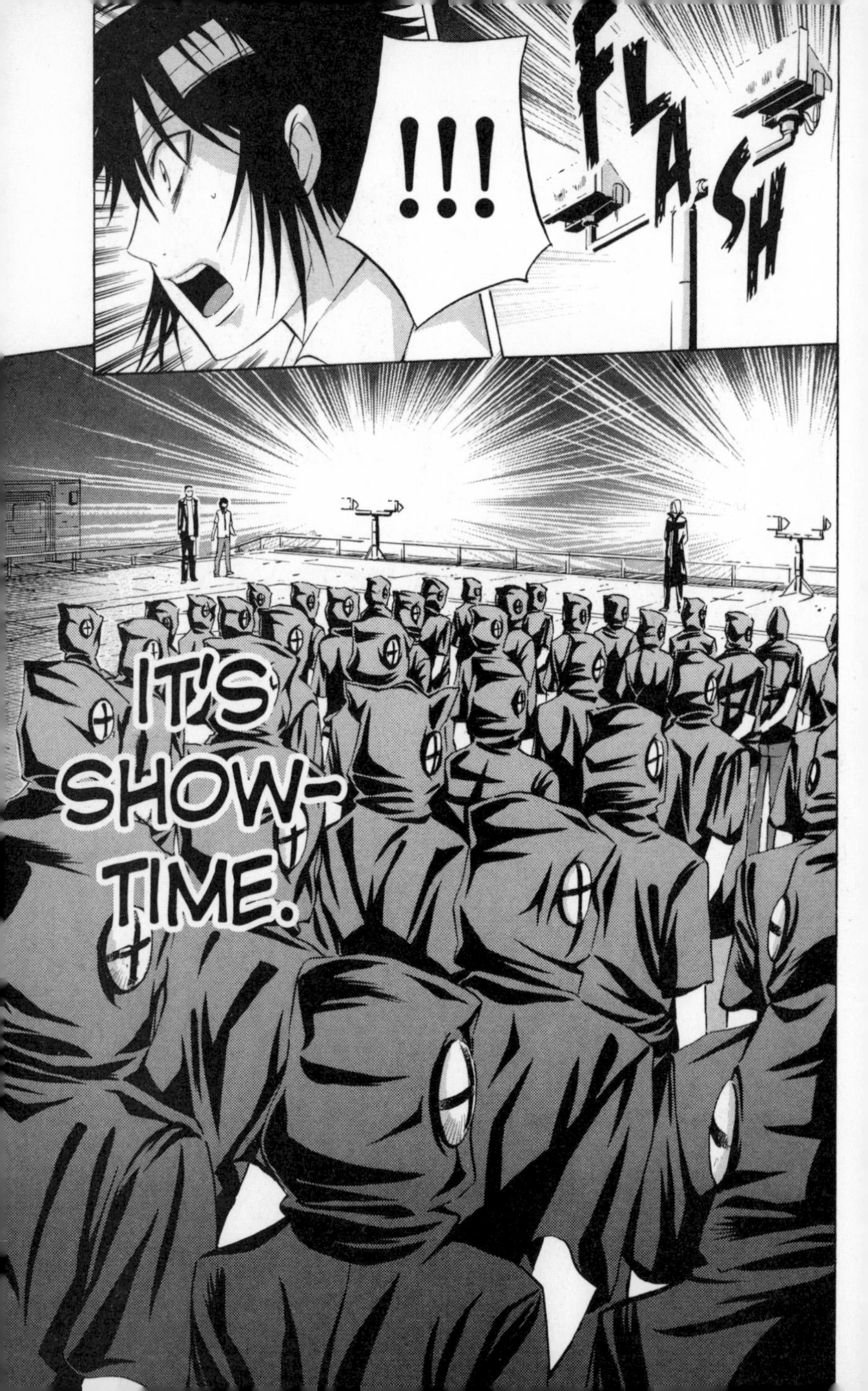
!!!
FLASH
IT'S SHOW-TIME.

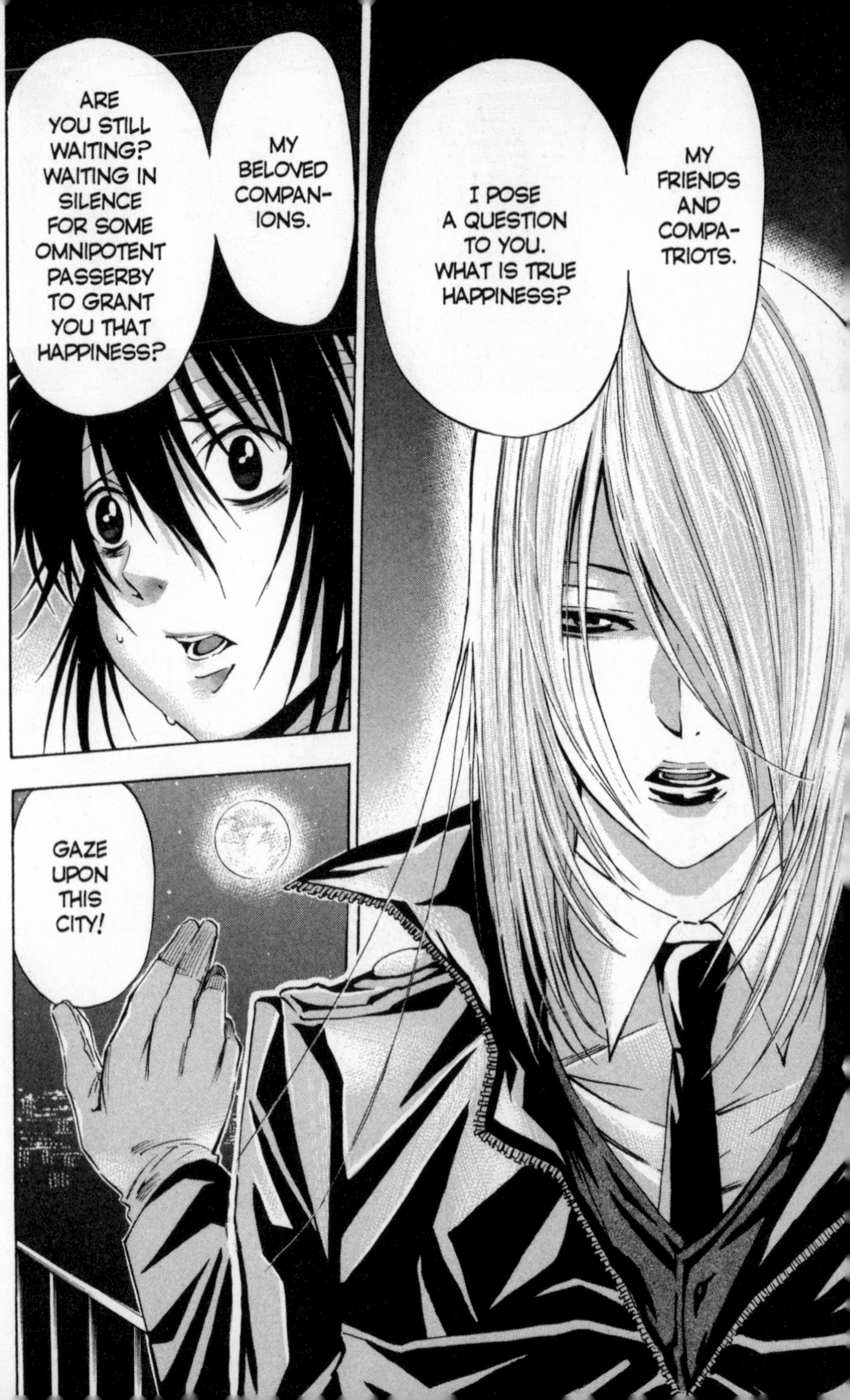
MY FRIENDS AND COMPATRIOTS.
I POSE A QUESTION TO YOU. WHAT IS TRUE HAPPINESS?
MY BELOVED COMPANIONS.
ARE YOU STILL WAITING? WAITING IN SILENCE FOR SOME OMNIPOTENT PASSERBY TO GRANT YOU THAT HAPPINESS?
GAZE UPON THIS CITY!

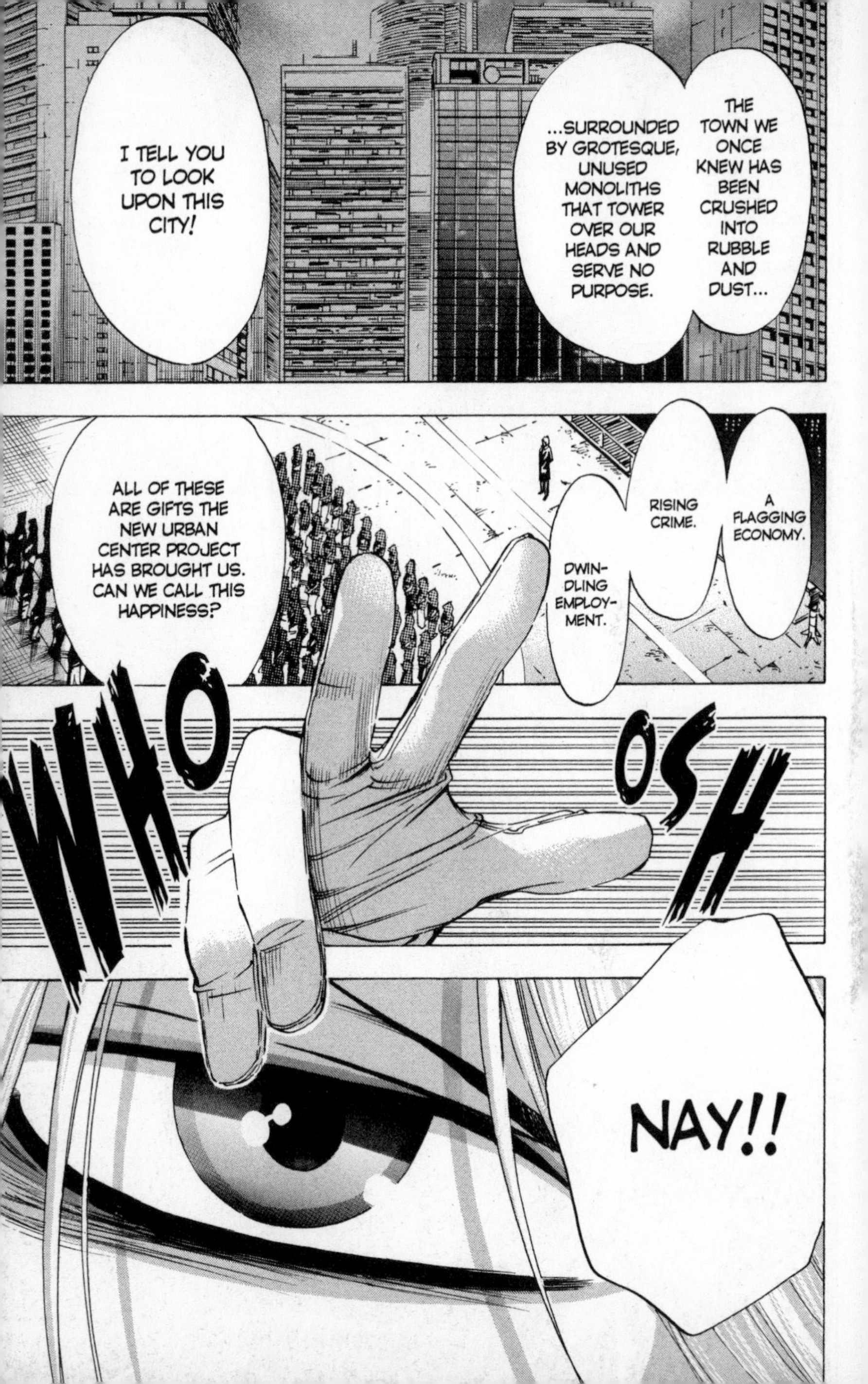
THE TOWN WE ONCE KNEW HAS BEEN CRUSHED INTO RUBBLE AND DUST...
...SURROUNDED BY GROTESQUE, UNUSED MONOLITHS THAT TOWER OVER OUR HEADS AND SERVE NO PURPOSE.
I TELL YOU TO LOOK UPON THIS CITY!
A FLAGGING ECONOMY.
RISING CRIME.
DWIN-DLING EMPLOY-MENT.
ALL OF THESE ARE GIFTS THE NEW URBAN CENTER PROJECT HAS BROUGHT US. CAN WE CALL THIS HAPPINESS?
WHOOSH
NAY!!

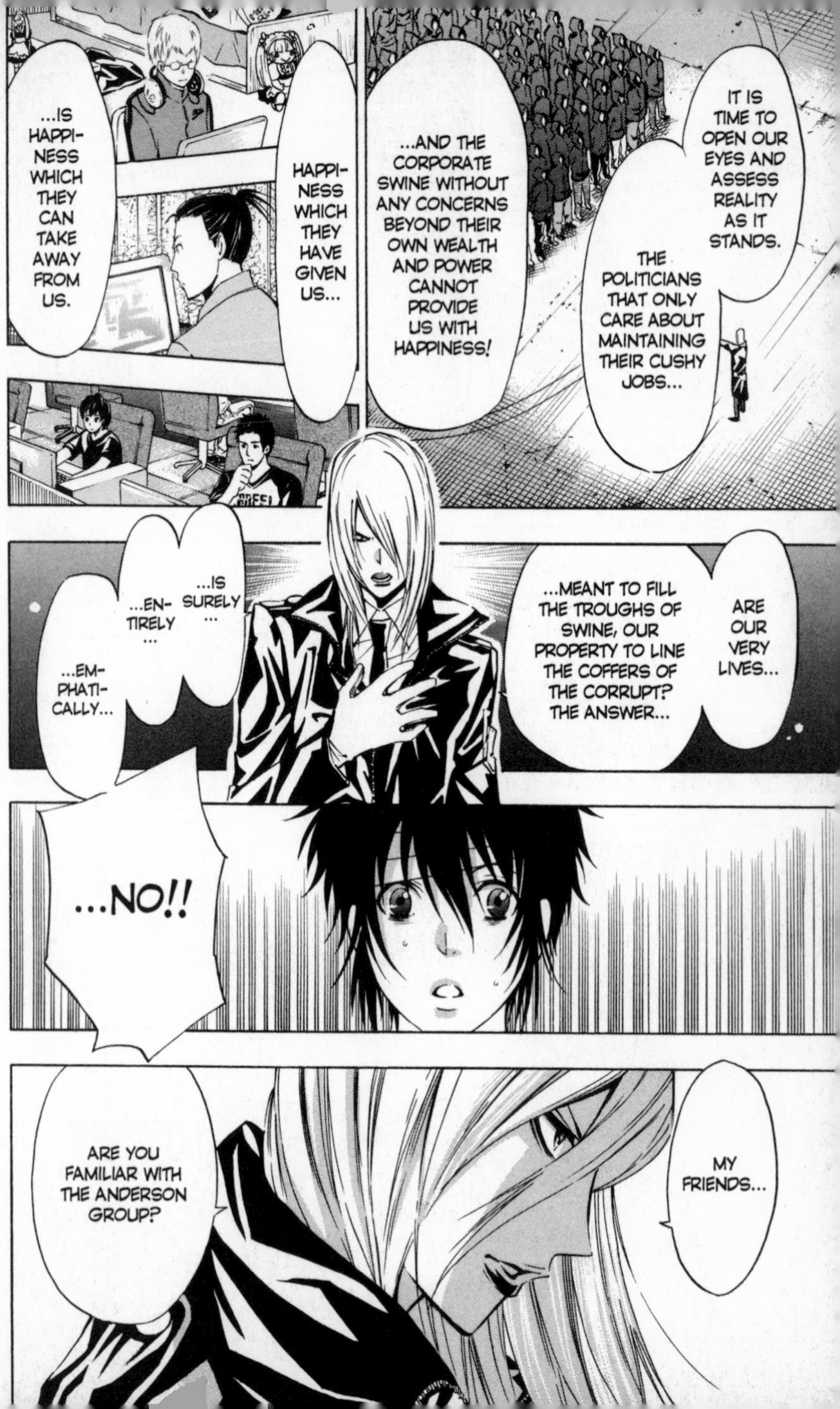
IT IS TIME TO OPEN OUR EYES AND ASSESS REALITY AS IT STANDS.
THE POLITICIANS THAT ONLY CARE ABOUT MAINTAINING THEIR CUSHY JOBS...
...AND THE CORPORATE SWINE WITHOUT ANY CONCERNS BEYOND THEIR OWN WEALTH AND POWER CANNOT PROVIDE US WITH HAPPINESS!
HAPPINESS WHICH THEY HAVE GIVEN US...
...IS HAPPINESS WHICH THEY CAN TAKE AWAY FROM US.
ARE OUR VERY LIVES...
...MEANT TO FILL THE TROUGHS OF SWINE, OUR PROPERTY TO LINE THE COFFERS OF THE CORRUPT? THE ANSWER...
...IS SURELY...
...ENTIRELY...
...EMPHATICALLY...
...NO!!
MY FRIENDS...
ARE YOU FAMILIAR WITH THE ANDERSON GROUP?

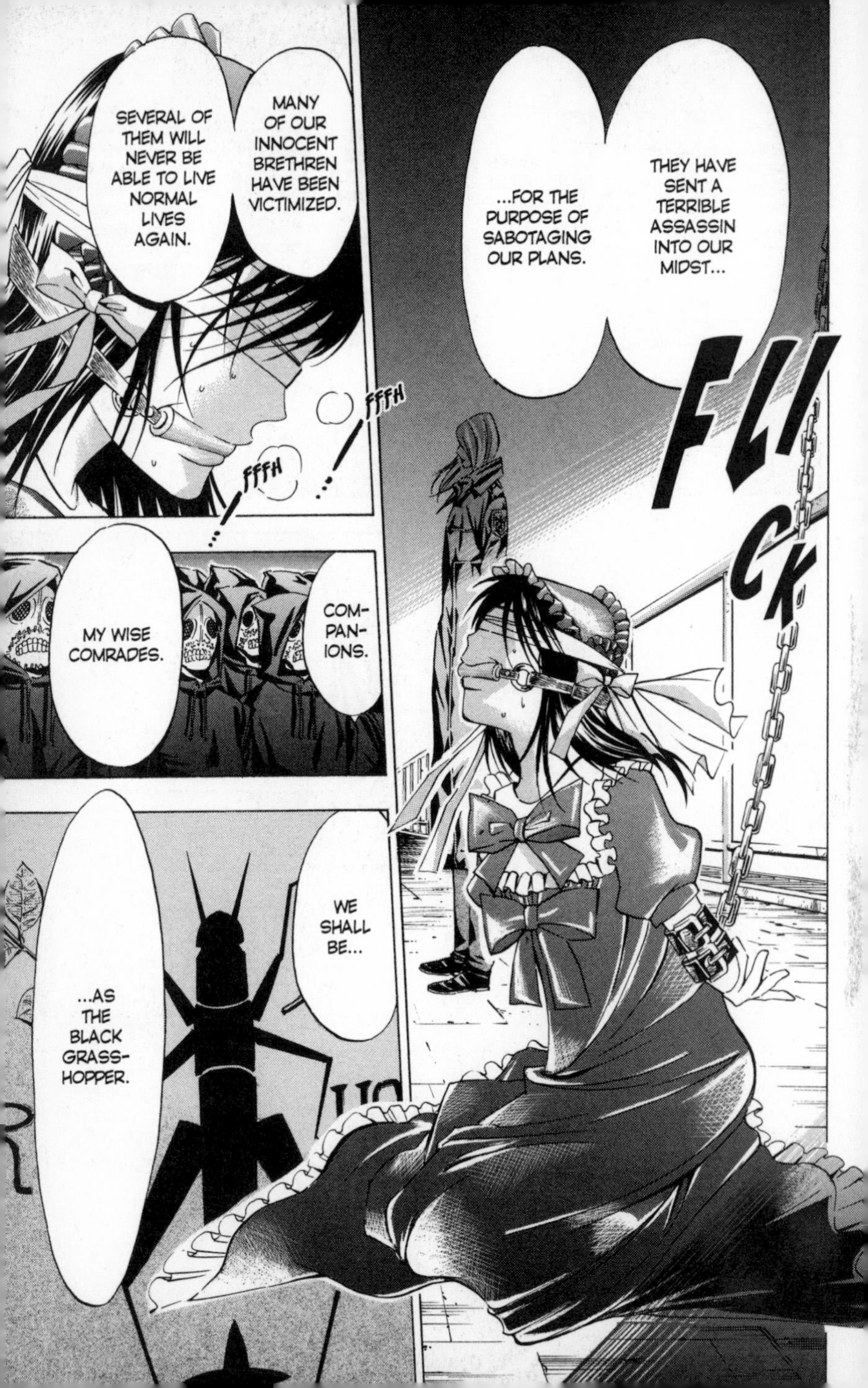
THEY HAVE SENT A TERRIBLE ASSASSIN INTO OUR MIDST...
...FOR THE PURPOSE OF SABOTAGING OUR PLANS.
FLICK
MANY OF OUR INNOCENT BRETHREN HAVE BEEN VICTIMIZED.
SEVERAL OF THEM WILL NEVER BE ABLE TO LIVE NORMAL LIVES AGAIN.
FFFH
FFFH
COMPANIONS.
MY WISE COMRADES.
WE SHALL BE...
...AS THE BLACK GRASSHOPPER.

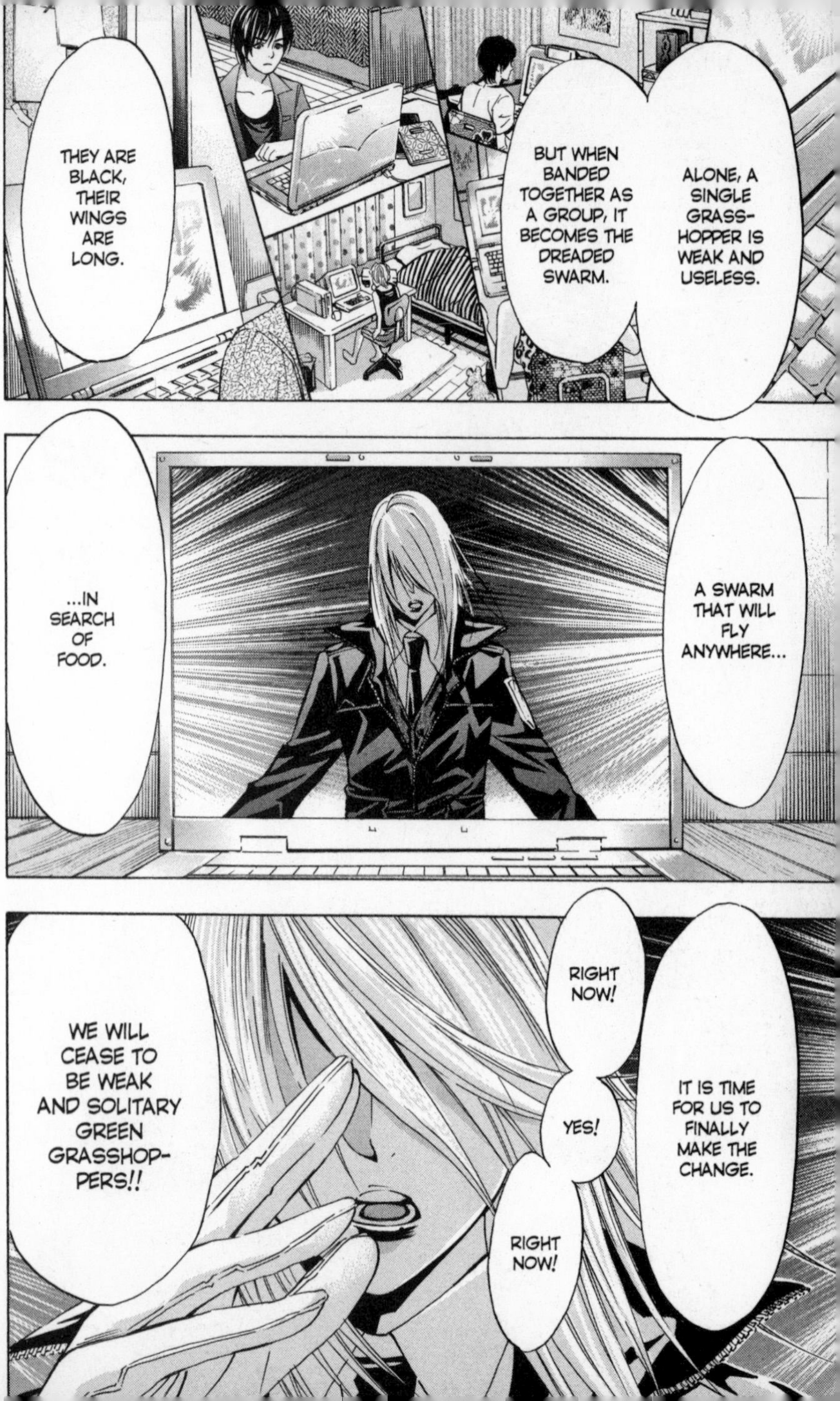
ALONE, A SINGLE GRASS-HOPPER IS WEAK AND USELESS.
BUT WHEN BANDED TOGETHER AS A GROUP, IT BECOMES THE DREADED SWARM.
THEY ARE BLACK, THEIR WINGS ARE LONG.
A SWARM THAT WILL FLY ANYWHERE...
...IN SEARCH OF FOOD.
IT IS TIME FOR US TO FINALLY MAKE THE CHANGE.
RIGHT NOW!
YES!
RIGHT NOW!
WE WILL CEASE TO BE WEAK AND SOLITARY GREEN GRASSHOP-PERS!!

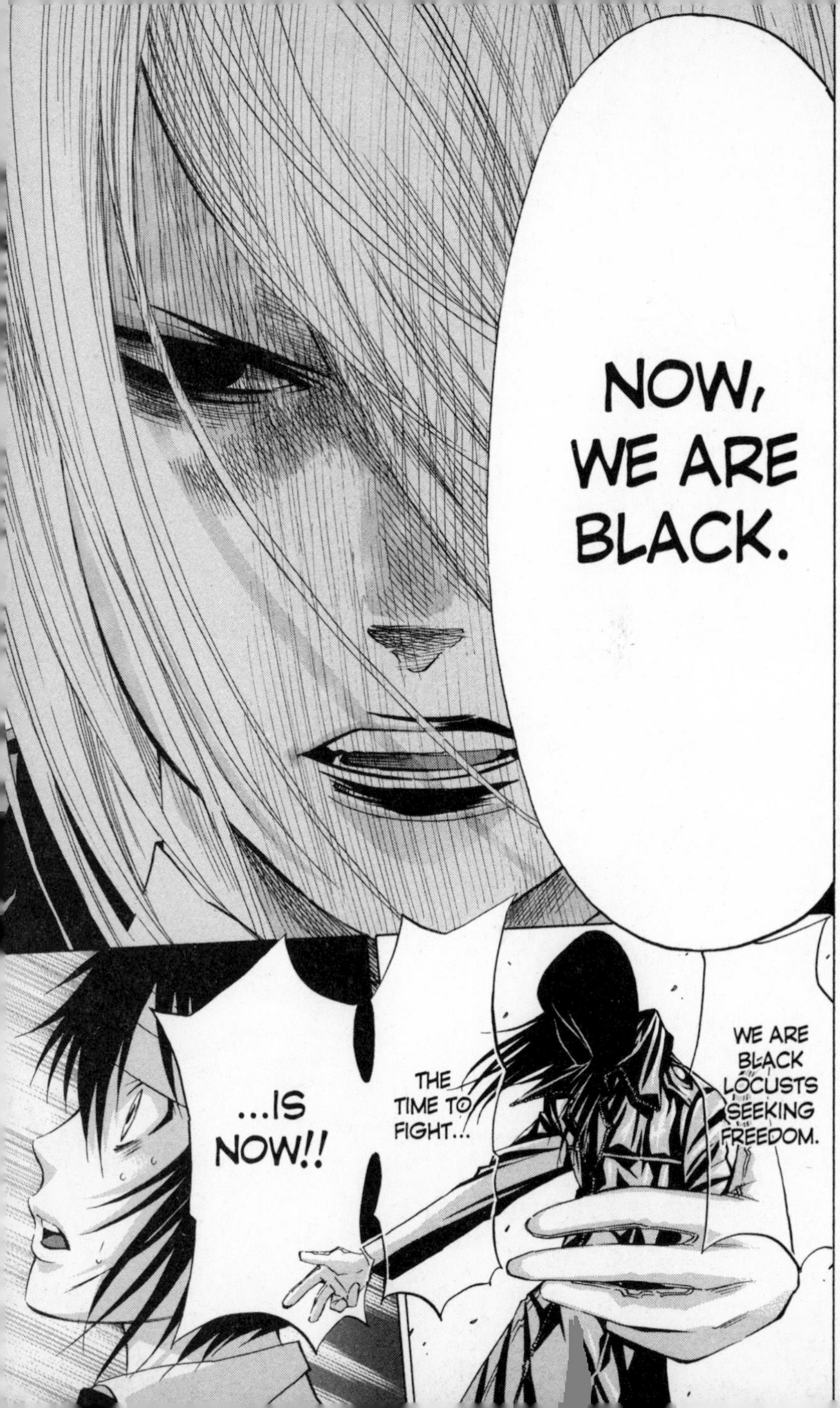
NOW, WE ARE BLACK.
WE ARE BLACK LOCUSTS SEEKING FREEDOM.
THE TIME TO FIGHT...
...IS NOW!!

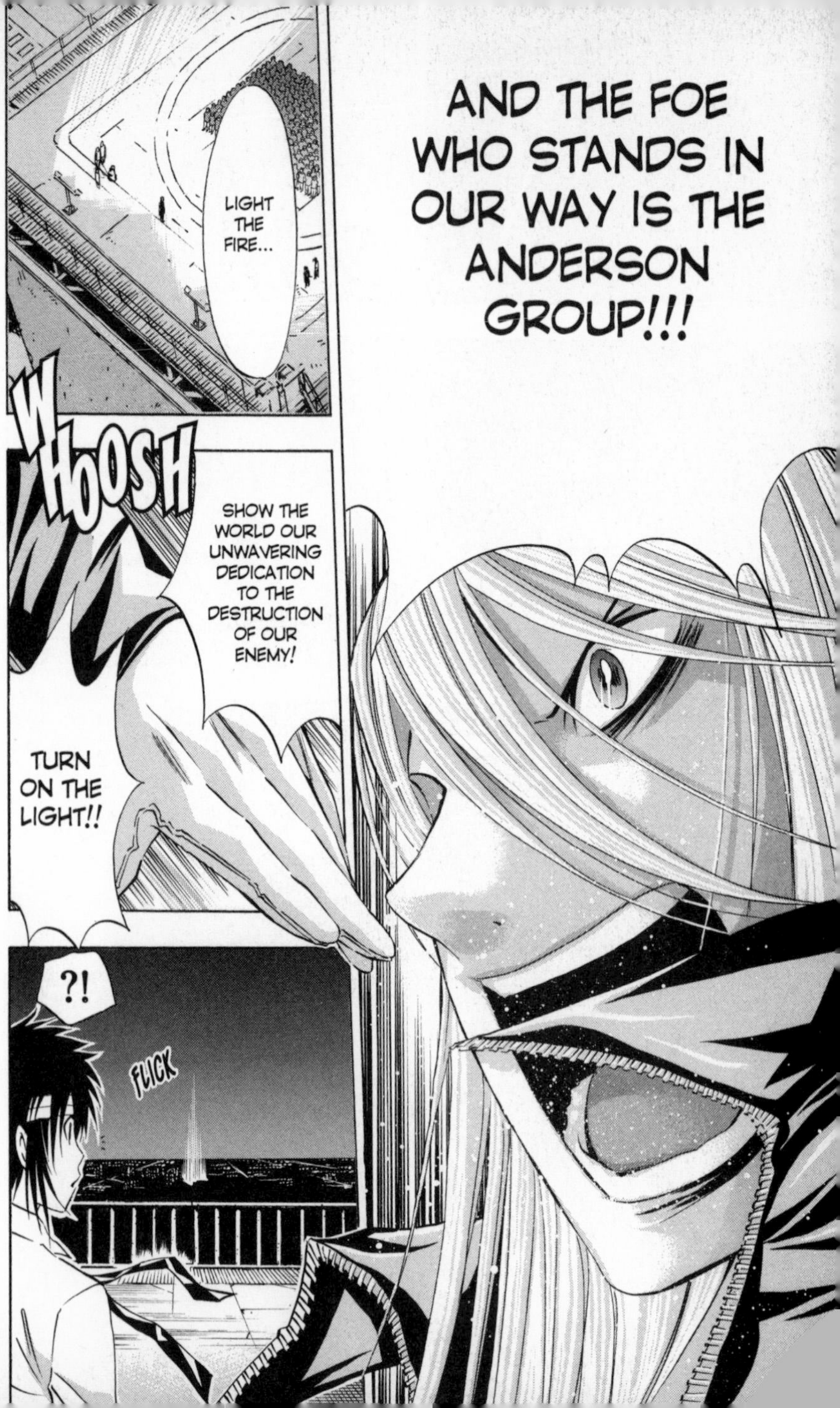
AND THE FOE WHO STANDS IN OUR WAY IS THE ANDERSON GROUP!!!
LIGHT THE FIRE...
WHOOSH
SHOW THE WORLD OUR UNWAVERING DEDICATION TO THE DESTRUCTION OF OUR ENEMY!
TURN ON THE LIGHT!!
?!
FLICK

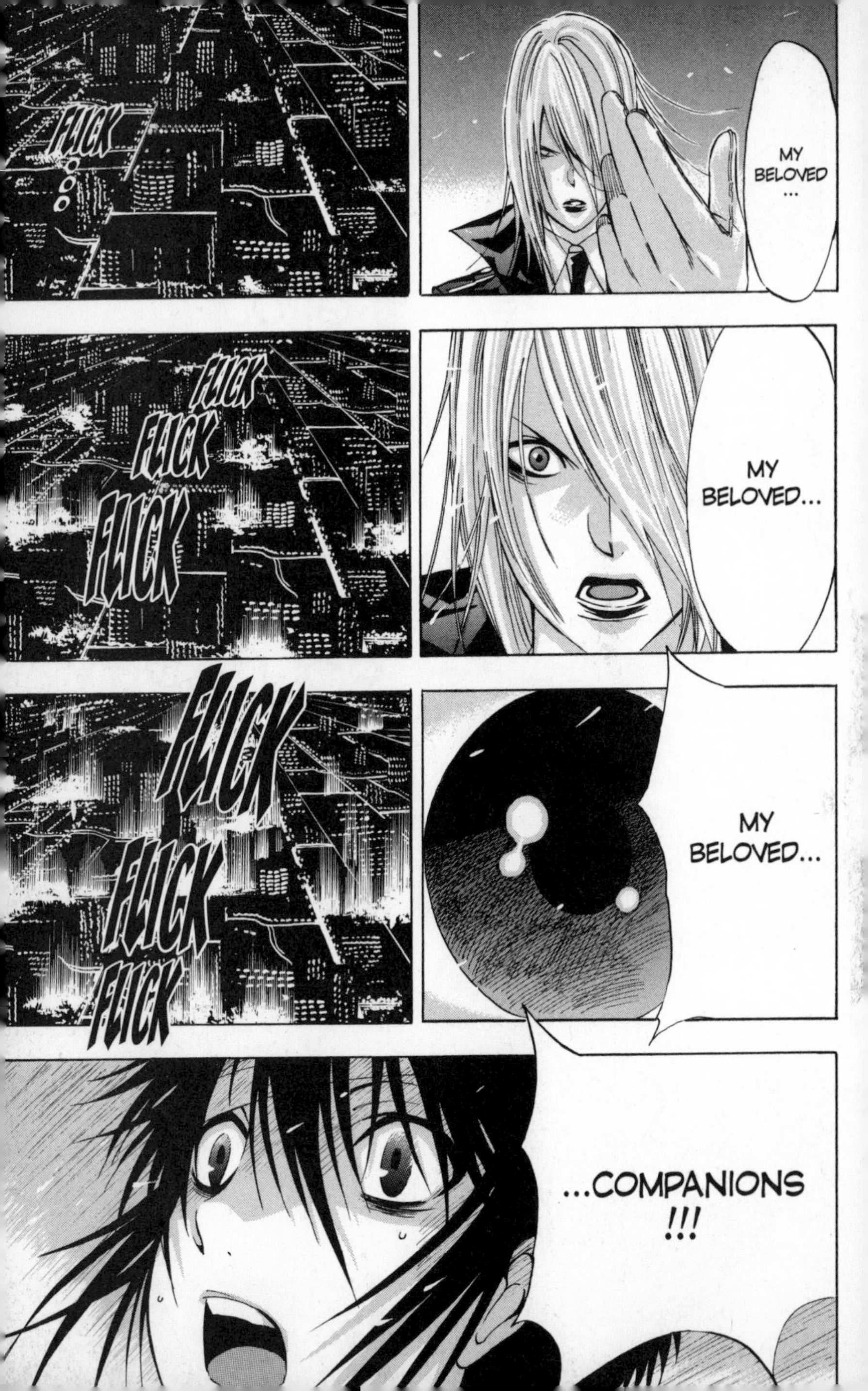

MY BELOVED ...
FLICK
MY BELOVED...
FLICK
FLICK
FLICK
MY BELOVED...
FLICK
FLICK
FLICK
...COMPANIONS !!!

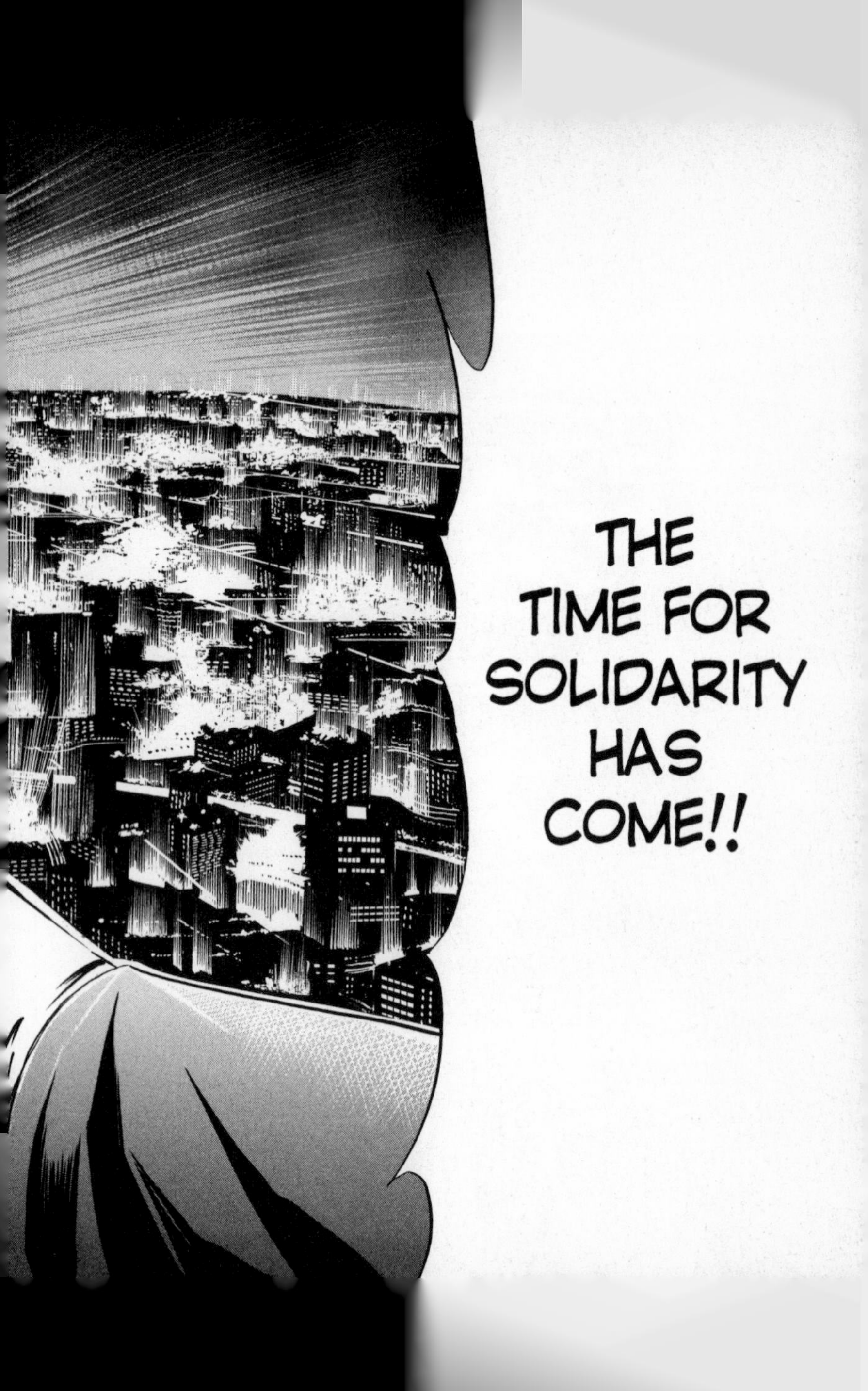
THE TIME FOR SOLIDARITY HAS COME!!

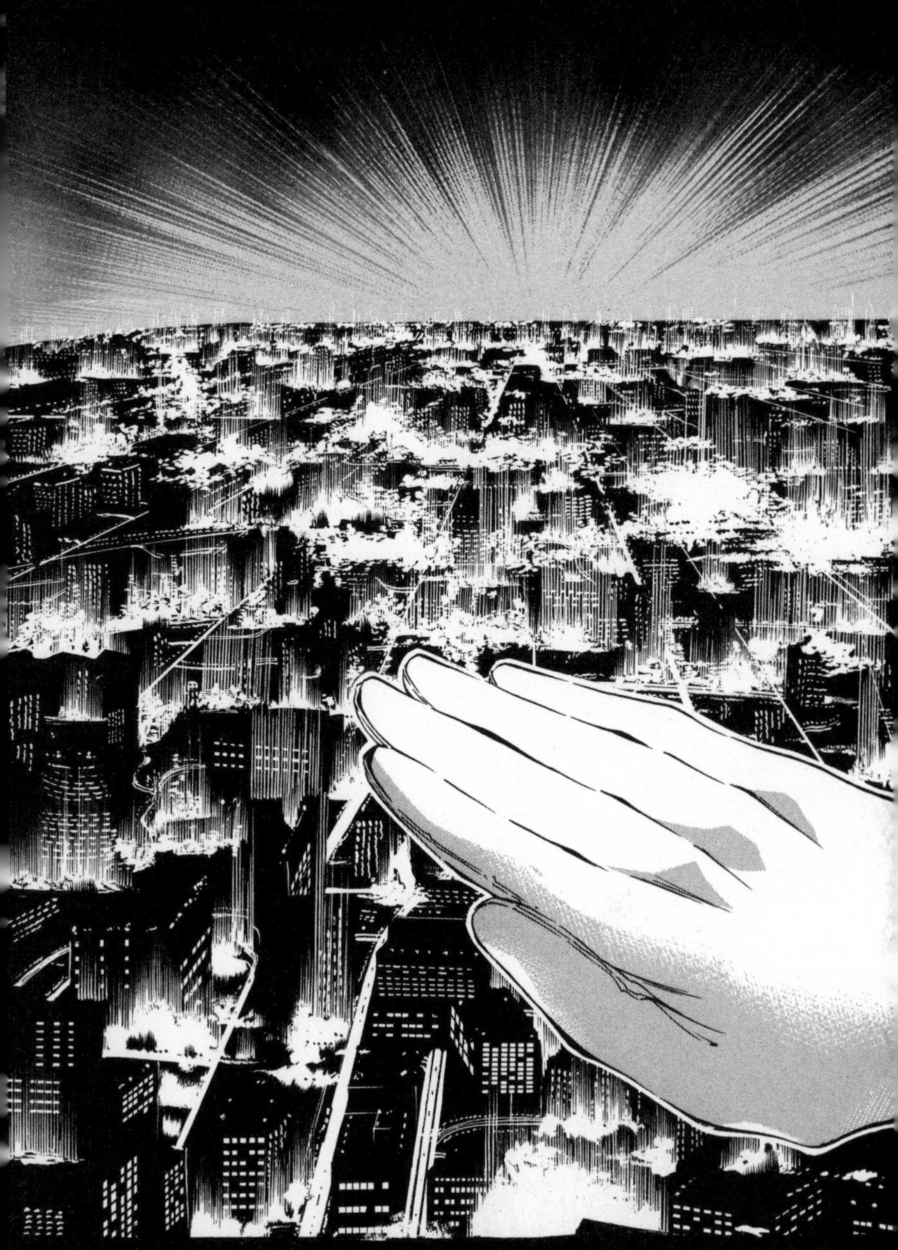

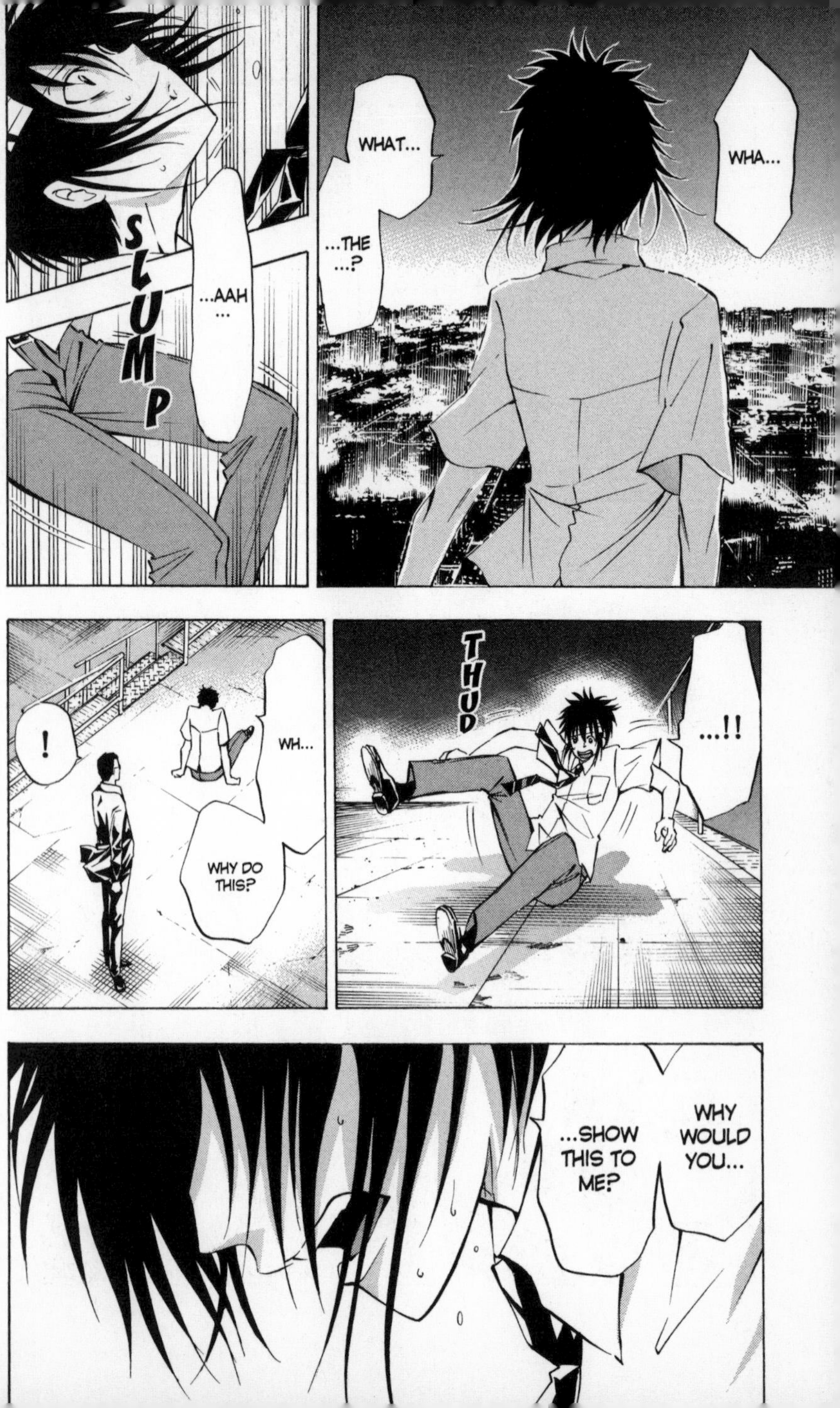
WHA...
WHAT...
...THE ...?
SLUMP
...AAH ...
THUD
...!!
WH...
WHY DO THIS?
!
WHY WOULD YOU...
...SHOW THIS TO ME?

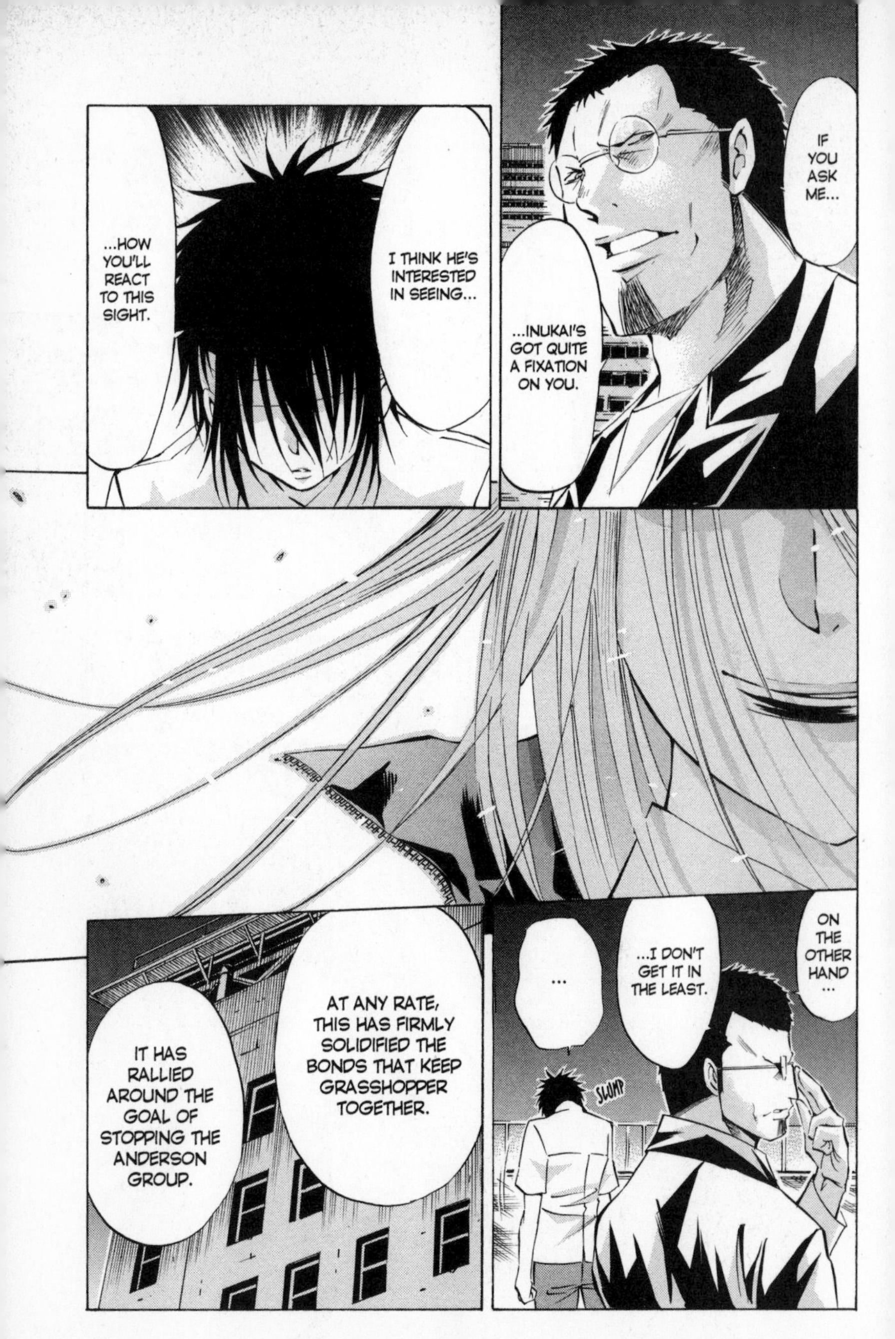
IF YOU ASK ME...
...INUKAI'S GOT QUITE A FIXATION ON YOU.
I THINK HE'S INTERESTED IN SEEING...
...HOW YOU'LL REACT TO THIS SIGHT.
ON THE OTHER HAND...
...I DON'T GET IT IN THE LEAST.
...
SLUMP
AT ANY RATE, THIS HAS FIRMLY SOLIDIFIED THE BONDS THAT KEEP GRASSHOPPER TOGETHER.
IT HAS RALLIED AROUND THE GOAL OF STOPPING THE ANDERSON GROUP.

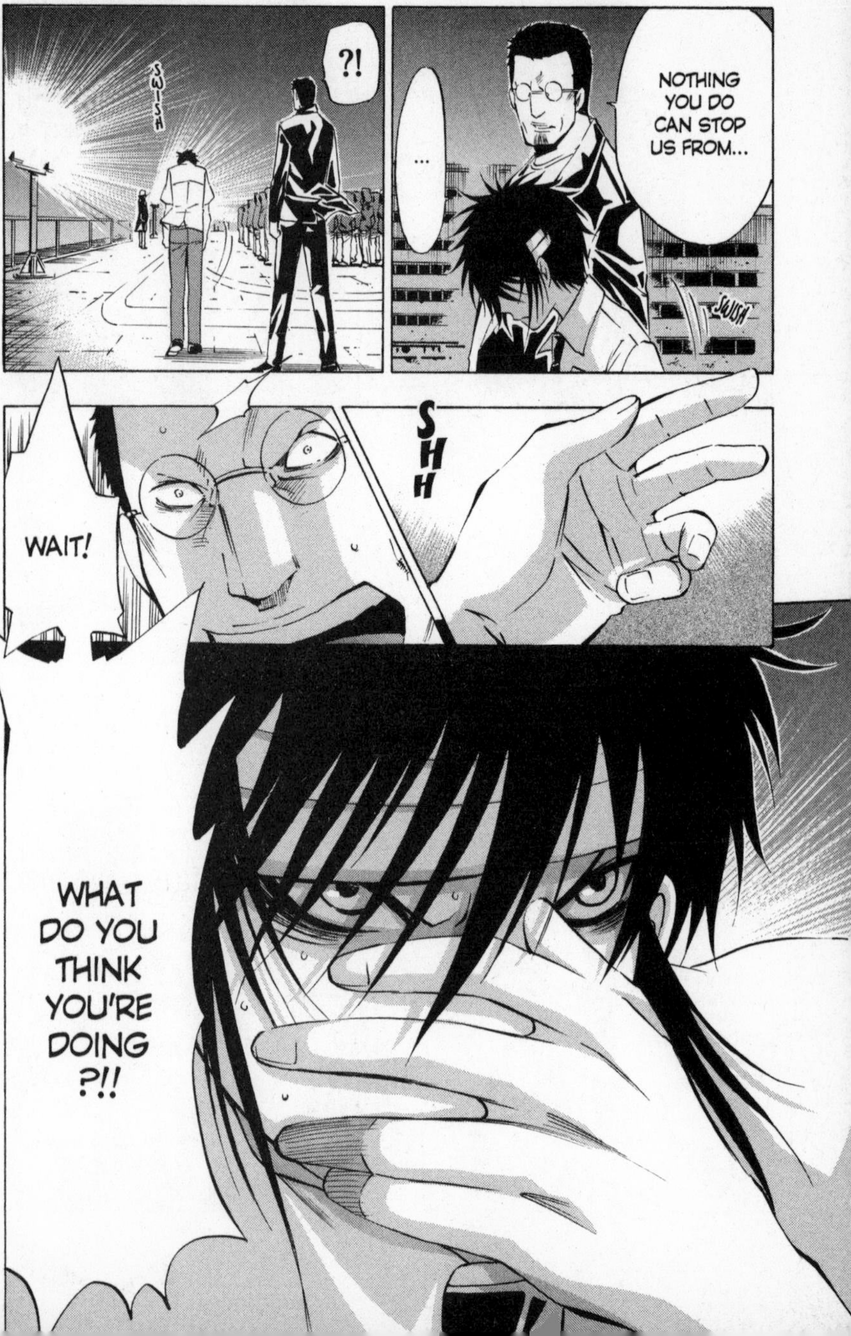
NOTHING YOU DO CAN STOP US FROM...
...
SWISH
?!
SWISH
SHH
WAIT!
WHAT DO YOU THINK YOU'RE DOING ?!!

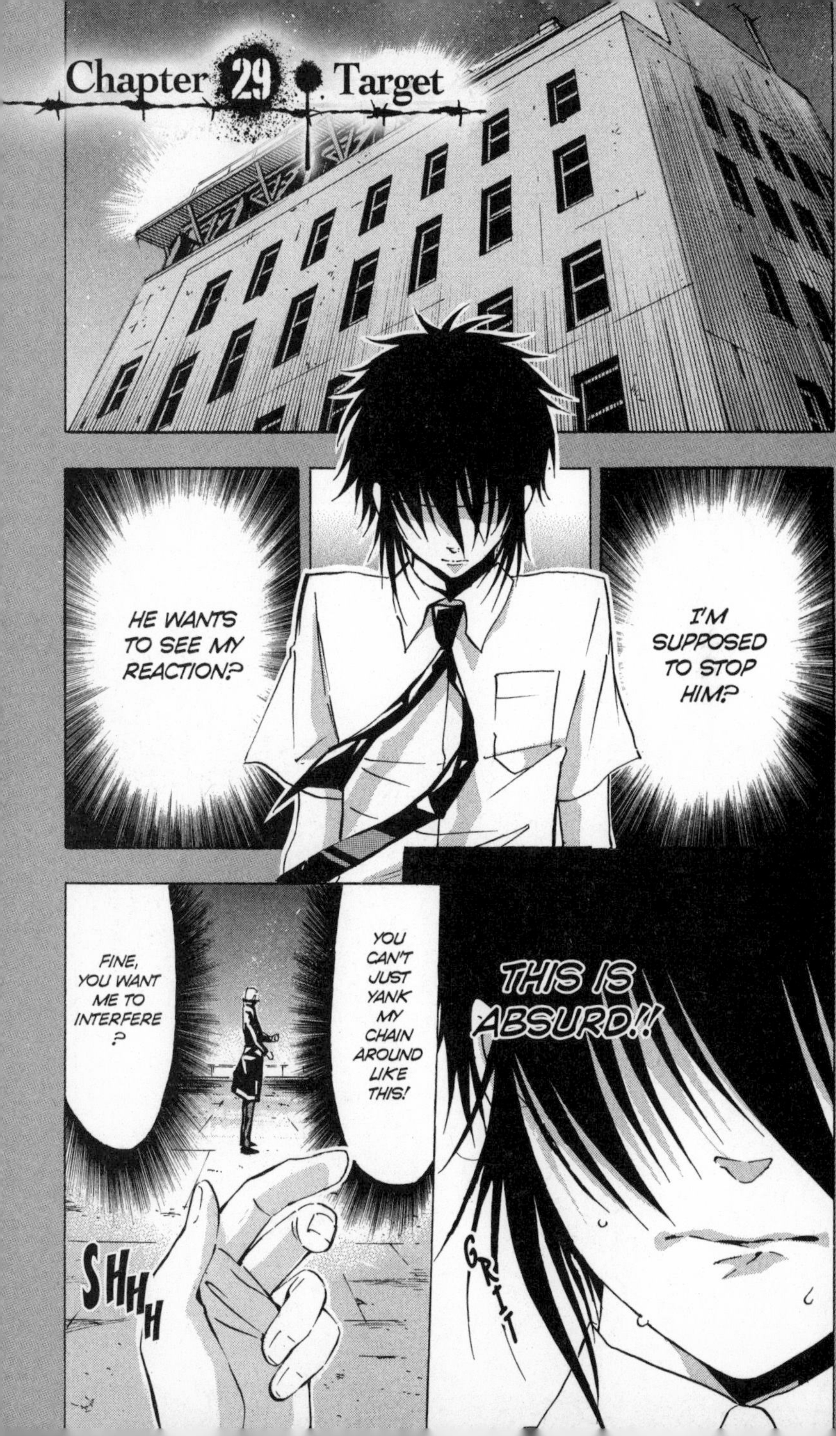
Chapter 29 Target
I'M SUPPOSED TO STOP HIM?
HE WANTS TO SEE MY REACTION?
THIS IS ABSURD!!
GRIIT
YOU CAN'T JUST YANK MY CHAIN AROUND LIKE THIS!
FINE, YOU WANT ME TO INTERFERE?
SHHH

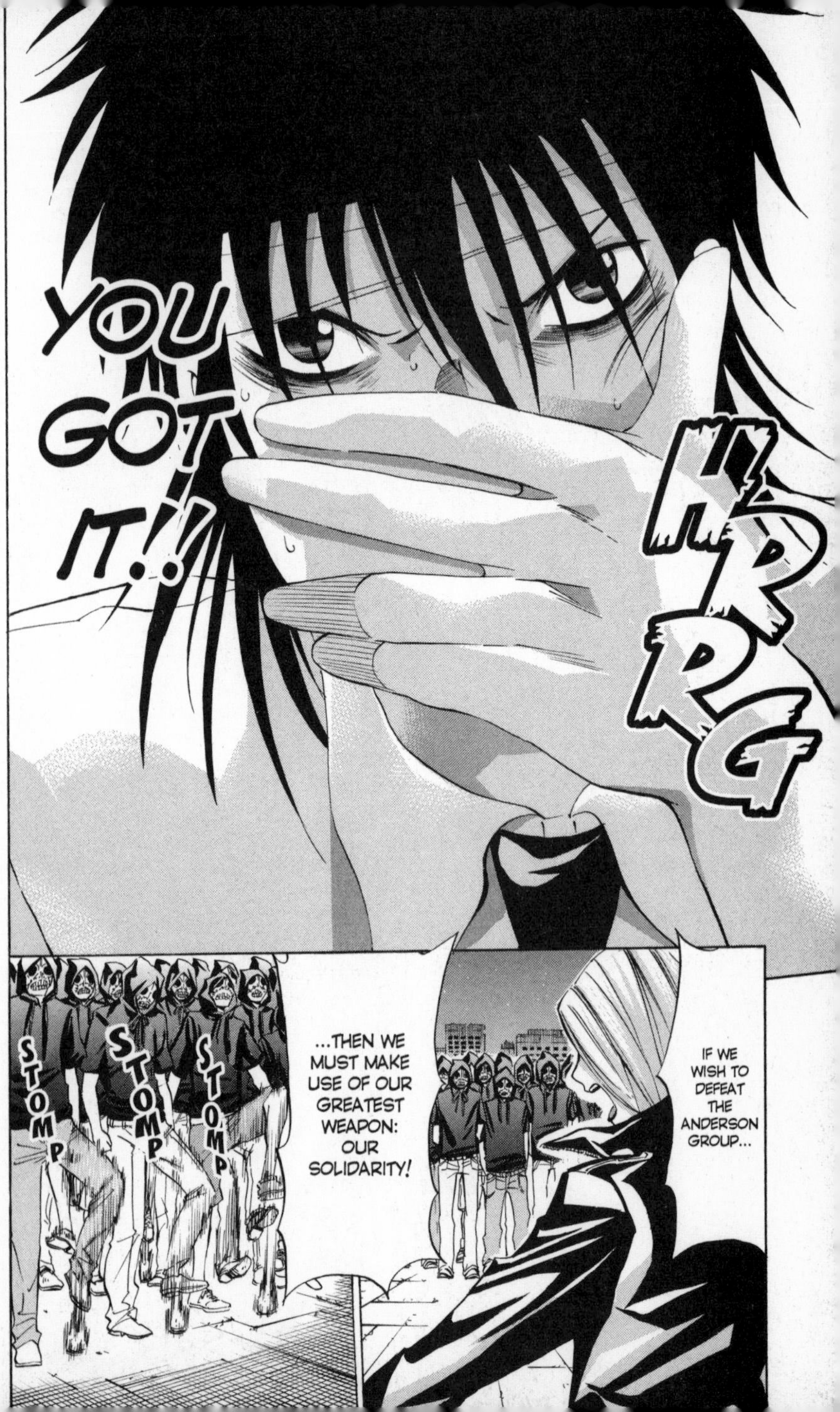
HRRG
YOU GOT IT!!
IF WE WISH TO DEFEAT THE ANDERSON GROUP...
...THEN WE MUST MAKE USE OF OUR GREATEST WEAPON: OUR SOLIDARITY!
STOMP
STOMP
STOMP

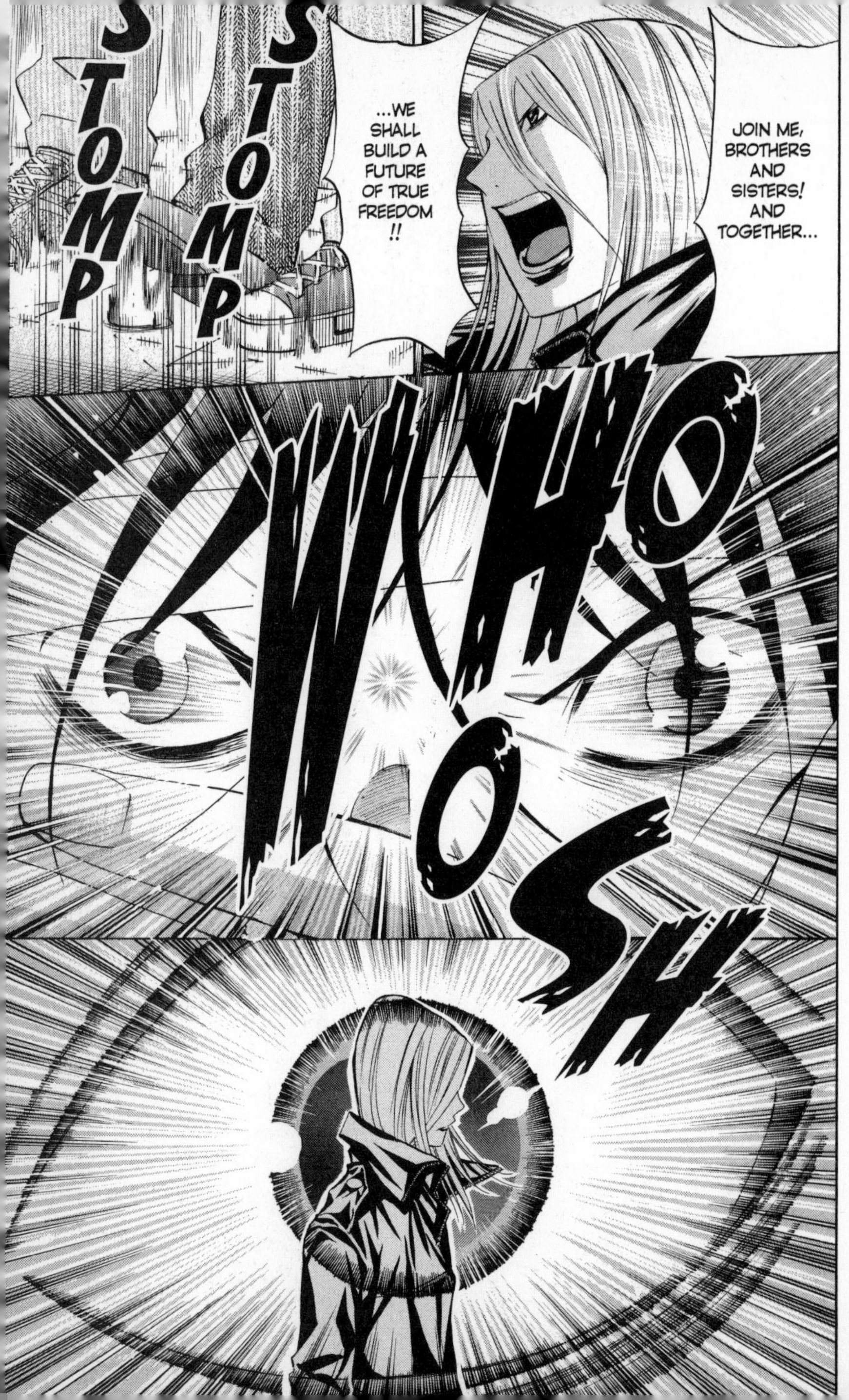
JOIN ME, BROTHERS AND SISTERS! AND TOGETHER...
...WE SHALL BUILD A FUTURE OF TRUE FREEDOM !!
STOMP
STOMP
WHOOSH

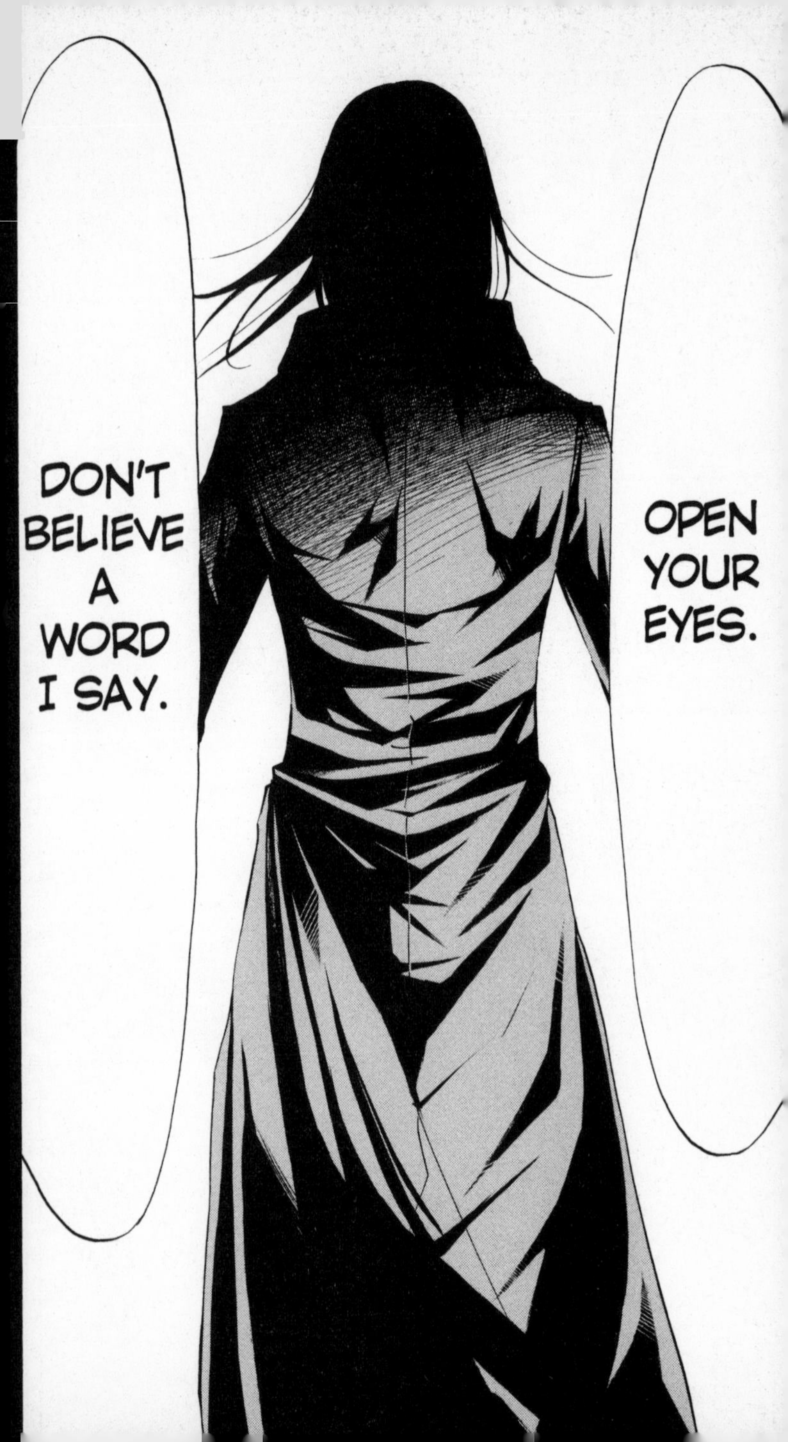
OPEN YOUR EYES.
DON'T BELIEVE A WORD I SAY.

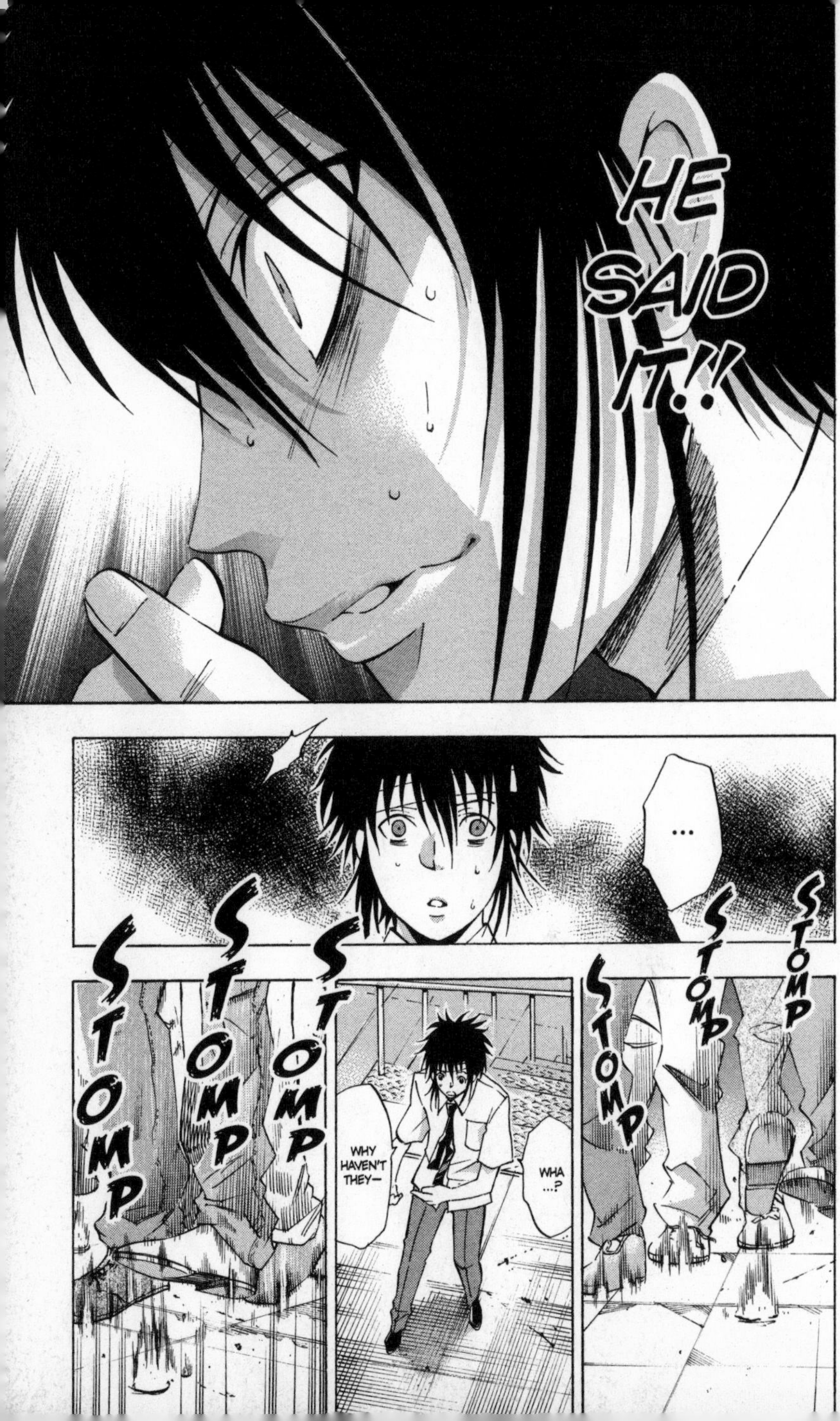
HE SAID IT!!
...
STOMP
STOMP
STOMP
WHA ...?
WHY HAVEN'T THEY—
STOMP
STOMP
STOMP

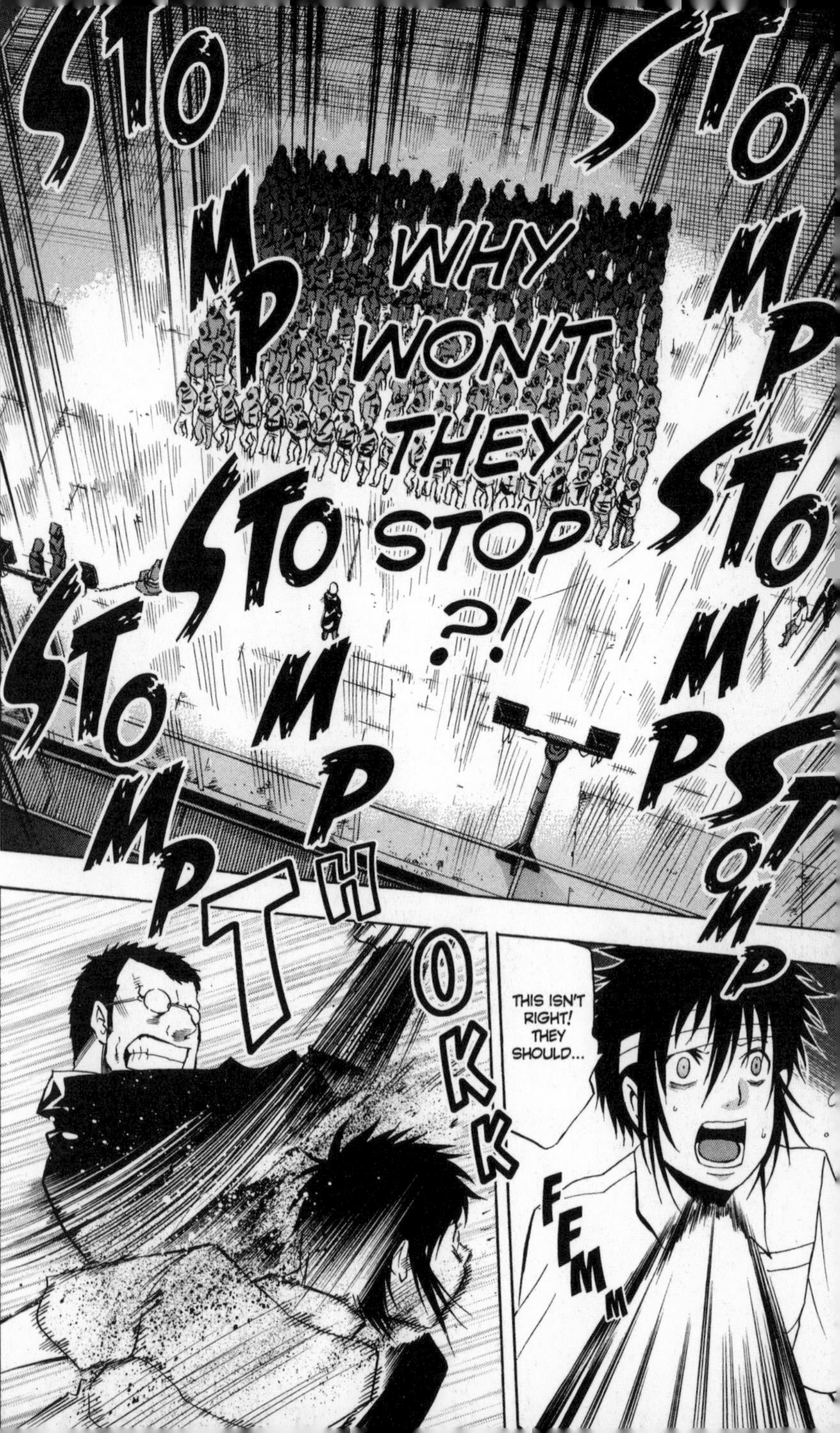
STOMP
STOMP
WHY WON'T THEY STOP?!
STOMP
STOMP
STOMP
STOMP
THIS ISN'T RIGHT! THEY SHOULD...
FEMM
THOKK

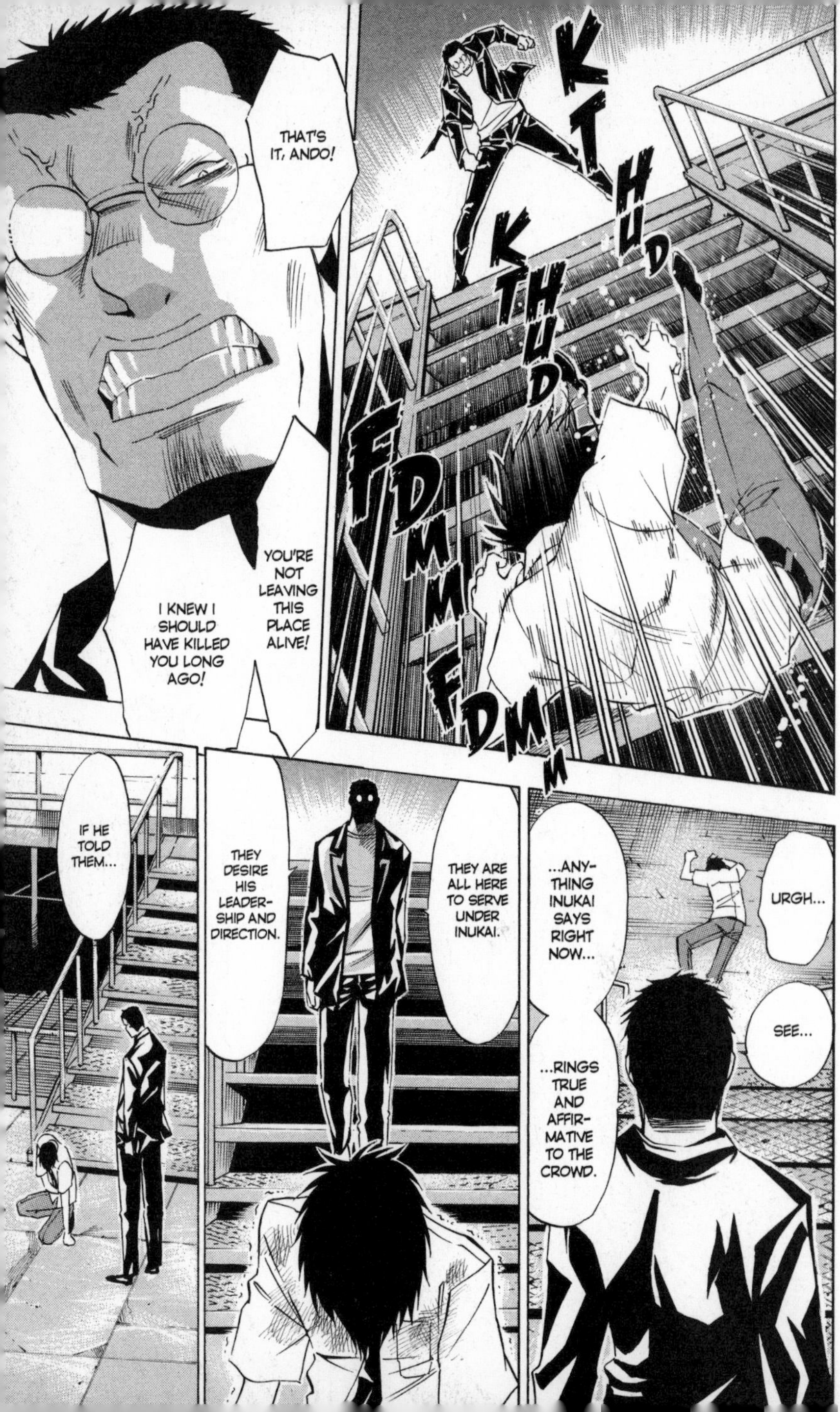
KTHUD
KTHUD
FDMM
FDMM
THAT'S IT, ANDO!
YOU'RE NOT LEAVING THIS PLACE ALIVE!
I KNEW I SHOULD HAVE KILLED YOU LONG AGO!
URGH...
SEE...
...ANY-THING INUKAI SAYS RIGHT NOW...
...RINGS TRUE AND AFFIR-MATIVE TO THE CROWD.
THEY ARE ALL HERE TO SERVE UNDER INUKAI.
THEY DESIRE HIS LEADER-SHIP AND DIRECTION.
IF HE TOLD THEM...

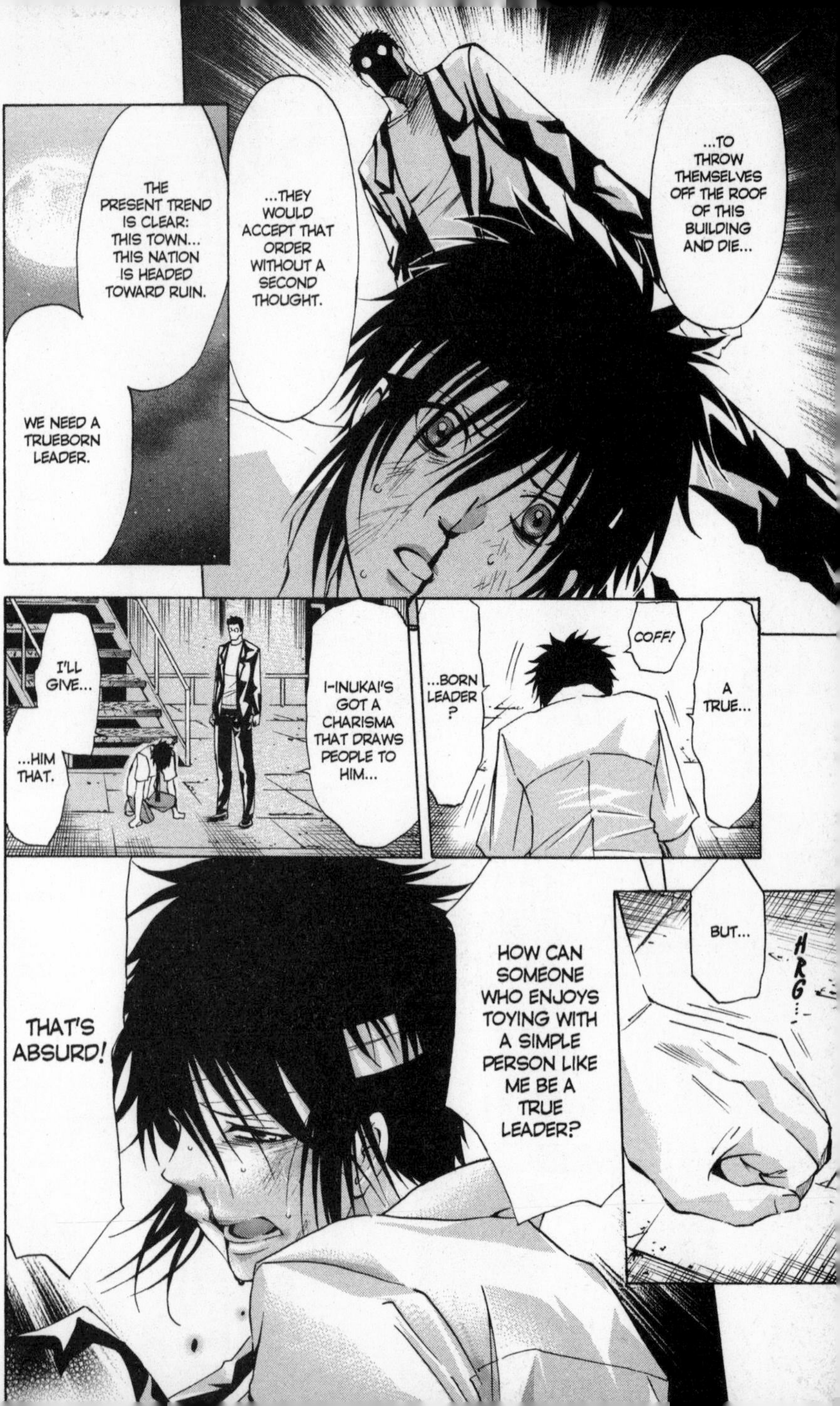
...TO THROW THEMSELVES OFF THE ROOF OF THIS BUILDING AND DIE...
...THEY WOULD ACCEPT THAT ORDER WITHOUT A SECOND THOUGHT.
THE PRESENT TREND IS CLEAR: THIS TOWN... THIS NATION IS HEADED TOWARD RUIN.
WE NEED A TRUEBORN LEADER.
A TRUE...
COFF!
...BORN LEADER?
I-INUKAI'S GOT A CHARISMA THAT DRAWS PEOPLE TO HIM...
I'LL GIVE...
...HIM THAT.
BUT...
HRG...
HOW CAN SOMEONE WHO ENJOYS TOYING WITH A SIMPLE PERSON LIKE ME BE A TRUE LEADER?
THAT'S ABSURD!

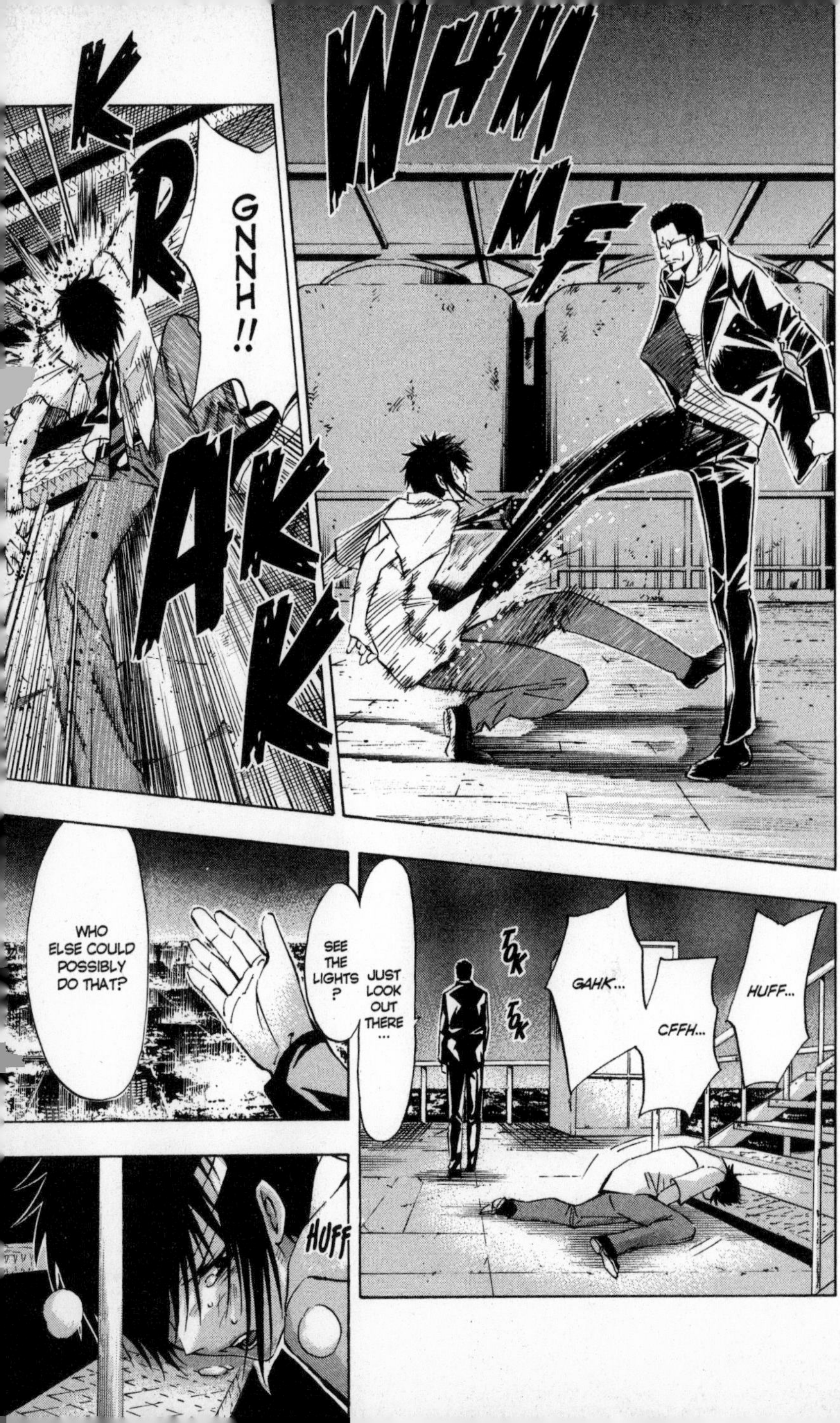
WHMMF
KRAKK
GNNH!!
HUFF...
GAHK...
CFFH...
TOK TOK
SEE THE LIGHTS? JUST LOOK OUT THERE...
WHO ELSE COULD POSSIBLY DO THAT?
HUFF

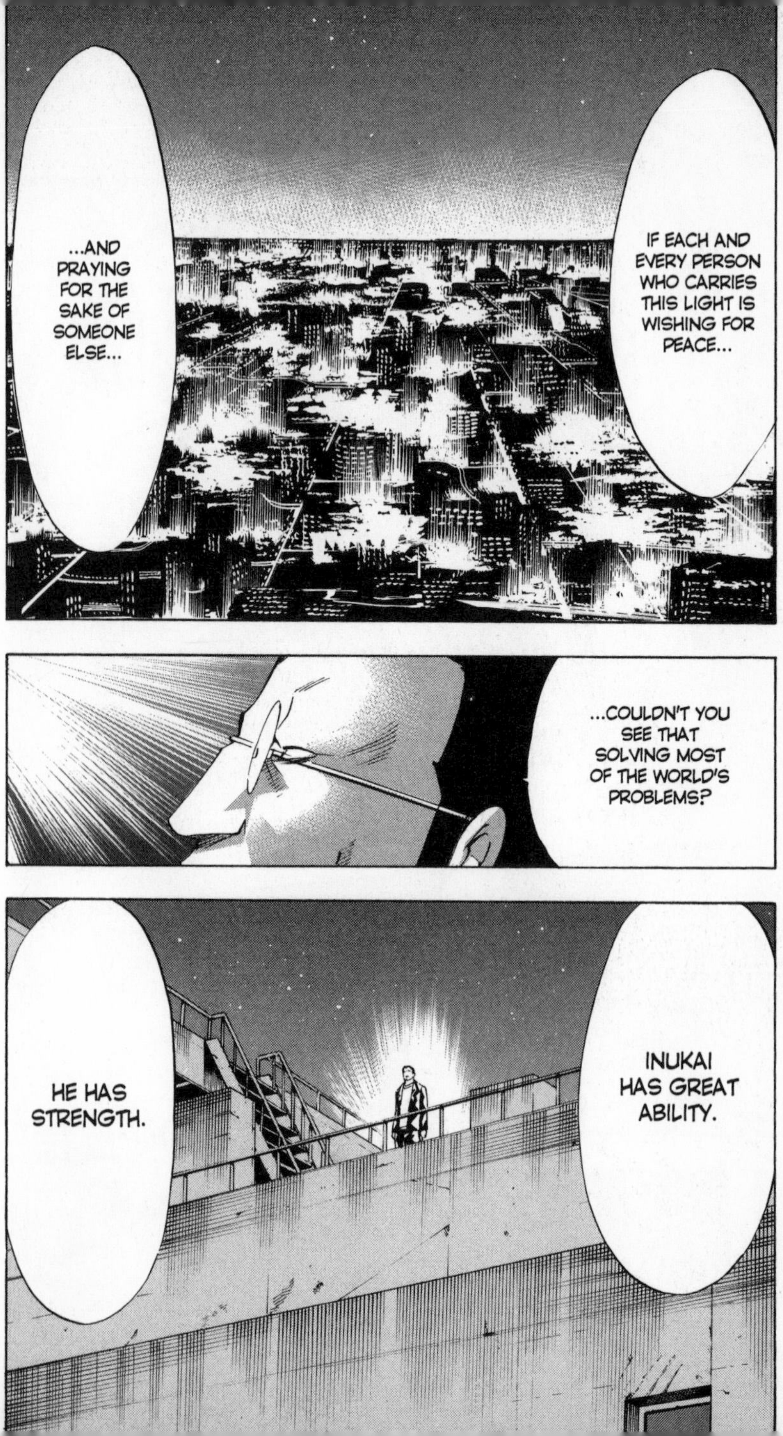
IF EACH AND EVERY PERSON WHO CARRIES THIS LIGHT IS WISHING FOR PEACE...
...AND PRAYING FOR THE SAKE OF SOMEONE ELSE...
...COULDN'T YOU SEE THAT SOLVING MOST OF THE WORLD'S PROBLEMS?
INUKAI HAS GREAT ABILITY.
HE HAS STRENGTH.

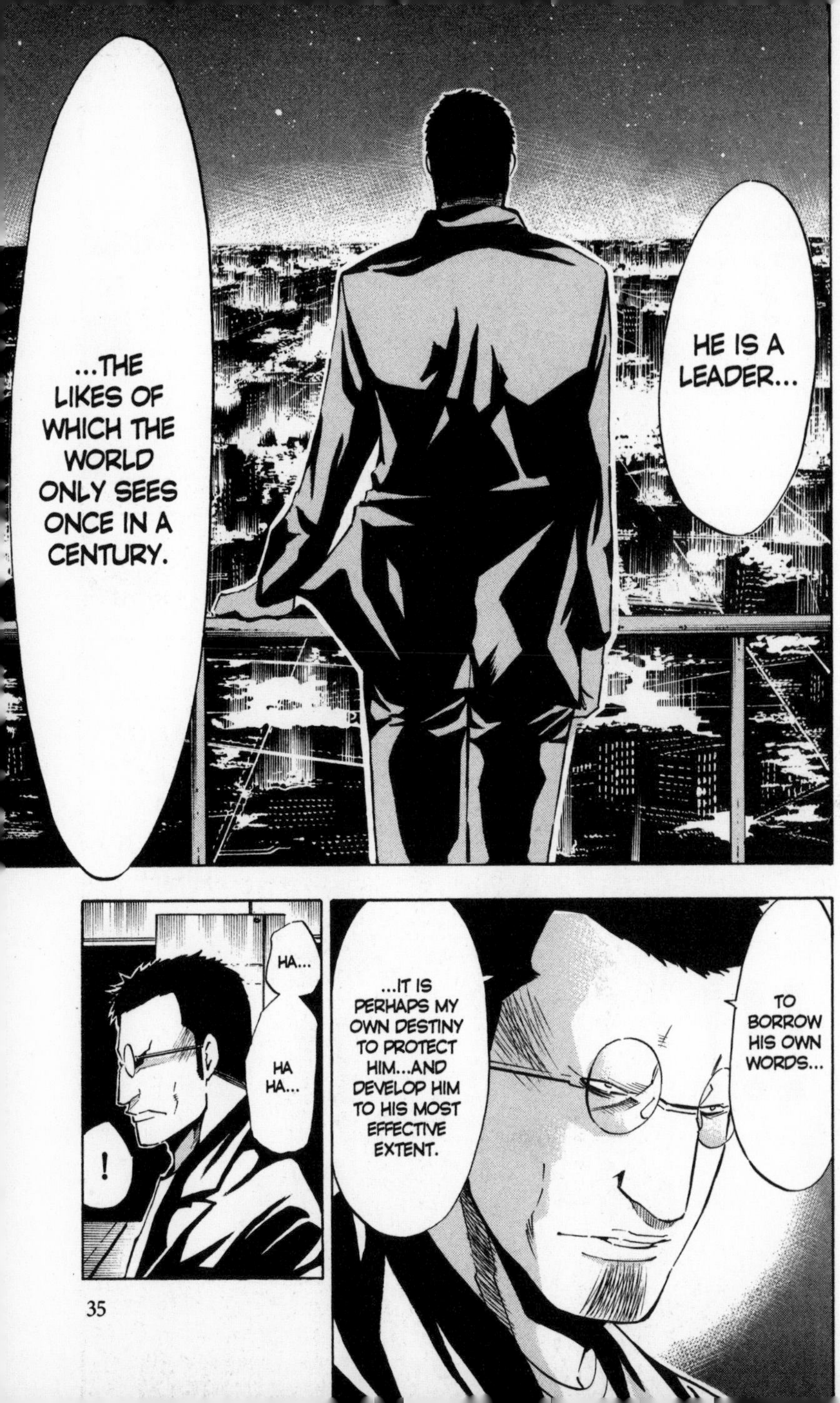
HE IS A LEADER...
...THE LIKES OF WHICH THE WORLD ONLY SEES ONCE IN A CENTURY.
TO BORROW HIS OWN WORDS...
...IT IS PERHAPS MY OWN DESTINY TO PROTECT HIM...AND DEVELOP HIM TO HIS MOST EFFECTIVE EXTENT.
HA...
HA HA...
!

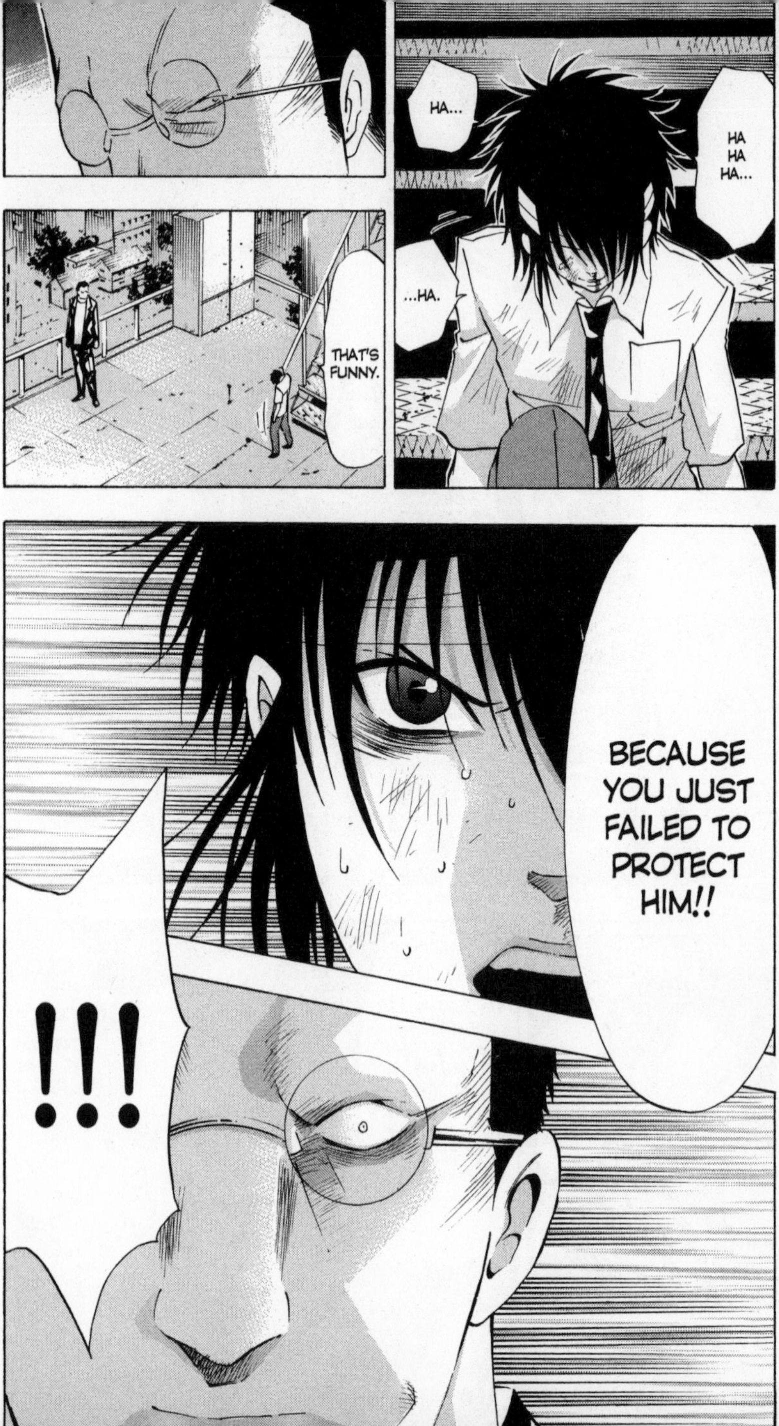
HA...
HA HA HA...
...HA.
THAT'S FUNNY.
BECAUSE YOU JUST FAILED TO PROTECT HIM!!
!!!

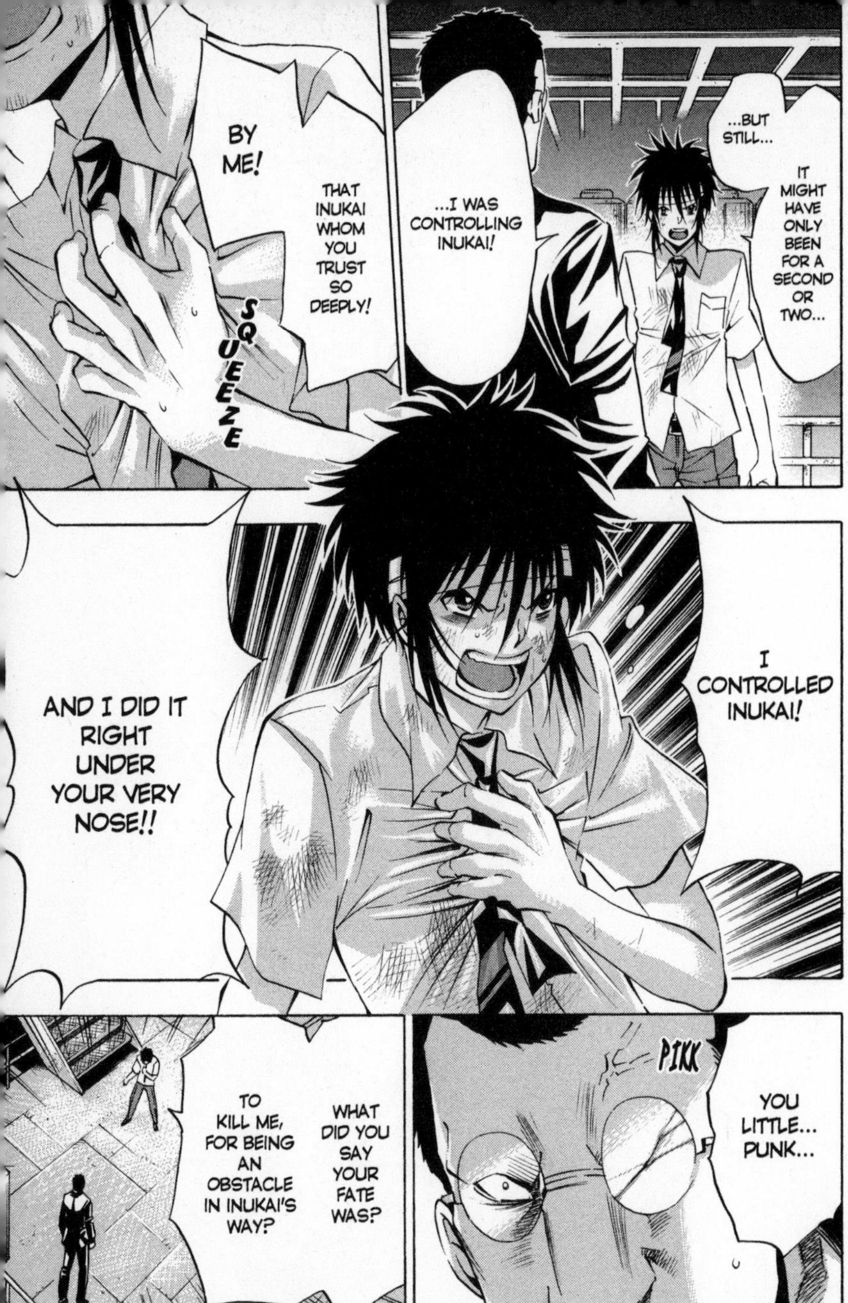
...BUT STILL...
IT MIGHT HAVE ONLY BEEN FOR A SECOND OR TWO...
...I WAS CONTROLLING INUKAI!
THAT INUKAI WHOM YOU TRUST SO DEEPLY!
BY ME!
SQUEEZE
I CONTROLLED INUKAI!
AND I DID IT RIGHT UNDER YOUR VERY NOSE!!
PIKK
YOU LITTLE... PUNK...
WHAT DID YOU SAY YOUR FATE WAS?
TO KILL ME, FOR BEING AN OBSTACLE IN INUKAI'S WAY?

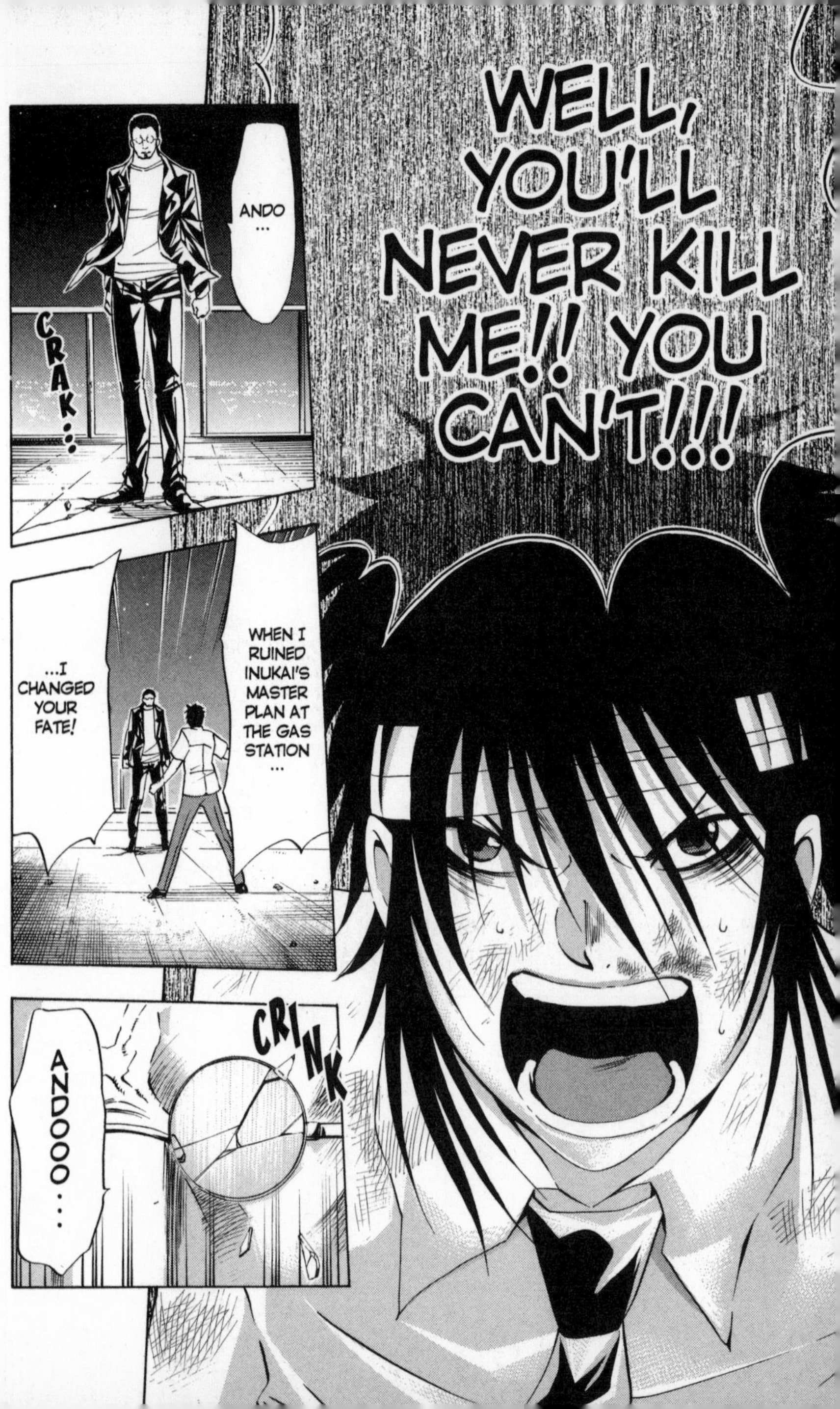
WELL, YOU'LL NEVER KILL ME!! YOU CAN'T!!!
ANDO ...
CRAK...
WHEN I RUINED INUKAI'S MASTER PLAN AT THE GAS STATION ...
...I CHANGED YOUR FATE!
CRINK
ANDOOO...

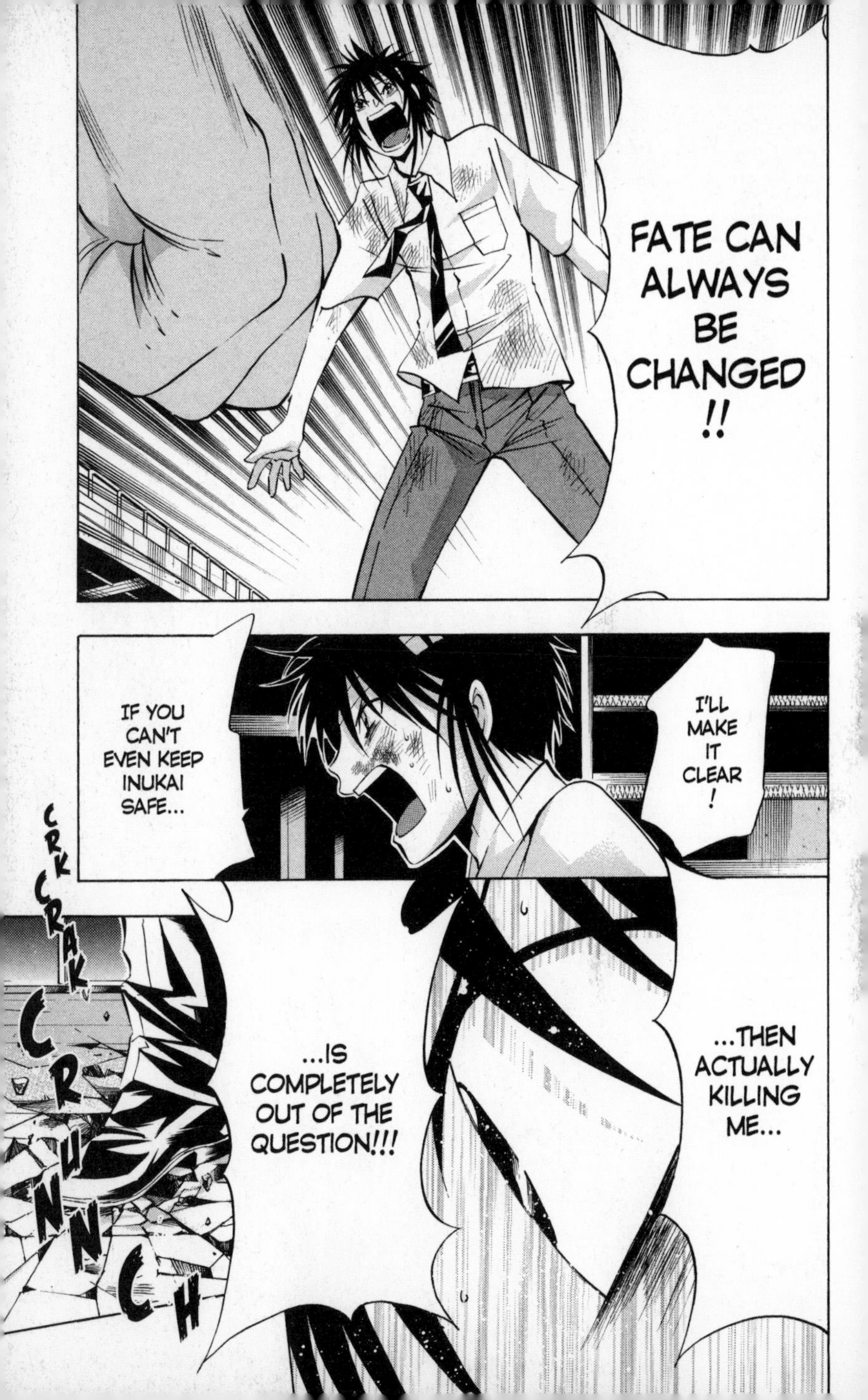
FATE CAN ALWAYS BE CHANGED!!
I'LL MAKE IT CLEAR!
IF YOU CAN'T EVEN KEEP INUKAI SAFE...
...THEN ACTUALLY KILLING ME...
...IS COMPLETELY OUT OF THE QUESTION!!!
CRK
CRAK
CRUNNCH

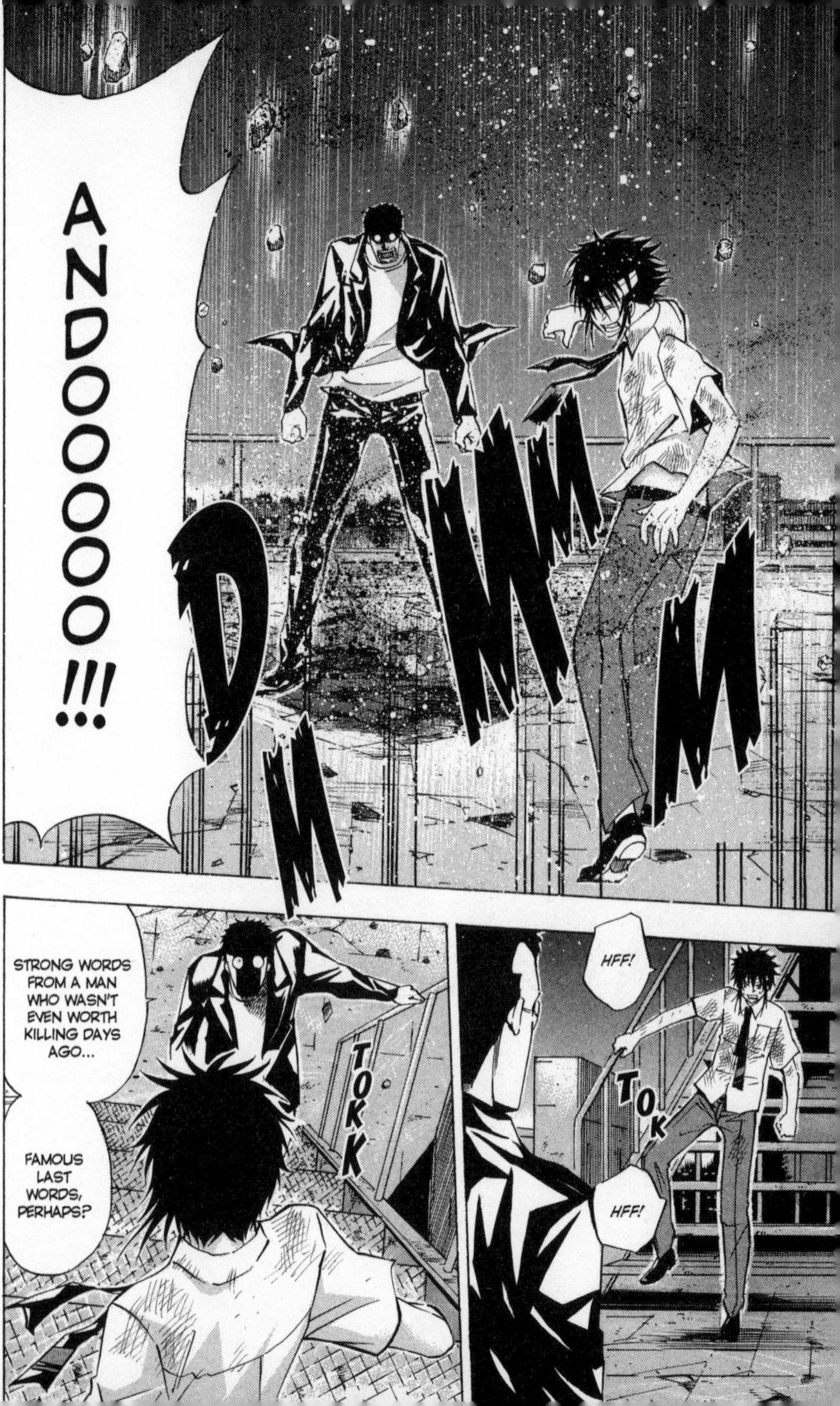
ANDOOOOOO!!!
DMMMMM
HFF!
TOK
HFF!
STRONG WORDS FROM A MAN WHO WASN'T EVEN WORTH KILLING DAYS AGO...
TOKK
FAMOUS LAST WORDS, PERHAPS?

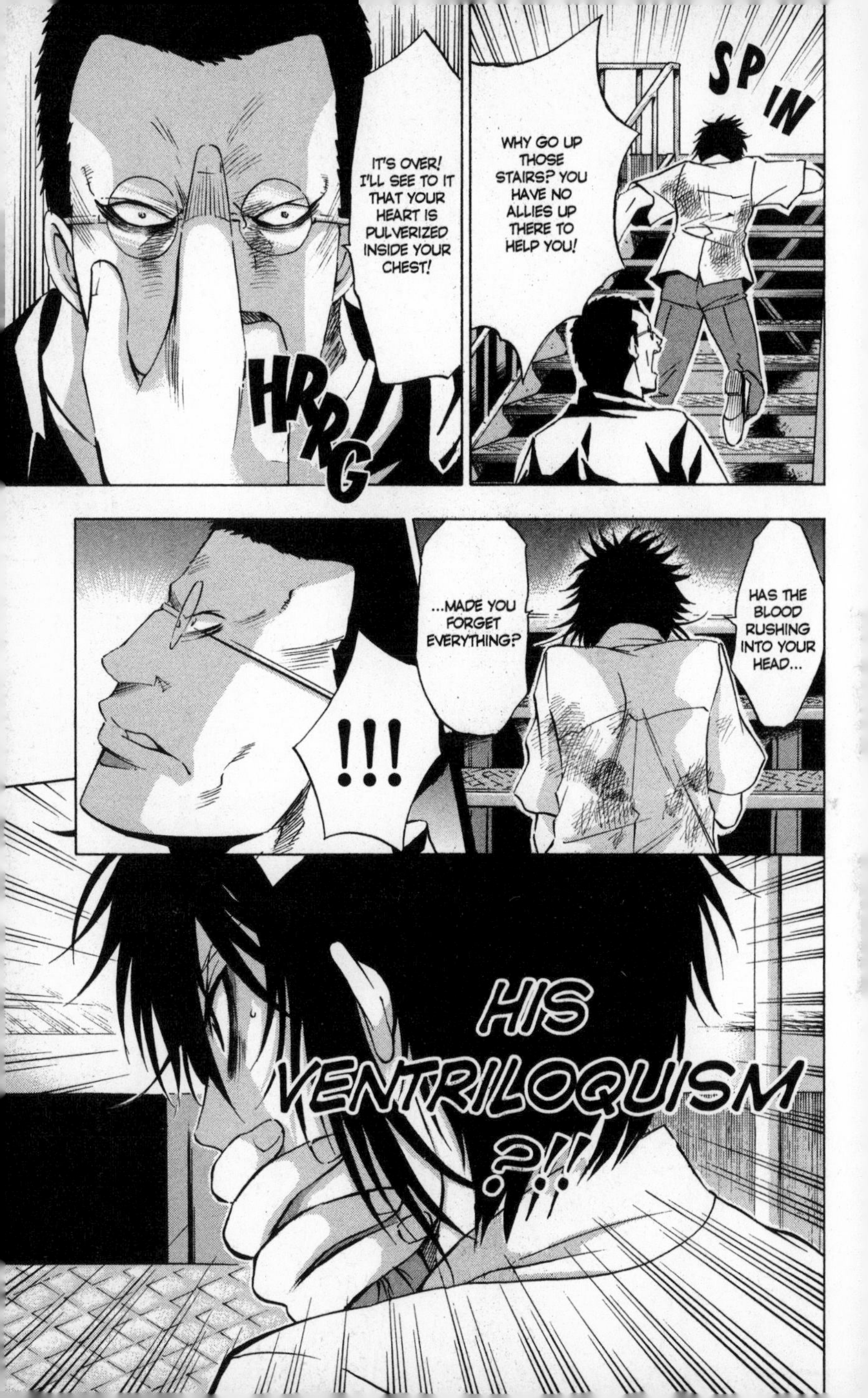
SPIN
WHY GO UP THOSE STAIRS? YOU HAVE NO ALLIES UP THERE TO HELP YOU!
IT'S OVER! I'LL SEE TO IT THAT YOUR HEART IS PULVERIZED INSIDE YOUR CHEST!
HRRG
HAS THE BLOOD RUSHING INTO YOUR HEAD...
...MADE YOU FORGET EVERYTHING?
!!!
HIS VENTRILOQUISM ?!!

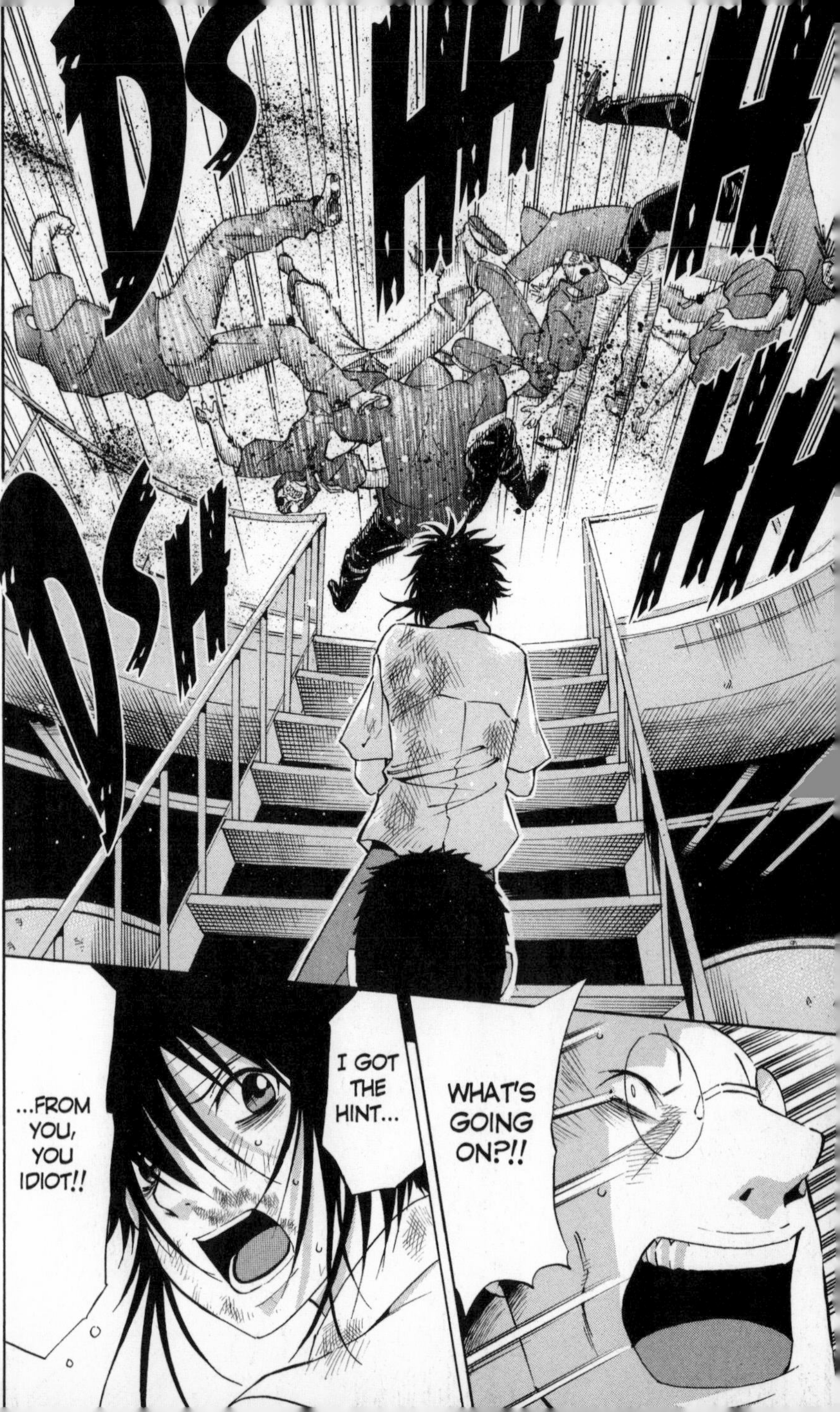
DSHHH-HHHH
DSH
WHAT'S GOING ON?!!
I GOT THE HINT...
...FROM YOU, YOU IDIOT!!

Chapter 30 • Inukai's Light and Ando's Isolation

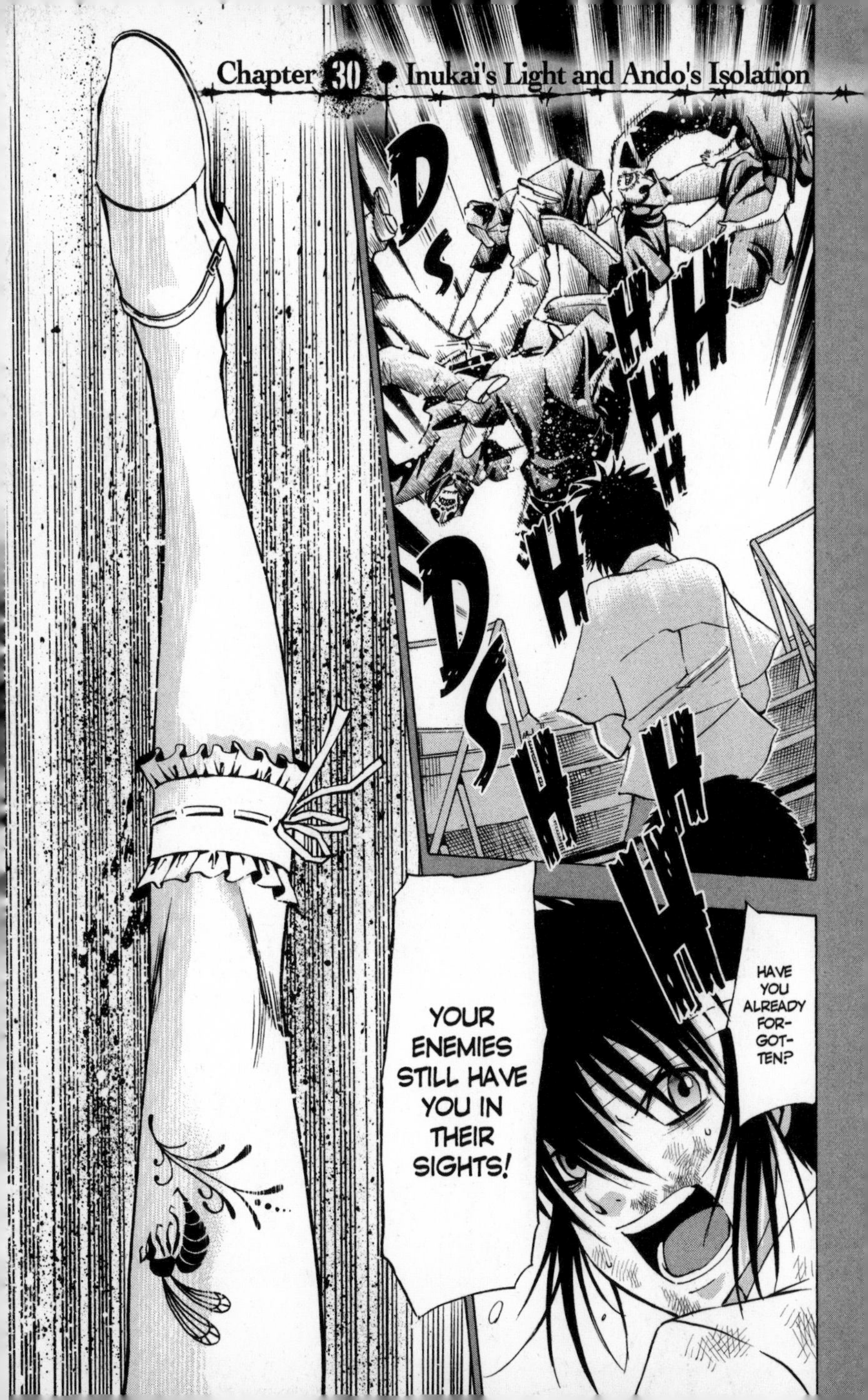
DSHHHHHH
DSHHHHHH
HAVE YOU ALREADY FOR-GOT-TEN?
YOUR ENEMIES STILL HAVE YOU IN THEIR SIGHTS!

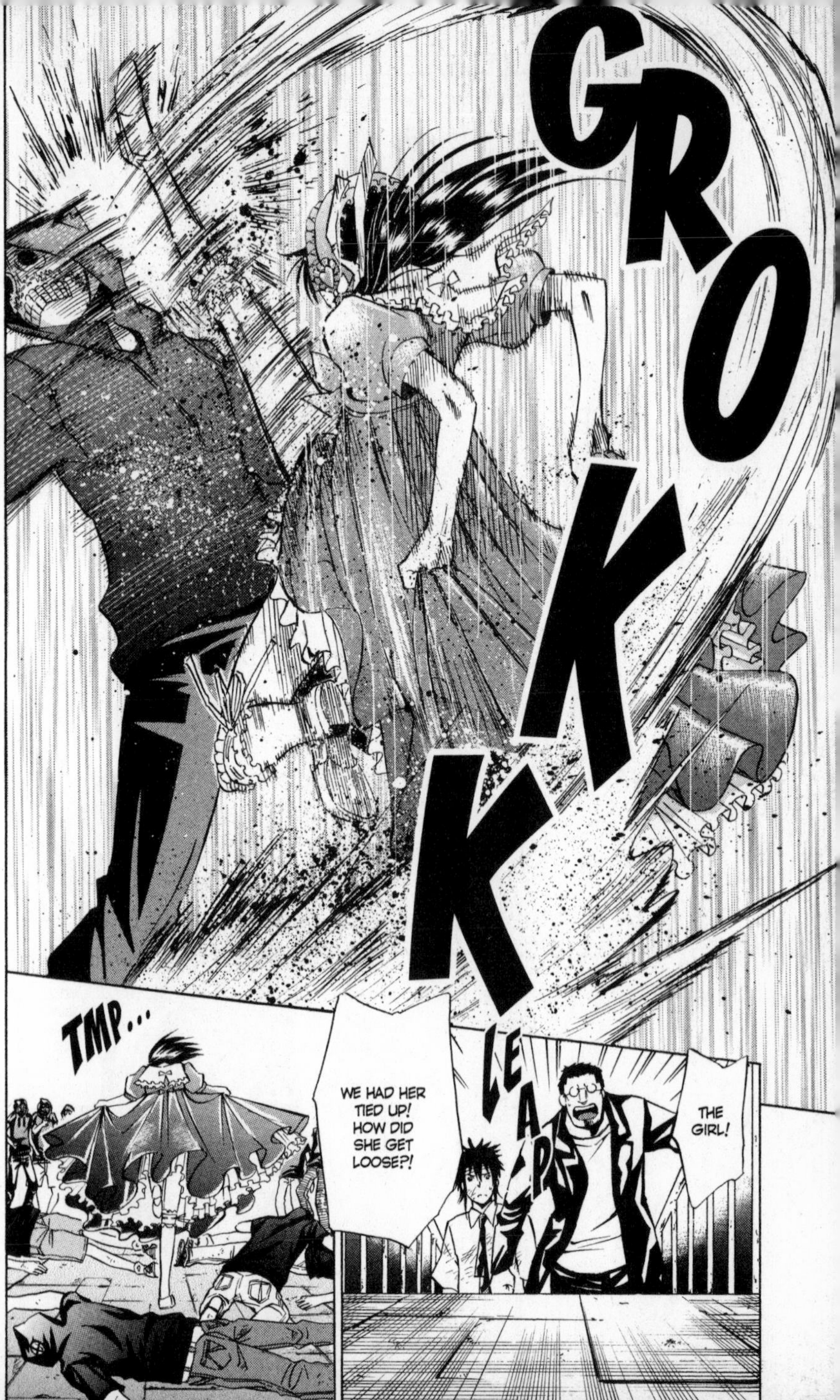
GROKKK
THE GIRL!
LEAP
WE HAD HER TIED UP! HOW DID SHE GET LOOSE?!
TMP...

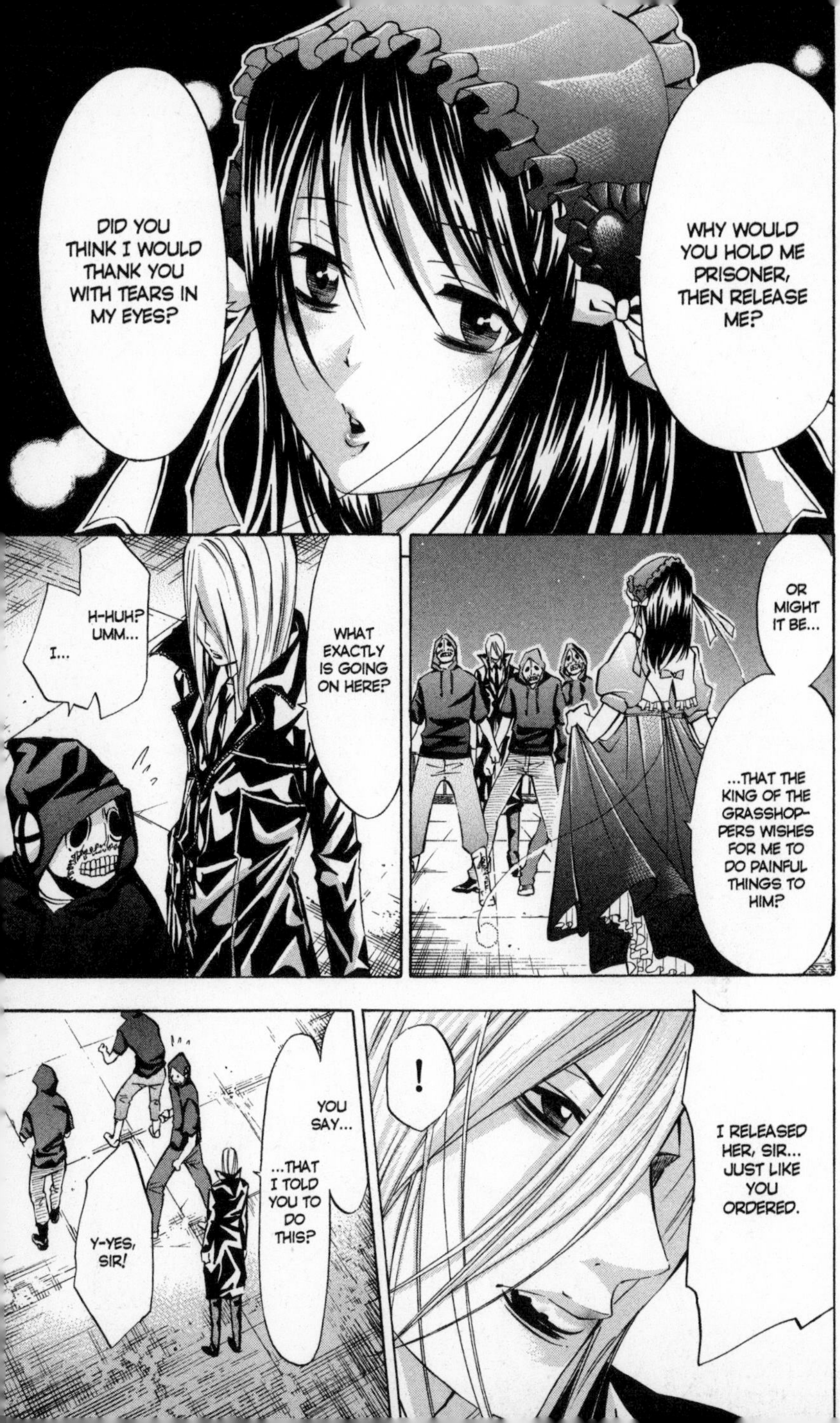
WHY WOULD YOU HOLD ME PRISONER, THEN RELEASE ME?
DID YOU THINK I WOULD THANK YOU WITH TEARS IN MY EYES?
OR MIGHT IT BE...
...THAT THE KING OF THE GRASSHOPPERS WISHES FOR ME TO DO PAINFUL THINGS TO HIM?
WHAT EXACTLY IS GOING ON HERE?
H-HUH? UMM... I...
I RELEASED HER, SIR... JUST LIKE YOU ORDERED.
!
YOU SAY... ...THAT I TOLD YOU TO DO THIS?
Y-YES, SIR!

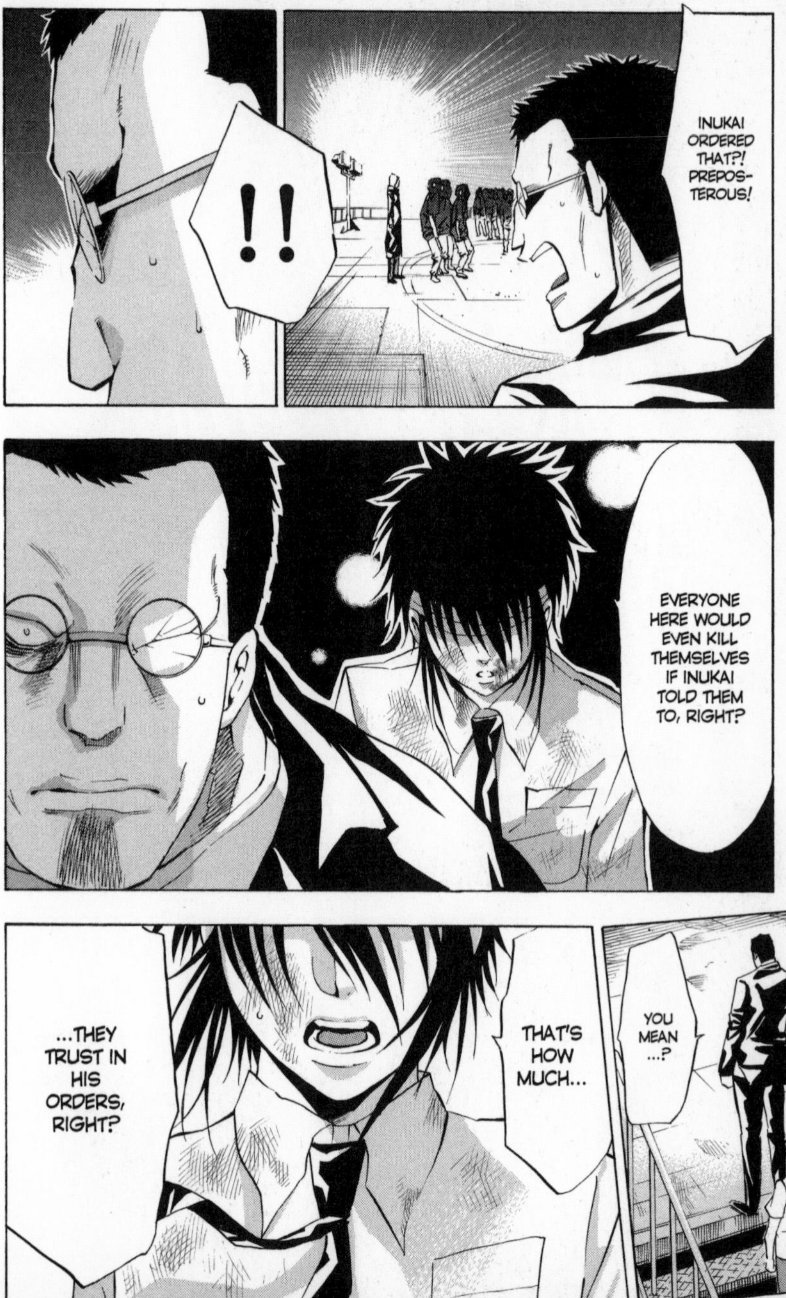
INUKAI ORDERED THAT?! PREPOSTEROUS!
!!
EVERYONE HERE WOULD EVEN KILL THEMSELVES IF INUKAI TOLD THEM TO, RIGHT?
YOU MEAN ...?
THAT'S HOW MUCH...
...THEY TRUST IN HIS ORDERS, RIGHT?

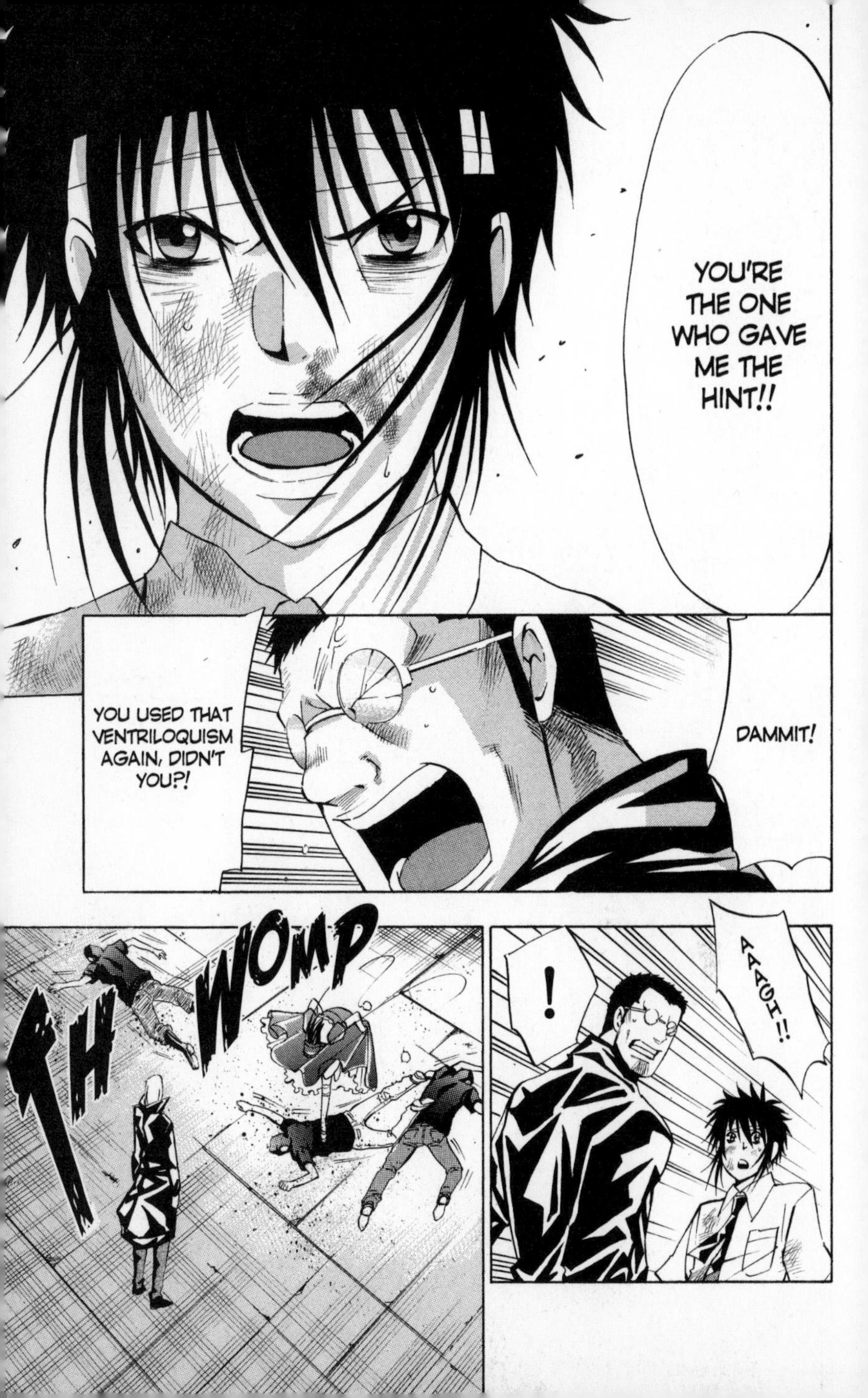
YOU'RE THE ONE WHO GAVE ME THE HINT!!
DAMMIT!
YOU USED THAT VENTRILOQUISM AGAIN, DIDN'T YOU?!
AAAGH!!
!
THWOMP

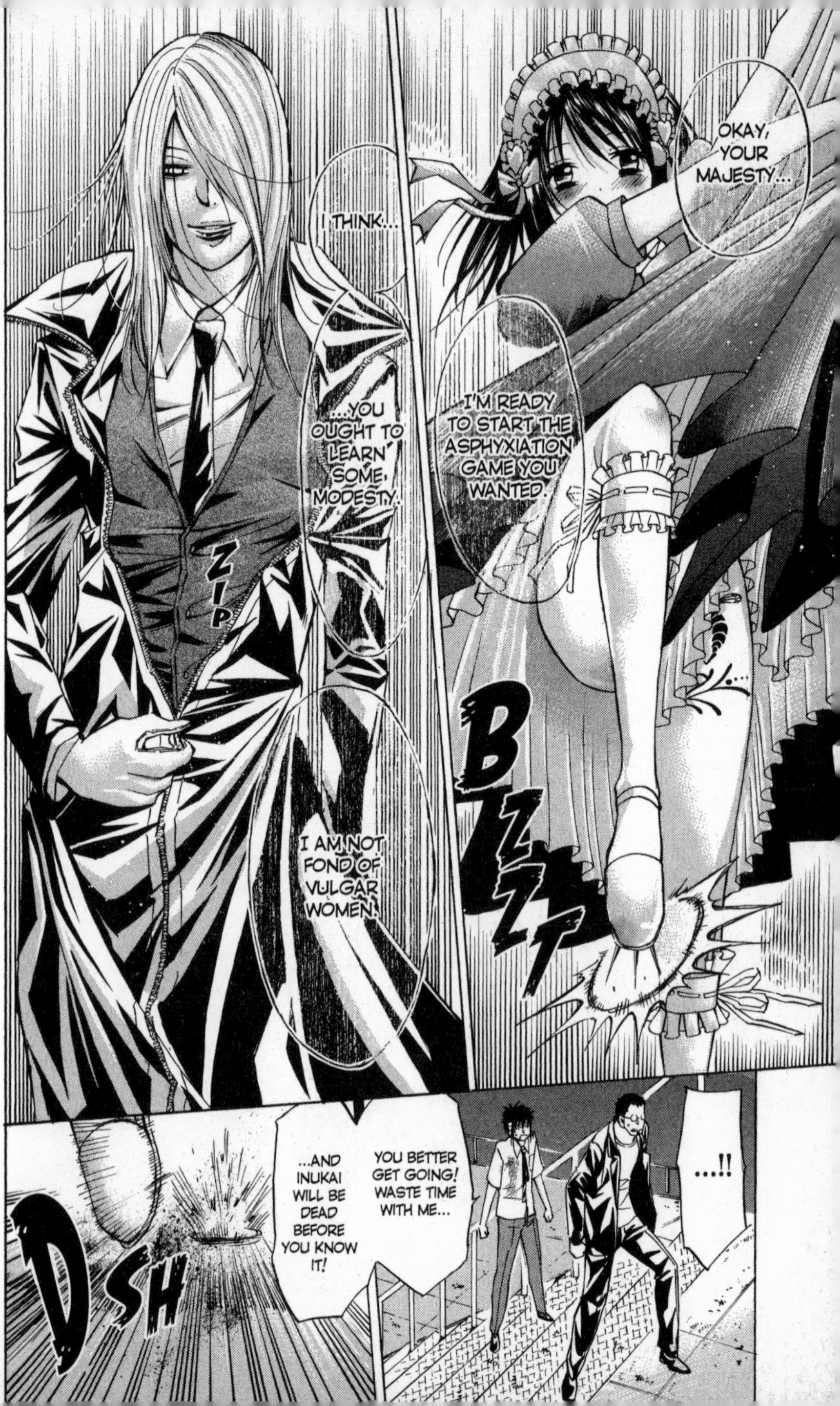
OKAY, YOUR MAJESTY...
I'M READY TO START THE ASPHYXIATION GAME YOU WANTED.
BZZZT
I THINK...
...YOU OUGHT TO LEARN SOME MODESTY.
ZIP
I AM NOT FOND OF VULGAR WOMEN.
...!!
YOU BETTER GET GOING! WASTE TIME WITH ME...
...AND INUKAI WILL BE DEAD BEFORE YOU KNOW IT!
DSH

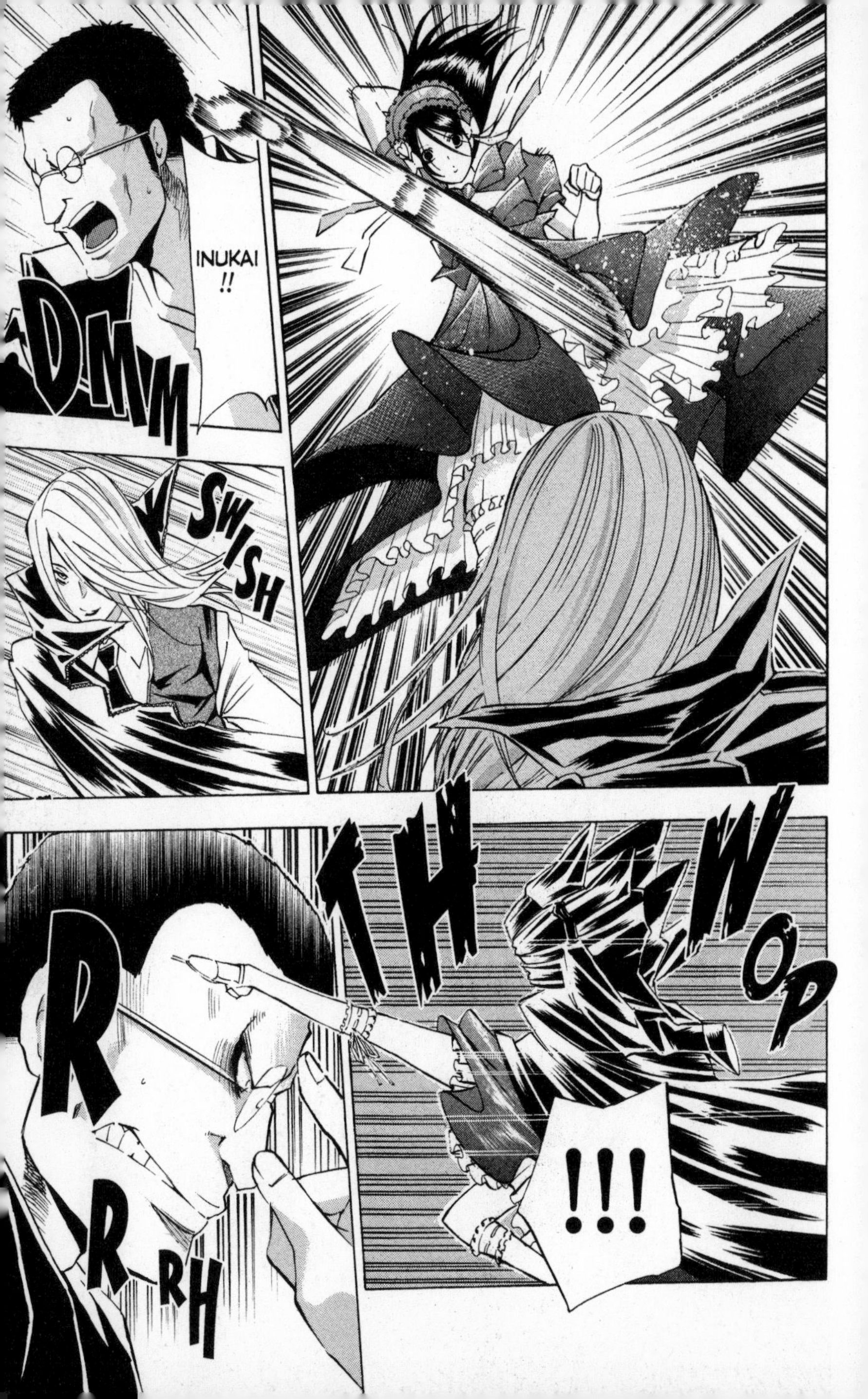
INUKAI !!
DMM
SWISH
THWOP
!!!
RRRH

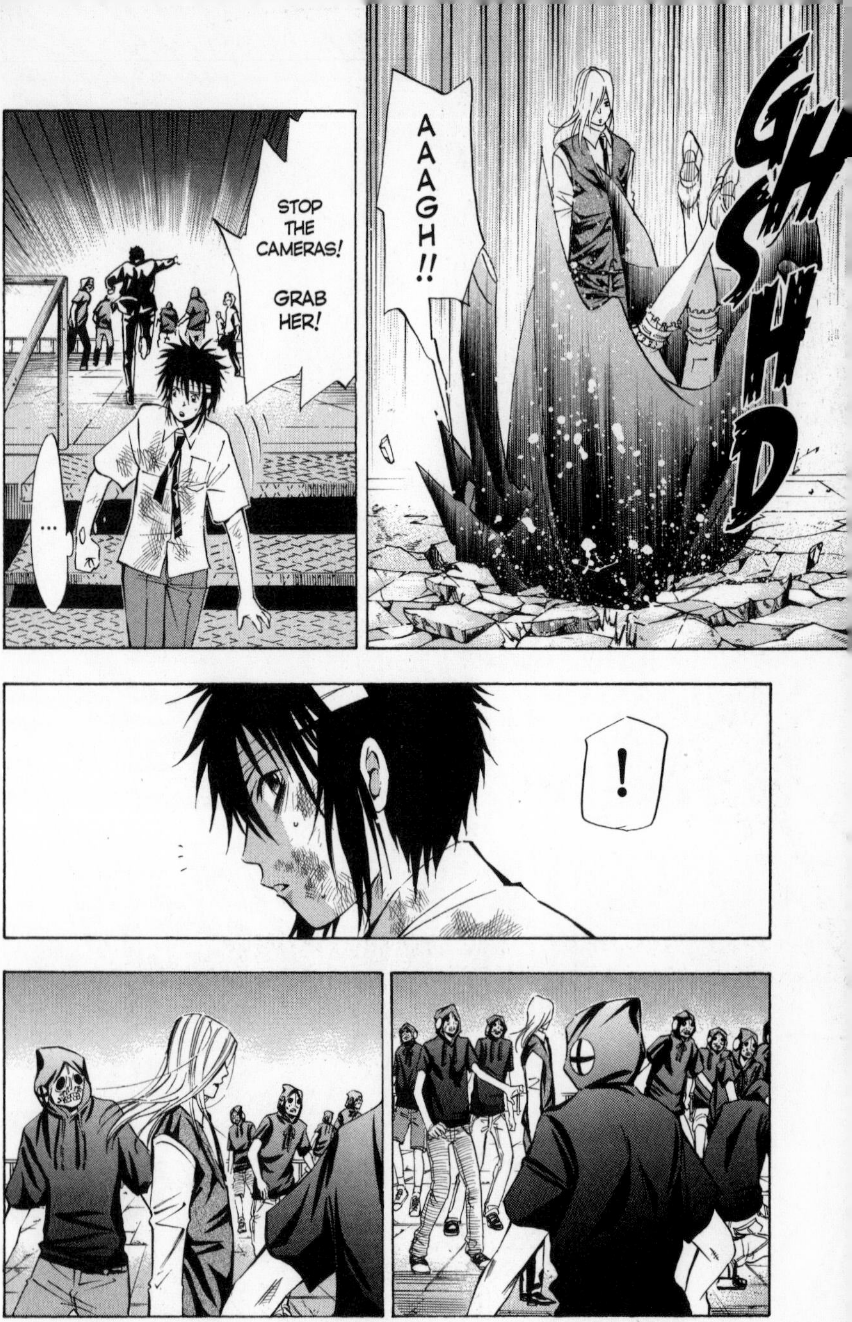
AAAGH!!
GHSHD
STOP THE CAMERAS!
GRAB HER!
...
!

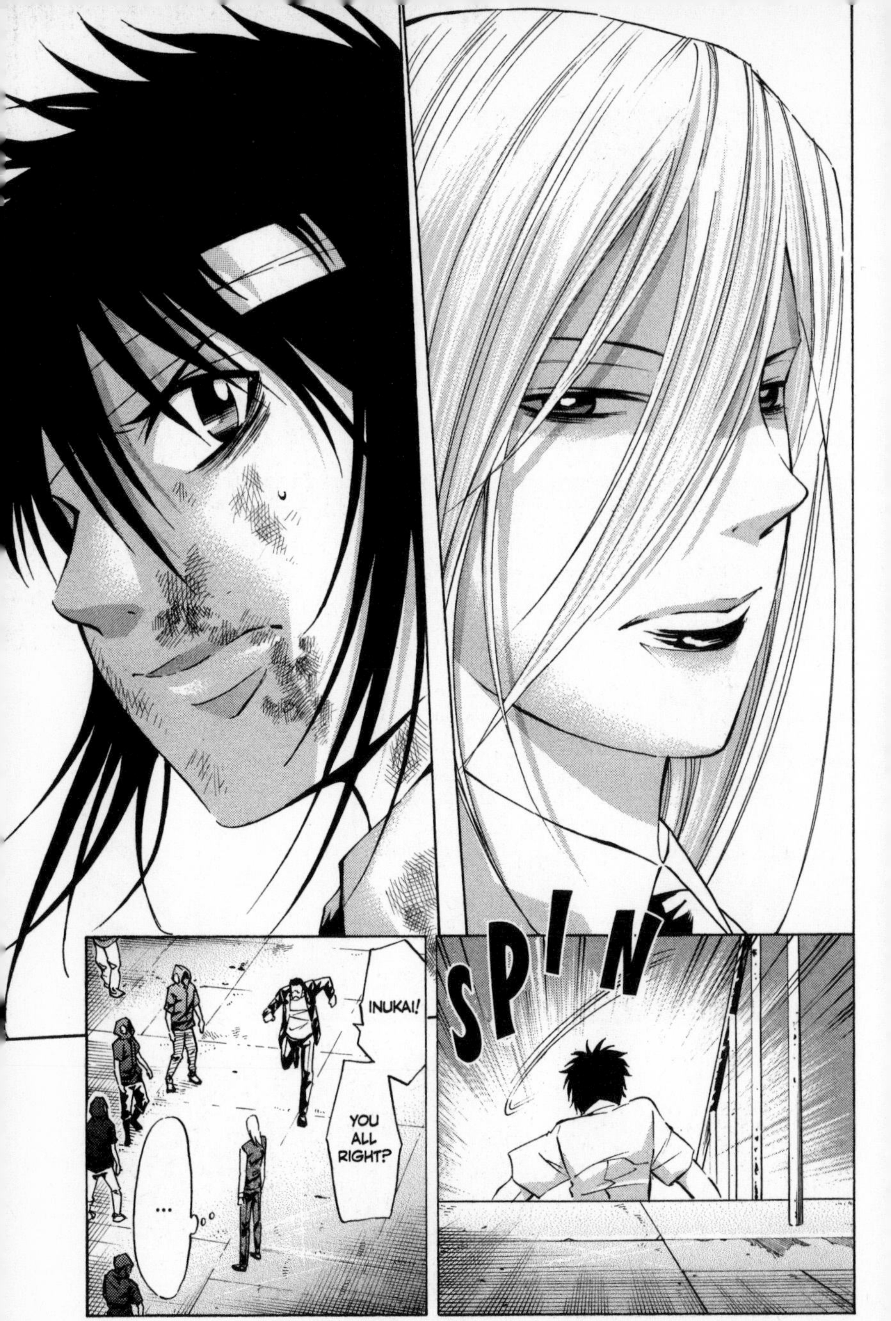
SPIN
INUKAI!
YOU ALL RIGHT?
...

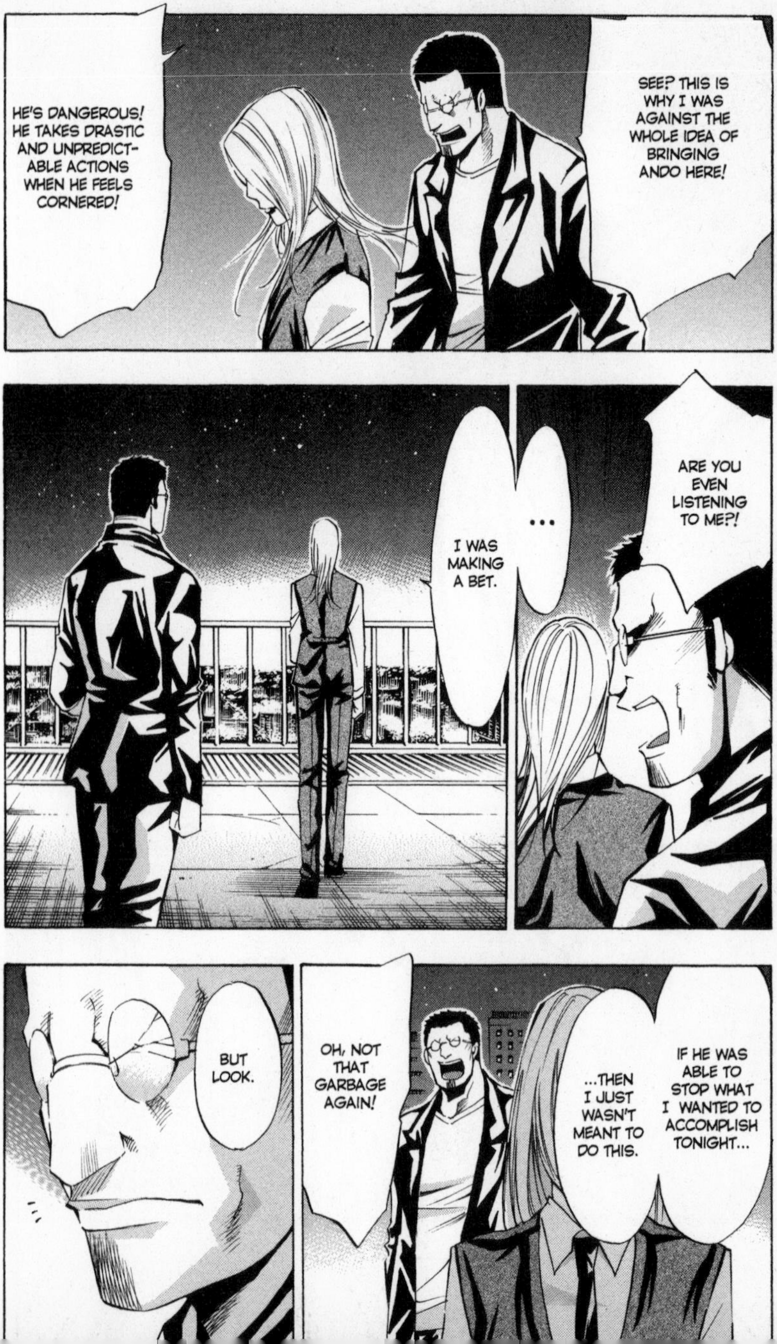
SEE? THIS IS WHY I WAS AGAINST THE WHOLE IDEA OF BRINGING ANDO HERE!
HE'S DANGEROUS! HE TAKES DRASTIC AND UNPREDICT-ABLE ACTIONS WHEN HE FEELS CORNERED!
ARE YOU EVEN LISTENING TO ME?!
...
I WAS MAKING A BET.
IF HE WAS ABLE TO STOP WHAT I WANTED TO ACCOMPLISH TONIGHT...
...THEN I JUST WASN'T MEANT TO DO THIS.
OH, NOT THAT GARBAGE AGAIN!
BUT LOOK.

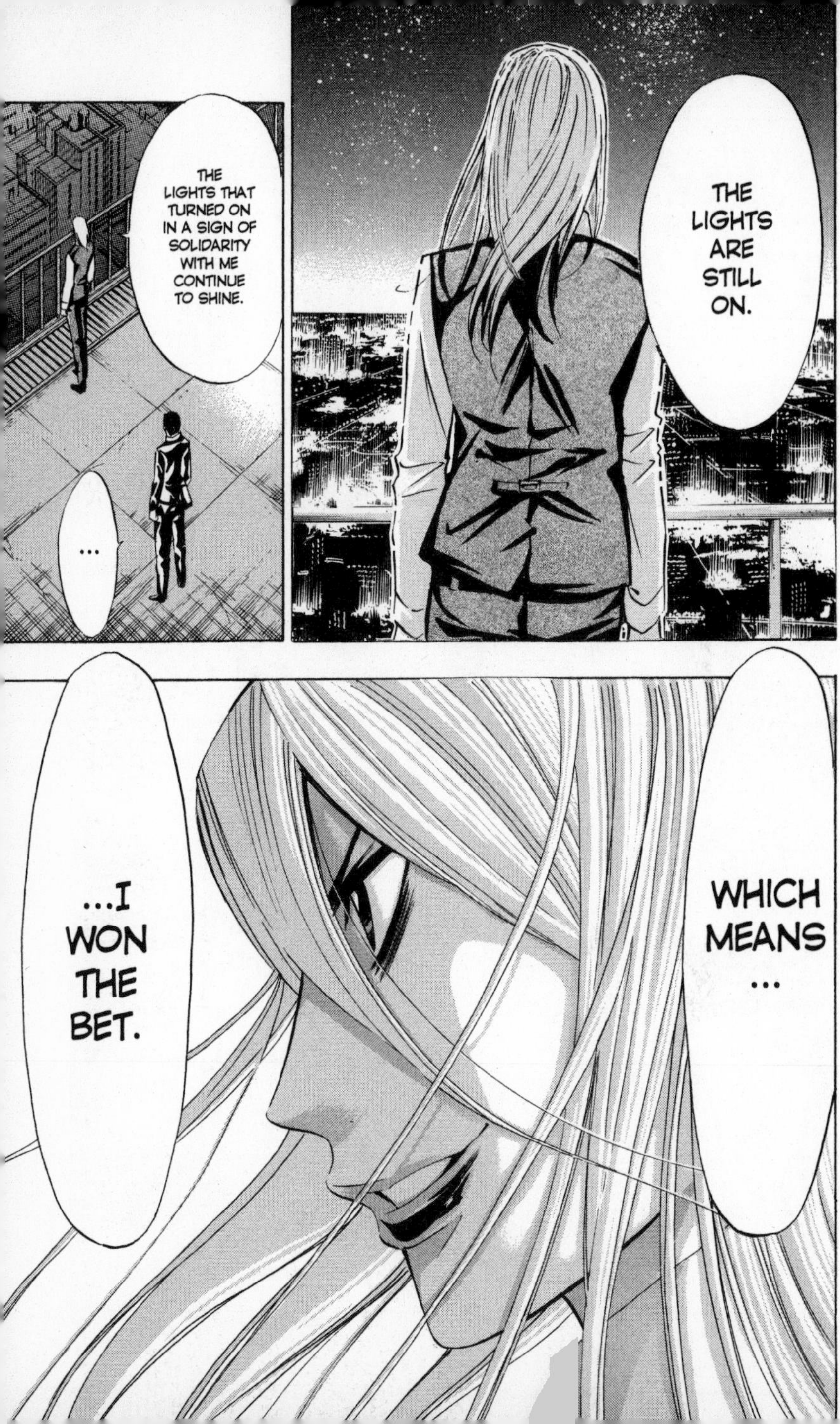
THE LIGHTS ARE STILL ON.
THE LIGHTS THAT TURNED ON IN A SIGN OF SOLIDARITY WITH ME CONTINUE TO SHINE.
...
WHICH MEANS ...
...I WON THE BET.

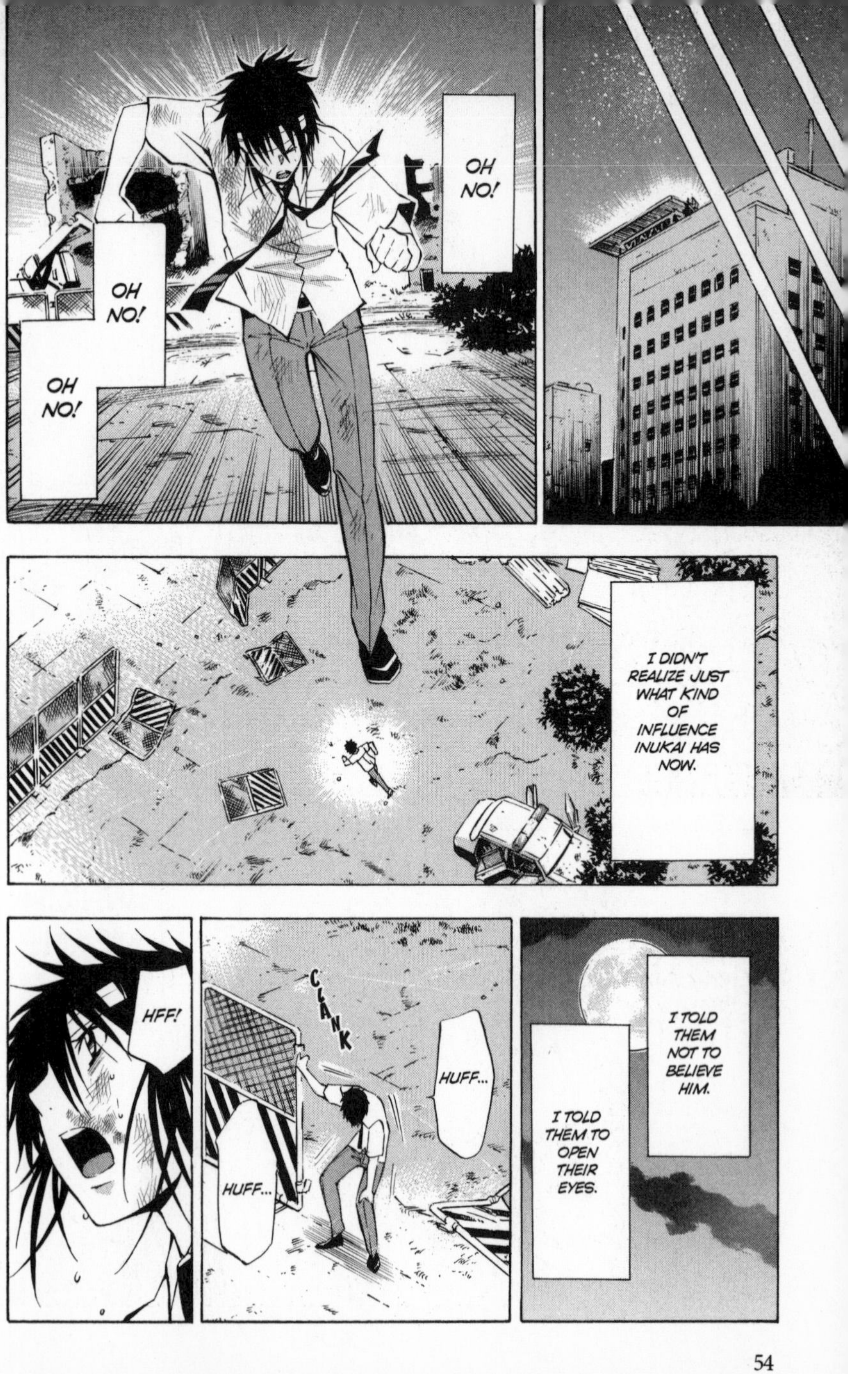
OH NO!
OH NO!
OH NO!
I DIDN'T REALIZE JUST WHAT KIND OF INFLUENCE INUKAI HAS NOW.
I TOLD THEM NOT TO BELIEVE HIM.
I TOLD THEM TO OPEN THEIR EYES.
CLANK
HUFF...
HUFF...
HFF!

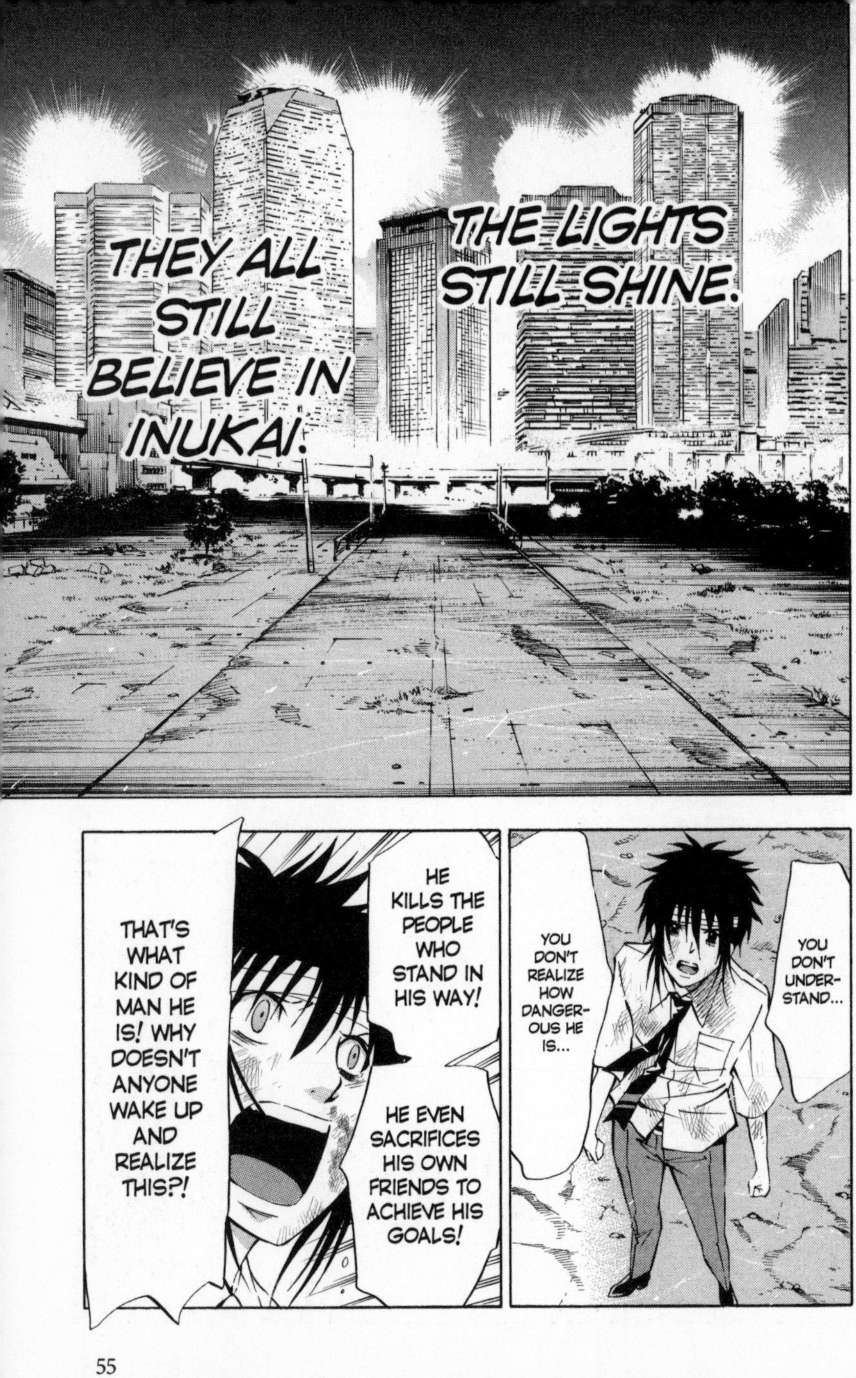
THE LIGHTS STILL SHINE.
THEY ALL STILL BELIEVE IN INUKAI.
YOU DON'T UNDER-STAND...
YOU DON'T REALIZE HOW DANGER-OUS HE IS...
HE KILLS THE PEOPLE WHO STAND IN HIS WAY!
HE EVEN SACRIFICES HIS OWN FRIENDS TO ACHIEVE HIS GOALS!
THAT'S WHAT KIND OF MAN HE IS! WHY DOESN'T ANYONE WAKE UP AND REALIZE THIS?!

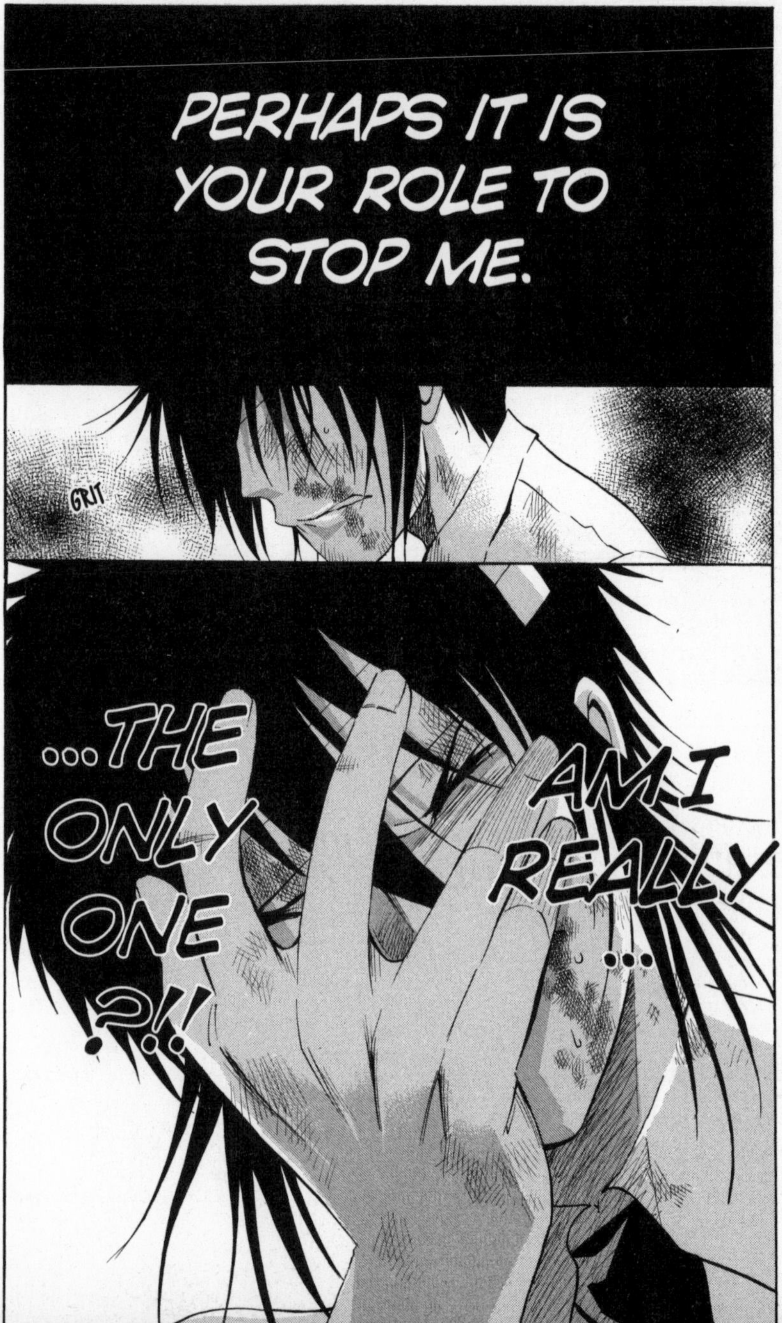
PERHAPS IT IS YOUR ROLE TO STOP ME.
GRIT
AM I REALLY ...
...THE ONLY ONE ?!!

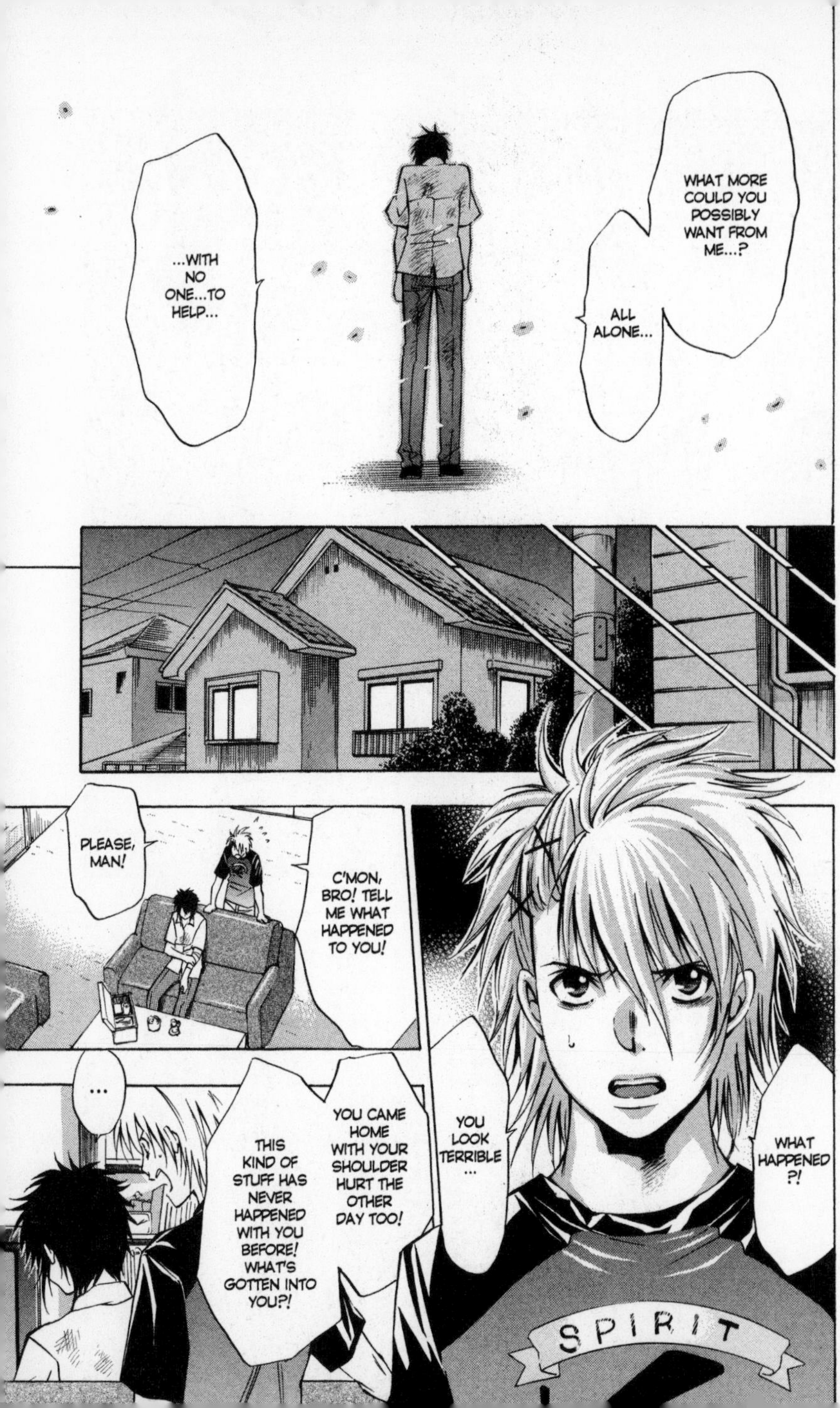
WHAT MORE COULD YOU POSSIBLY WANT FROM ME...?
ALL ALONE...
...WITH NO ONE...TO HELP...
WHAT HAPPENED?!
YOU LOOK TERRIBLE...
C'MON, BRO! TELL ME WHAT HAPPENED TO YOU!
PLEASE, MAN!
YOU CAME HOME WITH YOUR SHOULDER HURT THE OTHER DAY TOO!
THIS KIND OF STUFF HAS NEVER HAPPENED WITH YOU BEFORE! WHAT'S GOTTEN INTO YOU?!
...
SPIRIT

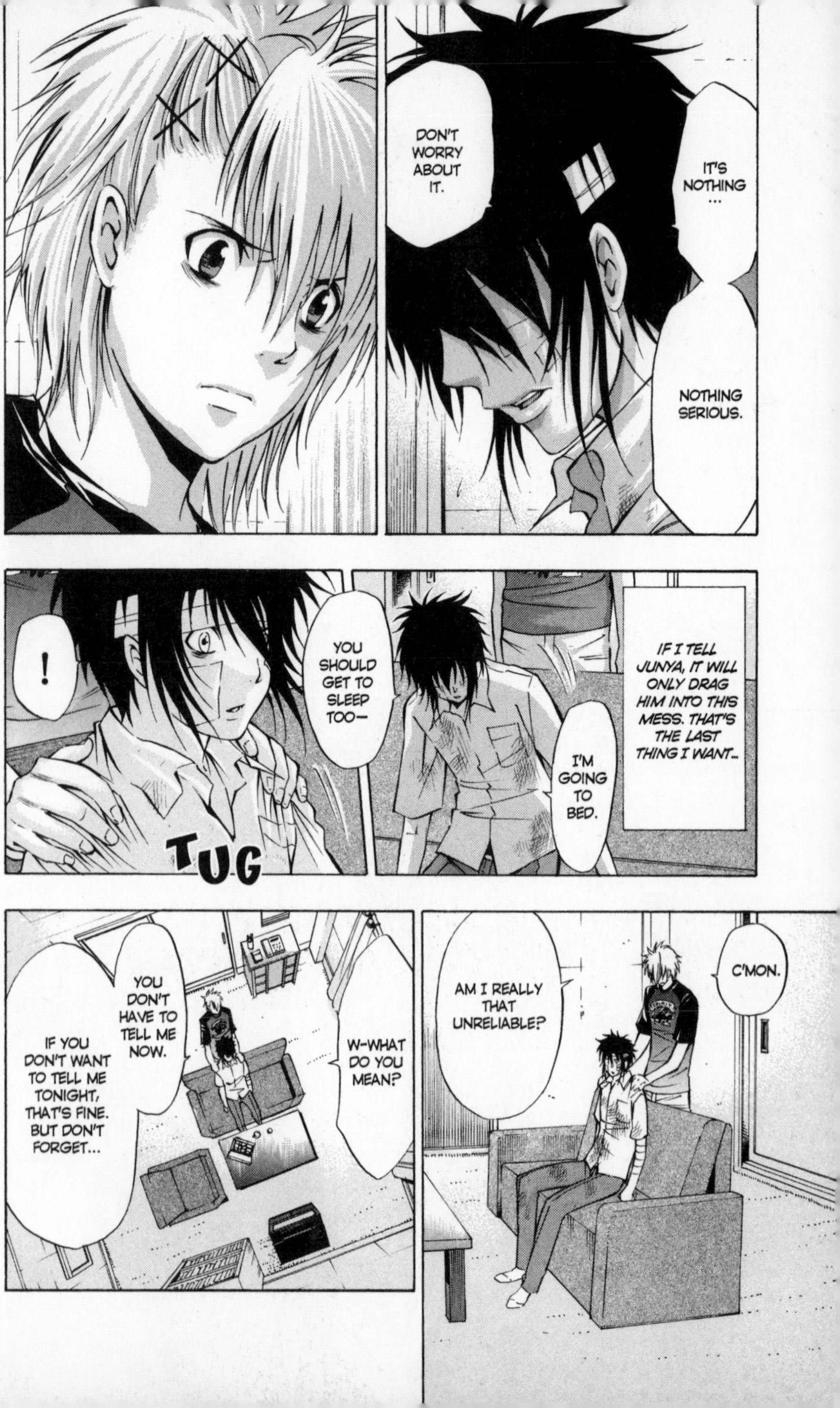
IT'S NOTHING ...
NOTHING SERIOUS.
DON'T WORRY ABOUT IT.
IF I TELL JUNYA, IT WILL ONLY DRAG HIM INTO THIS MESS. THAT'S THE LAST THING I WANT...
I'M GOING TO BED.
YOU SHOULD GET TO SLEEP TOO—
!
TUG
C'MON.
AM I REALLY THAT UNRELIABLE?
W-WHAT DO YOU MEAN?
YOU DON'T HAVE TO TELL ME NOW.
IF YOU DON'T WANT TO TELL ME TONIGHT, THAT'S FINE. BUT DON'T FORGET...

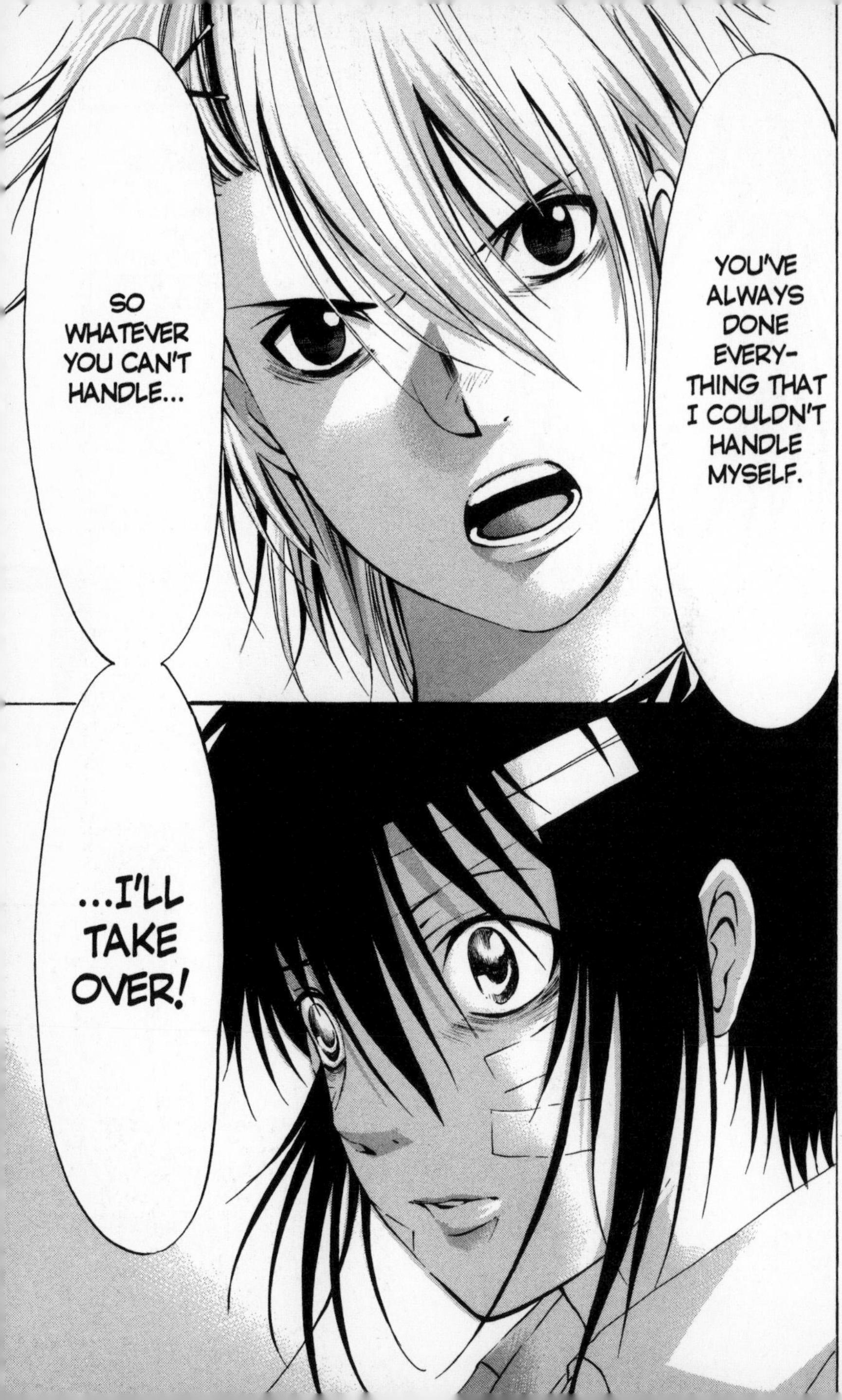
YOU'VE ALWAYS DONE EVERY-THING THAT I COULDN'T HANDLE MYSELF.
SO WHATEVER YOU CAN'T HANDLE...
...I'LL TAKE OVER!

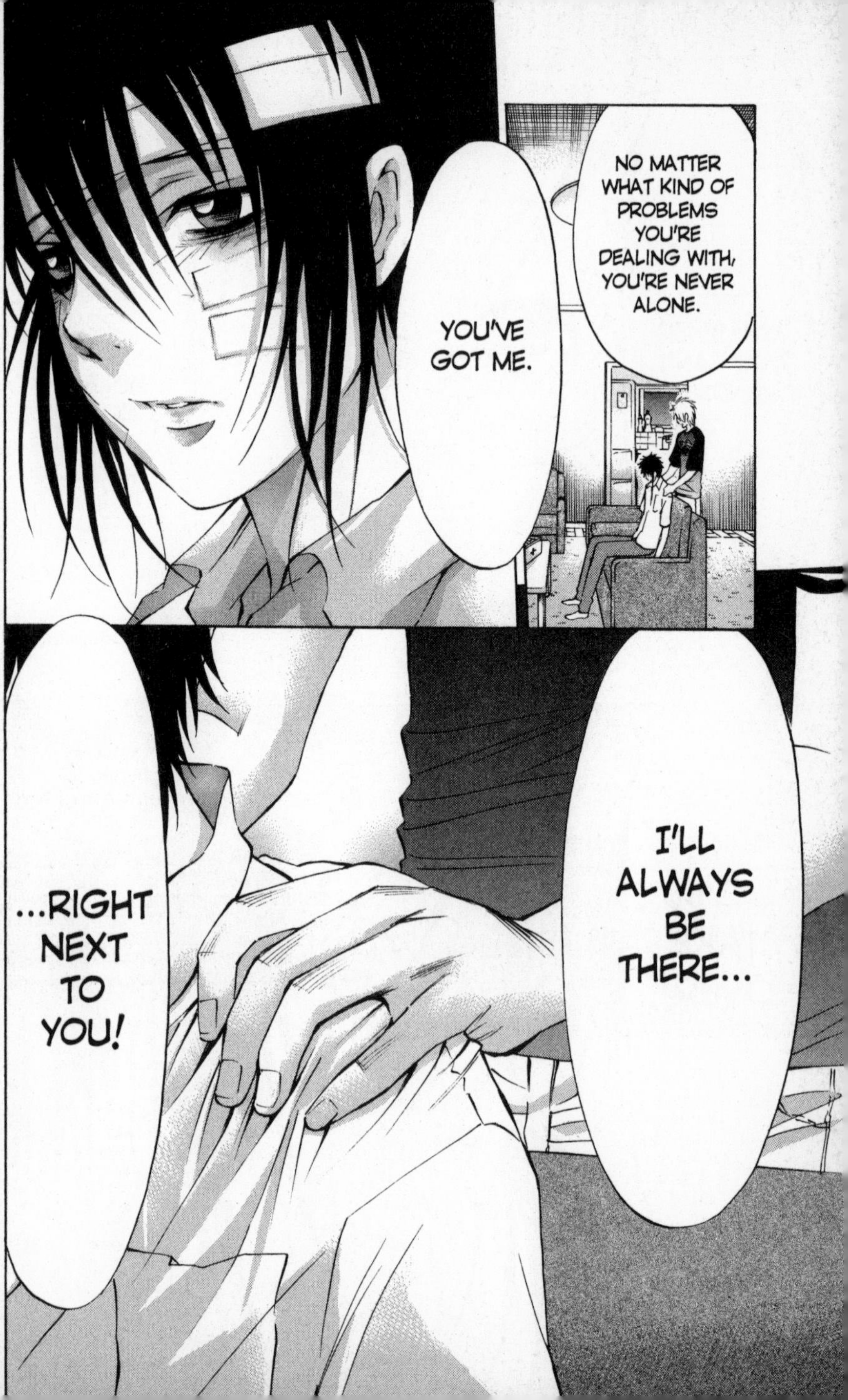
NO MATTER WHAT KIND OF PROBLEMS YOU'RE DEALING WITH, YOU'RE NEVER ALONE.
YOU'VE GOT ME.
I'LL ALWAYS BE THERE...
...RIGHT NEXT TO YOU!

Chapter 31 • The Scars of a Single Night

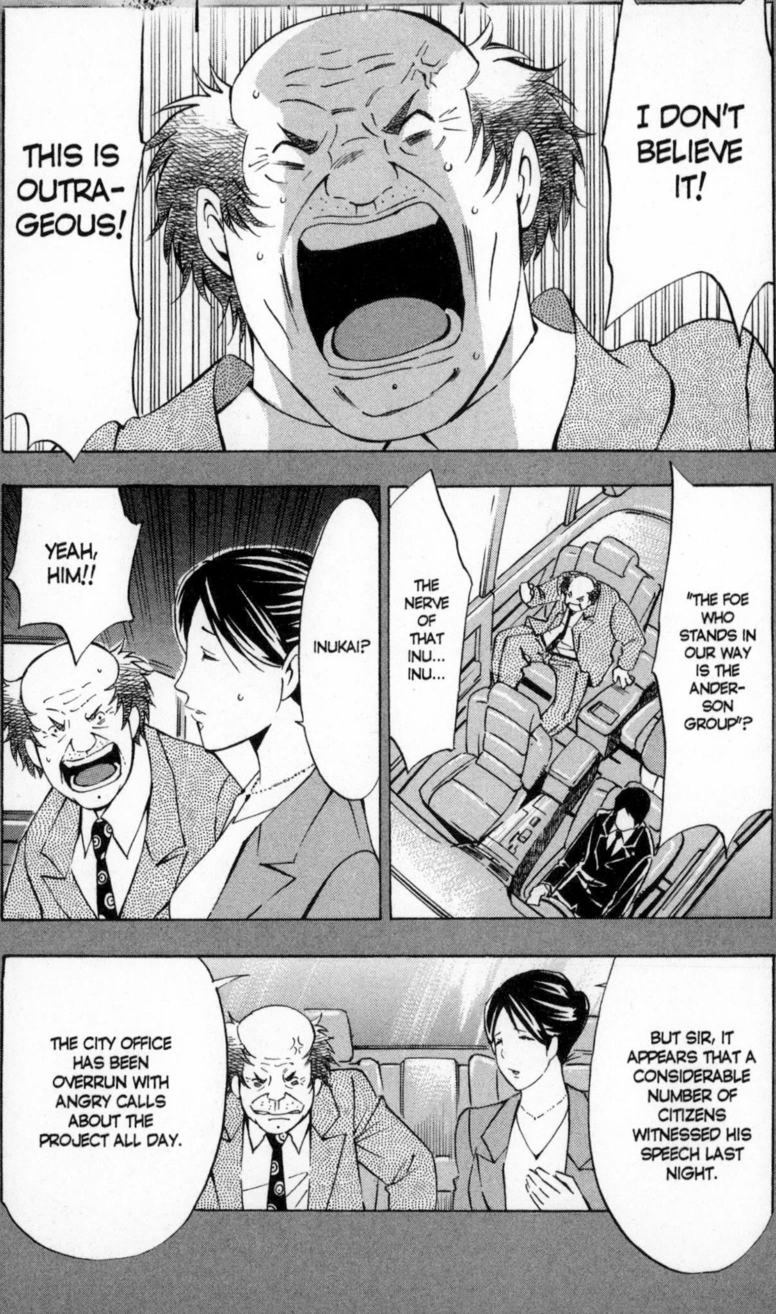

I DON'T BELIEVE IT!
THIS IS OUTRA-GEOUS!
"THE FOE WHO STANDS IN OUR WAY IS THE ANDER-SON GROUP"?
THE NERVE OF THAT INU... INU...
INUKAI?
YEAH, HIM!!
BUT SIR, IT APPEARS THAT A CONSIDERABLE NUMBER OF CITIZENS WITNESSED HIS SPEECH LAST NIGHT.
THE CITY OFFICE HAS BEEN OVERRUN WITH ANGRY CALLS ABOUT THE PROJECT ALL DAY.

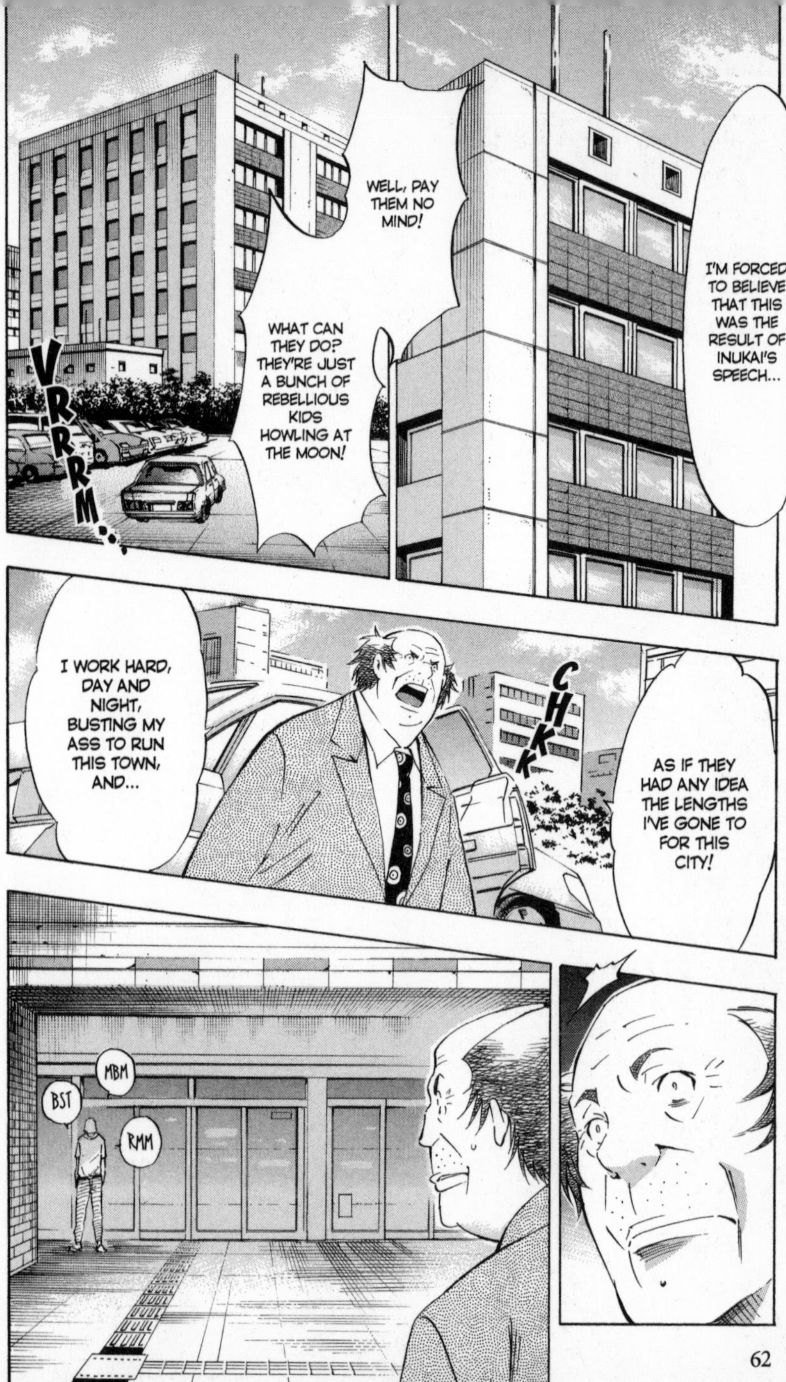
I'M FORCED TO BELIEVE THAT THIS WAS THE RESULT OF INUKAI'S SPEECH...
WELL, PAY THEM NO MIND!
WHAT CAN THEY DO? THEY'RE JUST A BUNCH OF REBELLIOUS KIDS HOWLING AT THE MOON!
VRRRM..
AS IF THEY HAD ANY IDEA THE LENGTHS I'VE GONE TO FOR THIS CITY!
CHKK
I WORK HARD, DAY AND NIGHT, BUSTING MY ASS TO RUN THIS TOWN, AND...
MBM
BST
RMM

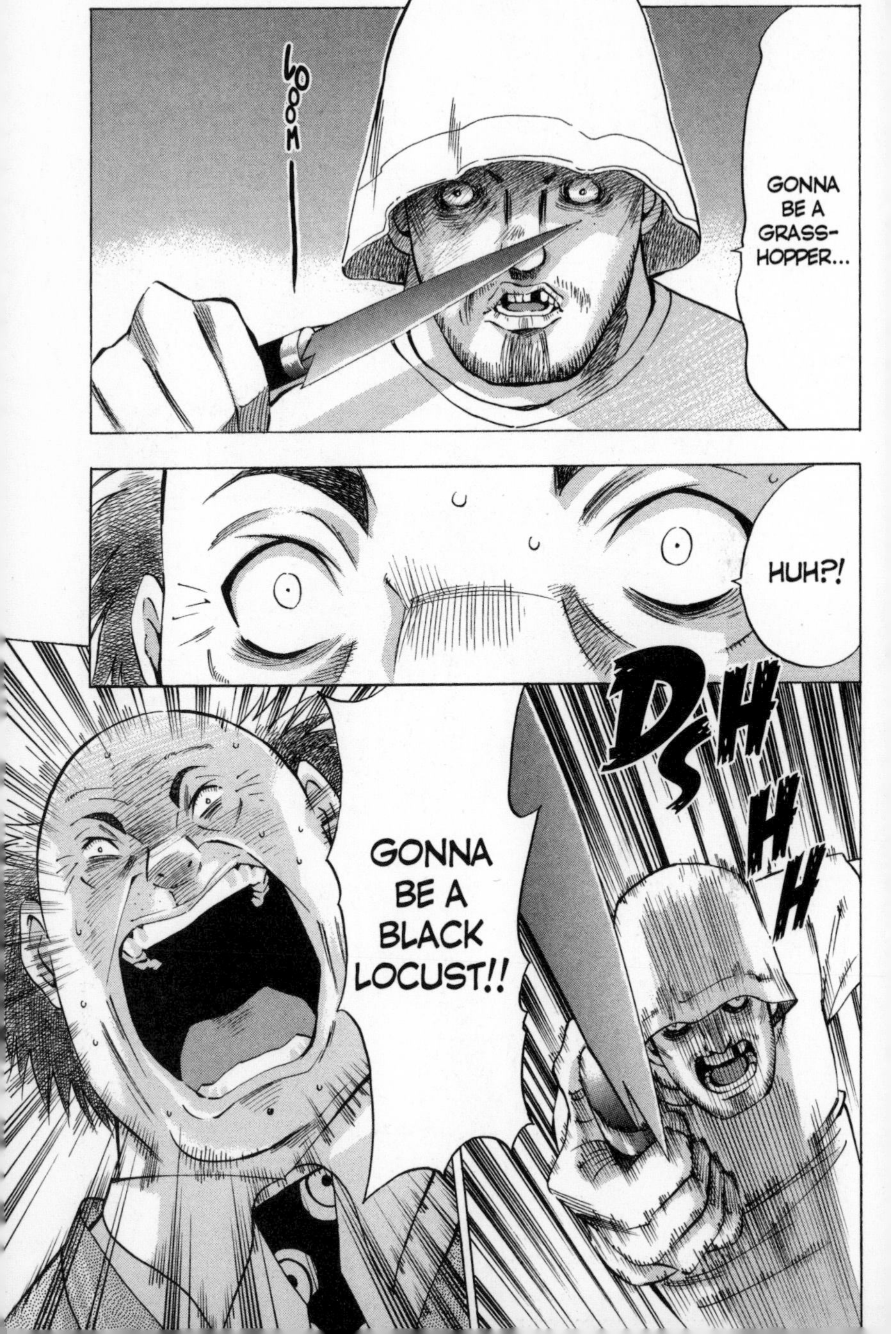
GONNA BE A GRASS-HOPPER...
VROOOM
HUH?!
DSHHHH
GONNA BE A BLACK LOCUST!!

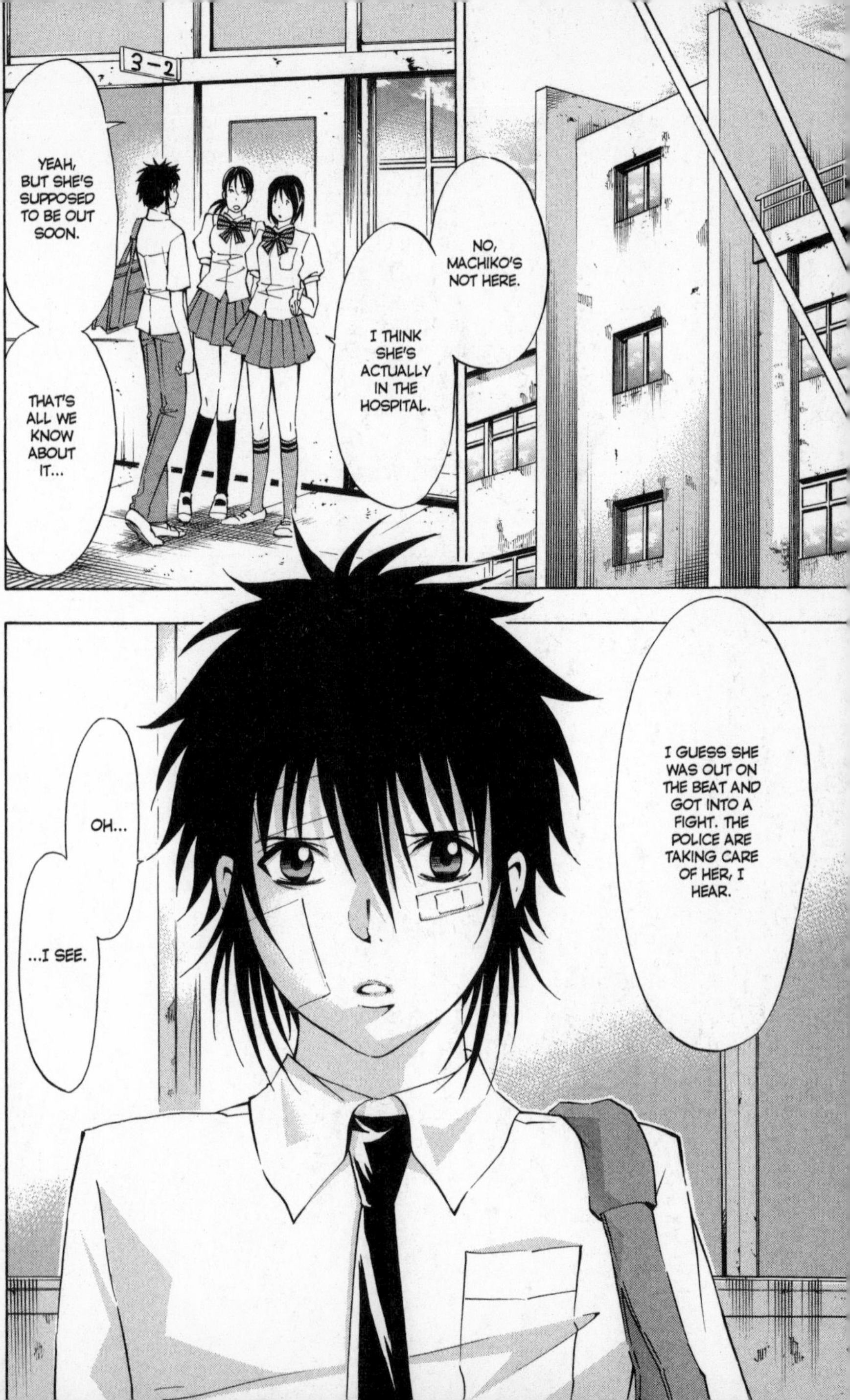
NO, MACHIKO'S NOT HERE.
I THINK SHE'S ACTUALLY IN THE HOSPITAL.
YEAH, BUT SHE'S SUPPOSED TO BE OUT SOON.
THAT'S ALL WE KNOW ABOUT IT...
I GUESS SHE WAS OUT ON THE BEAT AND GOT INTO A FIGHT. THE POLICE ARE TAKING CARE OF HER, I HEAR.
OH...
...I SEE.

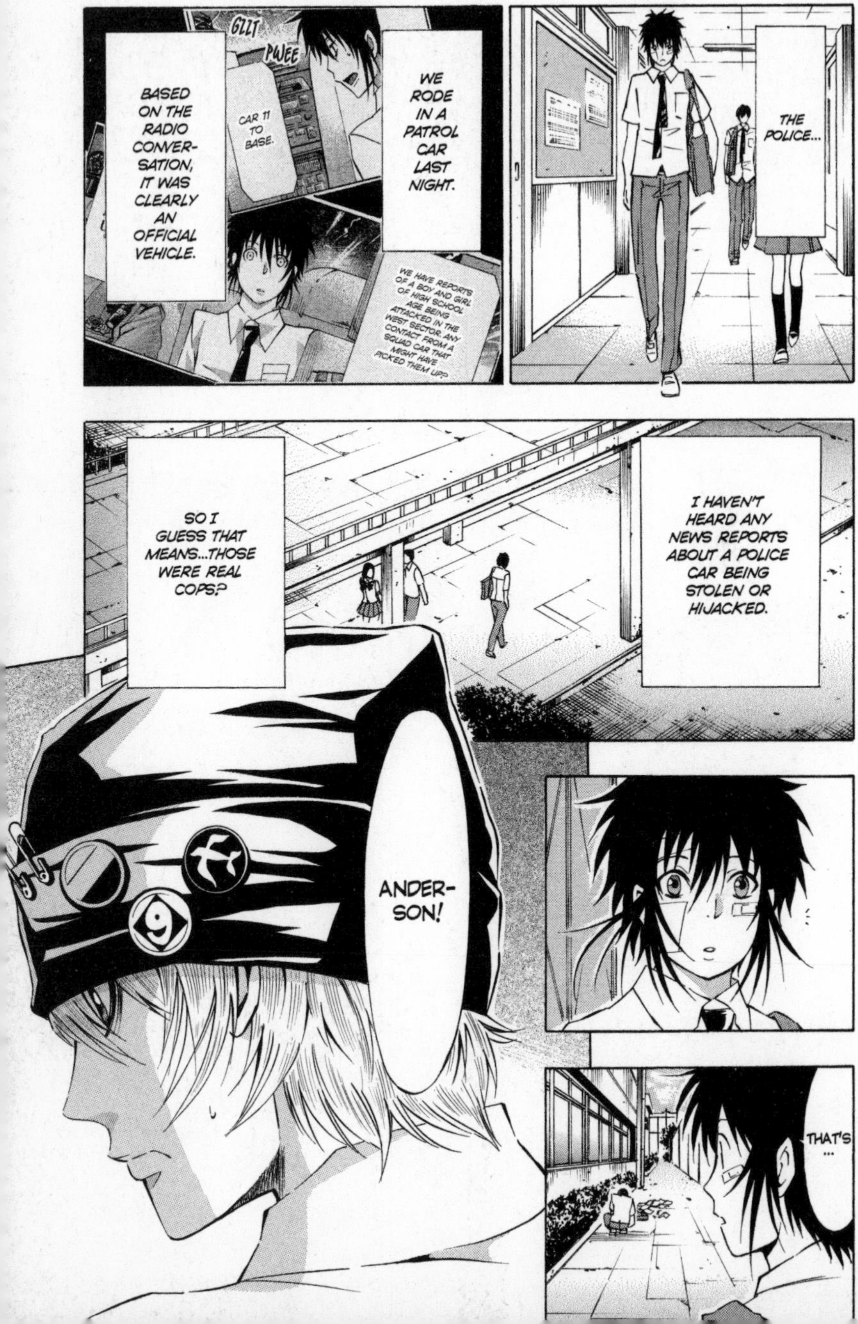
THE POLICE...
WE RODE IN A PATROL CAR LAST NIGHT.
GZZT
PWEE
CAR 11 TO BASE.
BASED ON THE RADIO CONVER-SATION, IT WAS CLEARLY AN OFFICIAL VEHICLE.
WE HAVE REPORTS OF A BOY AND GIRL OF HIGH SCHOOL AGE BEING ATTACKED IN THE WEST SECTOR. ANY CONTACT FROM A SQUAD CAR THAT MIGHT HAVE PICKED THEM UP?
I HAVEN'T HEARD ANY NEWS REPORTS ABOUT A POLICE CAR BEING STOLEN OR HIJACKED.
SO I GUESS THAT MEANS...THOSE WERE REAL COPS?
THAT'S ...
ANDER-SON!

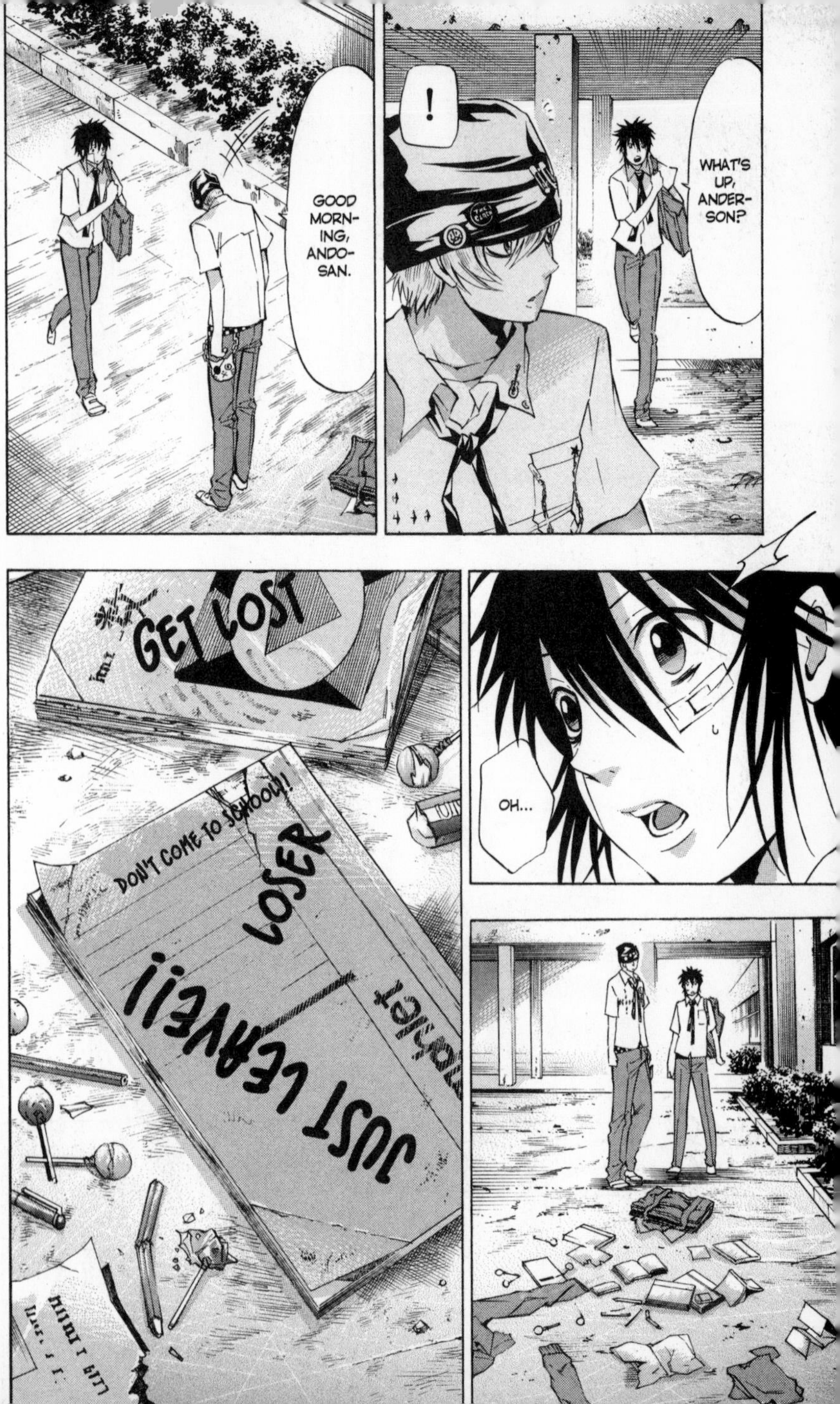
WHAT'S UP, ANDER-SON?
!
GOOD MORN-ING, ANDO-SAN.
OH...
GET LOST
DON'T COME TO SCHOOL!!
LOSER
JUST LEAVE!!

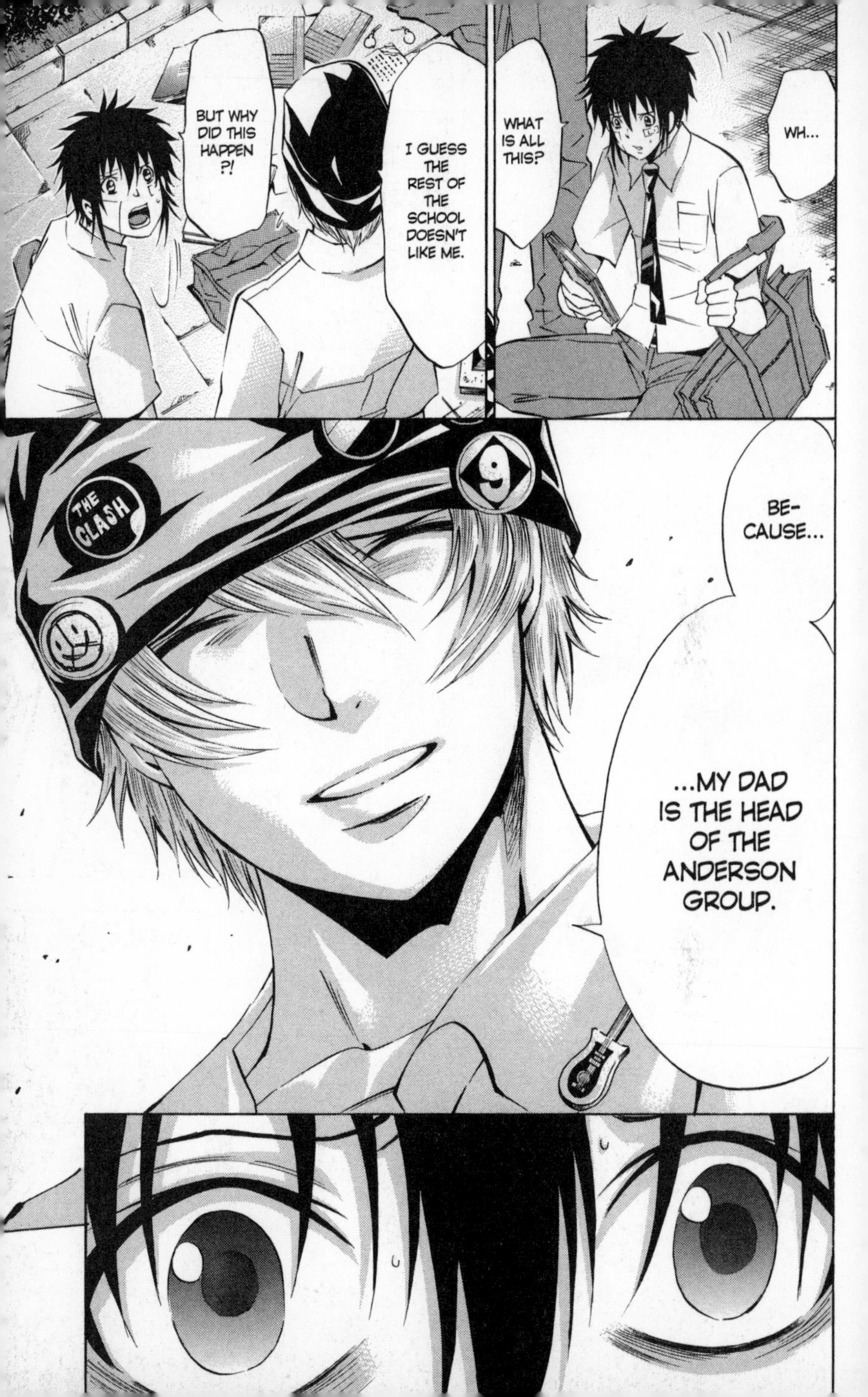
WH...
WHAT IS ALL THIS?
I GUESS THE REST OF THE SCHOOL DOESN'T LIKE ME.
BUT WHY DID THIS HAPPEN ?!
BE-CAUSE...
...MY DAD IS THE HEAD OF THE ANDERSON GROUP.

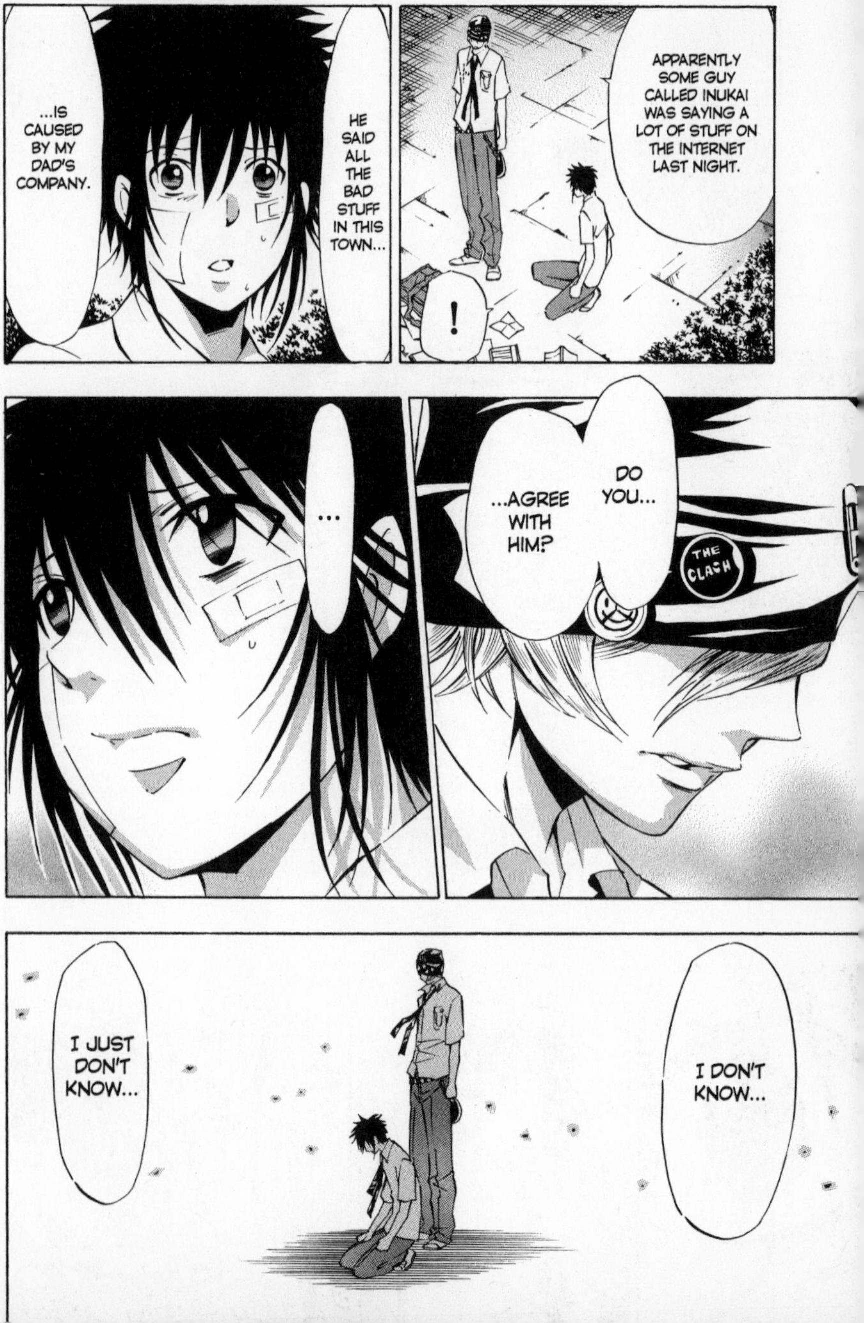
APPARENTLY SOME GUY CALLED INUKAI WAS SAYING A LOT OF STUFF ON THE INTERNET LAST NIGHT.
!
HE SAID ALL THE BAD STUFF IN THIS TOWN...
...IS CAUSED BY MY DAD'S COMPANY.
DO YOU...
...AGREE WITH HIM?
THE CLASH
...
I DON'T KNOW...
I JUST DON'T KNOW...

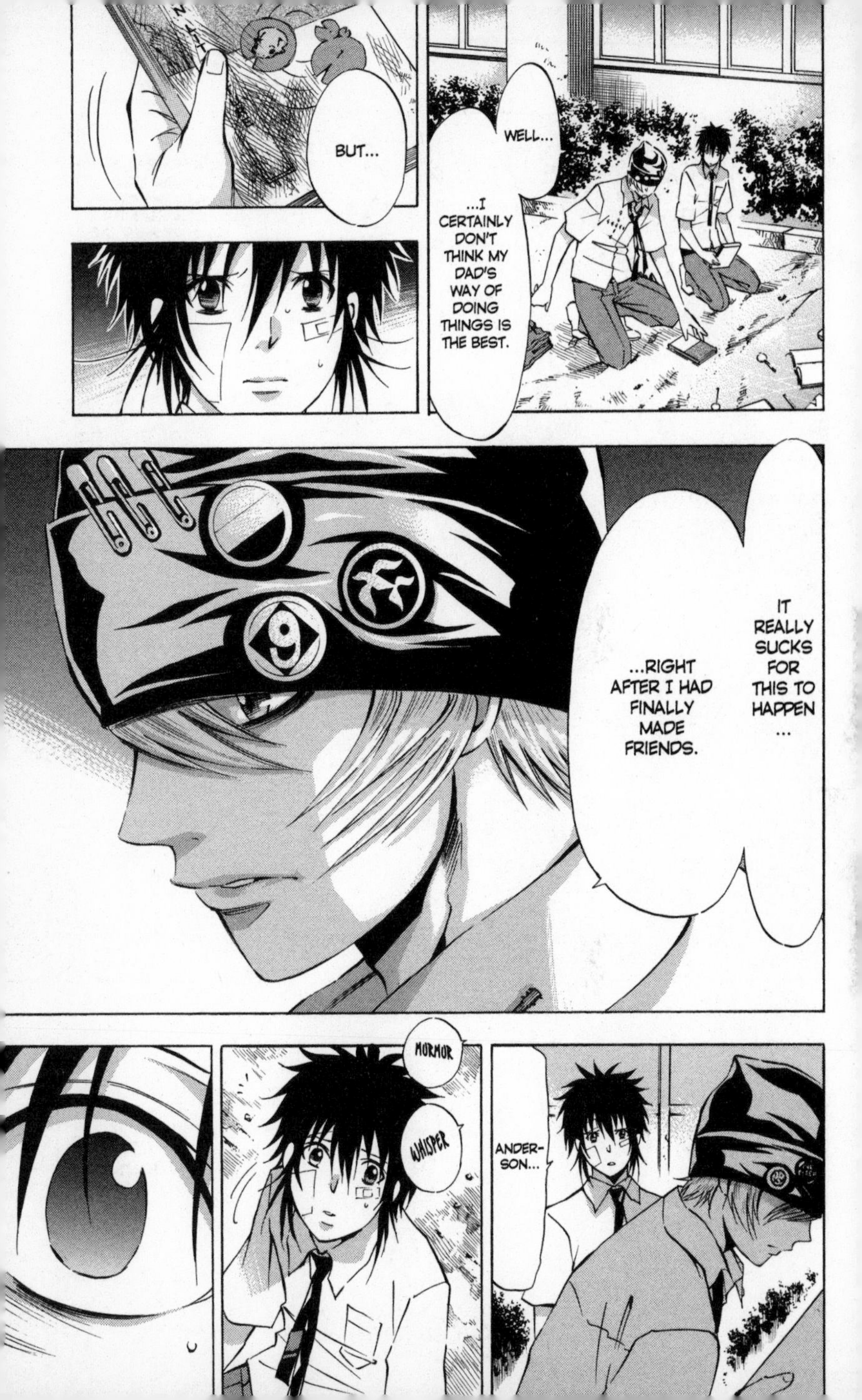
WELL...
...I CERTAINLY DON'T THINK MY DAD'S WAY OF DOING THINGS IS THE BEST.
BUT...
IT REALLY SUCKS FOR THIS TO HAPPEN ...
...RIGHT AFTER I HAD FINALLY MADE FRIENDS.
ANDER-SON...
MURMUR
WHISPER

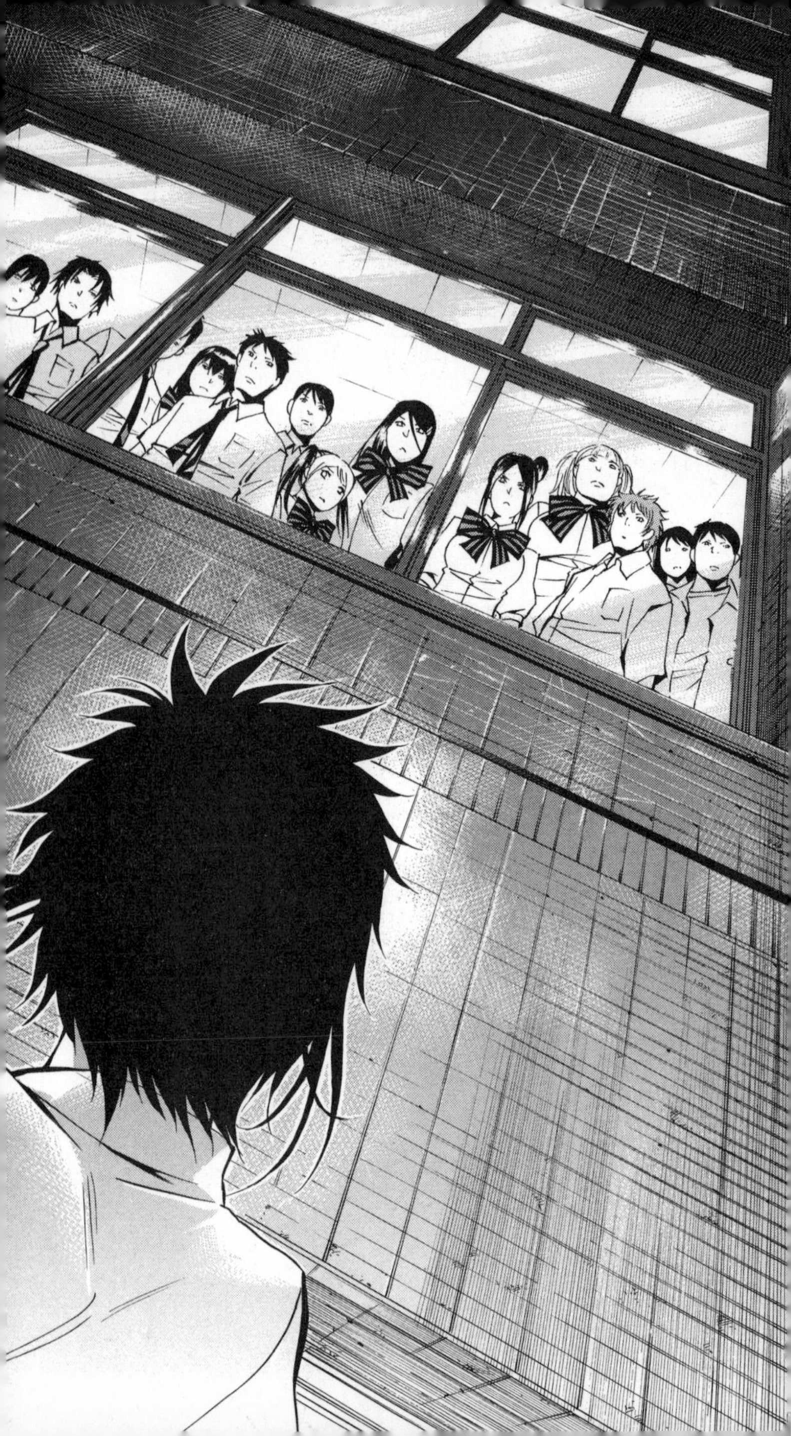

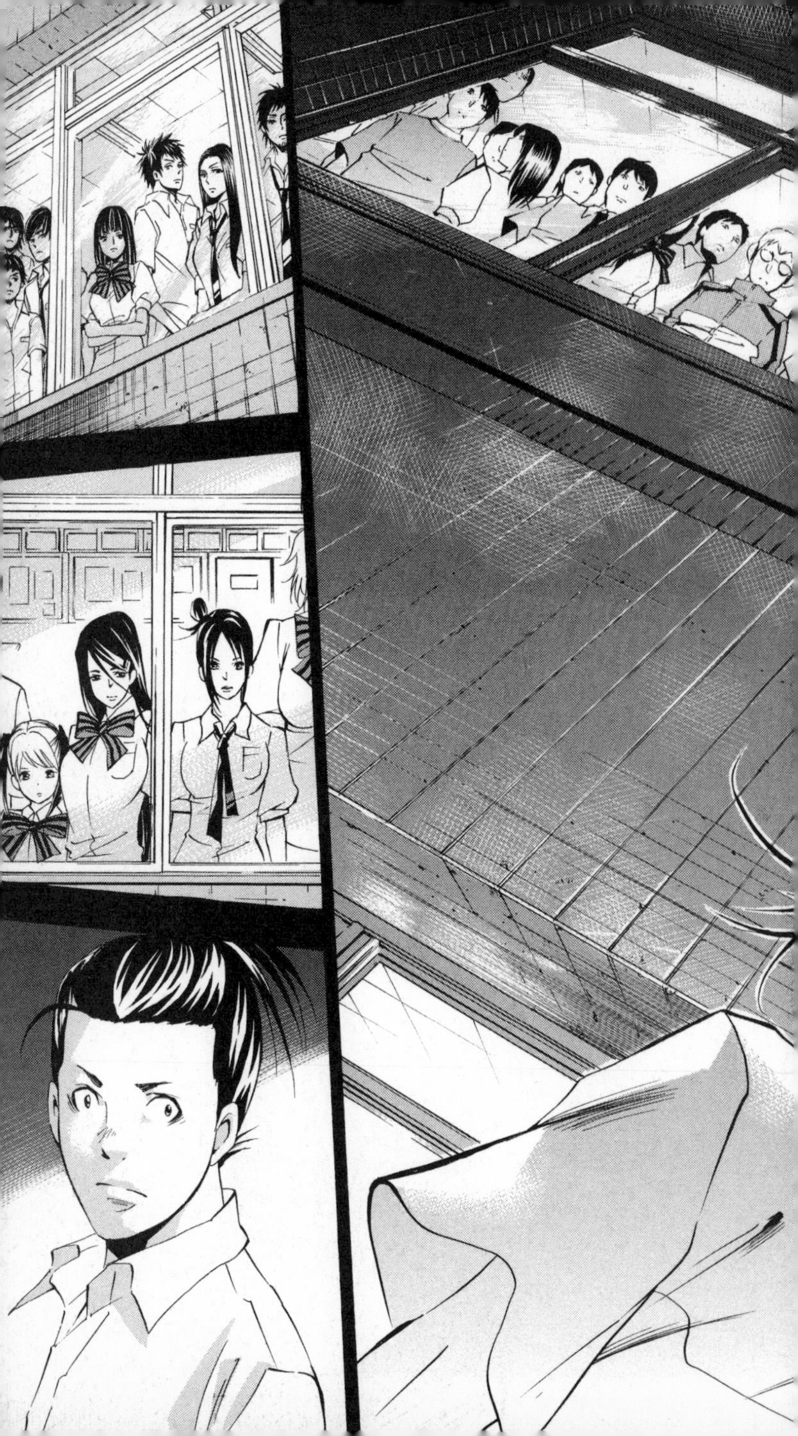

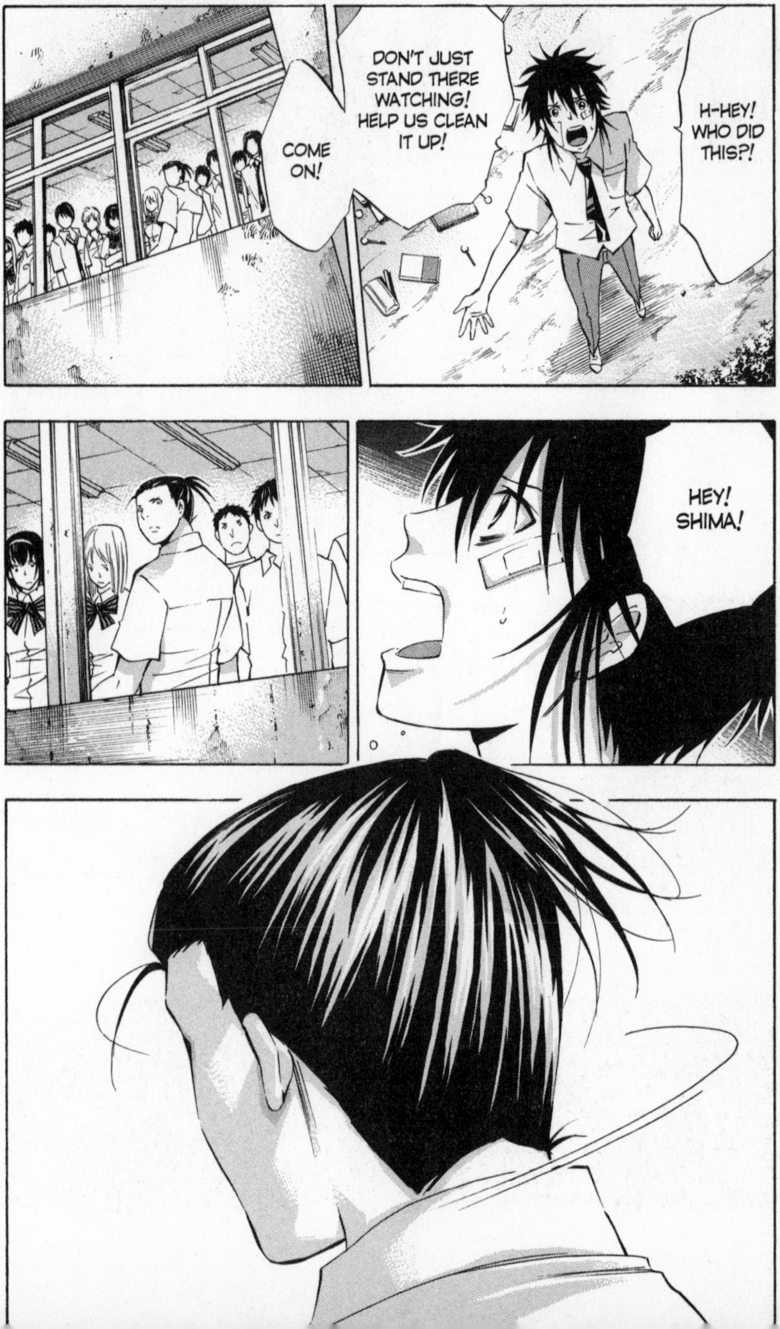
H-HEY! WHO DID THIS?!
DON'T JUST STAND THERE WATCHING! HELP US CLEAN IT UP!
COME ON!
HEY! SHIMA!

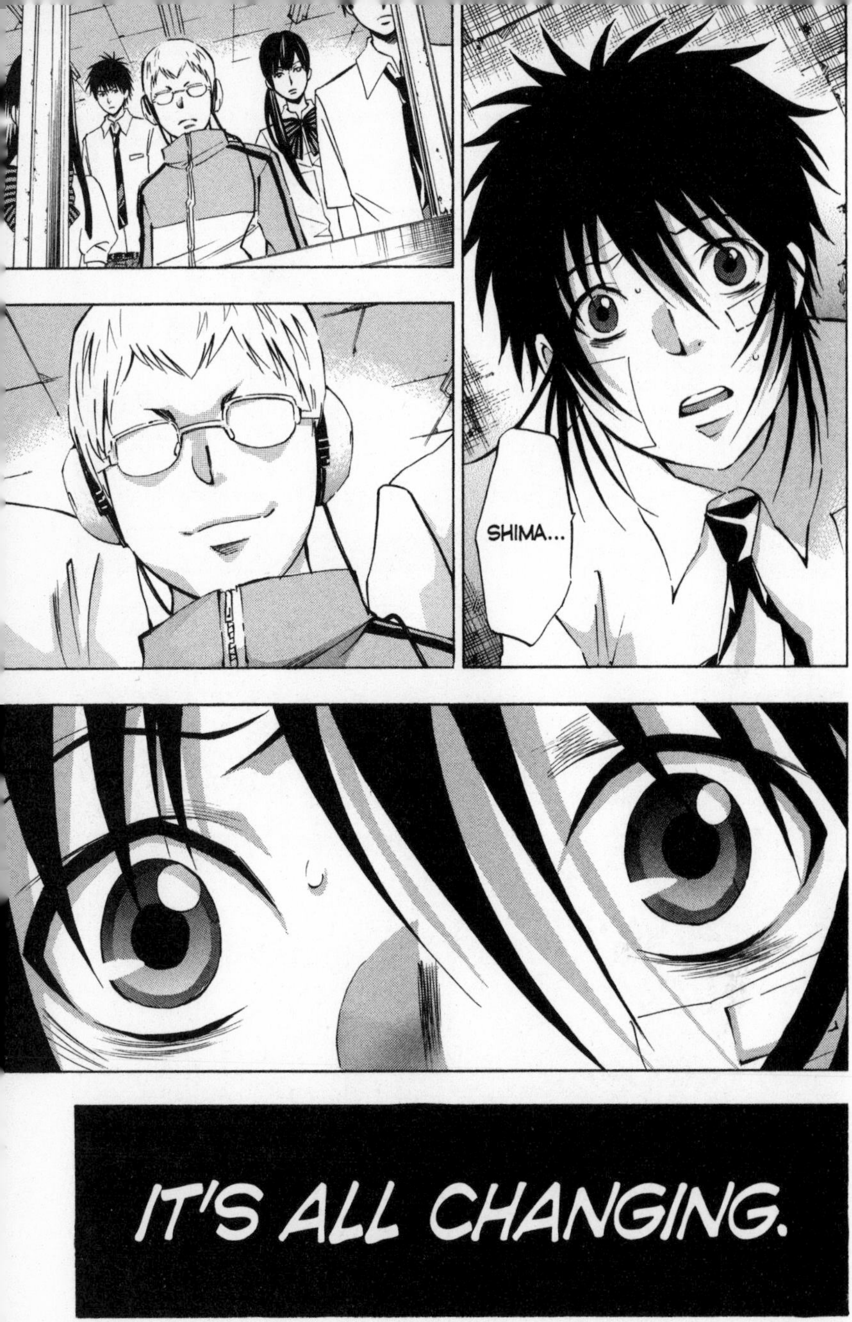
SHIMA...
IT'S ALL CHANGING.

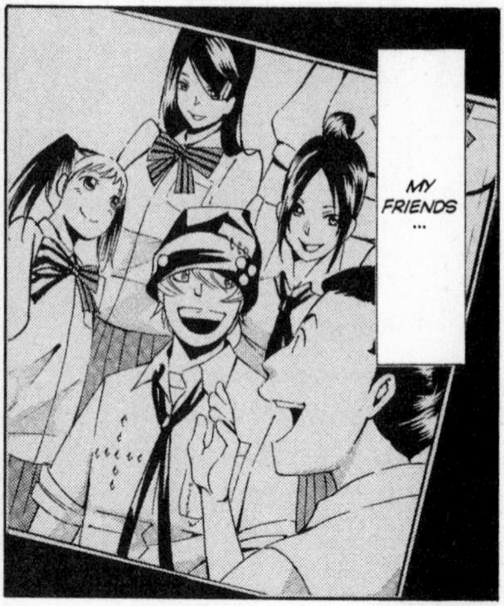
MY FRIENDS
...

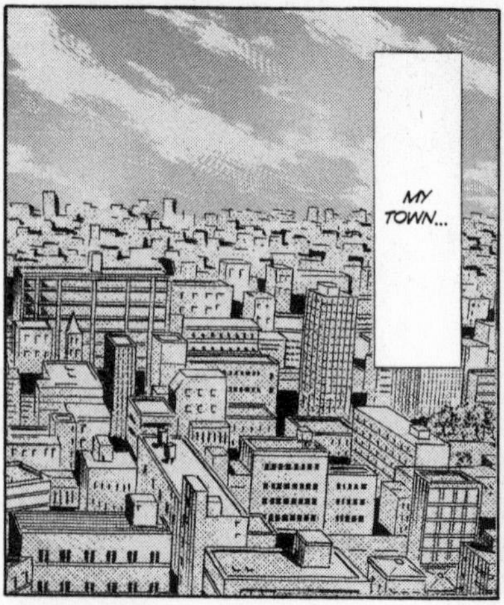
MY TOWN...

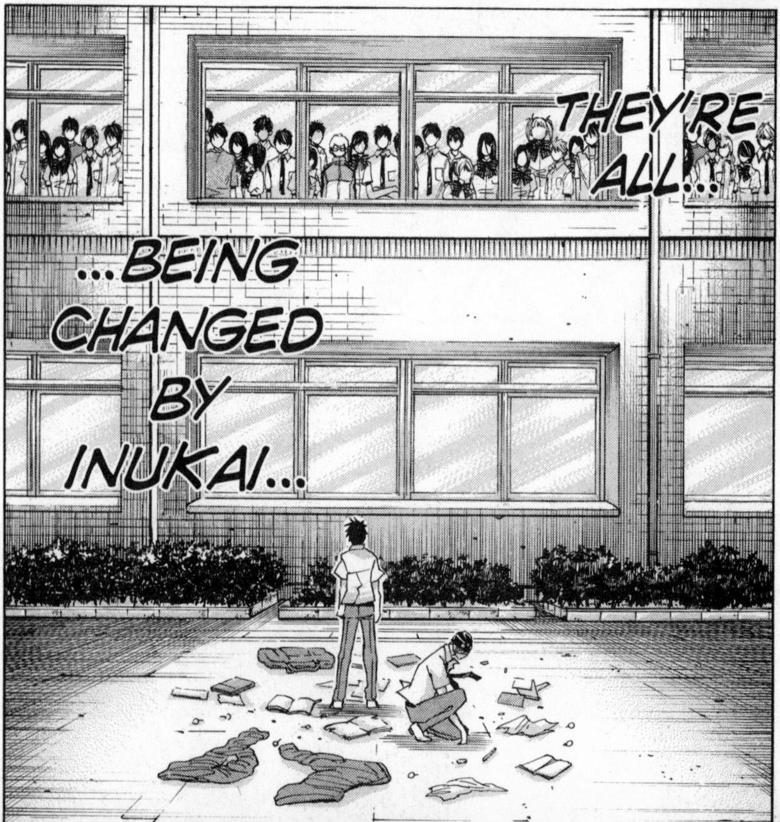
THEY'RE ALL...
...BEING CHANGED BY INUKAI...

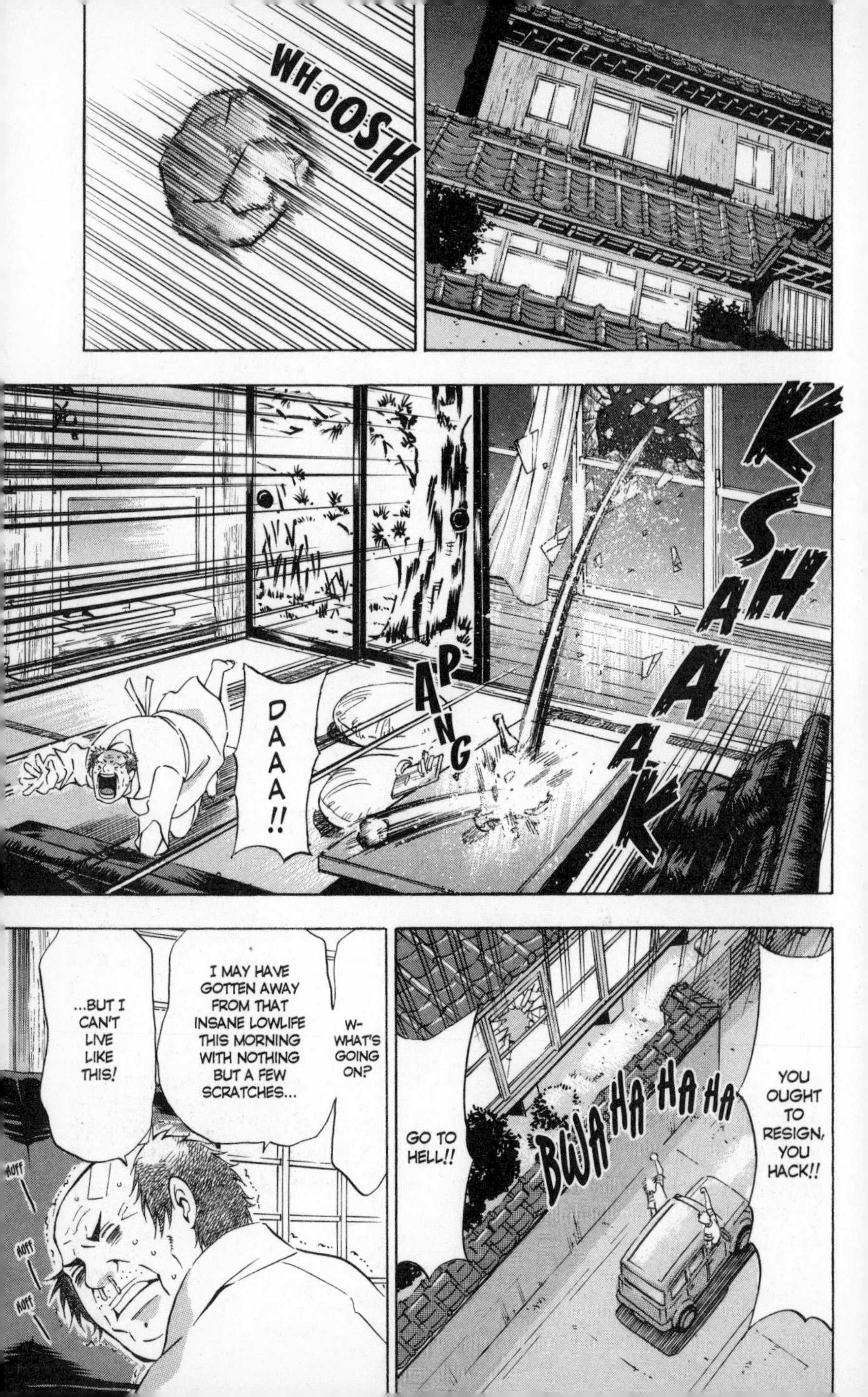
WHOOSH
KSHAAAAK
PANG
DAAAA!!
YOU OUGHT TO RESIGN, YOU HACK!!
BWAHAHAHAHA
GO TO HELL!!
W-WHAT'S GOING ON?
I MAY HAVE GOTTEN AWAY FROM THAT INSANE LOWLIFE THIS MORNING WITH NOTHING BUT A FEW SCRATCHES...
...BUT I CAN'T LIVE LIKE THIS!
HUFF
HUFF
HUFF

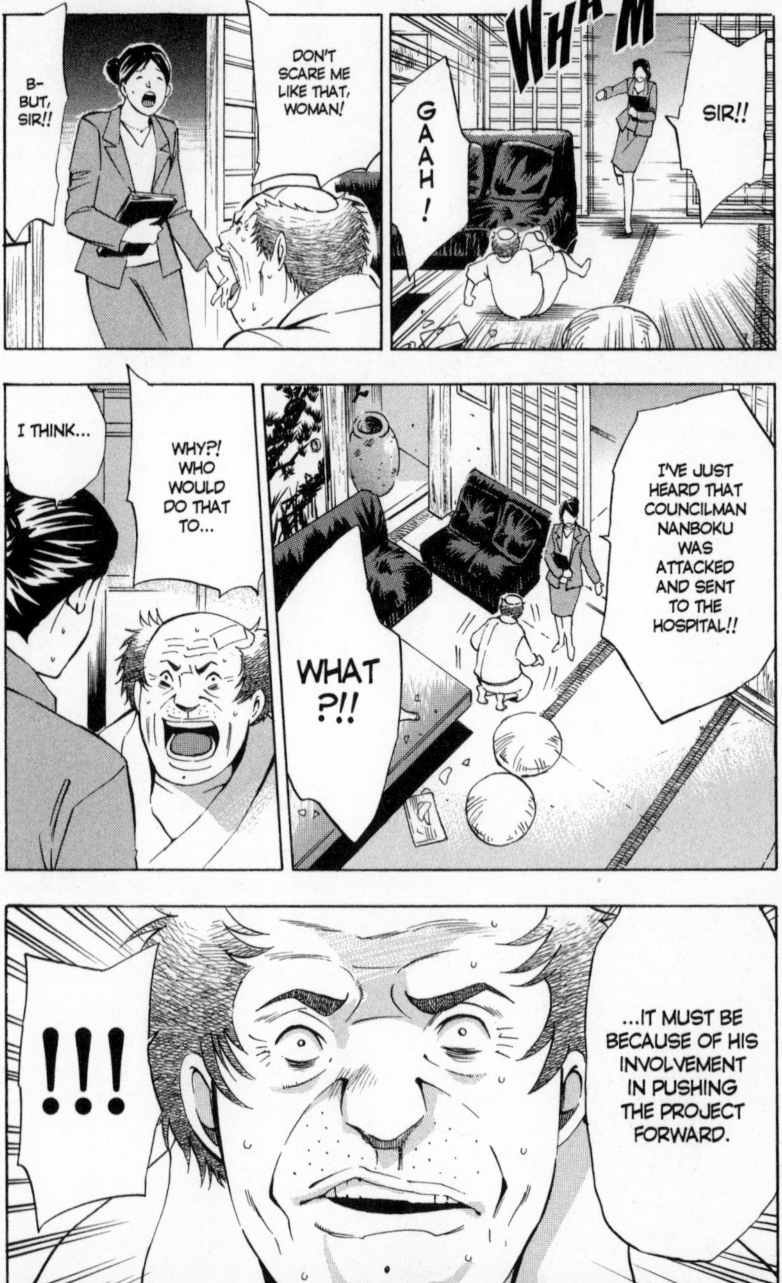
WHAM
SIR!!
GAAH!
DON'T SCARE ME LIKE THAT, WOMAN!
B-BUT, SIR!!
I'VE JUST HEARD THAT COUNCILMAN NANBOKU WAS ATTACKED AND SENT TO THE HOSPITAL!!
WHAT?!!
WHY?! WHO WOULD DO THAT TO...
I THINK...
...IT MUST BE BECAUSE OF HIS INVOLVEMENT IN PUSHING THE PROJECT FORWARD.
!!!

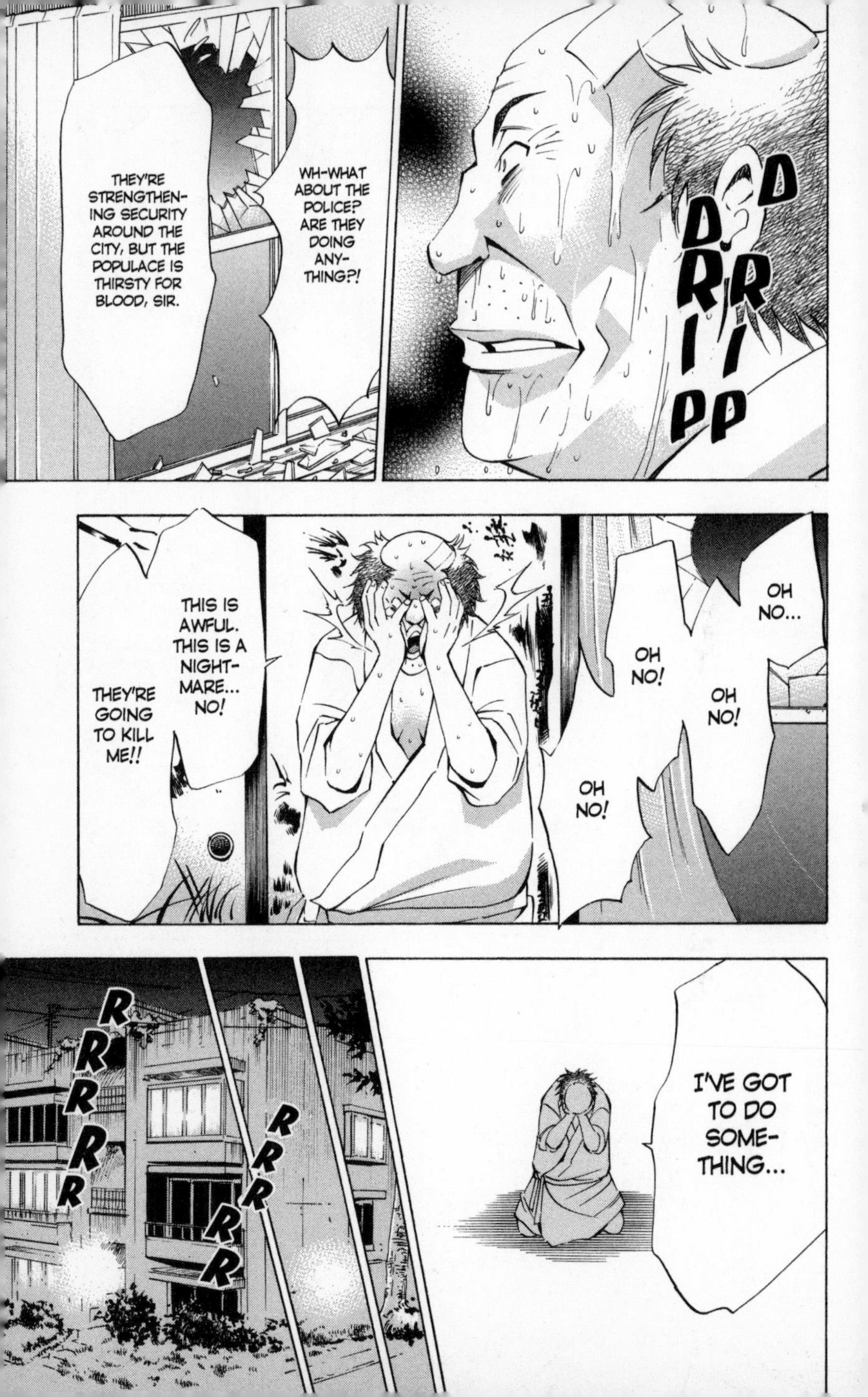
DRIPP
DRIPP
WH-WHAT ABOUT THE POLICE? ARE THEY DOING ANY-THING?!
THEY'RE STRENGTHEN-ING SECURITY AROUND THE CITY, BUT THE POPULACE IS THIRSTY FOR BLOOD, SIR.
OH NO...
OH NO!
OH NO!
OH NO!
THIS IS AWFUL. THIS IS A NIGHT-MARE... NO!
THEY'RE GOING TO KILL ME!!
I'VE GOT TO DO SOME-THING...
RRRRRR
RRRRRR

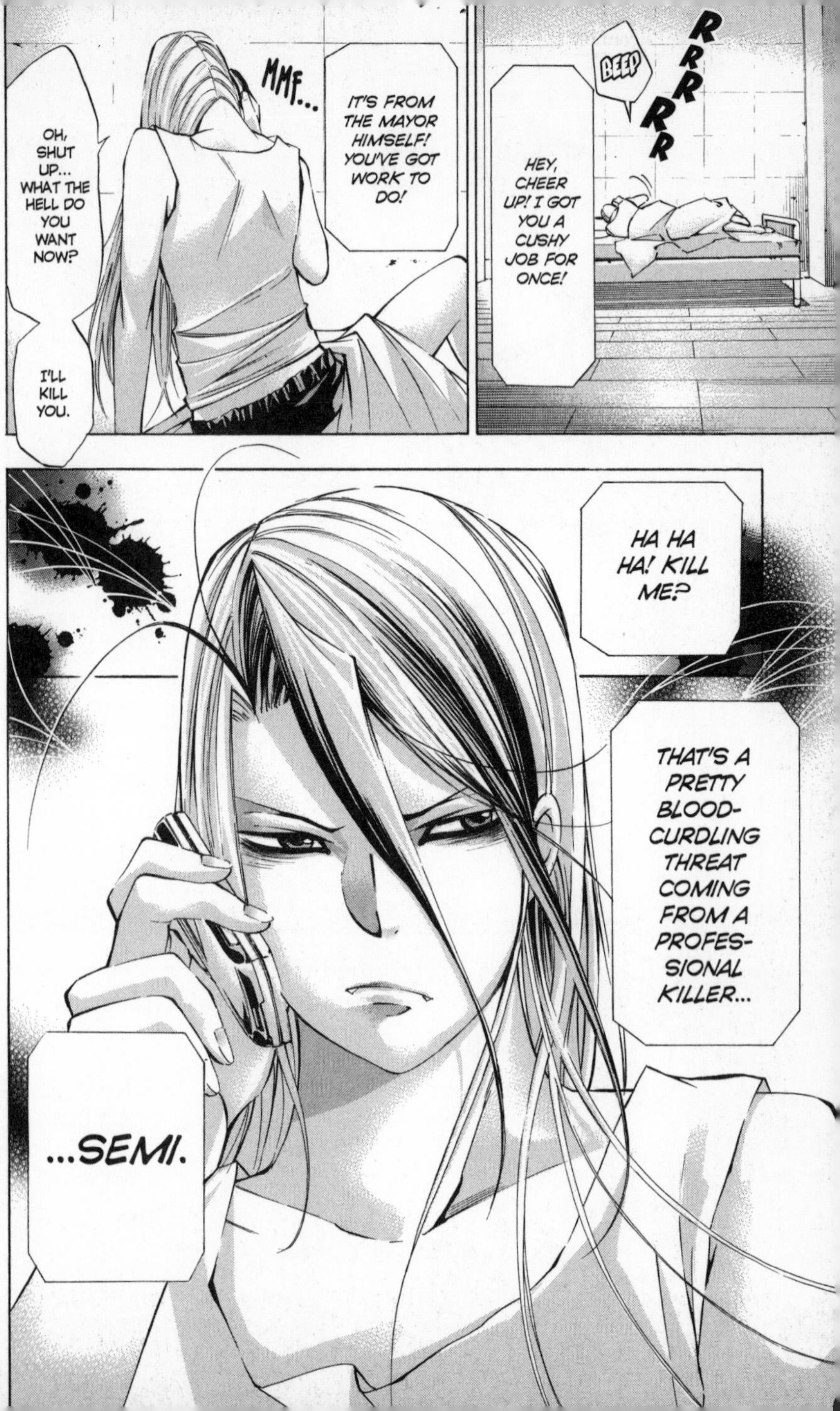
BEEP
RRRR
HEY, CHEER UP! I GOT YOU A CUSHY JOB FOR ONCE!
IT'S FROM THE MAYOR HIMSELF! YOU'VE GOT WORK TO DO!
MMF...
OH, SHUT UP... WHAT THE HELL DO YOU WANT NOW?
I'LL KILL YOU.
HA HA HA! KILL ME?
THAT'S A PRETTY BLOOD-CURDLING THREAT COMING FROM A PROFES-SIONAL KILLER...
...SEMI.

Chapter 32 • Encounter

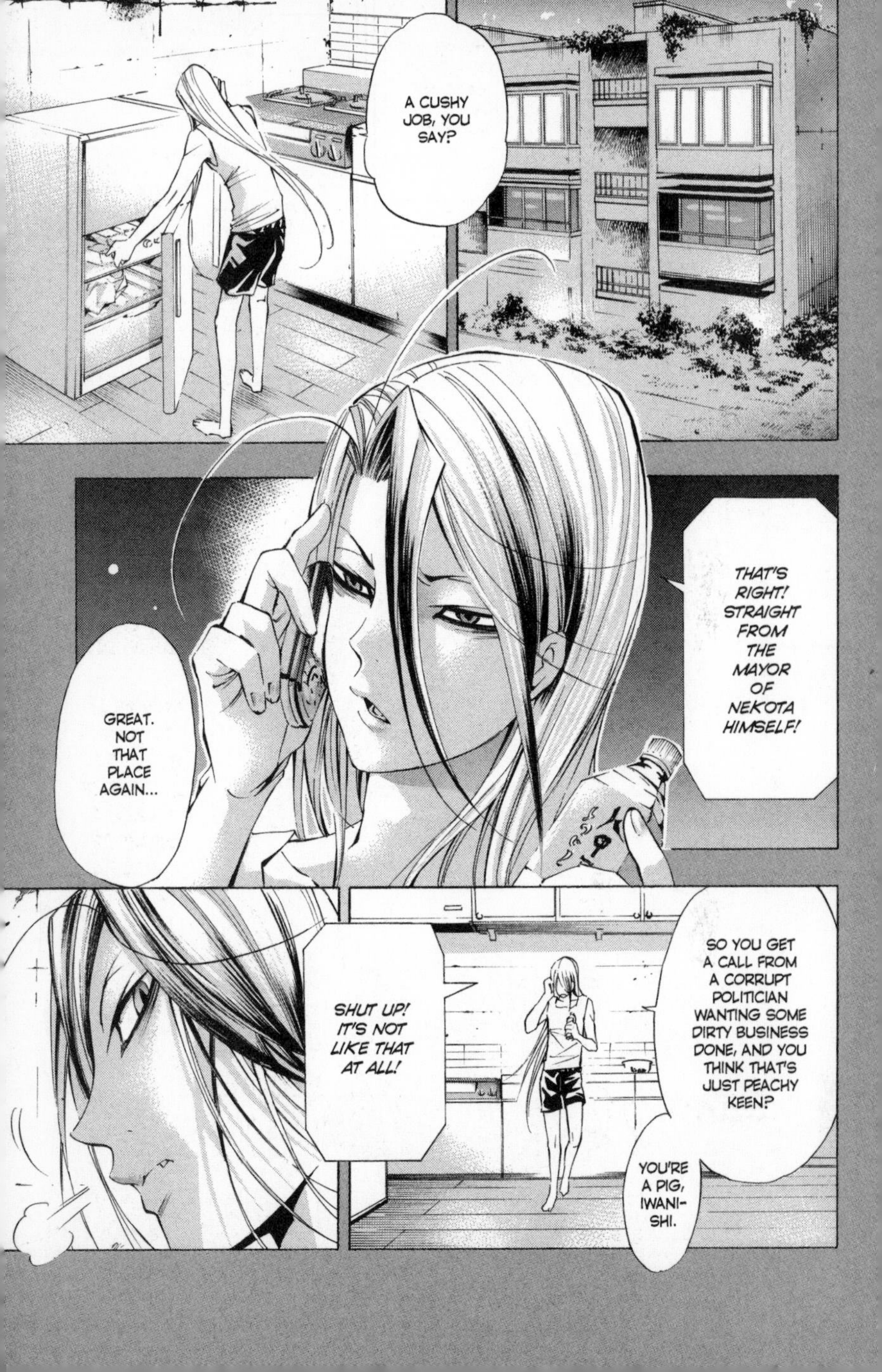
A CUSHY JOB, YOU SAY?
THAT'S RIGHT! STRAIGHT FROM THE MAYOR OF NEKOTA HIMSELF!
GREAT. NOT THAT PLACE AGAIN...
SO YOU GET A CALL FROM A CORRUPT POLITICIAN WANTING SOME DIRTY BUSINESS DONE, AND YOU THINK THAT'S JUST PEACHY KEEN?
YOU'RE A PIG, IWANI-SHI.
SHUT UP! IT'S NOT LIKE THAT AT ALL!

Chapter 32 • Encounter

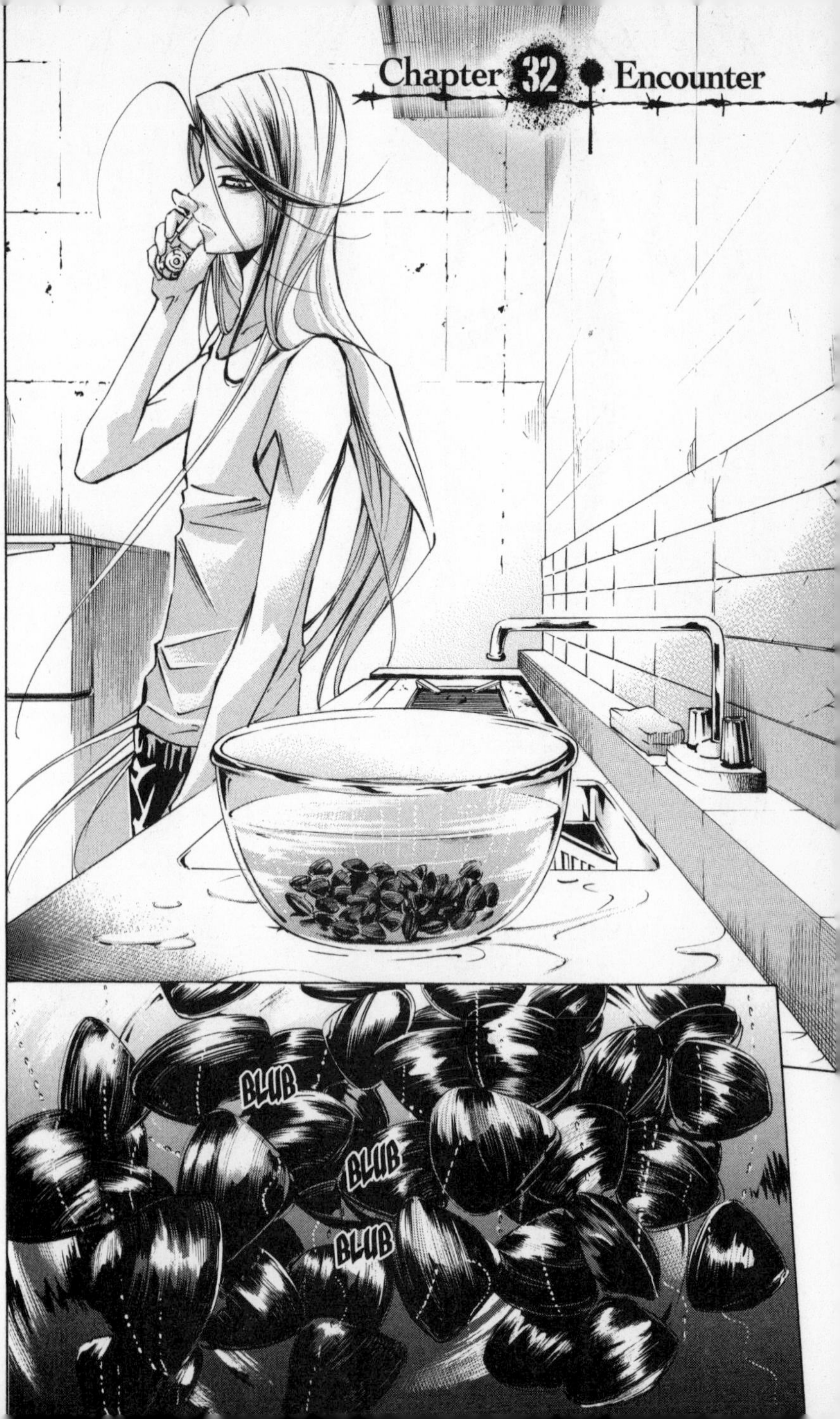
BLUB
BLUB
BLUB

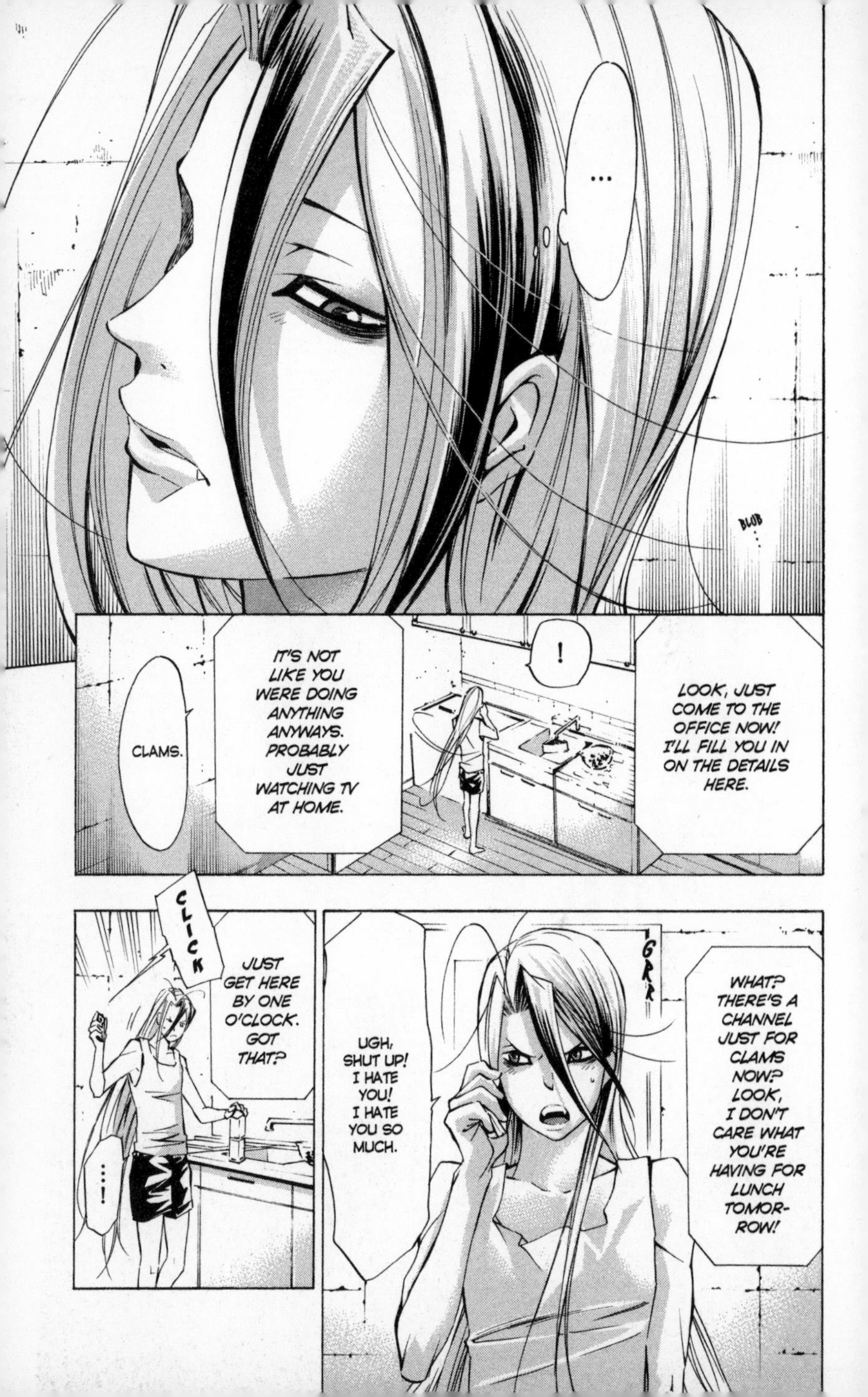
...
BLUB
LOOK, JUST COME TO THE OFFICE NOW! I'LL FILL YOU IN ON THE DETAILS HERE.
!
IT'S NOT LIKE YOU WERE DOING ANYTHING ANYWAYS. PROBABLY JUST WATCHING TV AT HOME.
CLAMS.
WHAT? THERE'S A CHANNEL JUST FOR CLAMS NOW? LOOK, I DON'T CARE WHAT YOU'RE HAVING FOR LUNCH TOMOR-ROW!
GRR
UGH, SHUT UP! I HATE YOU! I HATE YOU SO MUCH.
CLICK
JUST GET HERE BY ONE O'CLOCK. GOT THAT?
...!

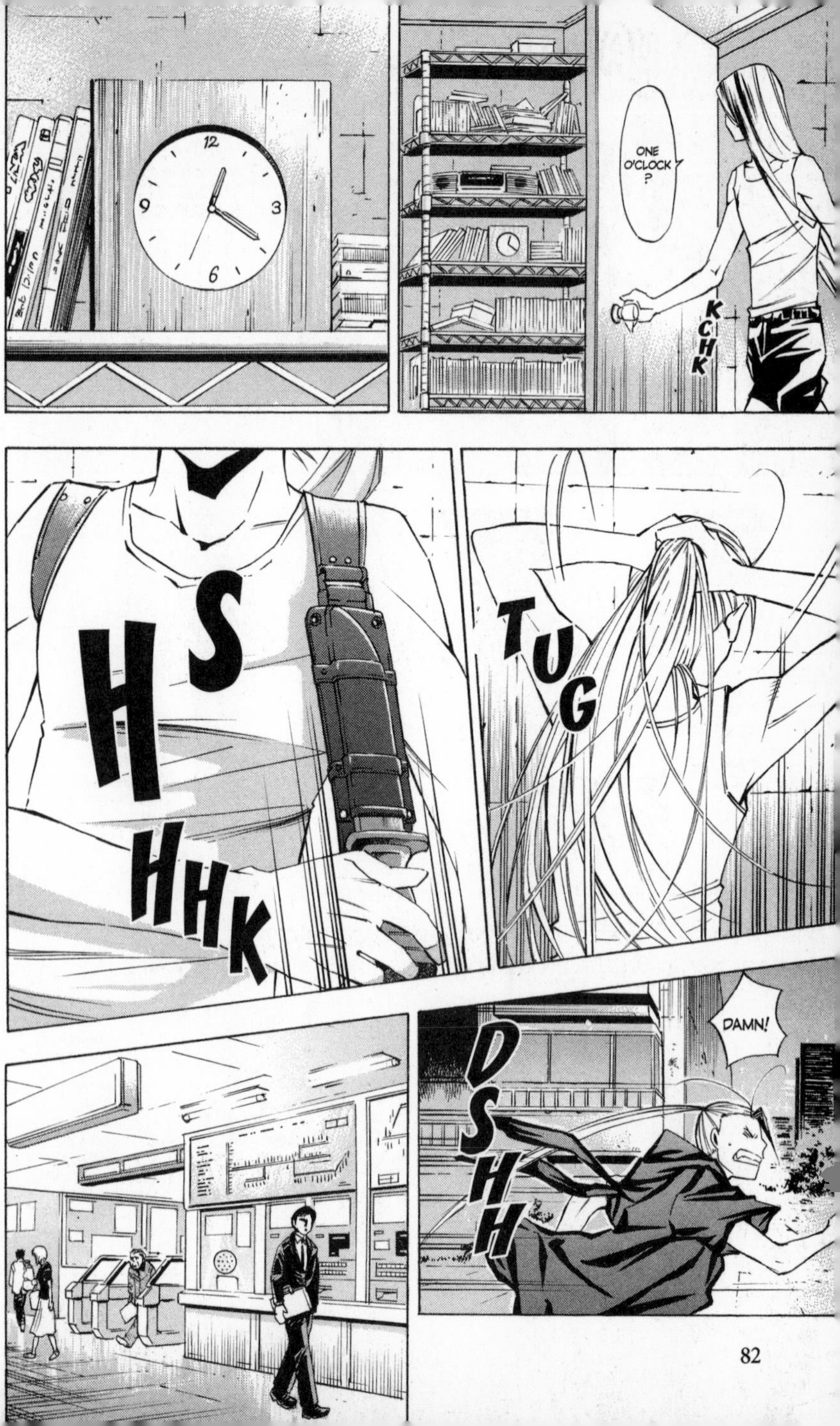
ONE O'CLOCK ?
KCHK
TUG
HSHHK
DAMN!
DSHH

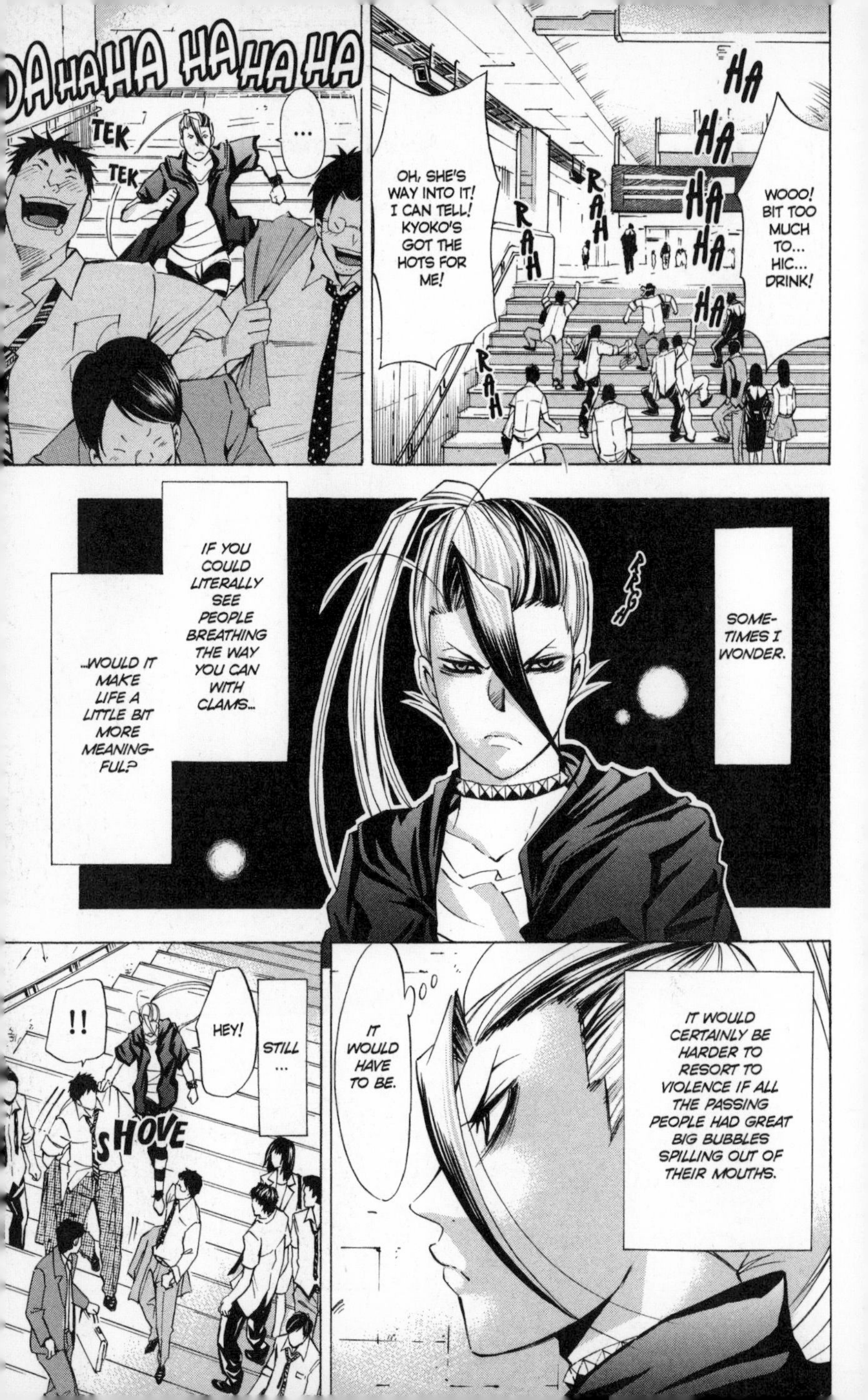
HA HA HA HA HA HA
WOOO! BIT TOO MUCH TO... HIC... DRINK!
OH, SHE'S WAY INTO IT! I CAN TELL! KYOKO'S GOT THE HOTS FOR ME!
RAH RAH
RAH RAH
RAH
DAHAHA HAHAHAHA
...
TEK
TEK
SOME-TIMES I WONDER.
IF YOU COULD LITERALLY SEE PEOPLE BREATHING THE WAY YOU CAN WITH CLAMS...
...WOULD IT MAKE LIFE A LITTLE BIT MORE MEANING-FUL?
IT WOULD CERTAINLY BE HARDER TO RESORT TO VIOLENCE IF ALL THE PASSING PEOPLE HAD GREAT BIG BUBBLES SPILLING OUT OF THEIR MOUTHS.
IT WOULD HAVE TO BE.
STILL ...
HEY!
!!
SHOVE

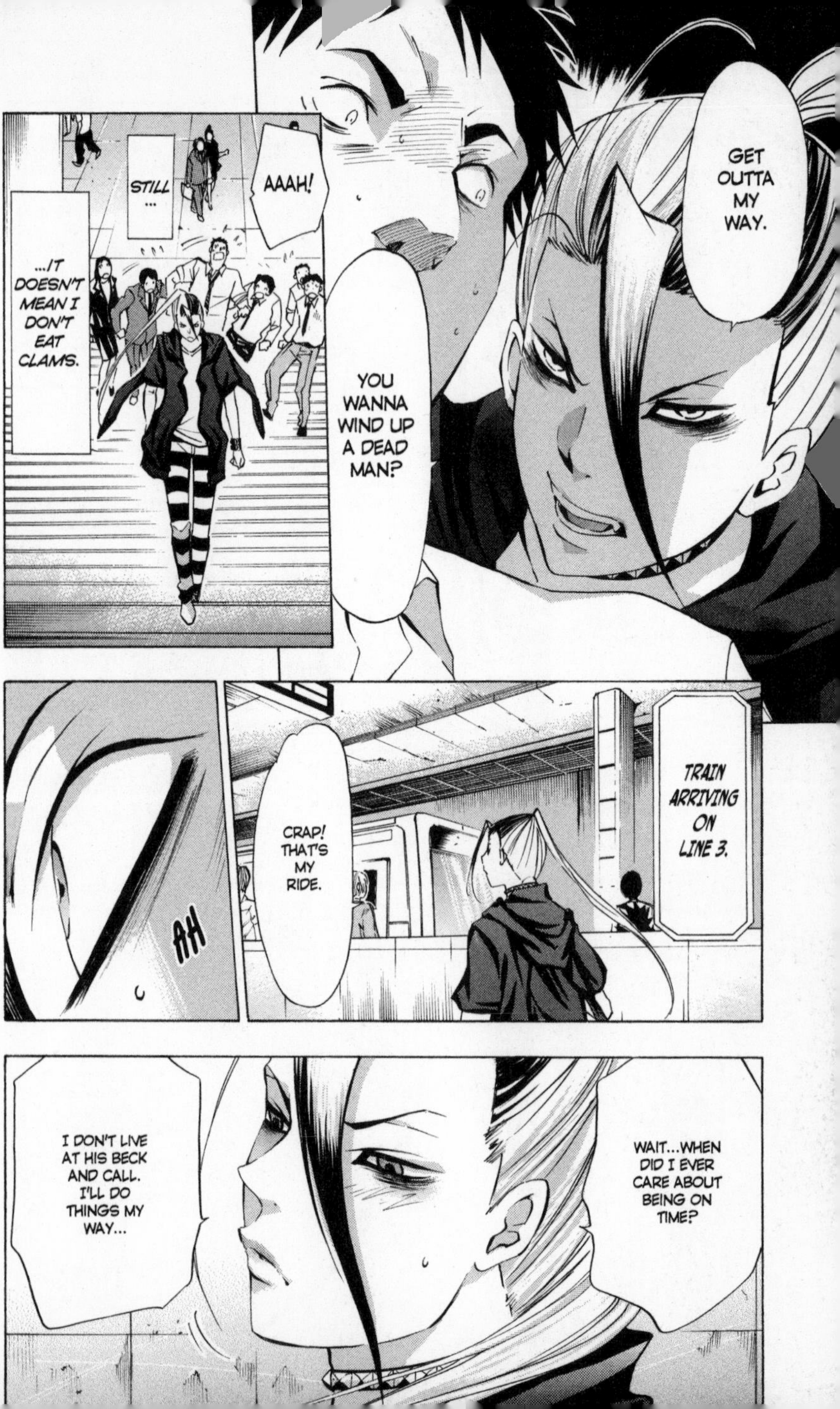
GET OUTTA MY WAY.
YOU WANNA WIND UP A DEAD MAN?
AAAH!
STILL...
...IT DOESN'T MEAN I DON'T EAT CLAMS.
TRAIN ARRIVING ON LINE 3.
CRAP! THAT'S MY RIDE.
AH
WAIT...WHEN DID I EVER CARE ABOUT BEING ON TIME?
I DON'T LIVE AT HIS BECK AND CALL. I'LL DO THINGS MY WAY...

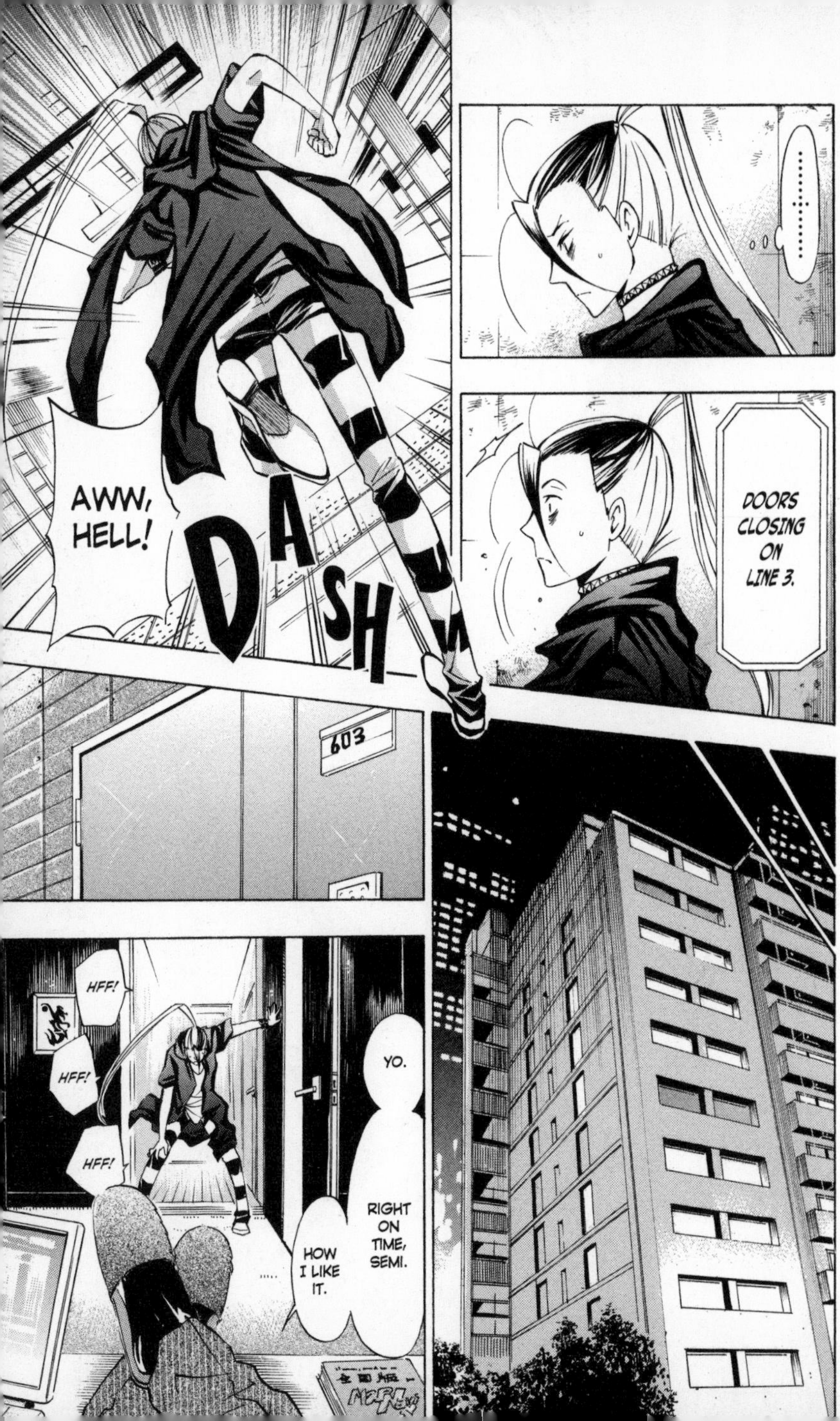
......
DOORS CLOSING ON LINE 3.
AWW, HELL!
DASH
603
YO.
RIGHT ON TIME, SEMI.
HOW I LIKE IT.
HFF!
HFF!
HFF!
.....

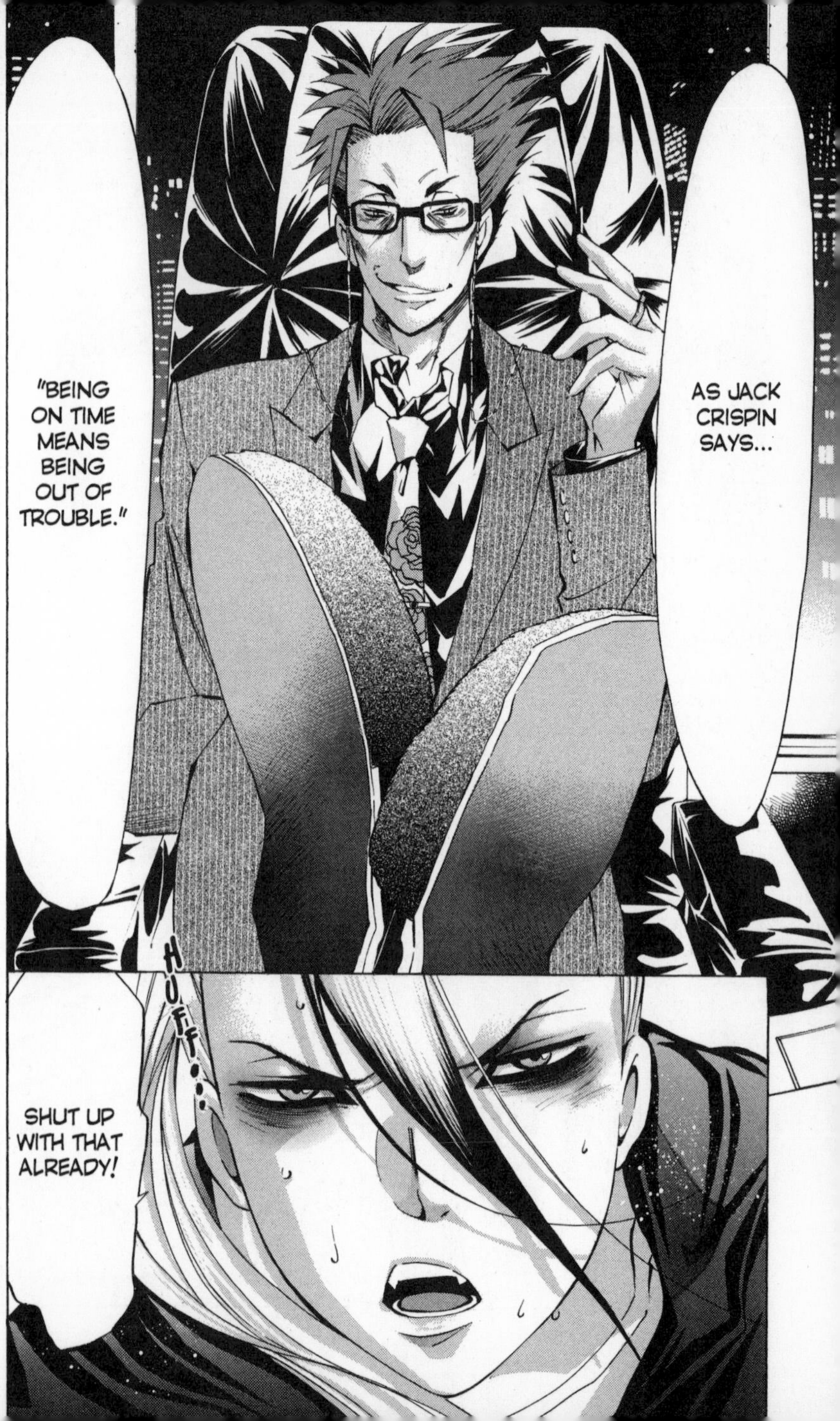
AS JACK CRISPIN SAYS...
"BEING ON TIME MEANS BEING OUT OF TROUBLE."
HUFF...
SHUT UP WITH THAT ALREADY!

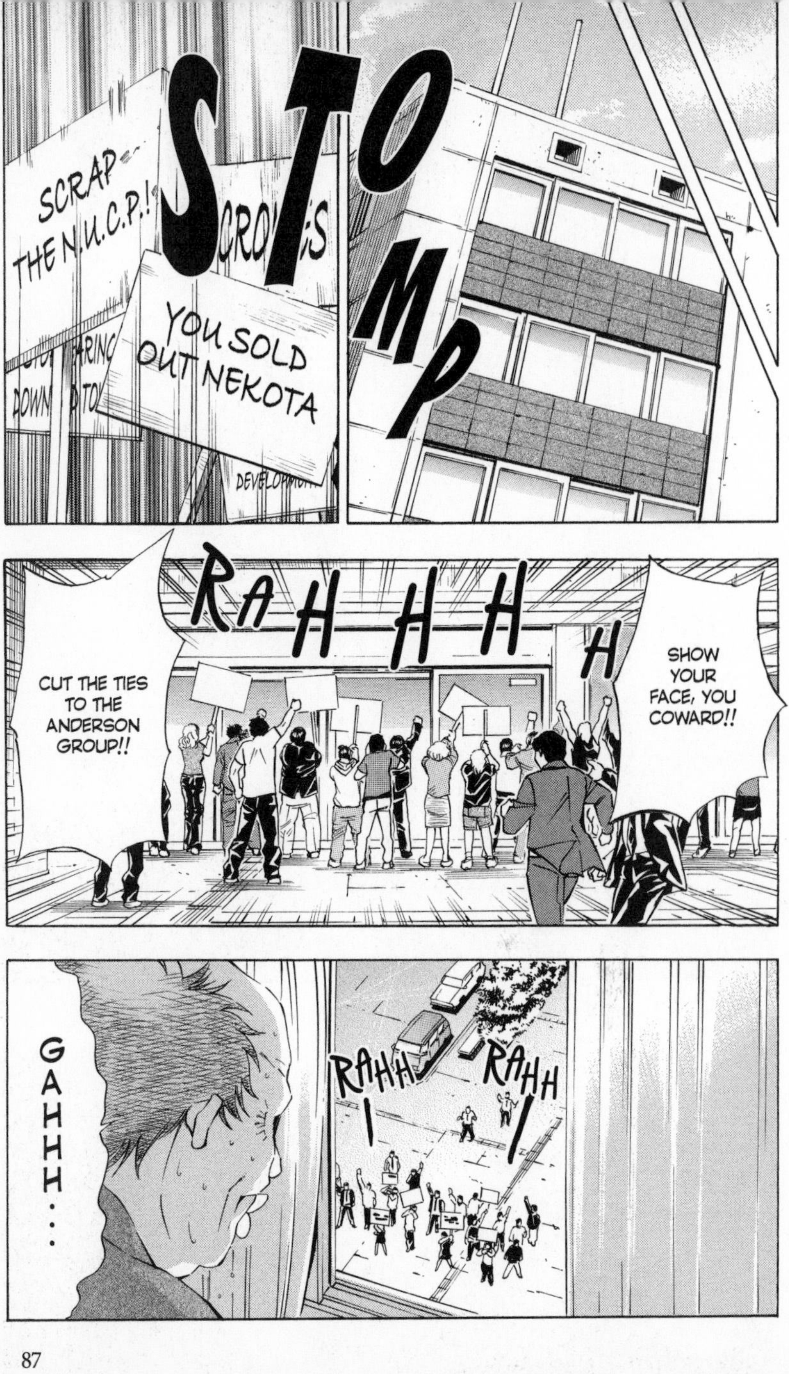
STOMP
SCRAP THE N.U.C.P.!
YOU SOLD OUT NEKOTA
SHOW YOUR FACE, YOU COWARD!!
RAHHHHH
CUT THE TIES TO THE ANDERSON GROUP!!
RAHH!
RAHH!
GAHHH...

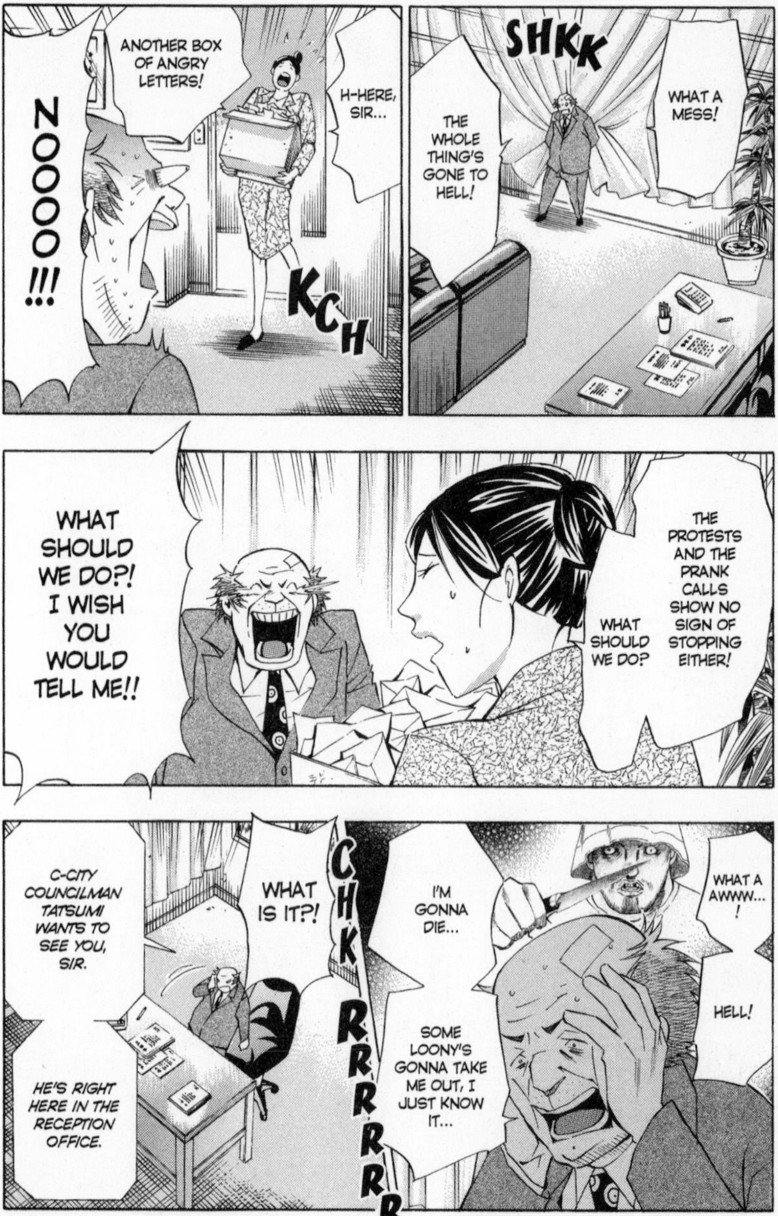
SHKK
WHAT A MESS!
THE WHOLE THING'S GONE TO HELL!
H-HERE, SIR...
ANOTHER BOX OF ANGRY LETTERS!
KCH
NOOOOO!!!
THE PROTESTS AND THE PRANK CALLS SHOW NO SIGN OF STOPPING EITHER!
WHAT SHOULD WE DO?
WHAT SHOULD WE DO?! I WISH YOU WOULD TELL ME!!
WHAT A AWWW... !
HELL!
I'M GONNA DIE...
SOME LOONY'S GONNA TAKE ME OUT, I JUST KNOW IT...
CHKRRRRRR
WHAT IS IT?!
C-CITY COUNCILMAN TATSUMI WANTS TO SEE YOU, SIR.
HE'S RIGHT HERE IN THE RECEPTION OFFICE.

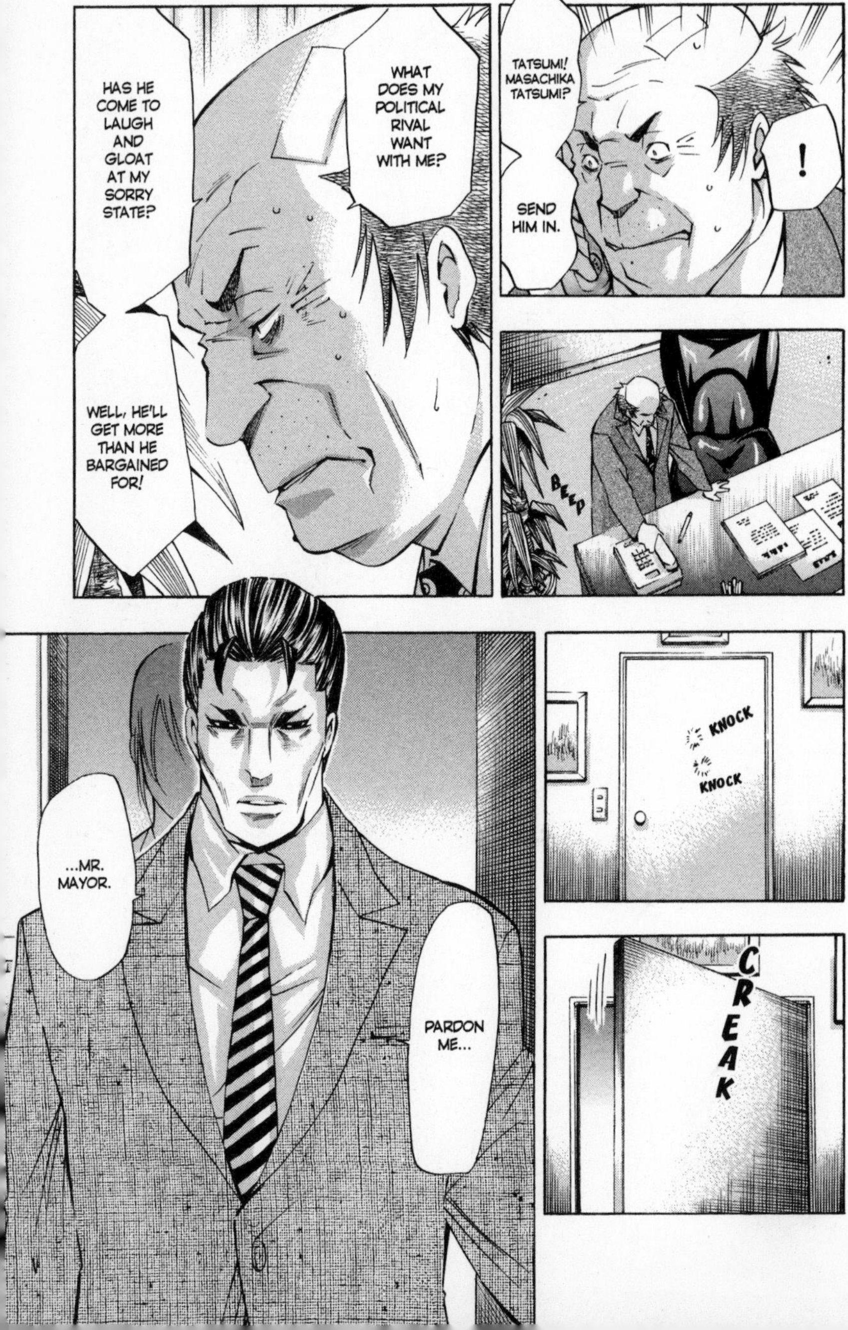
TATSUMI! MASACHIKA TATSUMI?
!
SEND HIM IN.
BEEP
WHAT DOES MY POLITICAL RIVAL WANT WITH ME?
HAS HE COME TO LAUGH AND GLOAT AT MY SORRY STATE?
WELL, HE'LL GET MORE THAN HE BARGAINED FOR!
KNOCK
KNOCK
CREAK
PARDON ME...
...MR. MAYOR.

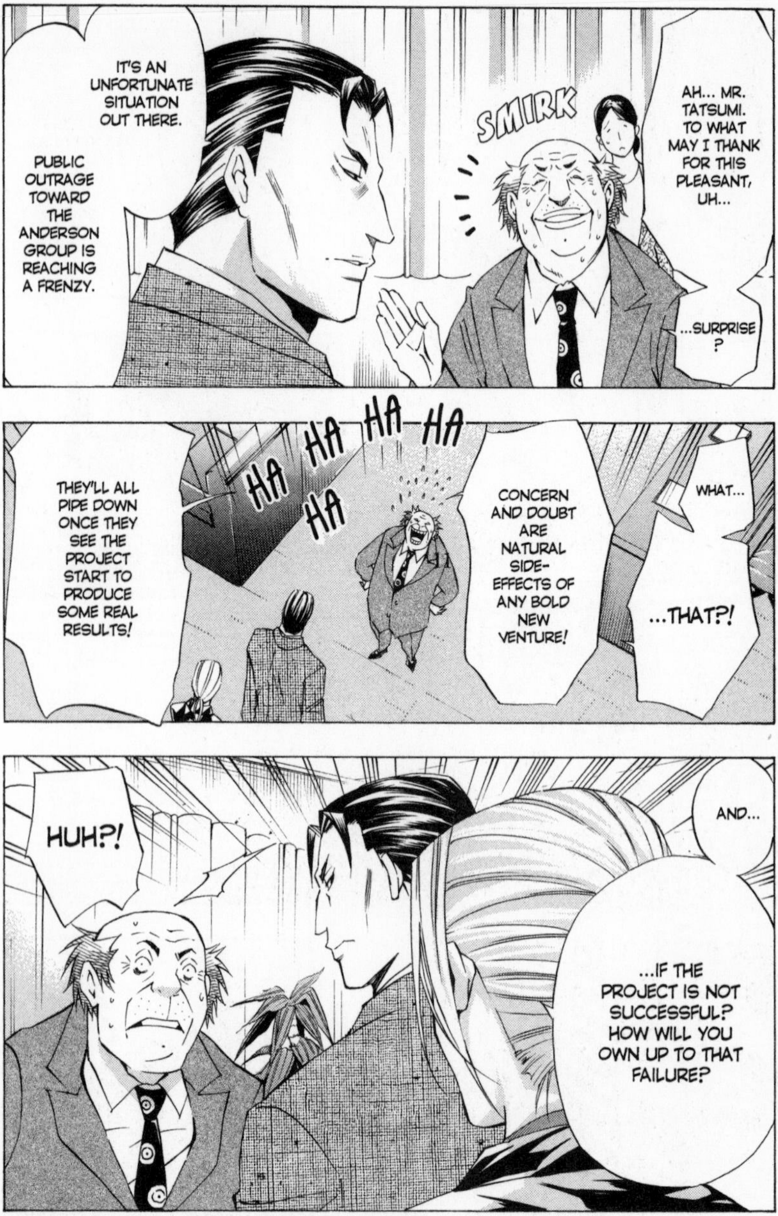

AH... MR. TATSUMI. TO WHAT MAY I THANK FOR THIS PLEASANT, UH...
...SURPRISE?
SMIRK
IT'S AN UNFORTUNATE SITUATION OUT THERE.
PUBLIC OUTRAGE TOWARD THE ANDERSON GROUP IS REACHING A FRENZY.
WHAT...
...THAT?!
CONCERN AND DOUBT ARE NATURAL SIDE-EFFECTS OF ANY BOLD NEW VENTURE!
HA HA HA HA HA
THEY'LL ALL PIPE DOWN ONCE THEY SEE THE PROJECT START TO PRODUCE SOME REAL RESULTS!
AND...
...IF THE PROJECT IS NOT SUCCESSFUL? HOW WILL YOU OWN UP TO THAT FAILURE?
HUH?!

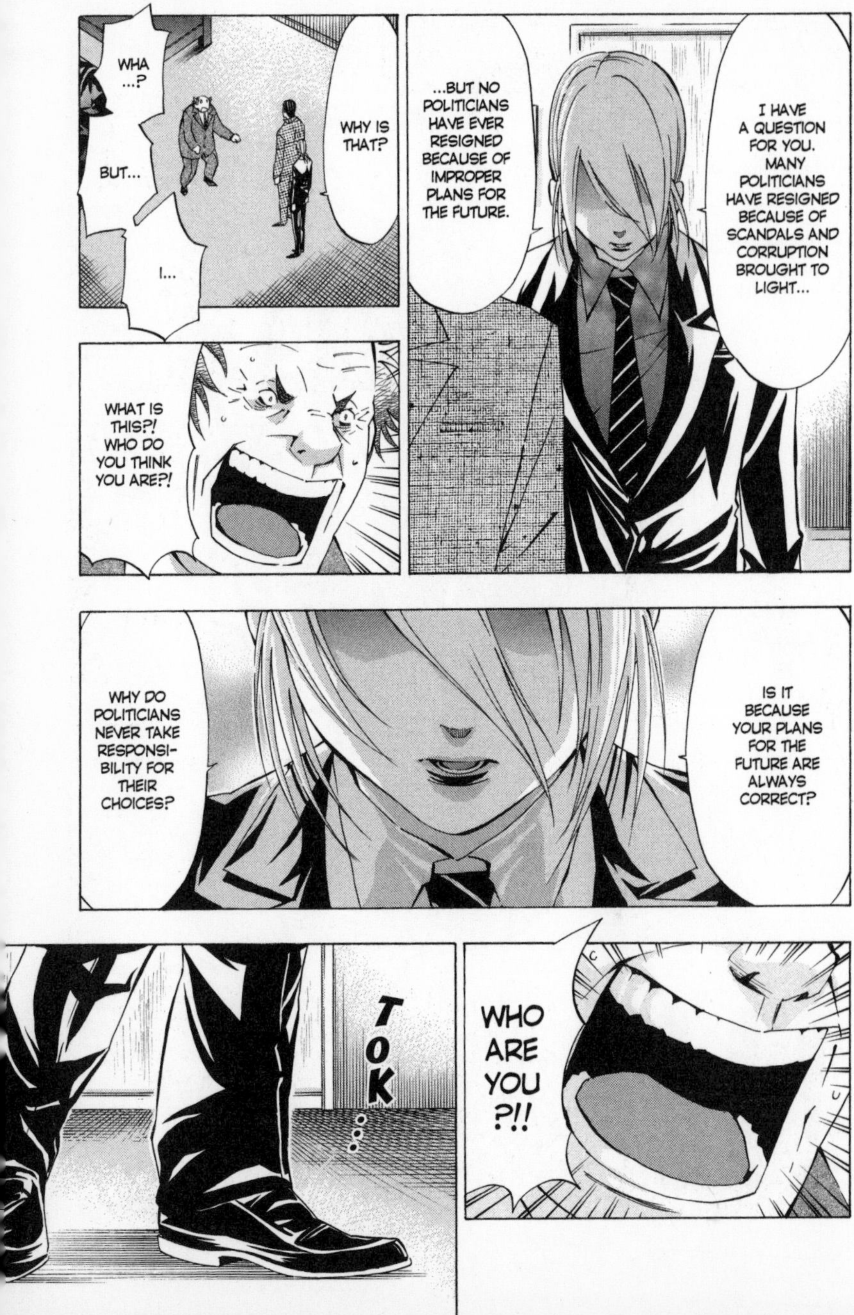
I HAVE A QUESTION FOR YOU. MANY POLITICIANS HAVE RESIGNED BECAUSE OF SCANDALS AND CORRUPTION BROUGHT TO LIGHT...
...BUT NO POLITICIANS HAVE EVER RESIGNED BECAUSE OF IMPROPER PLANS FOR THE FUTURE.
WHY IS THAT?
WHA ...?
BUT...
I...
WHAT IS THIS?! WHO DO YOU THINK YOU ARE?!
IS IT BECAUSE YOUR PLANS FOR THE FUTURE ARE ALWAYS CORRECT?
WHY DO POLITICIANS NEVER TAKE RESPONSI-BILITY FOR THEIR CHOICES?
WHO ARE YOU ?!!
TOK...

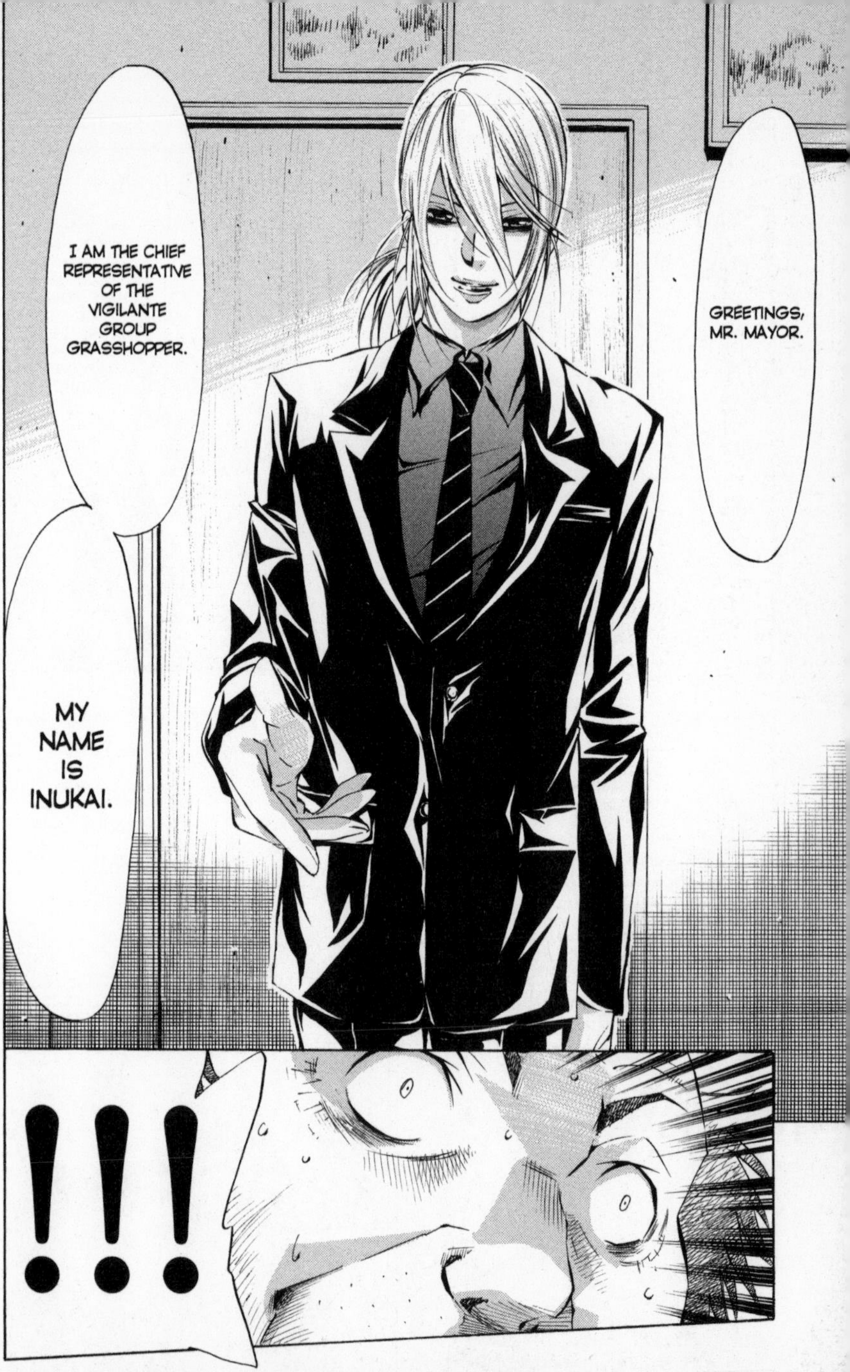
GREETINGS, MR. MAYOR.
I AM THE CHIEF REPRESENTATIVE OF THE VIGILANTE GROUP GRASSHOPPER.
MY NAME IS INUKAI.
!!!

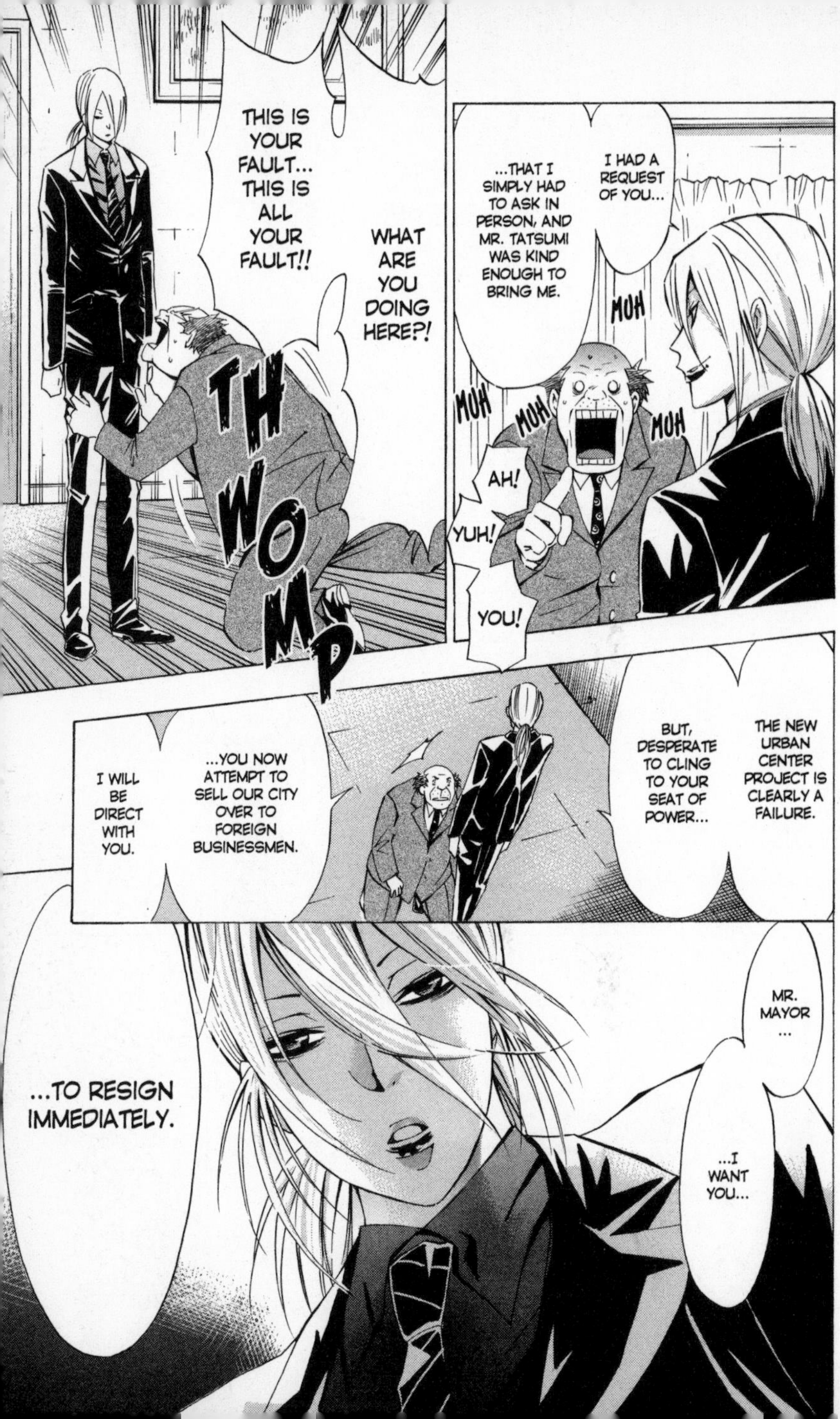
I HAD A REQUEST OF YOU...
...THAT I SIMPLY HAD TO ASK IN PERSON, AND MR. TATSUMI WAS KIND ENOUGH TO BRING ME.
MUH
MUH
MUH
MUH
AH!
YUH!
YOU!
WHAT ARE YOU DOING HERE?!
THIS IS YOUR FAULT... THIS IS ALL YOUR FAULT!!
THWOMP
THE NEW URBAN CENTER PROJECT IS CLEARLY A FAILURE.
BUT, DESPERATE TO CLING TO YOUR SEAT OF POWER...
...YOU NOW ATTEMPT TO SELL OUR CITY OVER TO FOREIGN BUSINESSMEN.
I WILL BE DIRECT WITH YOU.
MR. MAYOR...
...I WANT YOU...
...TO RESIGN IMMEDIATELY.

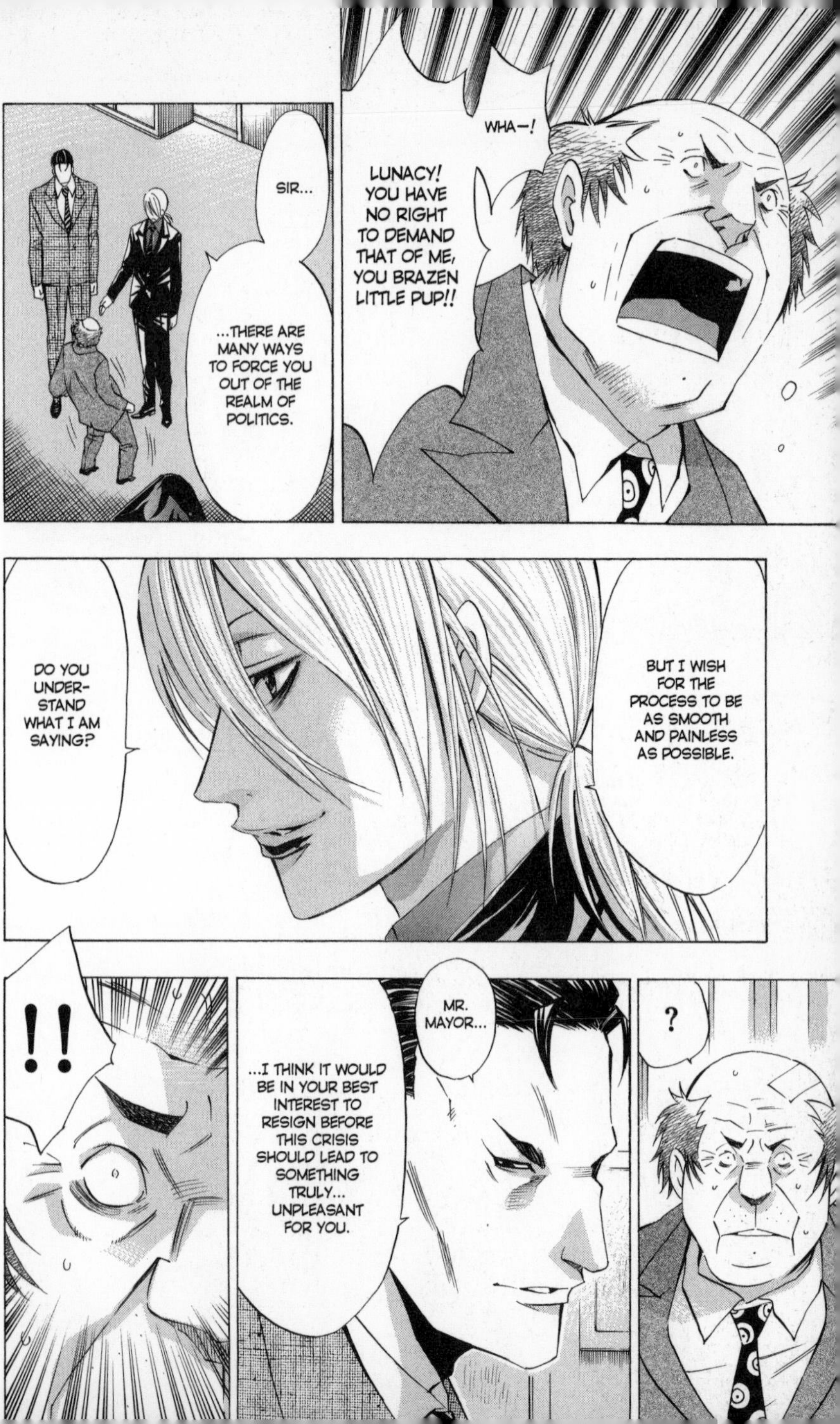
WHA—!
LUNACY! YOU HAVE NO RIGHT TO DEMAND THAT OF ME, YOU BRAZEN LITTLE PUP!!
SIR...
...THERE ARE MANY WAYS TO FORCE YOU OUT OF THE REALM OF POLITICS.
BUT I WISH FOR THE PROCESS TO BE AS SMOOTH AND PAINLESS AS POSSIBLE.
DO YOU UNDER-STAND WHAT I AM SAYING?
?
MR. MAYOR...
...I THINK IT WOULD BE IN YOUR BEST INTEREST TO RESIGN BEFORE THIS CRISIS SHOULD LEAD TO SOMETHING TRULY... UNPLEASANT FOR YOU.
!!

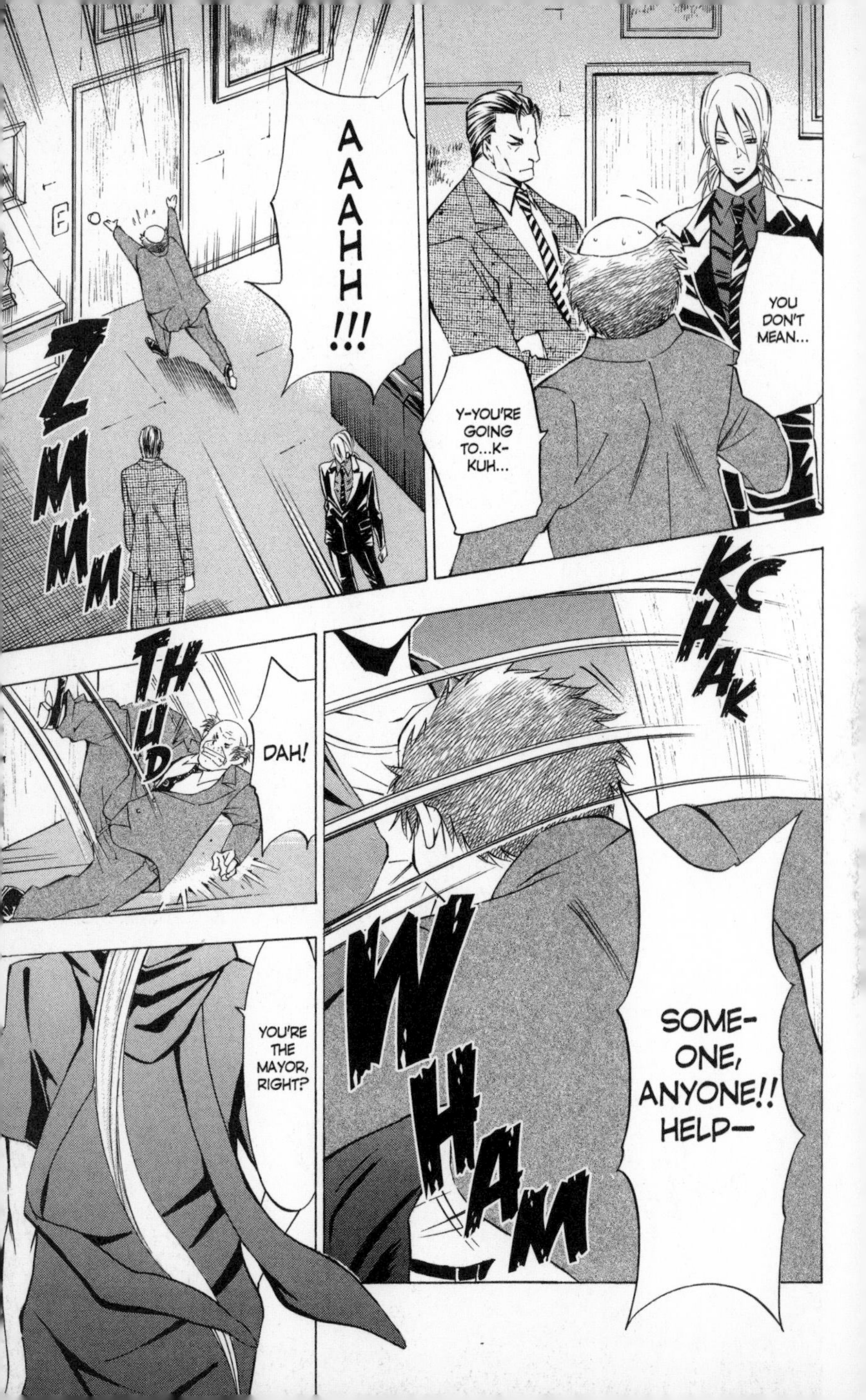
YOU DON'T MEAN...
Y-YOU'RE GOING TO...K-KUH...
AAAHH!!!
ZMMMN
KCHAK
WHAM
SOME-ONE, ANYONE!! HELP—
THUD
DAH!
YOU'RE THE MAYOR, RIGHT?

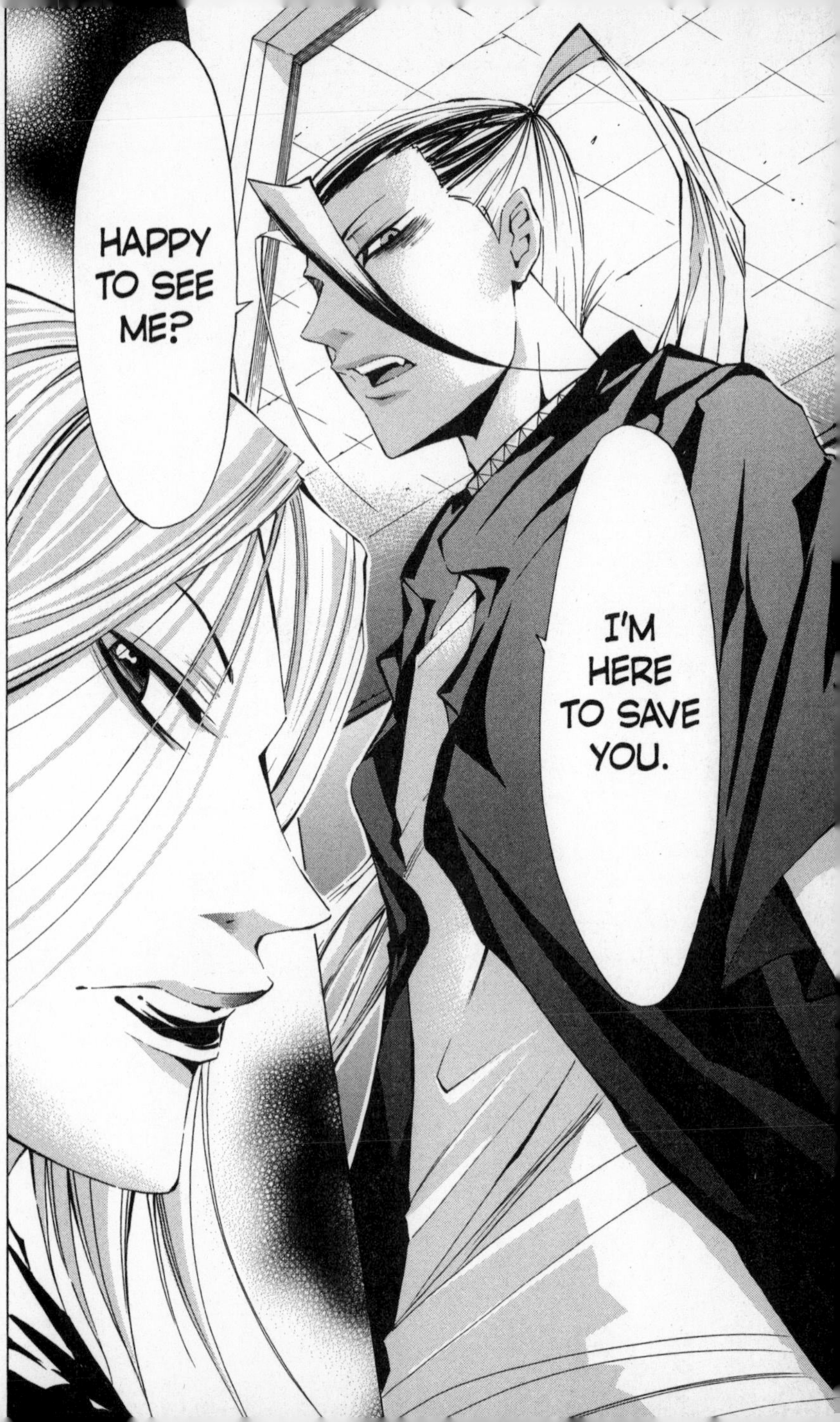
HAPPY TO SEE ME?
I'M HERE TO SAVE YOU.

Chapter 33 Cry of the Bystander

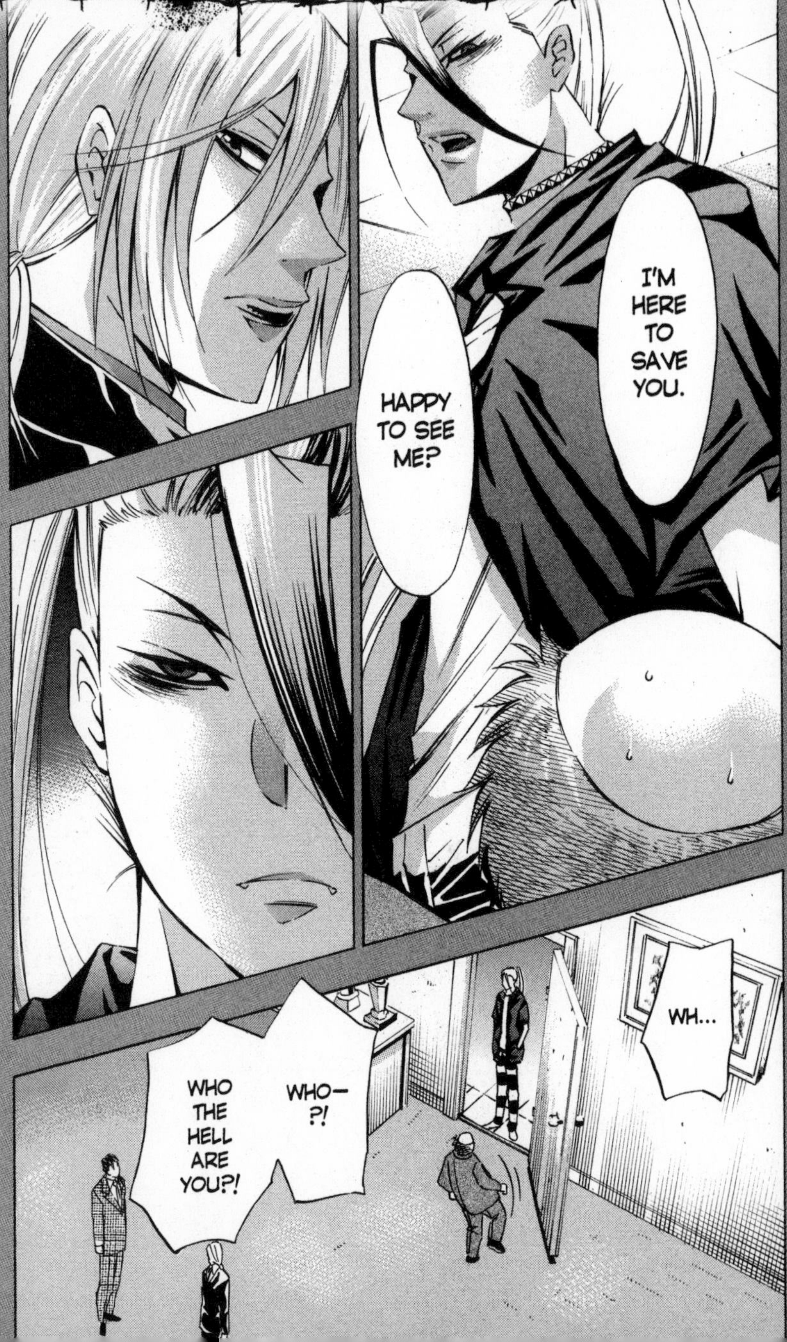
I'M HERE TO SAVE YOU.
HAPPY TO SEE ME?
WH...
WHO—?!
WHO THE HELL ARE YOU?!

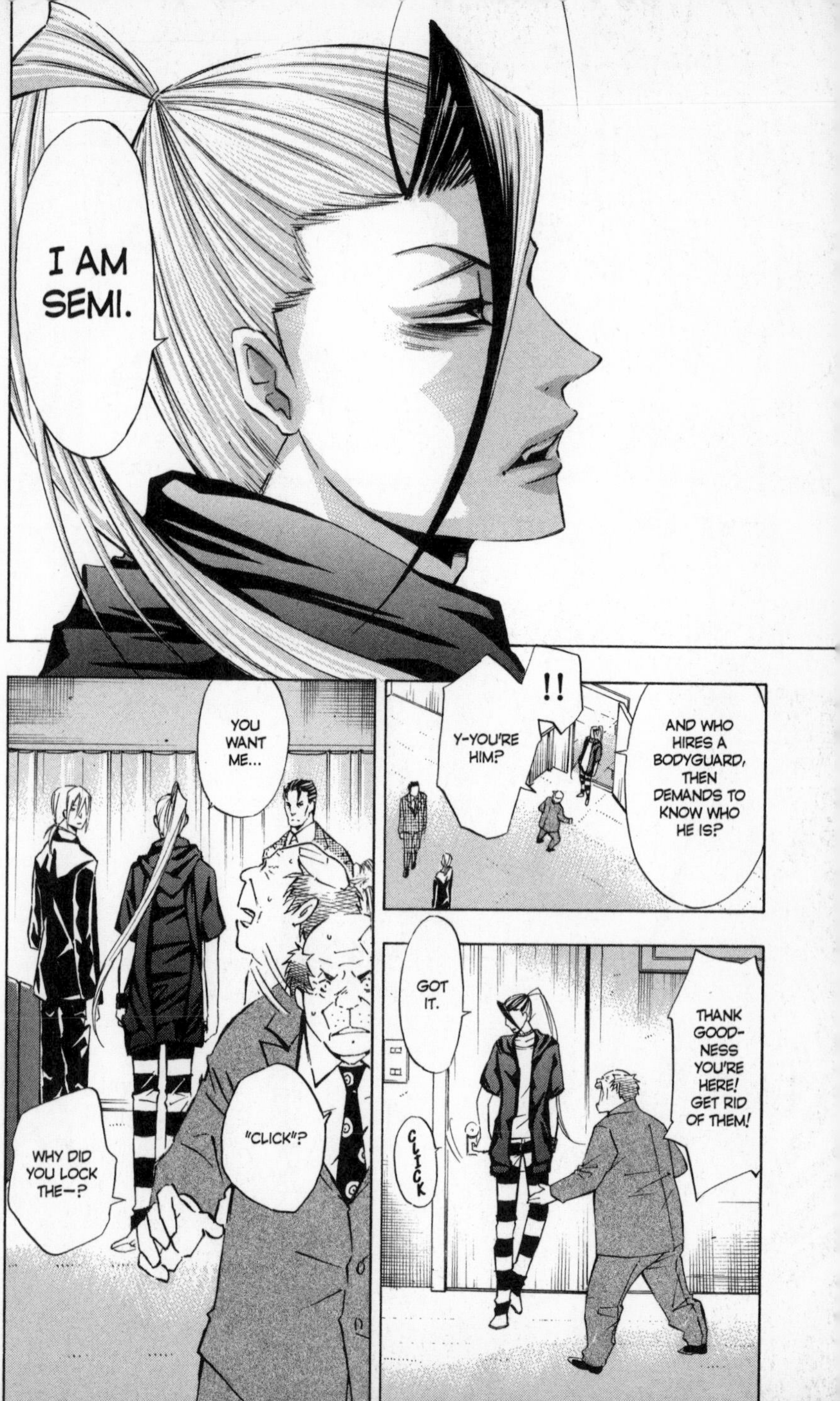
I AM SEMI.
AND WHO HIRES A BODYGUARD, THEN DEMANDS TO KNOW WHO HE IS?
!!
Y-YOU'RE HIM?
THANK GOODNESS YOU'RE HERE! GET RID OF THEM!
GOT IT.
CLICK
YOU WANT ME...
"CLICK"?
WHY DID YOU LOCK THE—?

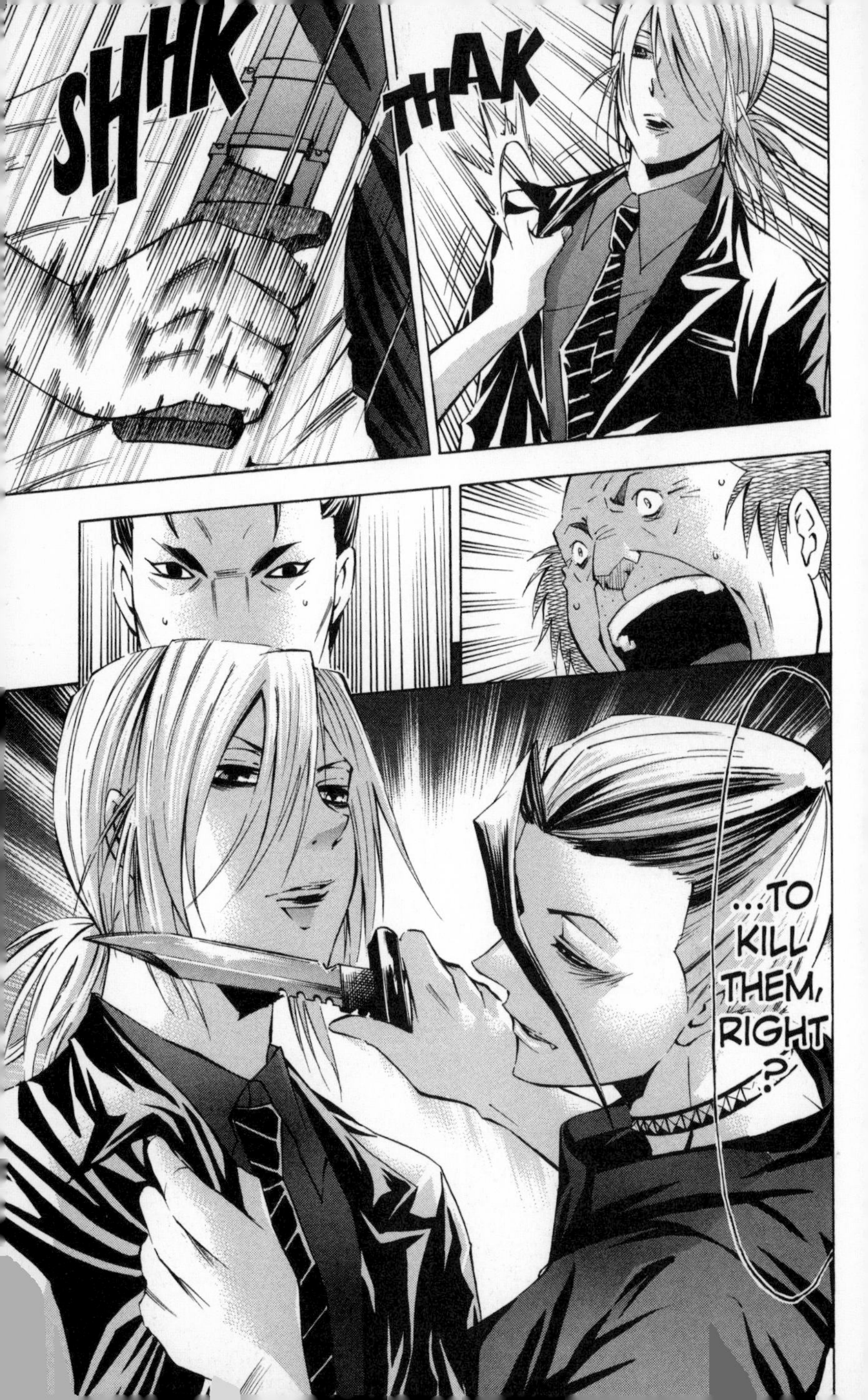
THAK
SHHK
...TO KILL THEM, RIGHT ?

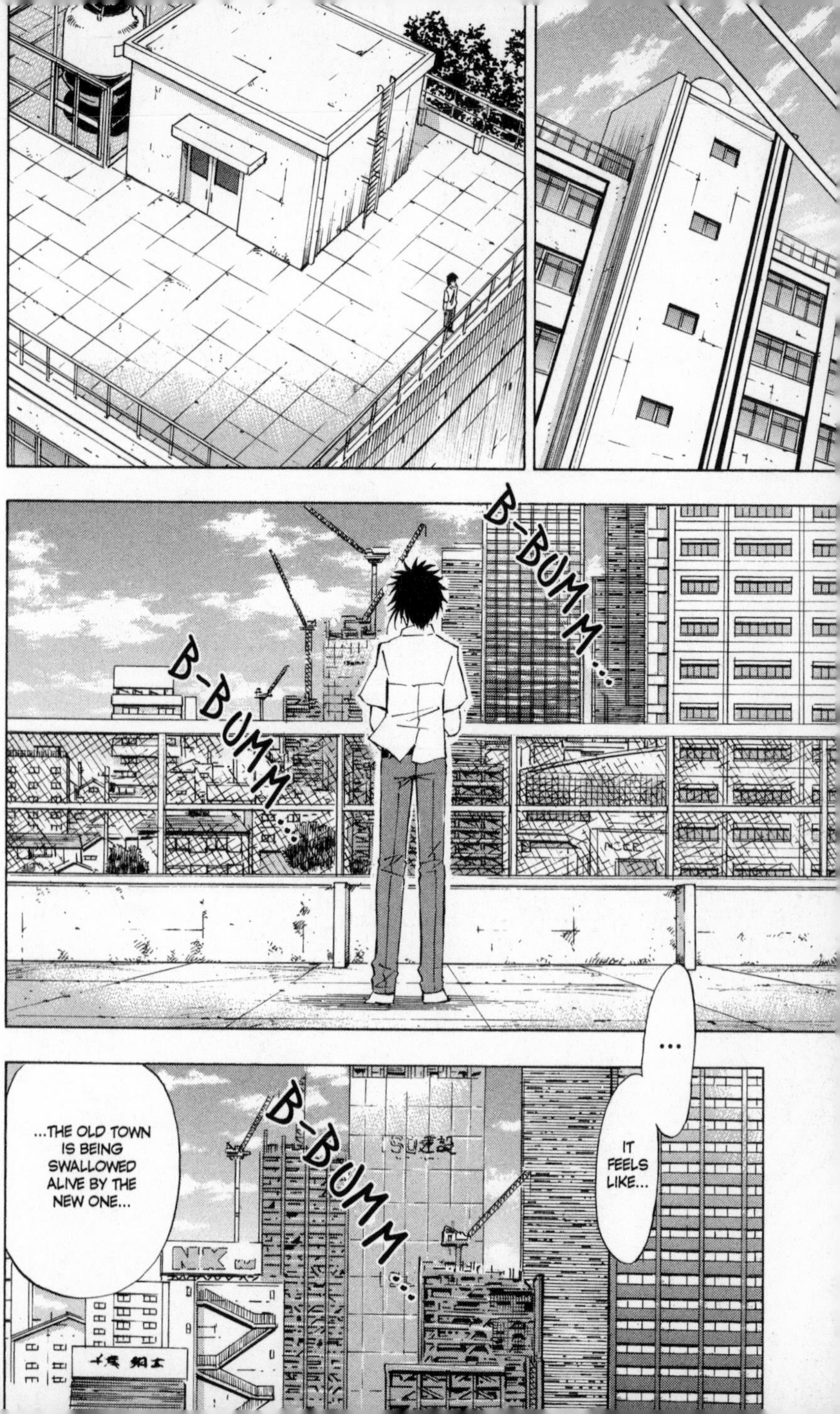
B-BUMMM...
B-BUMMM...
...
IT FEELS LIKE...
B-BUMMM...
...THE OLD TOWN IS BEING SWALLOWED ALIVE BY THE NEW ONE...

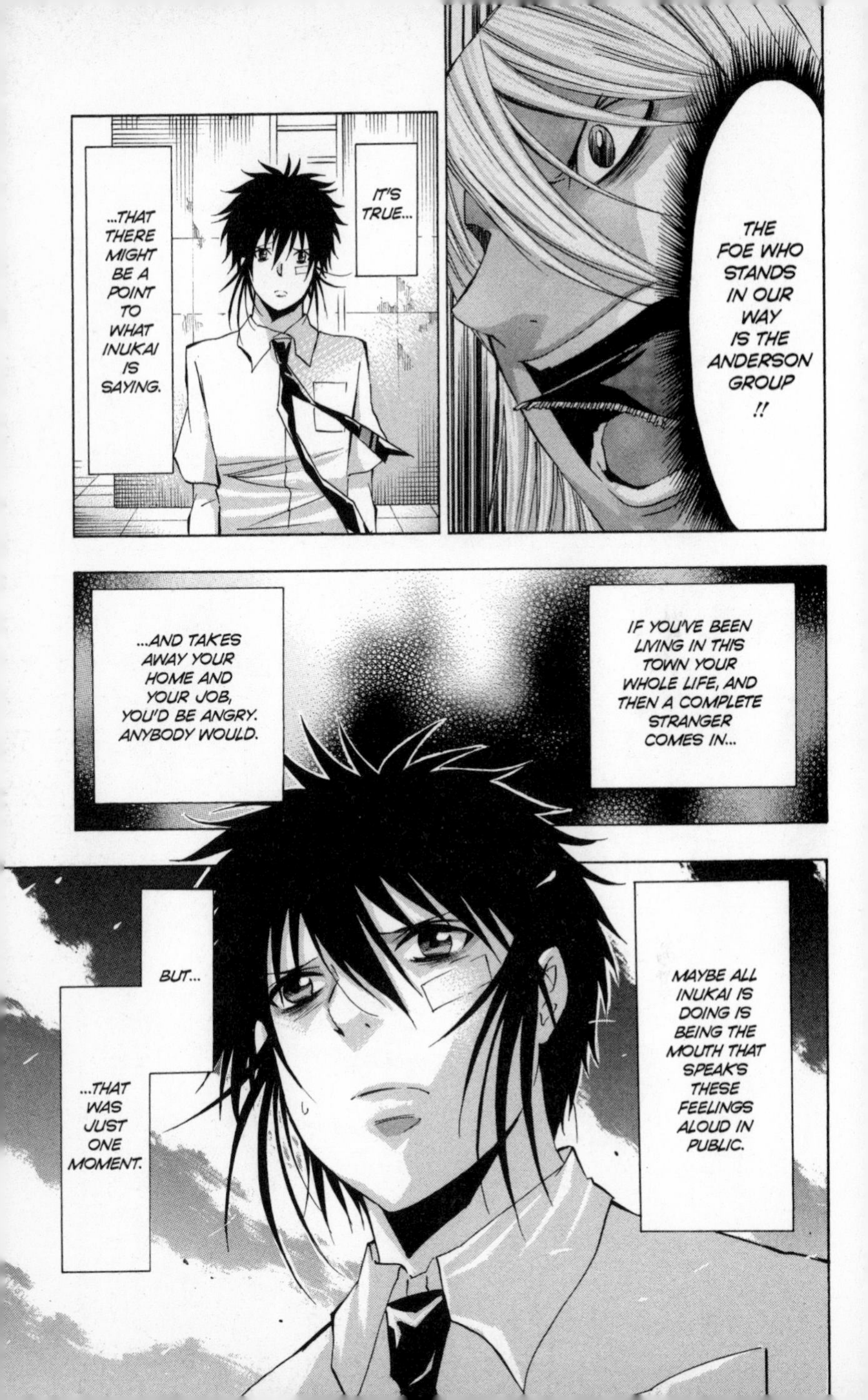
THE FOE WHO STANDS IN OUR WAY IS THE ANDERSON GROUP !!
IT'S TRUE...
...THAT THERE MIGHT BE A POINT TO WHAT INUKAI IS SAYING.
IF YOU'VE BEEN LIVING IN THIS TOWN YOUR WHOLE LIFE, AND THEN A COMPLETE STRANGER COMES IN...
...AND TAKES AWAY YOUR HOME AND YOUR JOB, YOU'D BE ANGRY. ANYBODY WOULD.
MAYBE ALL INUKAI IS DOING IS BEING THE MOUTH THAT SPEAKS THESE FEELINGS ALOUD IN PUBLIC.
BUT...
...THAT WAS JUST ONE MOMENT.

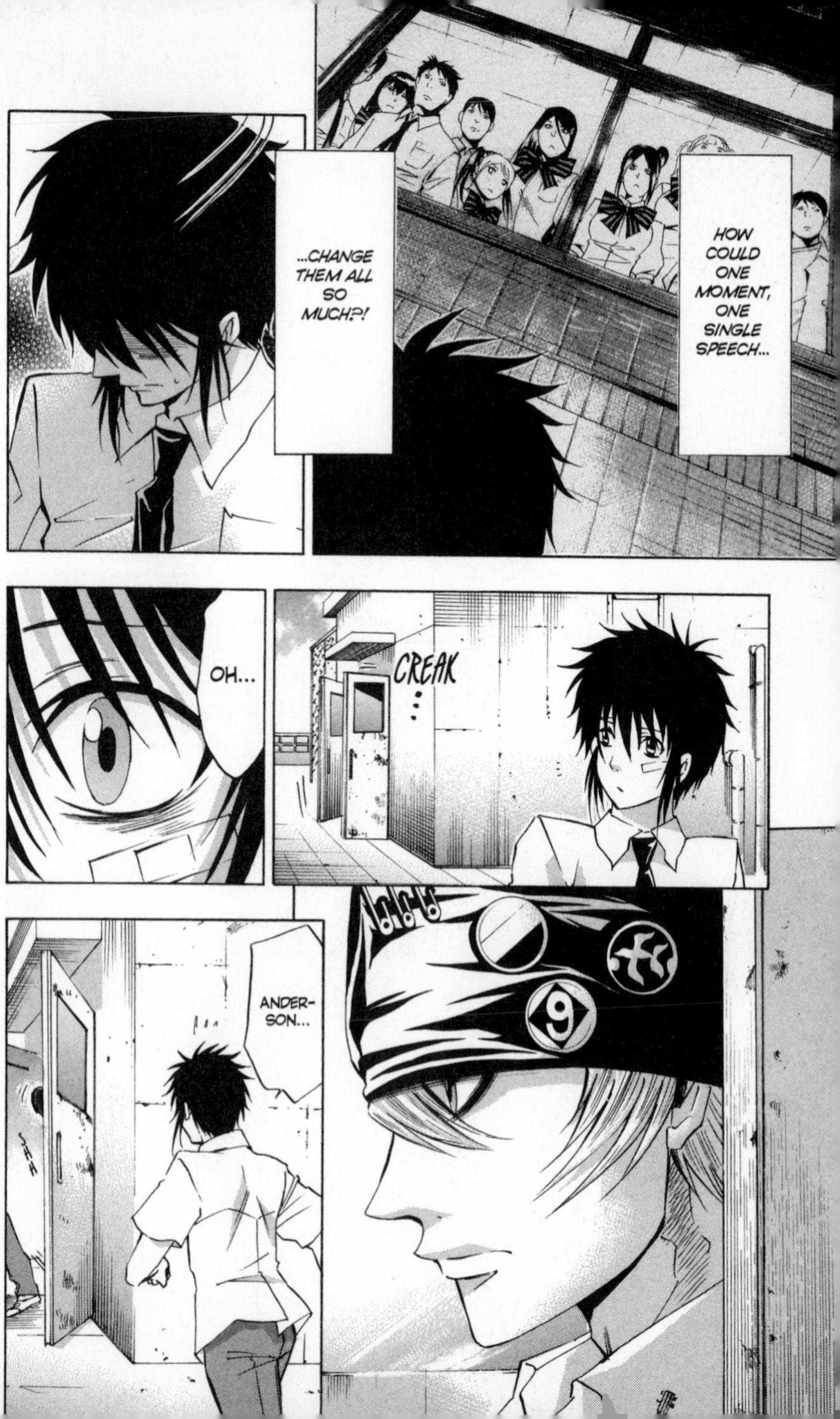
HOW COULD ONE MOMENT, ONE SINGLE SPEECH...
...CHANGE THEM ALL SO MUCH?!
CREAK
OH...
ANDER-SON...
SHH

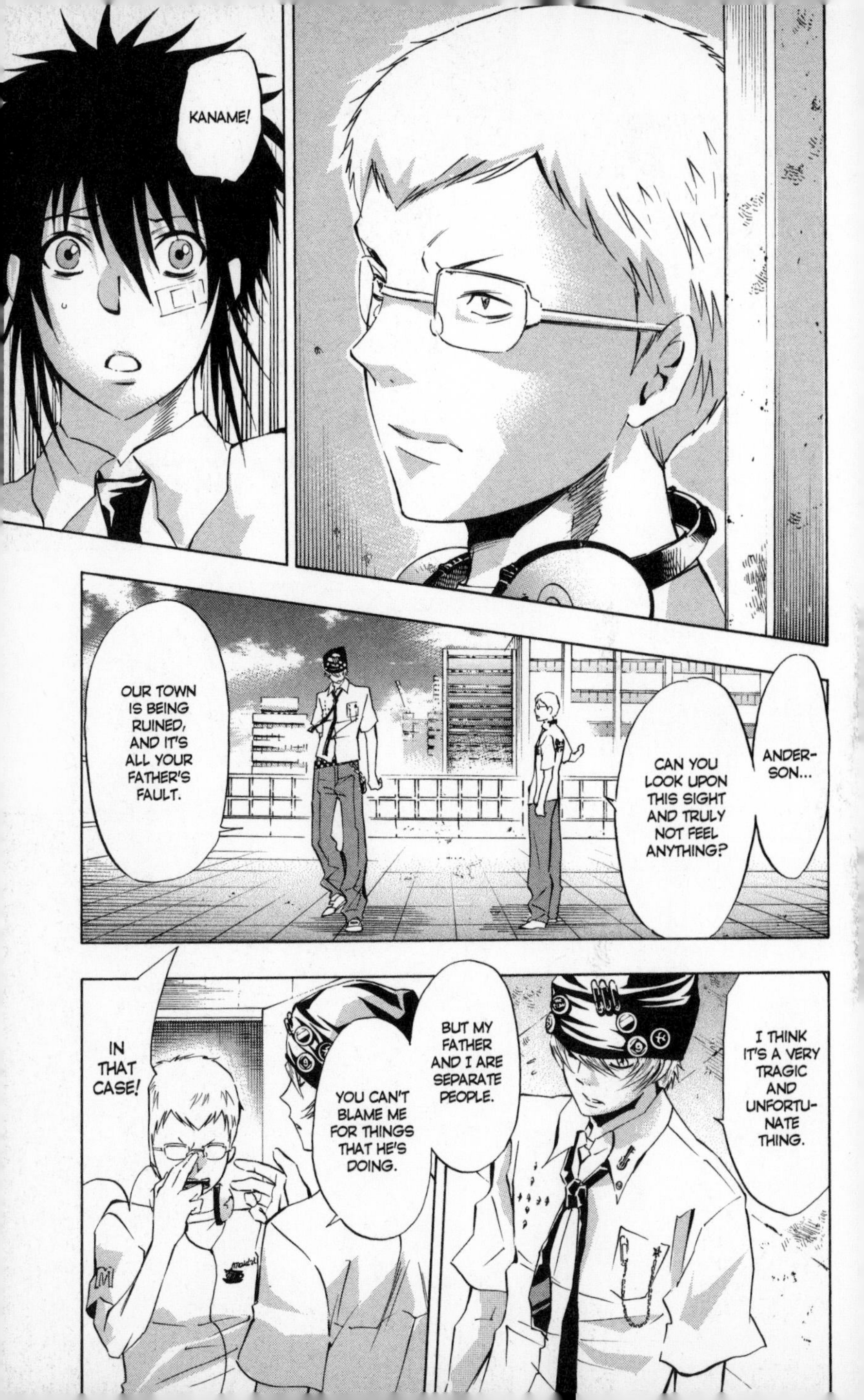
KANAME!
ANDER-SON...
CAN YOU LOOK UPON THIS SIGHT AND TRULY NOT FEEL ANYTHING?
OUR TOWN IS BEING RUINED, AND IT'S ALL YOUR FATHER'S FAULT.
I THINK IT'S A VERY TRAGIC AND UNFORTU-NATE THING.
BUT MY FATHER AND I ARE SEPARATE PEOPLE.
YOU CAN'T BLAME ME FOR THINGS THAT HE'S DOING.
IN THAT CASE!

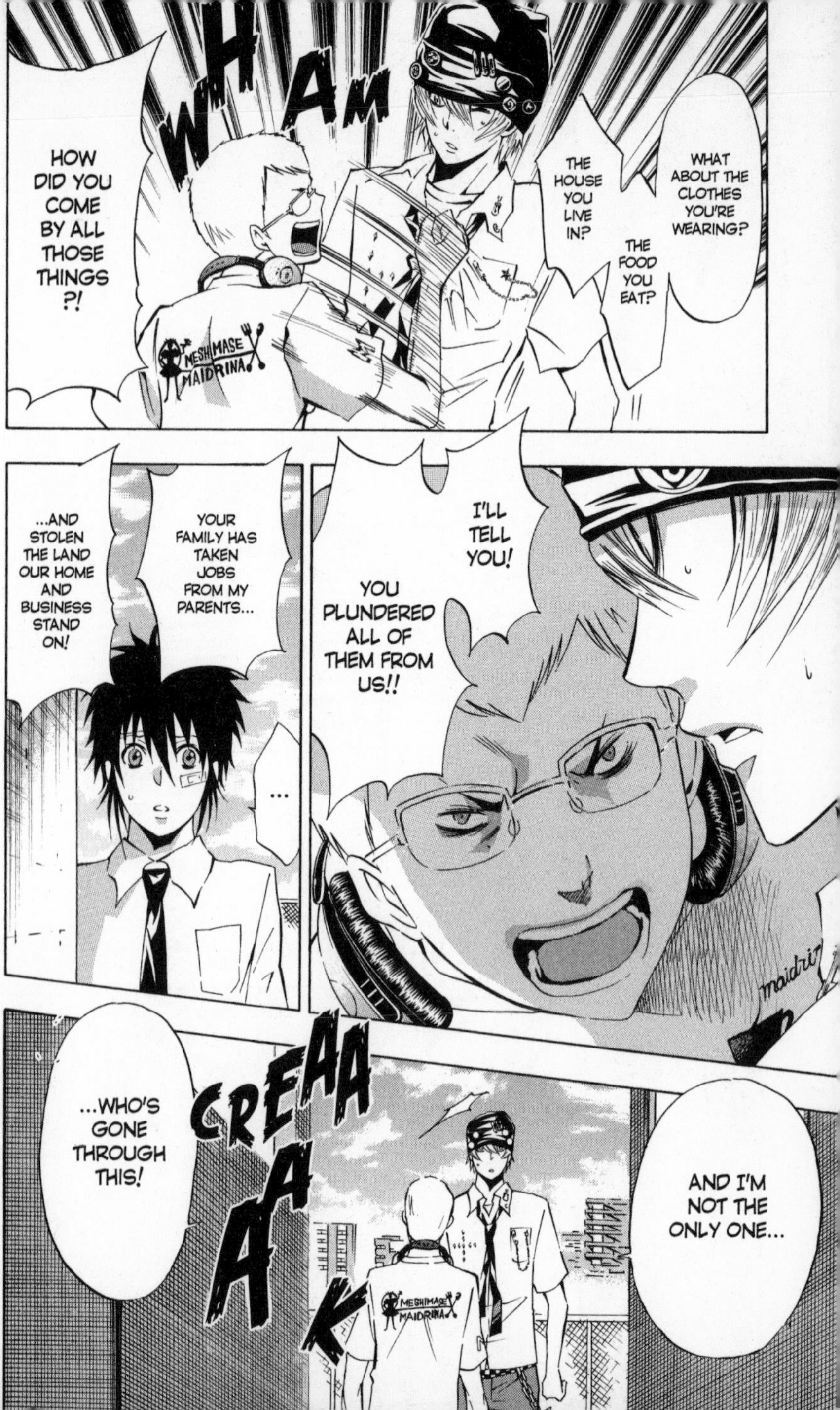
WHAT ABOUT THE CLOTHES YOU'RE WEARING?
THE FOOD YOU EAT?
THE HOUSE YOU LIVE IN?
WHAM
HOW DID YOU COME BY ALL THOSE THINGS?!
MESHIMASE MAIDRINA
I'LL TELL YOU!
YOU PLUNDERED ALL OF THEM FROM US!!
YOUR FAMILY HAS TAKEN JOBS FROM MY PARENTS...
...AND STOLEN THE LAND OUR HOME AND BUSINESS STAND ON!
...
AND I'M NOT THE ONLY ONE...
CREAAAAK
...WHO'S GONE THROUGH THIS!
MESHIMASE MAIDRINA

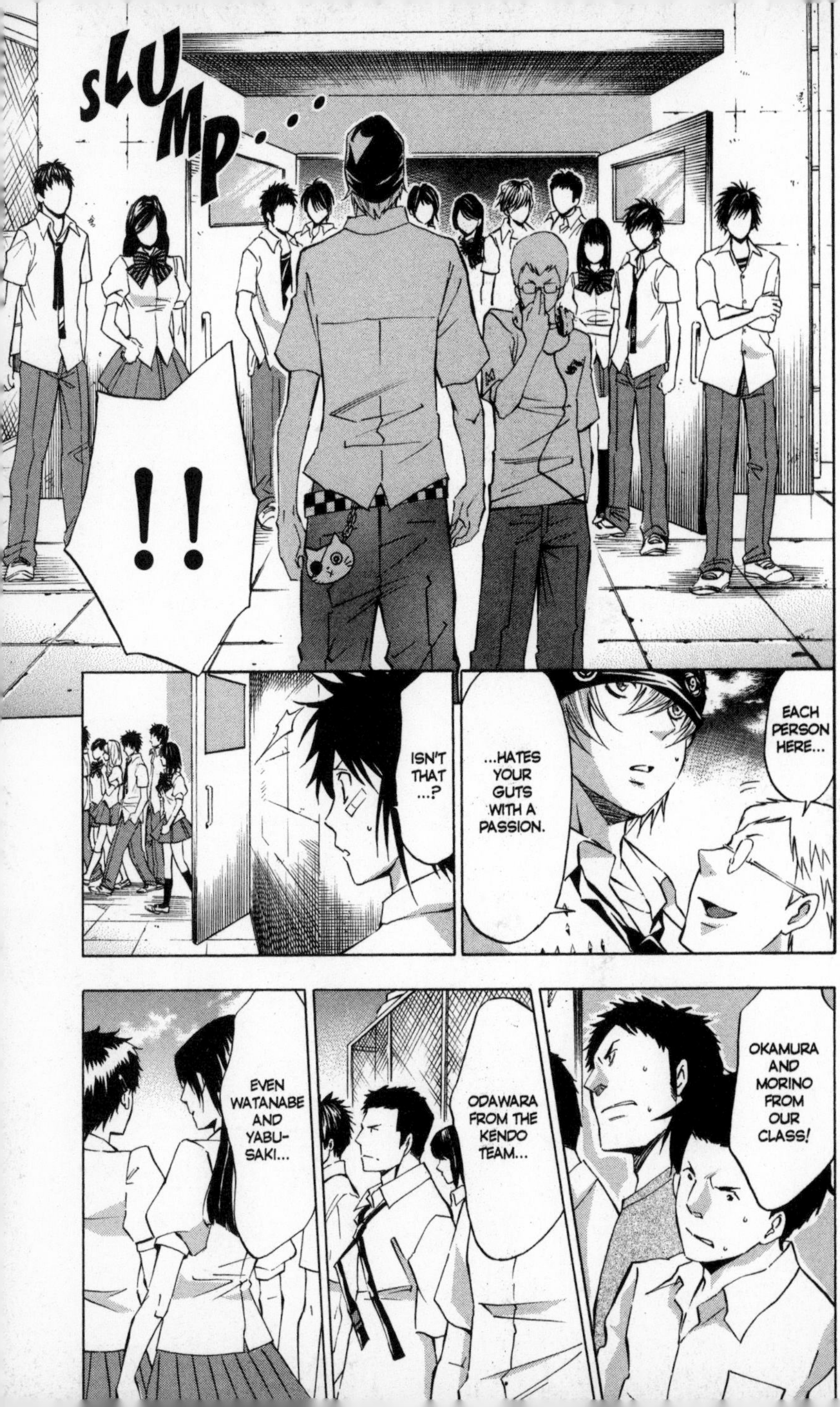
SLUMP...
!!
EACH PERSON HERE...
...HATES YOUR GUTS WITH A PASSION.
ISN'T THAT ...?
OKAMURA AND MORINO FROM OUR CLASS!
ODAWARA FROM THE KENDO TEAM...
EVEN WATANABE AND YABU-SAKI...

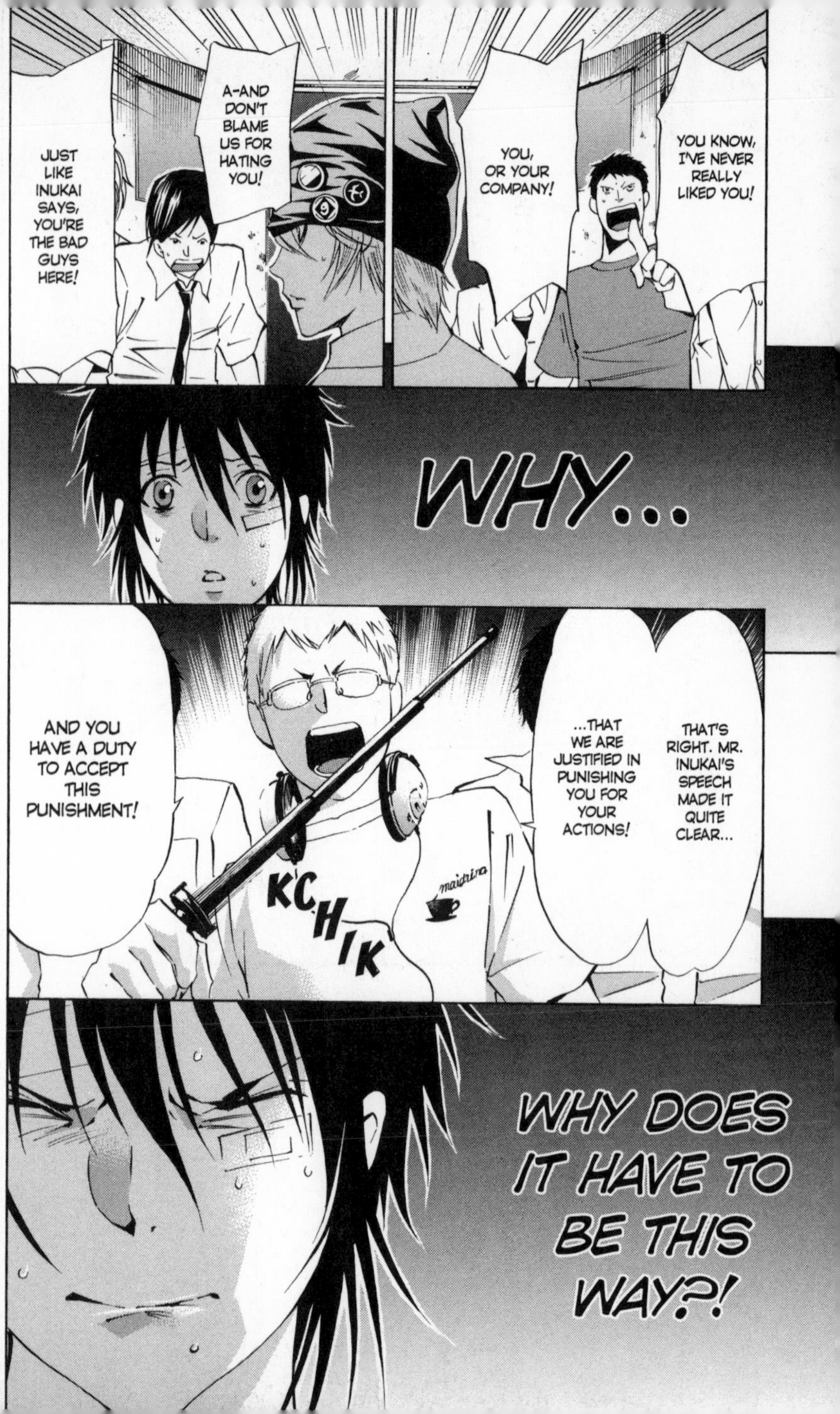
YOU KNOW, I'VE NEVER REALLY LIKED YOU!
YOU, OR YOUR COMPANY!
A-AND DON'T BLAME US FOR HATING YOU!
JUST LIKE INUKAI SAYS, YOU'RE THE BAD GUYS HERE!
WHY...
THAT'S RIGHT. MR. INUKAI'S SPEECH MADE IT QUITE CLEAR...
...THAT WE ARE JUSTIFIED IN PUNISHING YOU FOR YOUR ACTIONS!
KCHIK
AND YOU HAVE A DUTY TO ACCEPT THIS PUNISHMENT!
WHY DOES IT HAVE TO BE THIS WAY?!

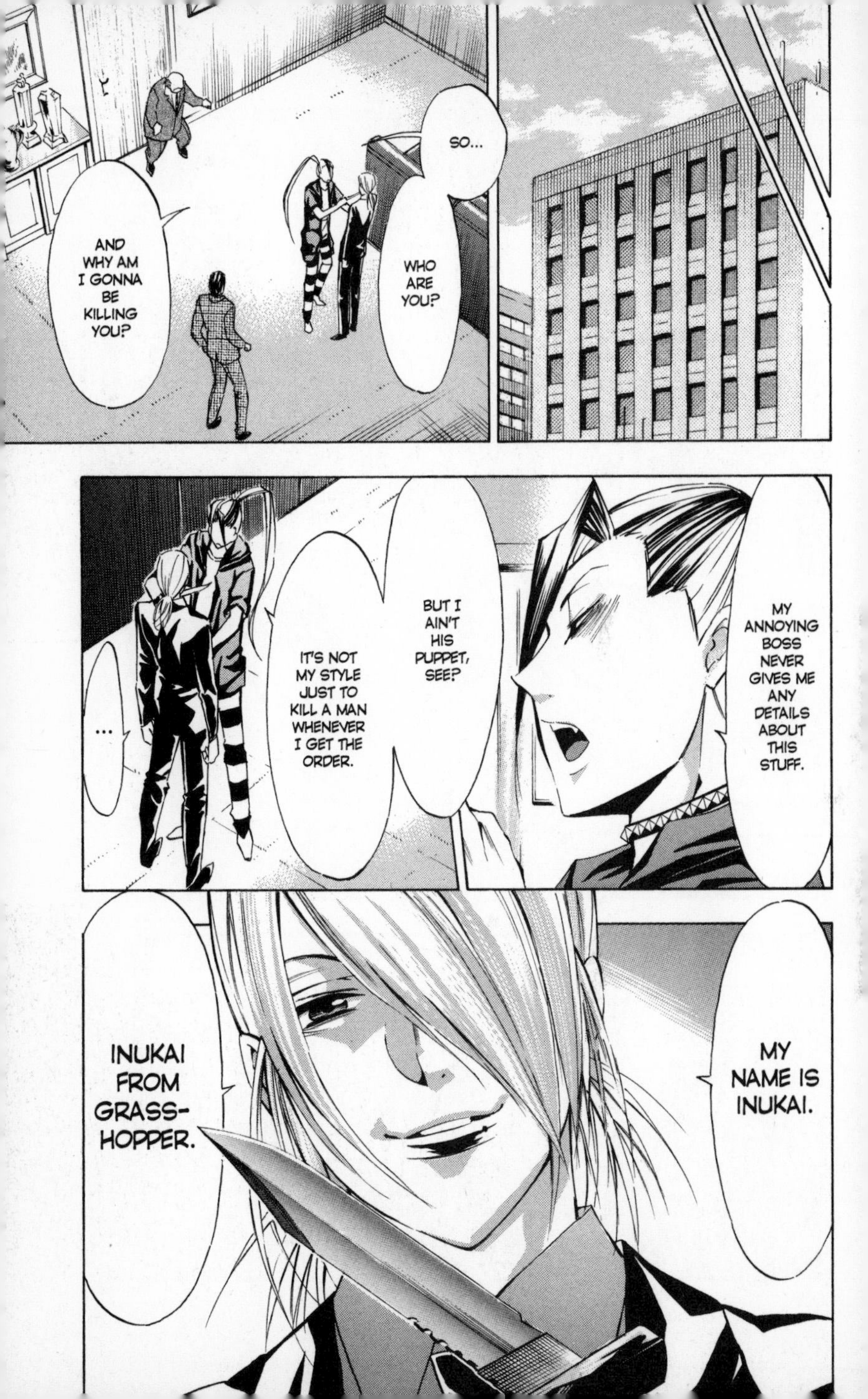
SO...
WHO ARE YOU?
AND WHY AM I GONNA BE KILLING YOU?
MY ANNOYING BOSS NEVER GIVES ME ANY DETAILS ABOUT THIS STUFF.
BUT I AIN'T HIS PUPPET, SEE?
IT'S NOT MY STYLE JUST TO KILL A MAN WHENEVER I GET THE ORDER.
...
MY NAME IS INUKAI.
INUKAI FROM GRASS-HOPPER.

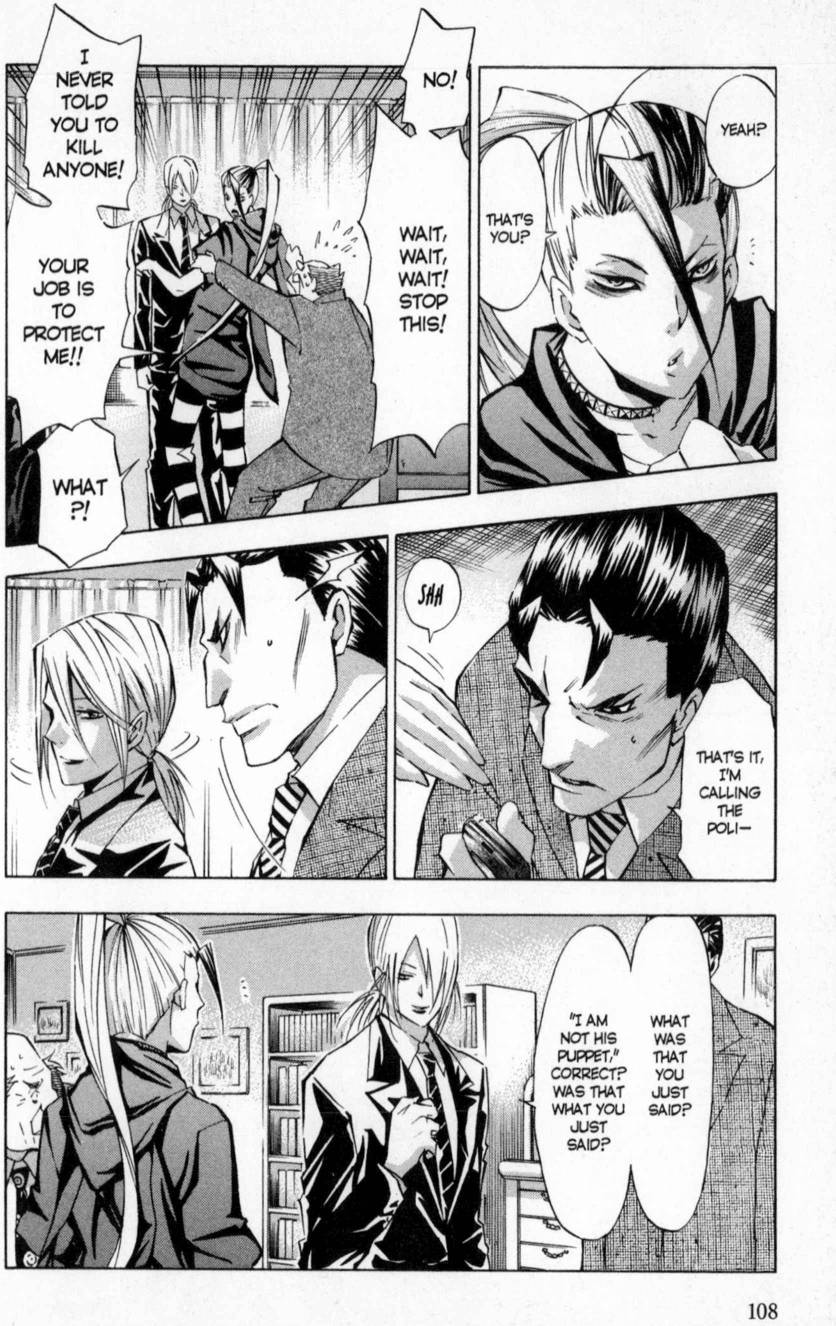
YEAH?
THAT'S YOU?
NO!
I NEVER TOLD YOU TO KILL ANYONE!
WAIT, WAIT, WAIT! STOP THIS!
YOUR JOB IS TO PROTECT ME!!
WHAT?!
SHH
THAT'S IT, I'M CALLING THE POLI—
WHAT WAS THAT YOU JUST SAID?
"I AM NOT HIS PUPPET," CORRECT? WAS THAT WHAT YOU JUST SAID?

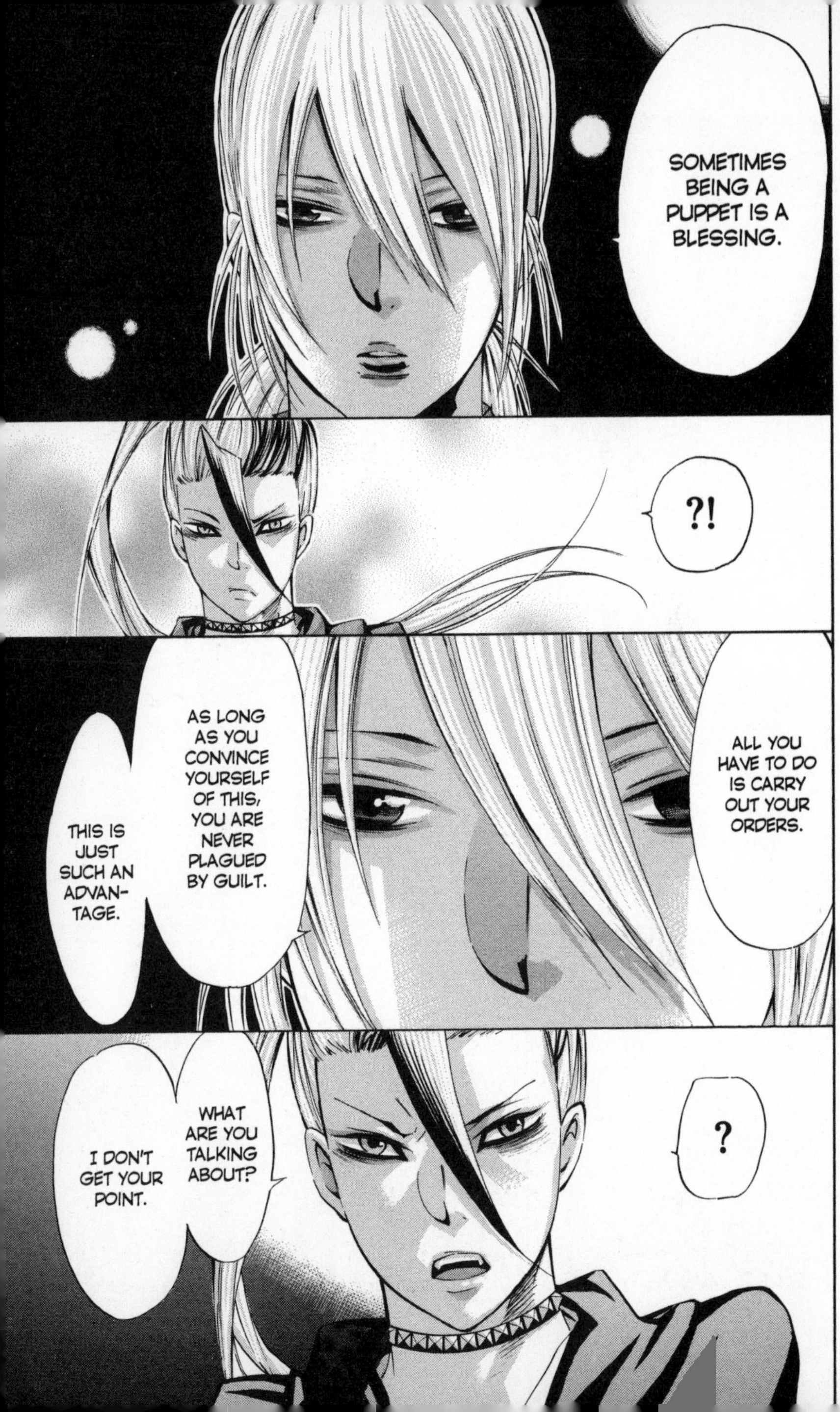
SOMETIMES BEING A PUPPET IS A BLESSING.
?!
ALL YOU HAVE TO DO IS CARRY OUT YOUR ORDERS.
AS LONG AS YOU CONVINCE YOURSELF OF THIS, YOU ARE NEVER PLAGUED BY GUILT.
THIS IS JUST SUCH AN ADVAN-TAGE.
?
WHAT ARE YOU TALKING ABOUT?
I DON'T GET YOUR POINT.

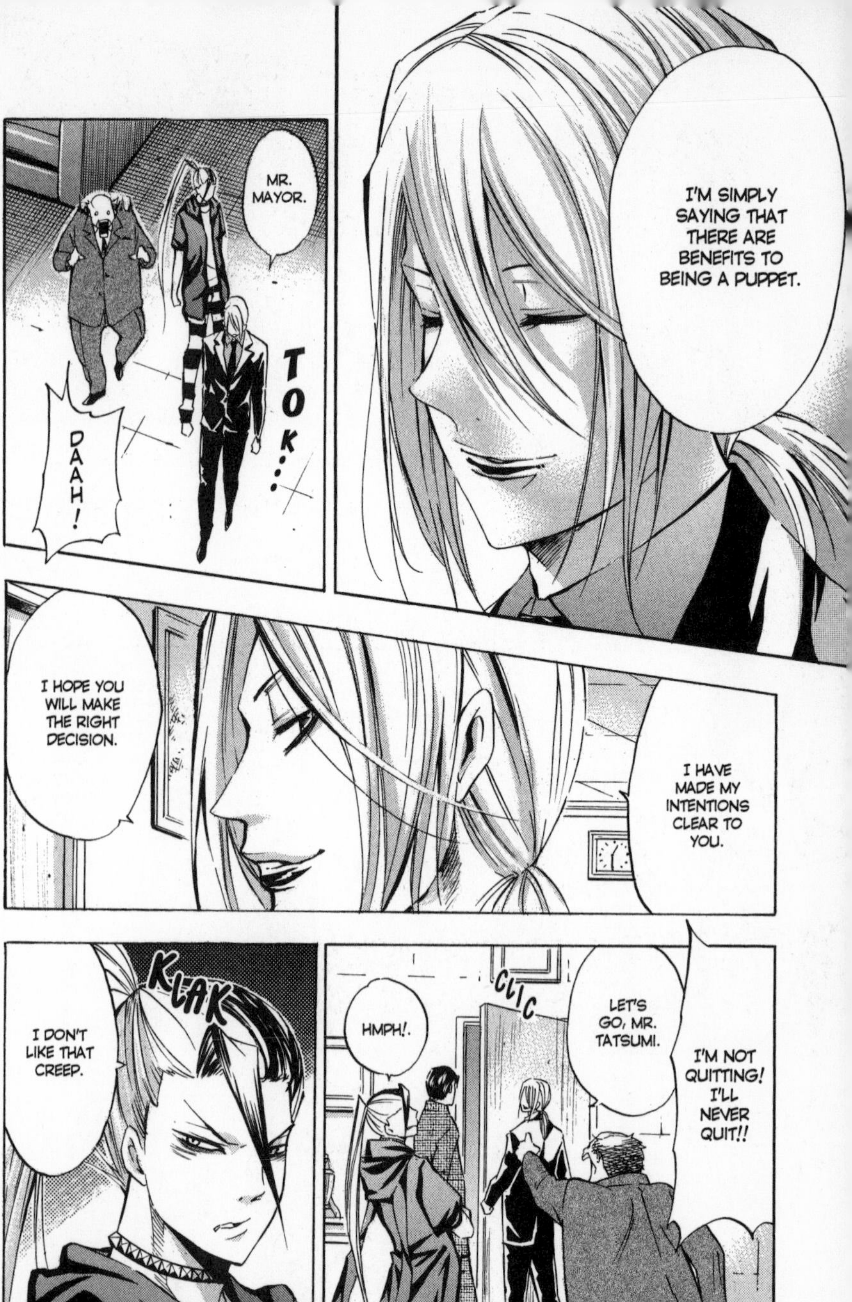
I'M SIMPLY SAYING THAT THERE ARE BENEFITS TO BEING A PUPPET.
MR. MAYOR.
TOK...
DAAH!
I HAVE MADE MY INTENTIONS CLEAR TO YOU.
I HOPE YOU WILL MAKE THE RIGHT DECISION.
I'M NOT QUITTING! I'LL NEVER QUIT!!
LET'S GO, MR. TATSUMI.
CLIC
HMPH!.
KLAK
I DON'T LIKE THAT CREEP.

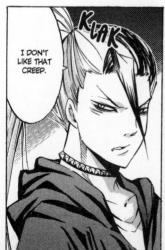

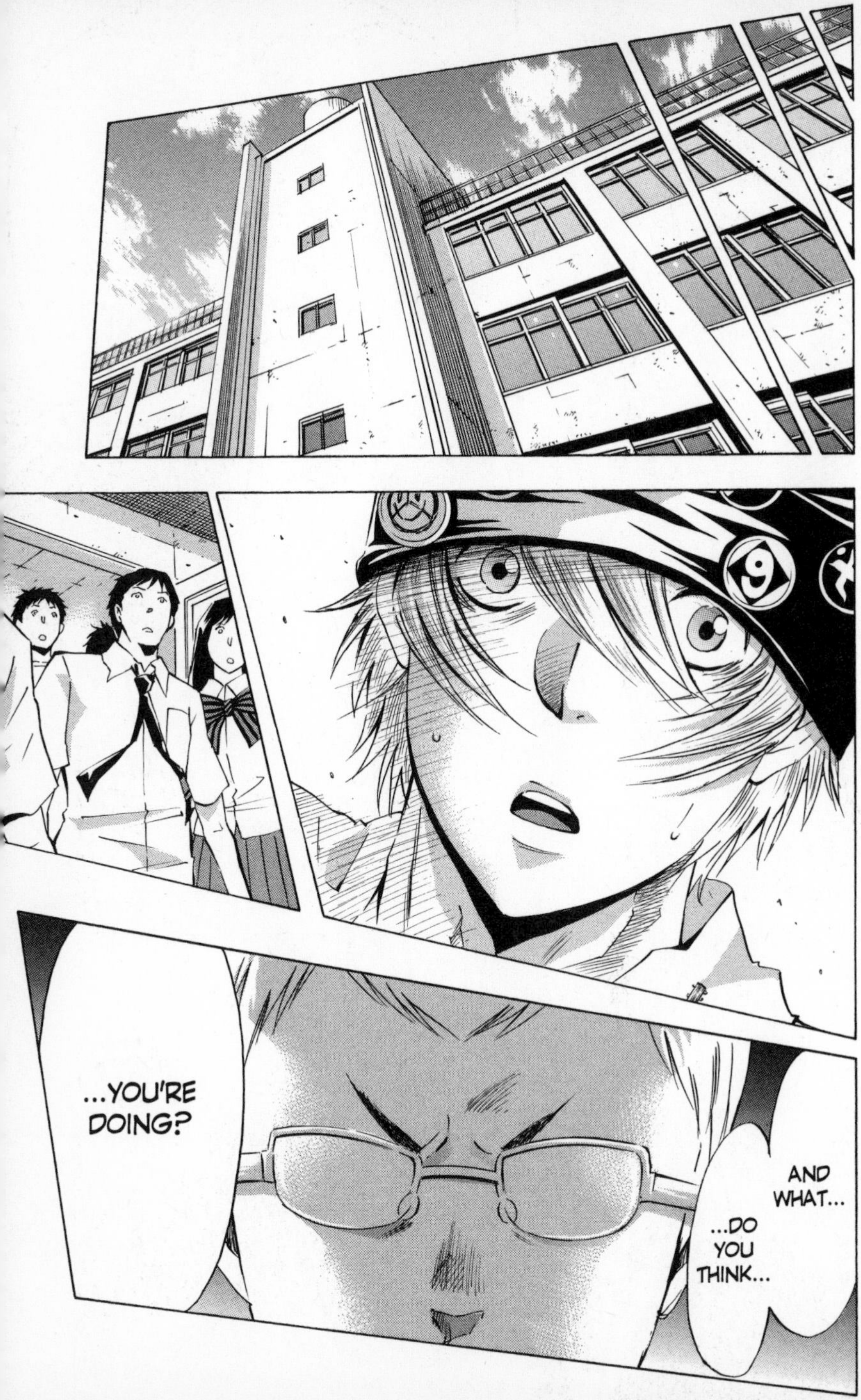
AND WHAT...
...DO YOU THINK...
...YOU'RE DOING?

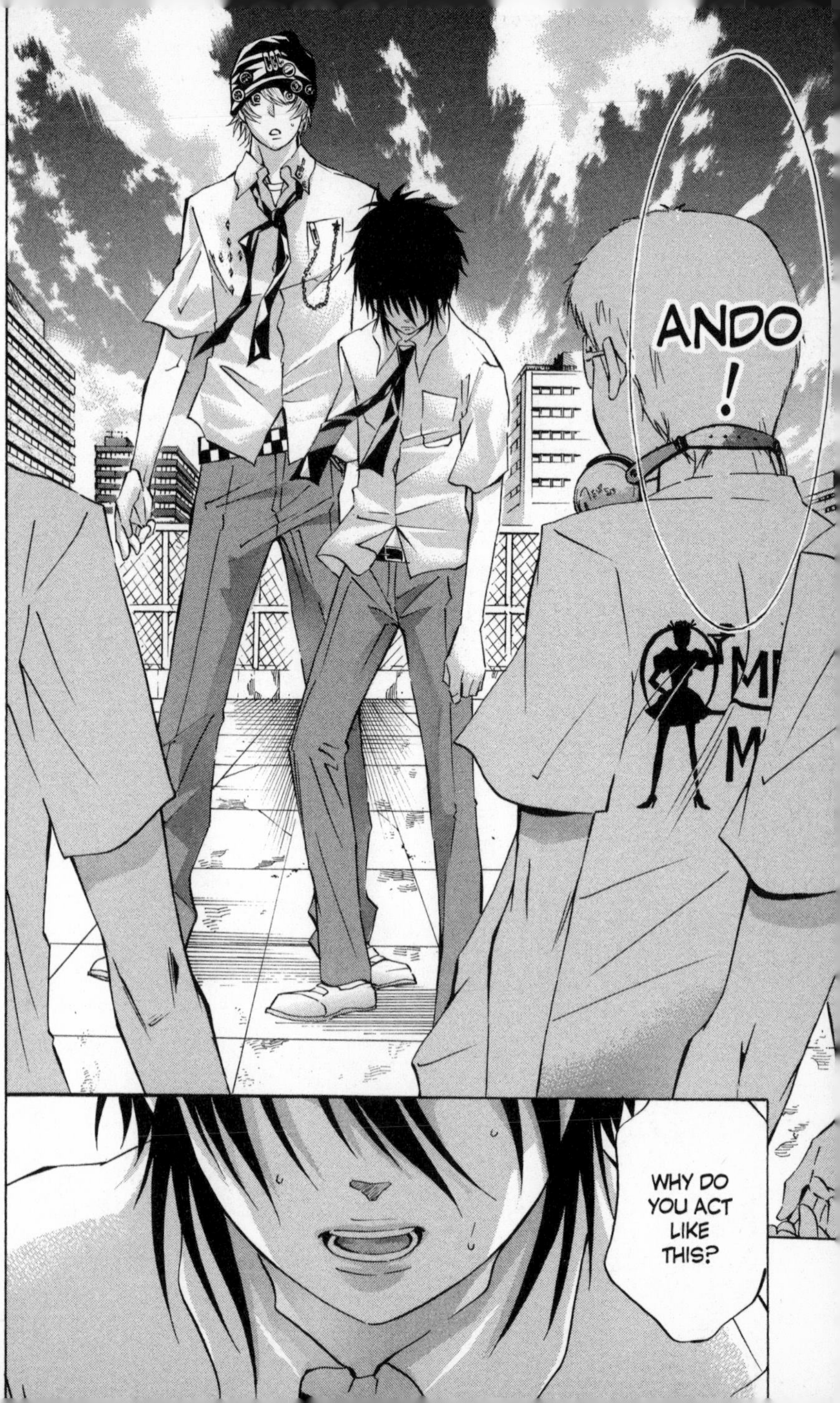
ANDO!
WHY DO YOU ACT LIKE THIS?

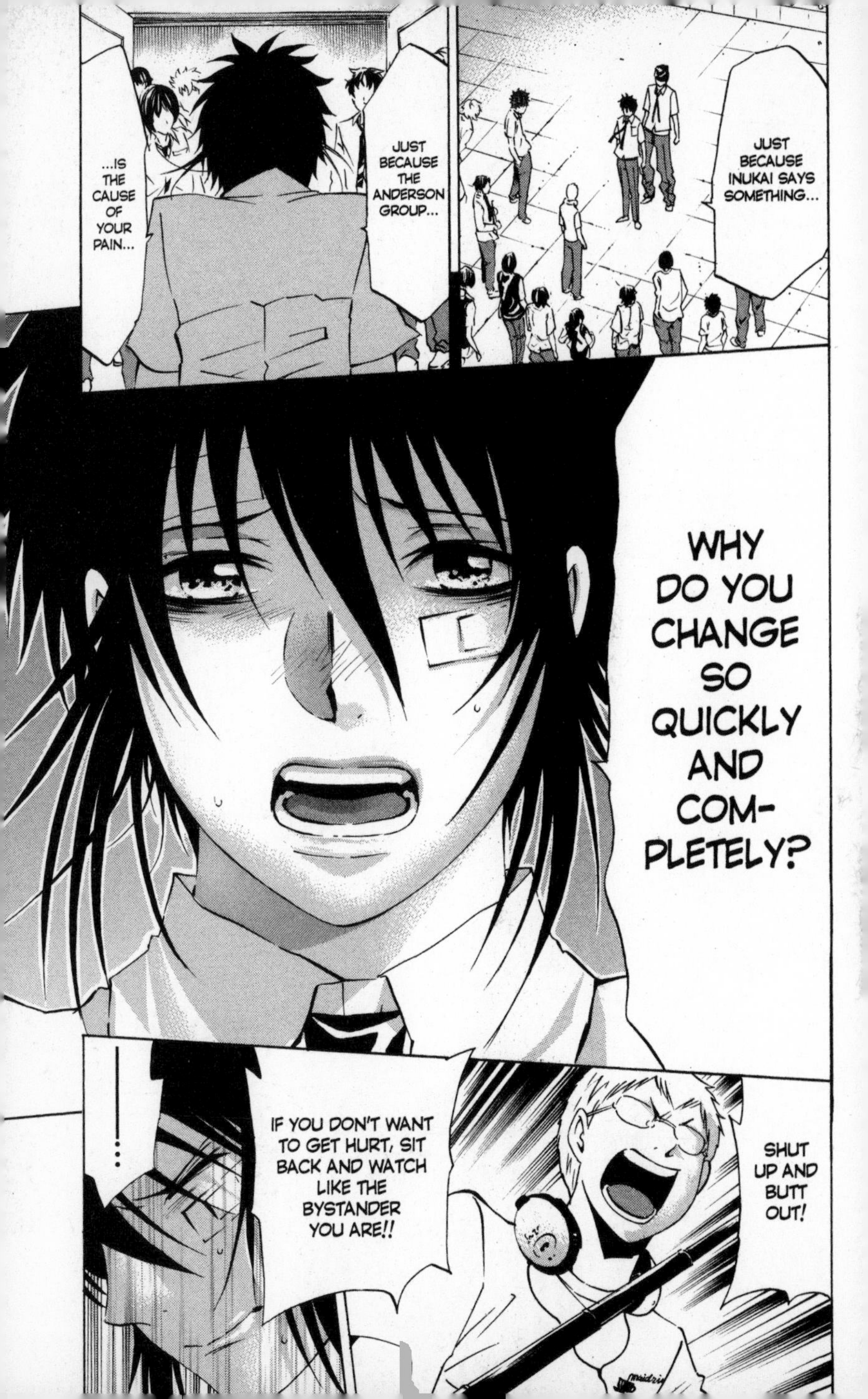
JUST BECAUSE INUKAI SAYS SOMETHING...
JUST BECAUSE THE ANDERSON GROUP...
...IS THE CAUSE OF YOUR PAIN...
WHY DO YOU CHANGE SO QUICKLY AND COM-PLETELY?
SHUT UP AND BUTT OUT!
IF YOU DON'T WANT TO GET HURT, SIT BACK AND WATCH LIKE THE BYSTANDER YOU ARE!!
...!

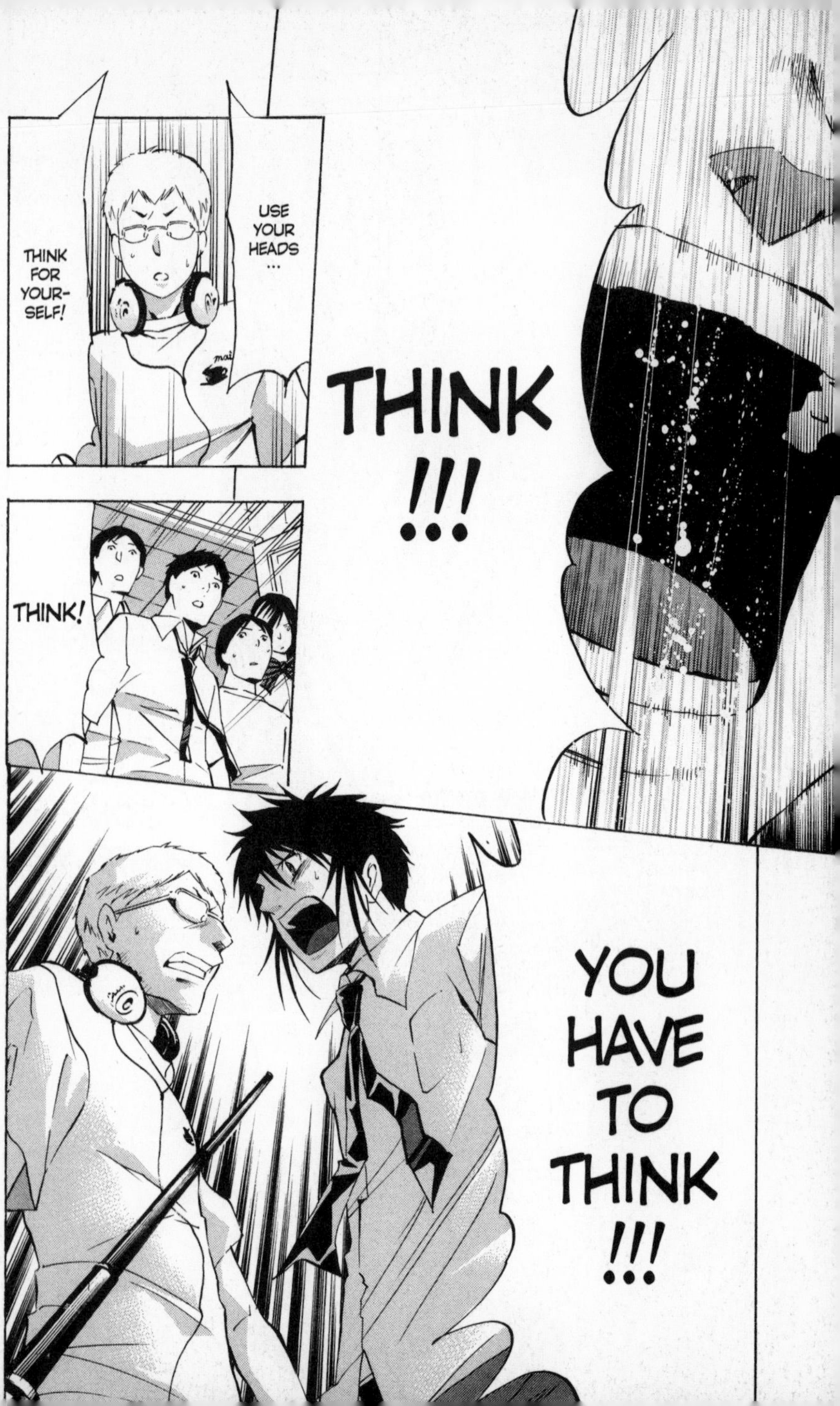
THINK!!!
USE YOUR HEADS...
THINK FOR YOURSELF!
THINK!
YOU HAVE TO THINK!!!

Chapter 34 Resignation and Conspiracy

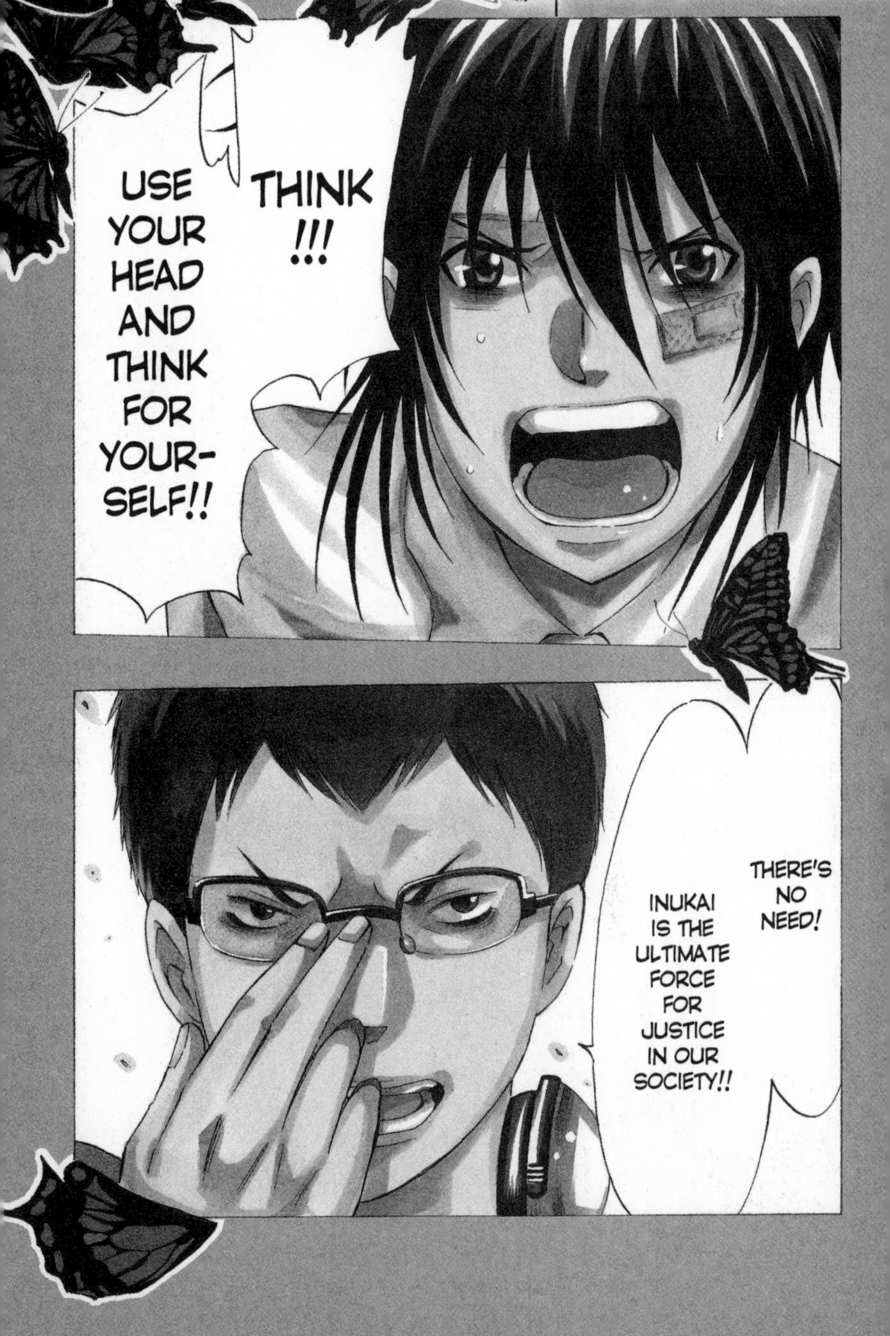
THINK!!!
USE YOUR HEAD AND THINK FOR YOUR-SELF!!
THERE'S NO NEED!
INUKAI IS THE ULTIMATE FORCE FOR JUSTICE IN OUR SOCIETY!!

Chapter 34 Resignation and Conspiracy

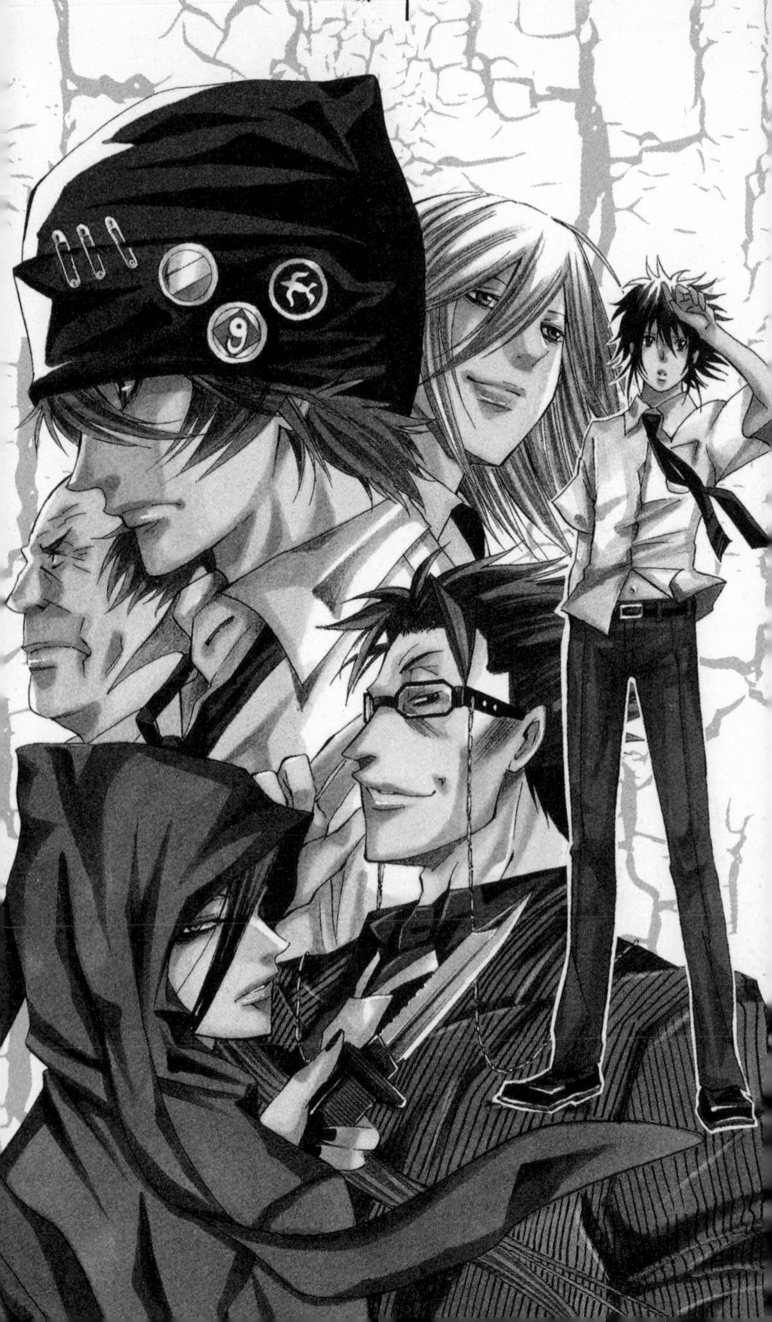

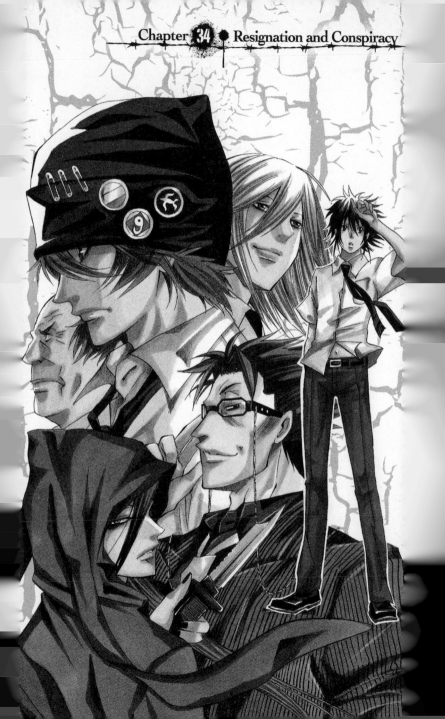

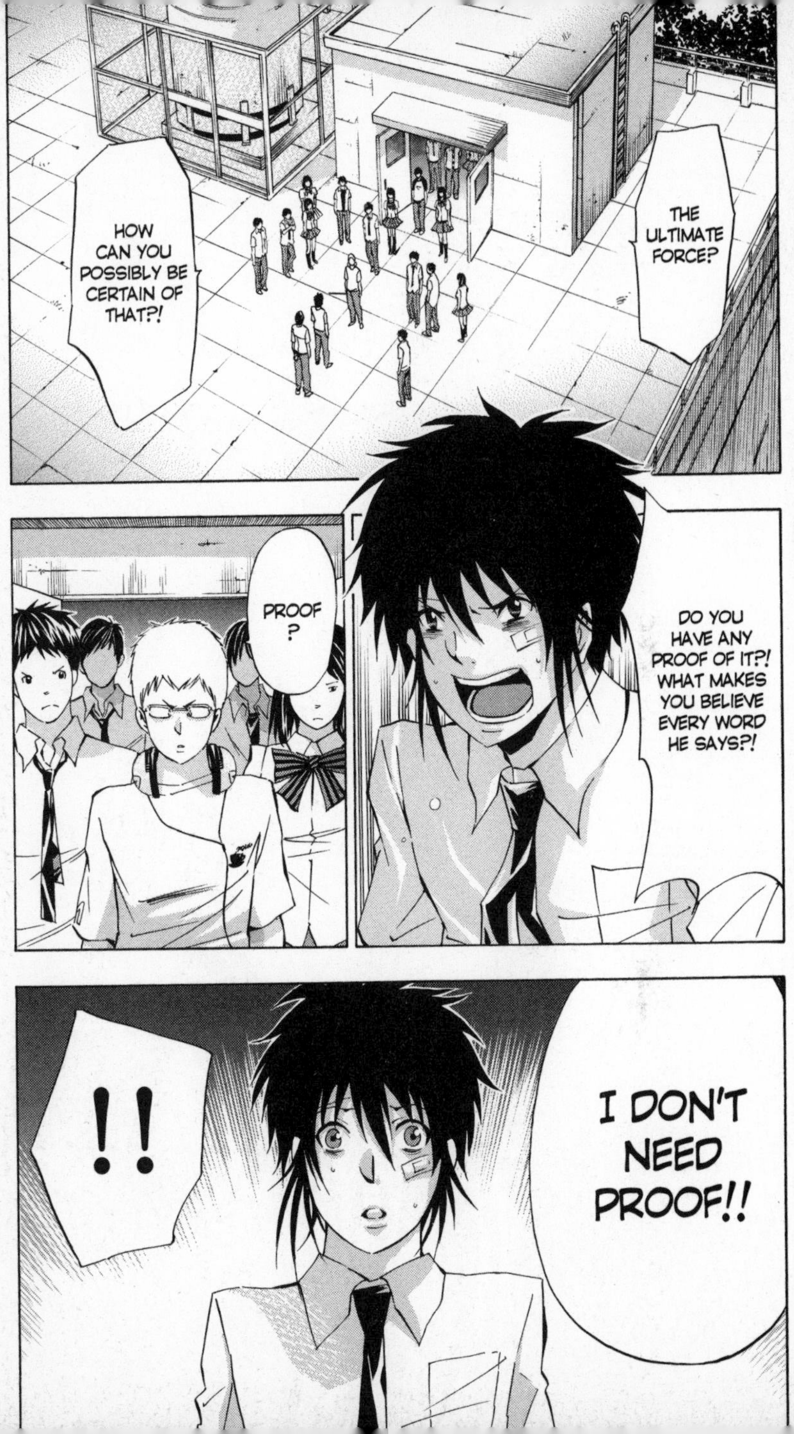
THE ULTIMATE FORCE?
HOW CAN YOU POSSIBLY BE CERTAIN OF THAT?!
DO YOU HAVE ANY PROOF OF IT?! WHAT MAKES YOU BELIEVE EVERY WORD HE SAYS?!
PROOF?
I DON'T NEED PROOF!!
!!

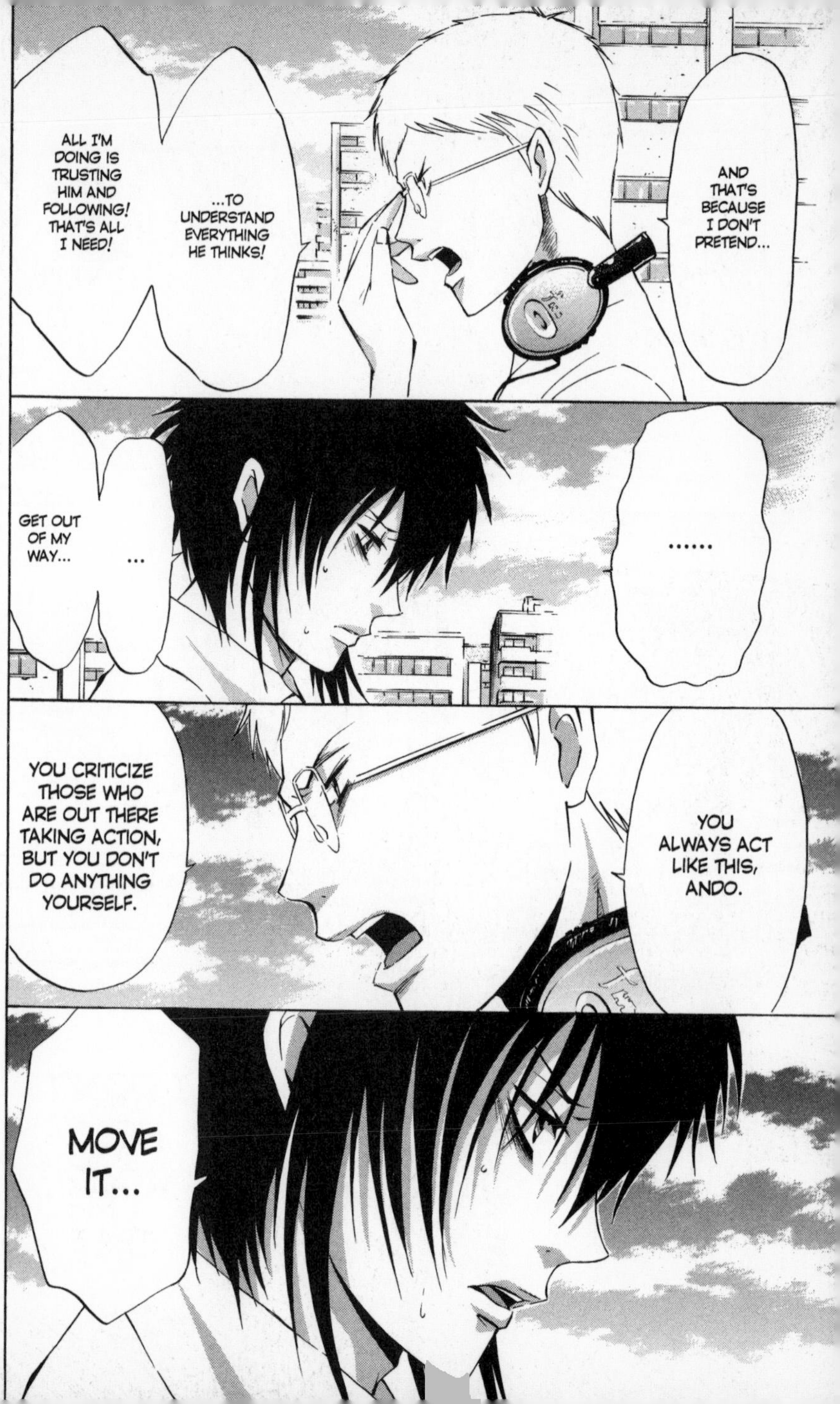
AND THAT'S BECAUSE I DON'T PRETEND...
...TO UNDERSTAND EVERYTHING HE THINKS!
ALL I'M DOING IS TRUSTING HIM AND FOLLOWING! THAT'S ALL I NEED!
......
...
GET OUT OF MY WAY...
YOU ALWAYS ACT LIKE THIS, ANDO.
YOU CRITICIZE THOSE WHO ARE OUT THERE TAKING ACTION, BUT YOU DON'T DO ANYTHING YOURSELF.
MOVE IT...

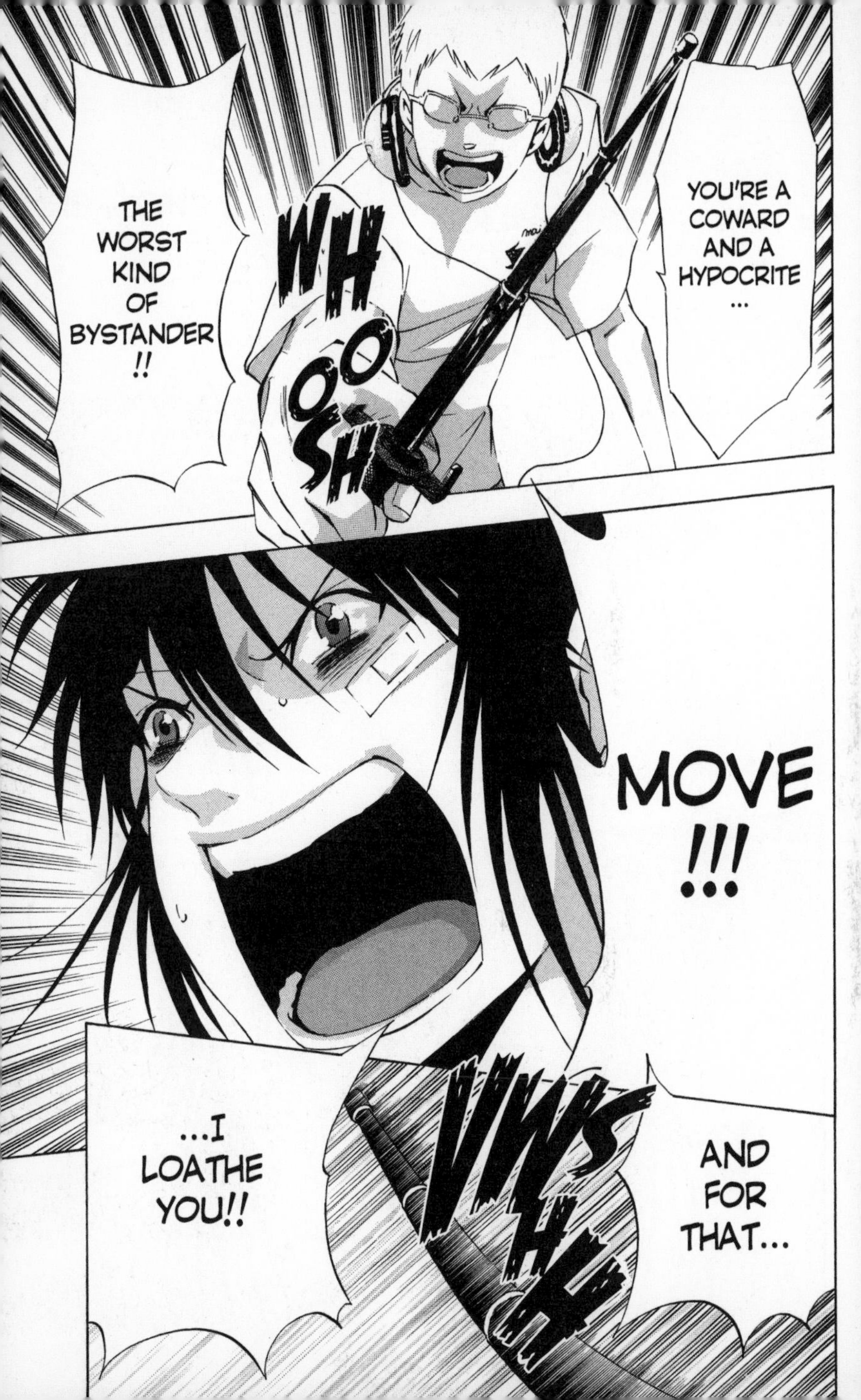
YOU'RE A COWARD AND A HYPOCRITE...
THE WORST KIND OF BYSTANDER!!
WHOOSH
MOVE!!!
AND FOR THAT...
...I LOATHE YOU!!

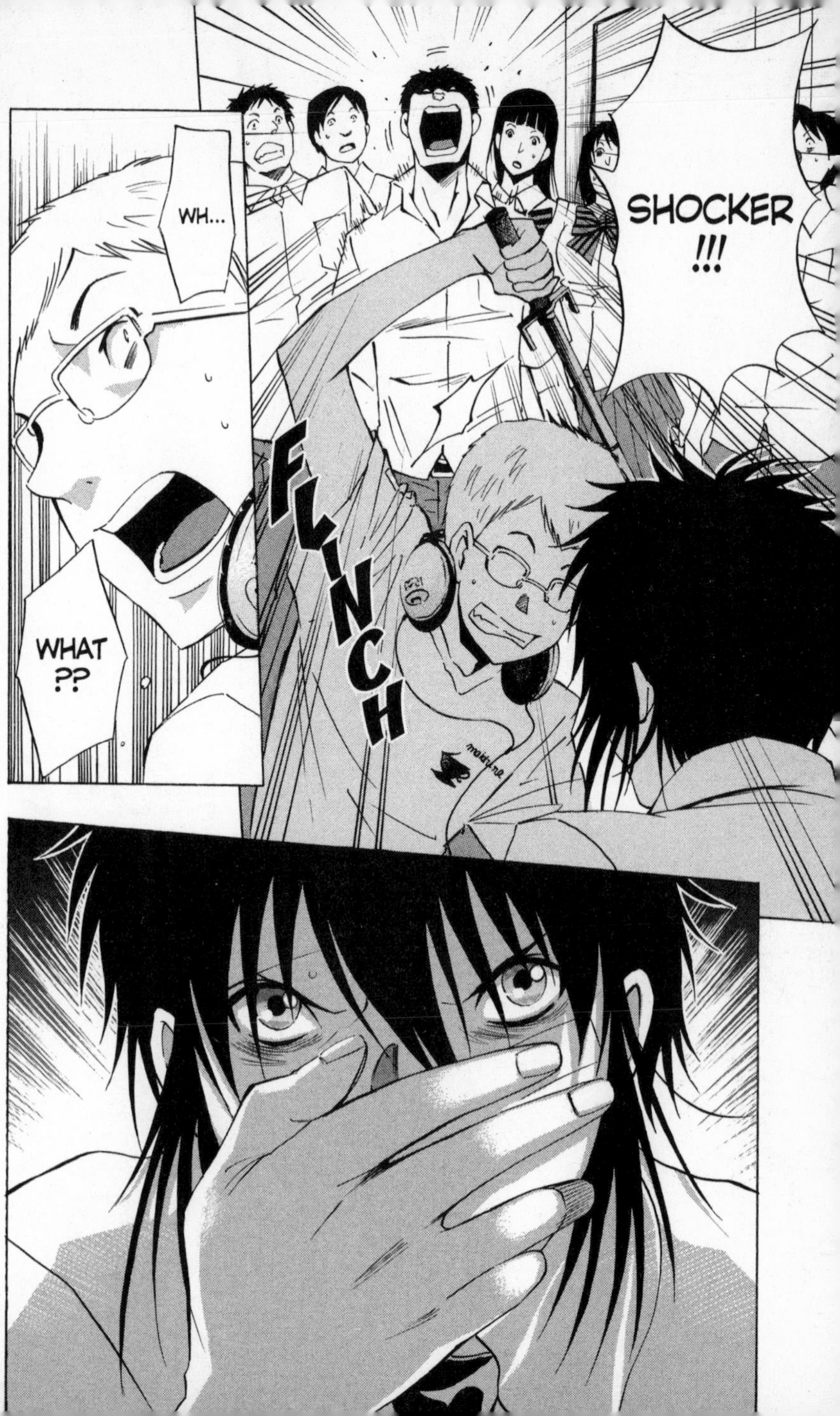
SHOCKER !!!
FLINCH
WH...
WHAT ??

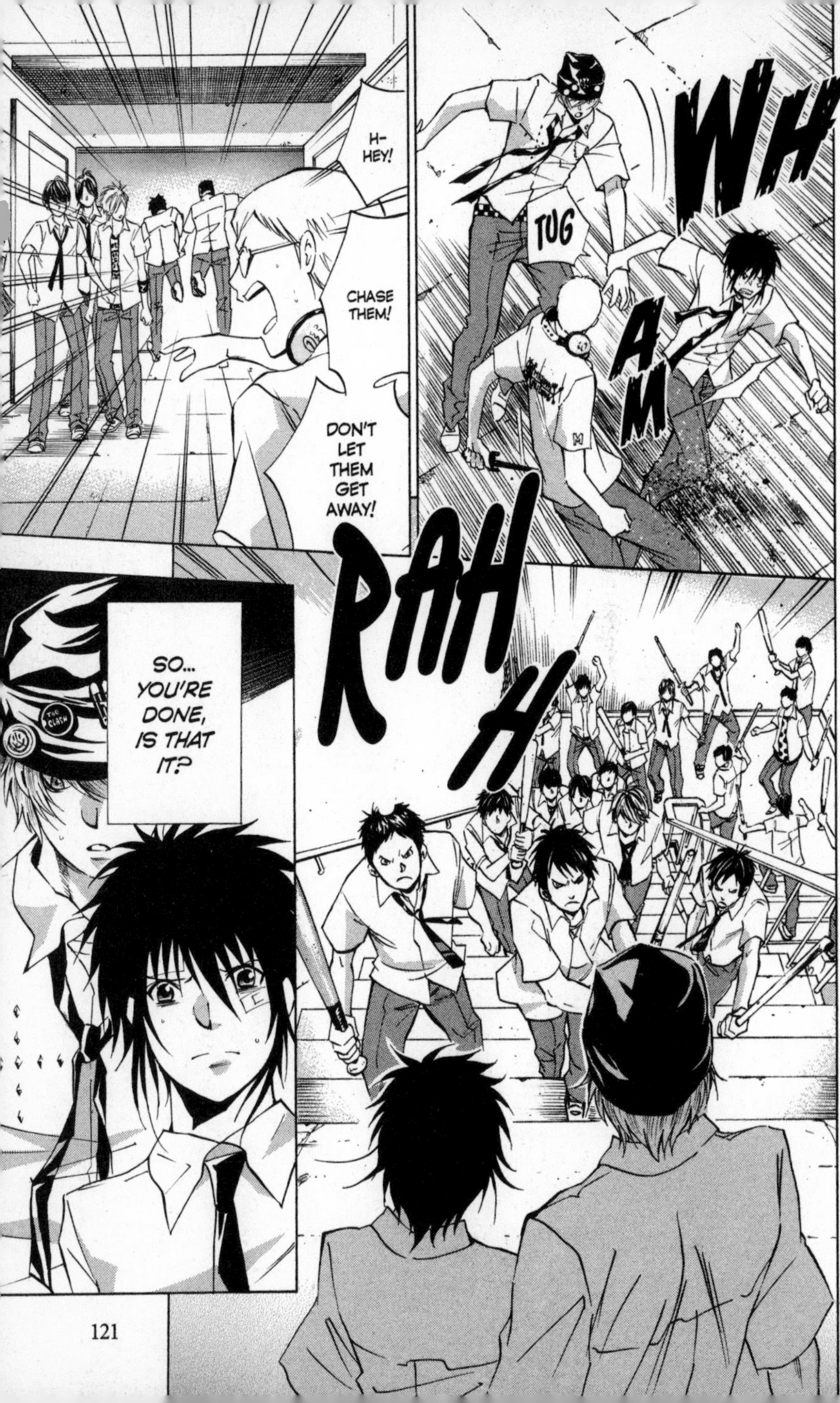
WHAM
TUG
H-HEY!
CHASE THEM!
DON'T LET THEM GET AWAY!
RAHH
SO... YOU'RE DONE, IS THAT IT?

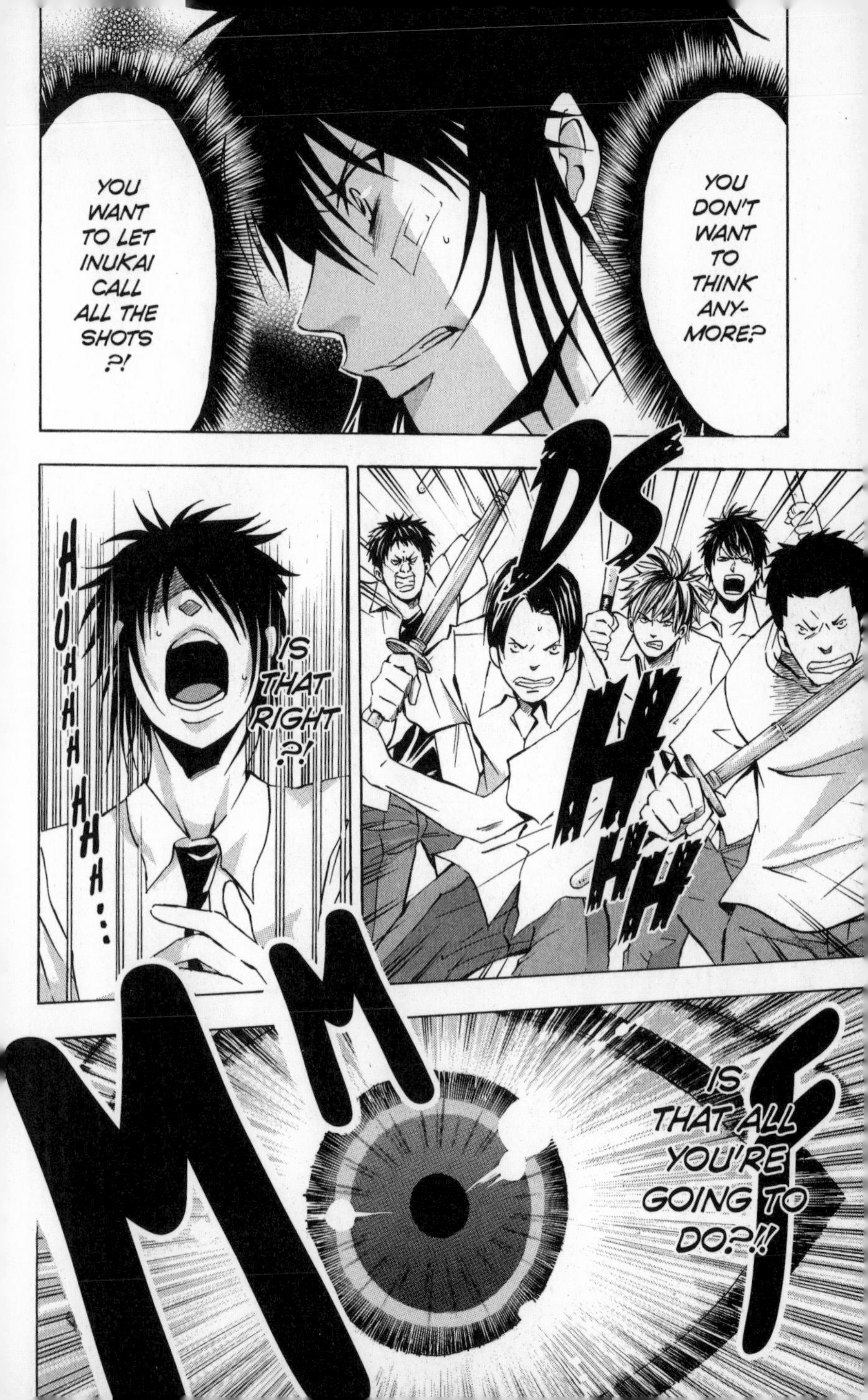
YOU DON'T WANT TO THINK ANY-MORE?
YOU WANT TO LET INUKAI CALL ALL THE SHOTS ?!
DSHHHH
IS THAT RIGHT ?!
HUHHHHHH...
IS THAT ALL YOU'RE GOING TO DO?!!
MMF

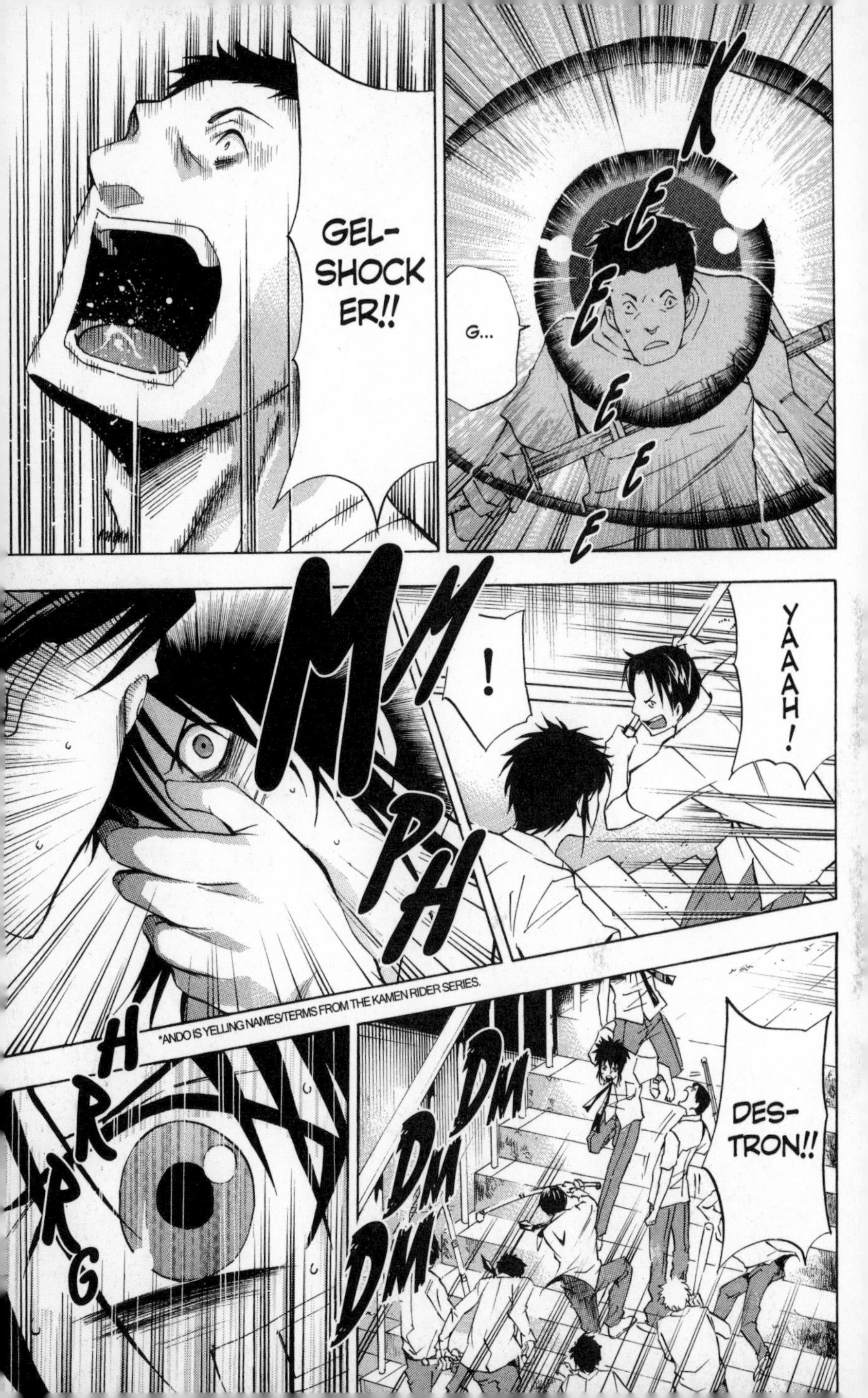
KEEEEEEE
G...
GEL-SHOCKER!!
YAAAH!
!
MMPH
*ANDO IS YELLING NAMES/TERMS FROM THE KAMEN RIDER SERIES.
DES-TRON!!
DM DM DM DM
HRRG

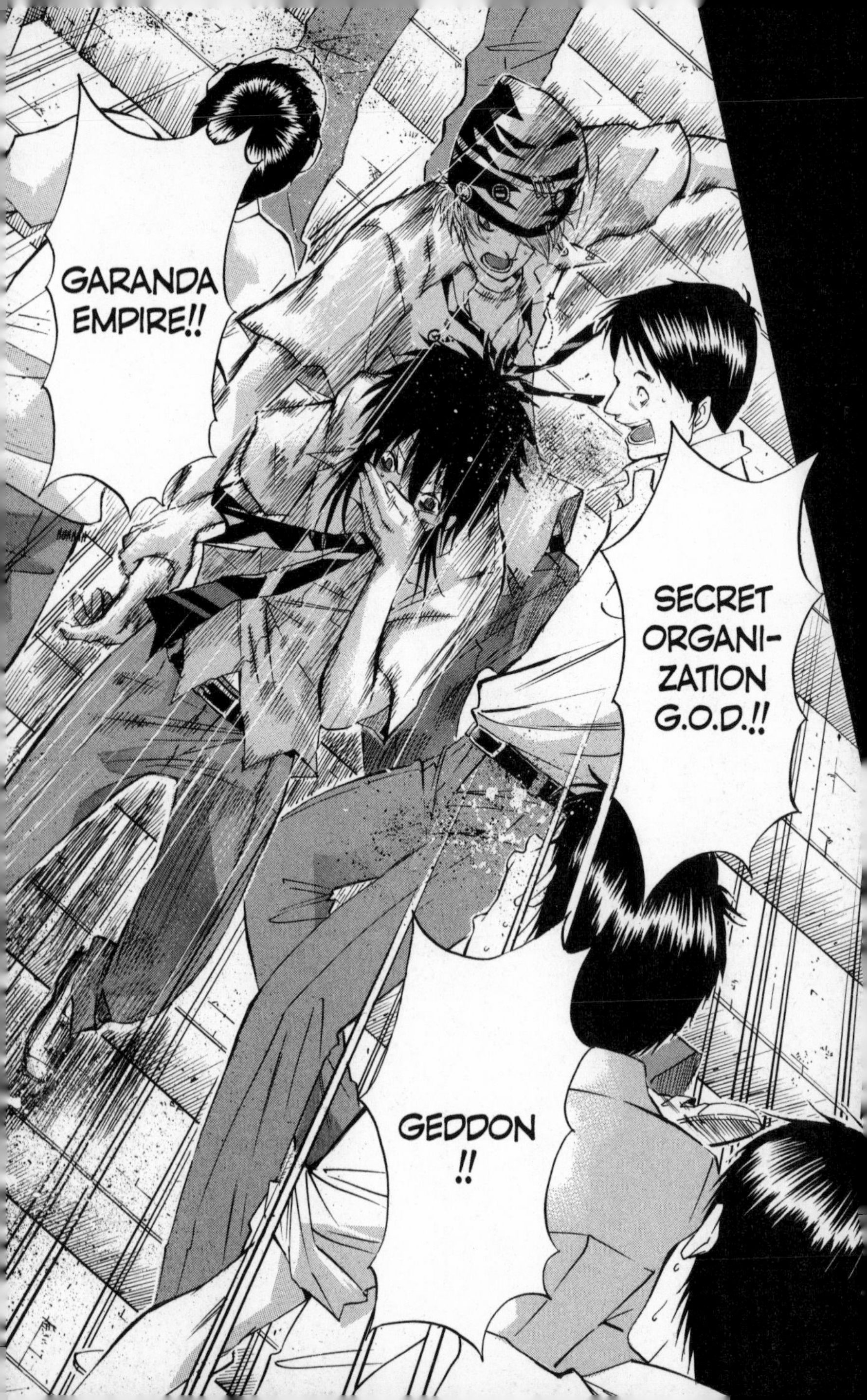
GARANDA EMPIRE!!
SECRET ORGANI-ZATION G.O.D.!!
GEDDON !!

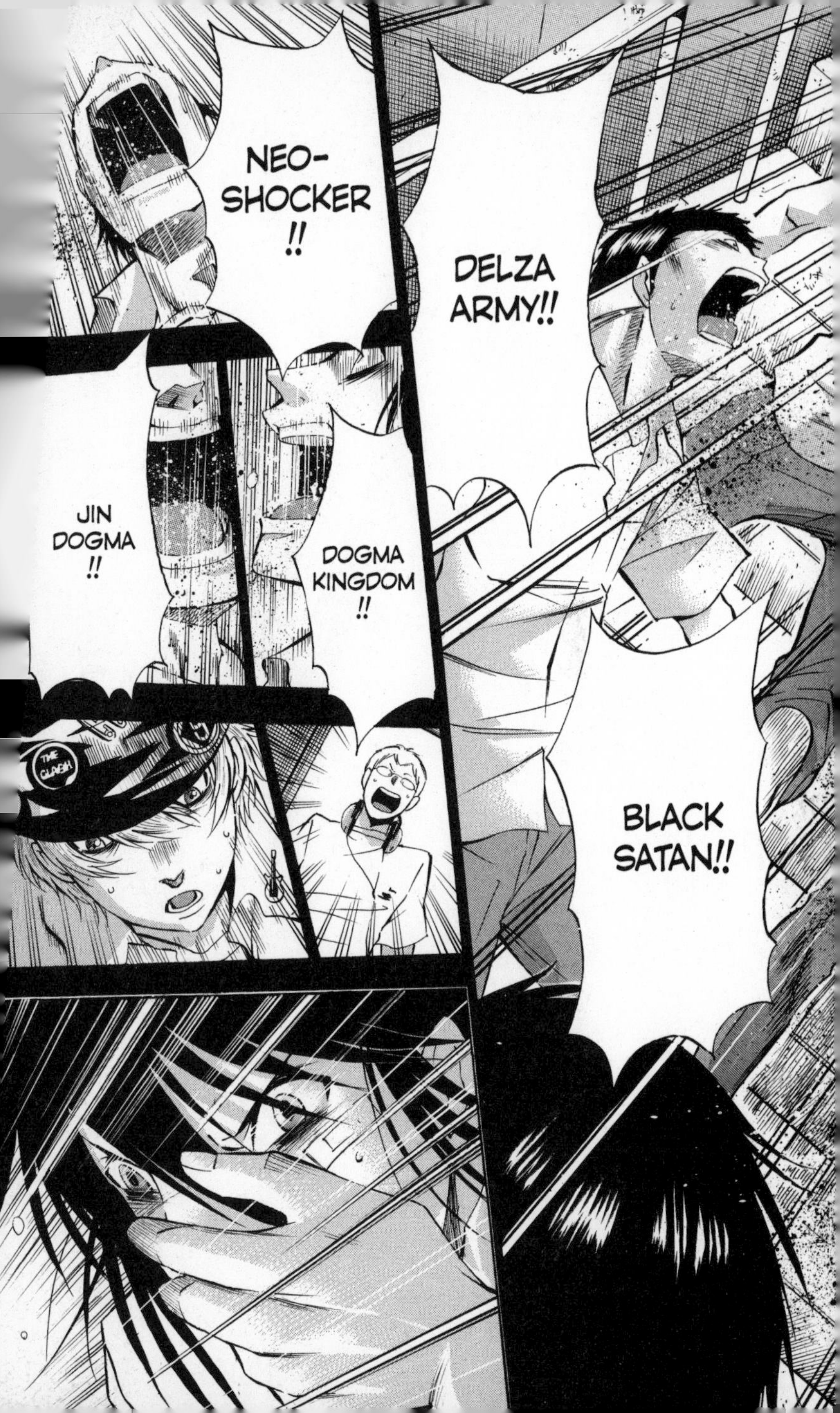
DELZA ARMY!!
BLACK SATAN!!
NEO-SHOCKER!!
DOGMA KINGDOM!!
JIN DOGMA!!
THE CLASH

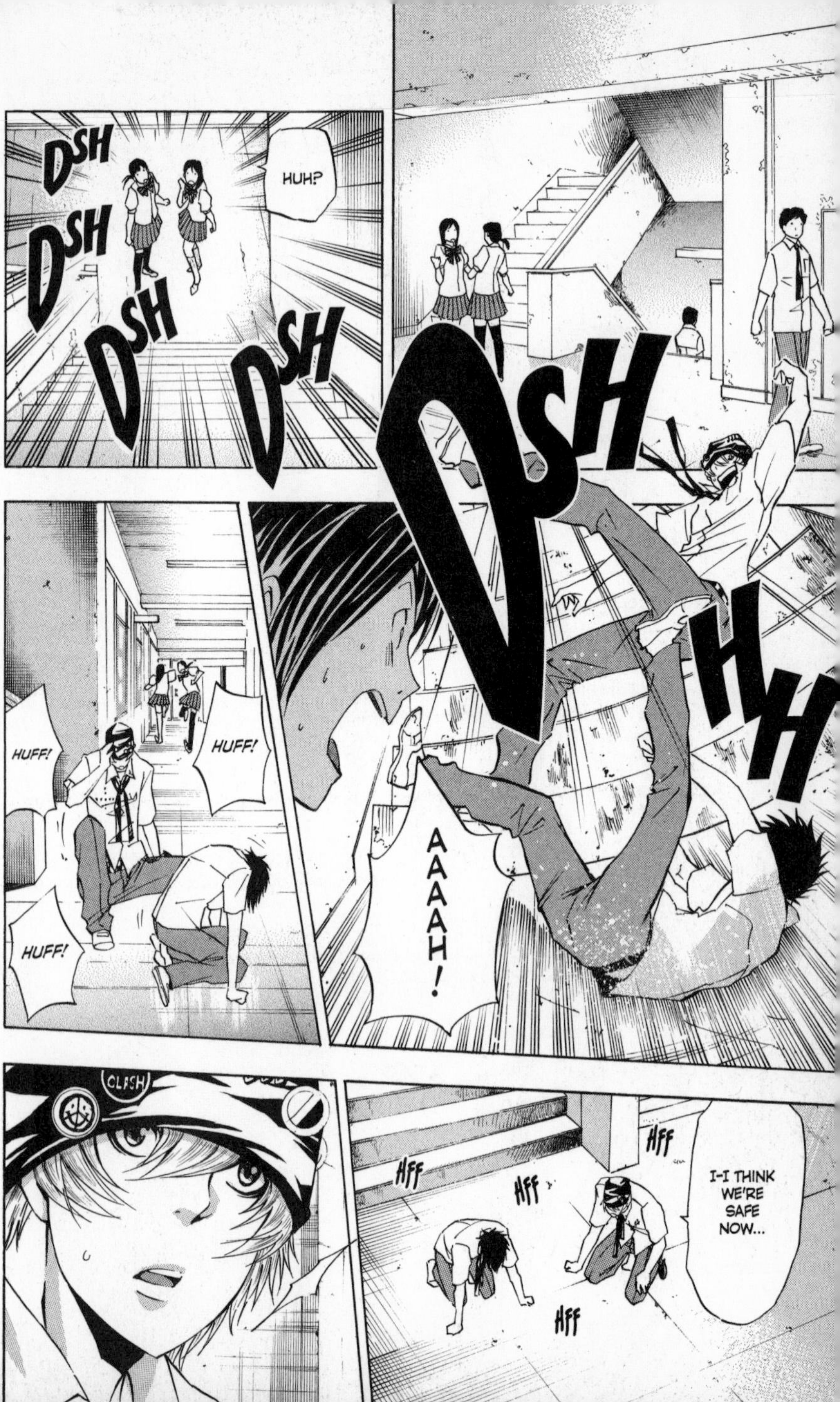
DSH
DSH
DSH
DSH
HUH?
DSHHHH
AAAAH!
HUFF!
HUFF!
HUFF!
HFF
HFF
HFF
HFF
I-I THINK WE'RE SAFE NOW...
CLASH

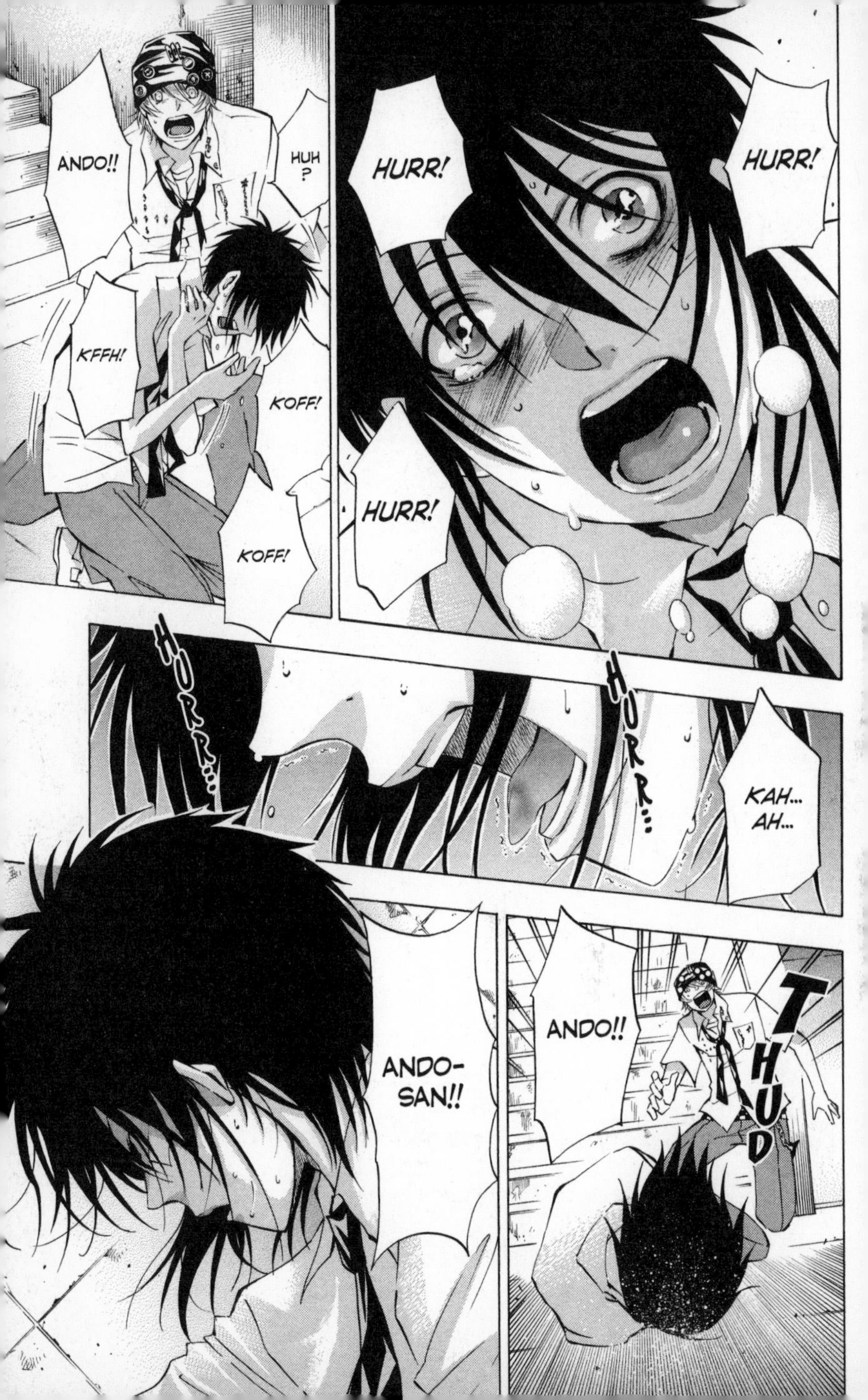
HURR!
HURR!
HURR!
HUH?
ANDO!!
KFFH!
KOFF!
KOFF!
KAH... AH...
HURR...
HURR...
THUD
ANDO!!
ANDO-SAN!!

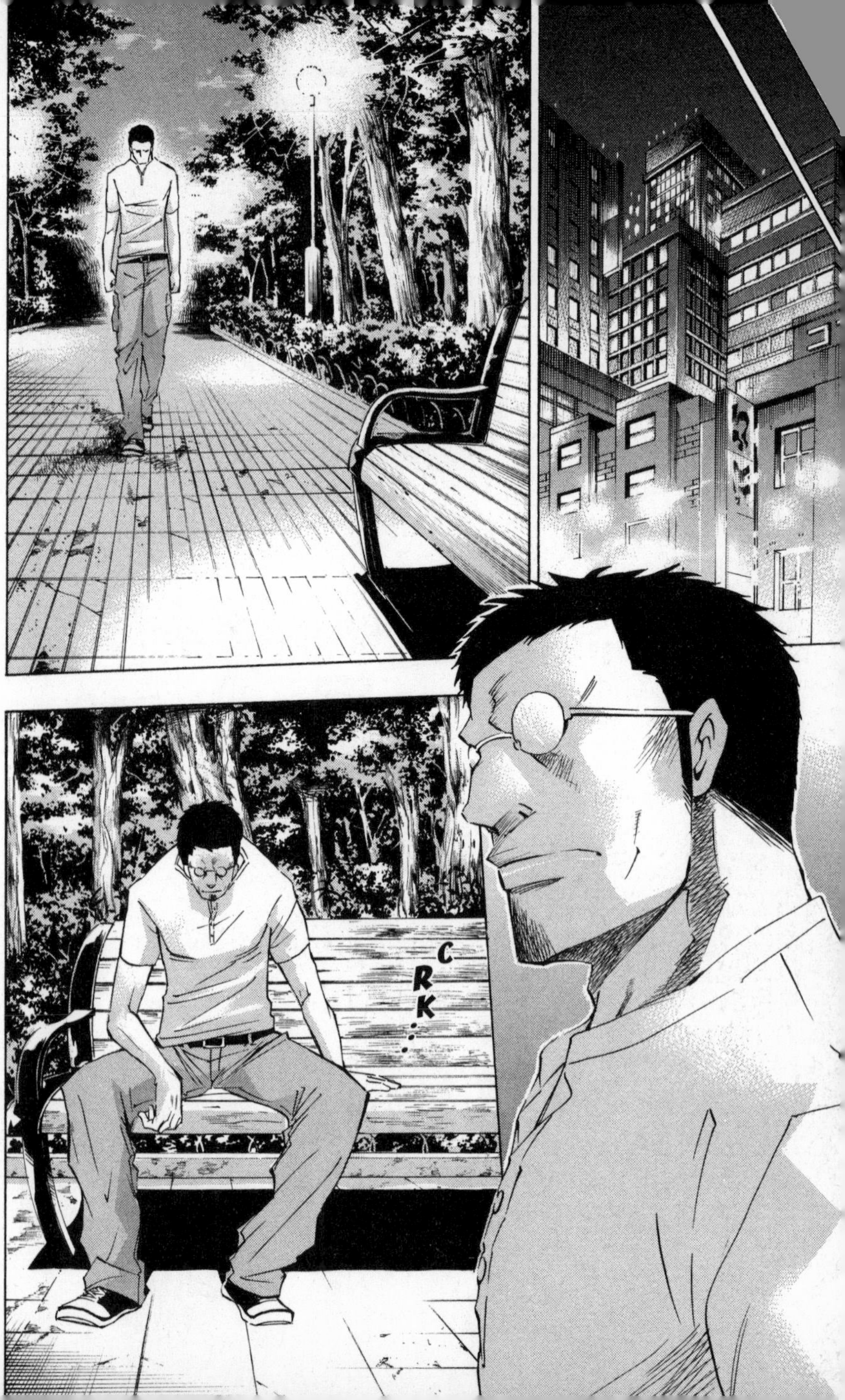
CRK...

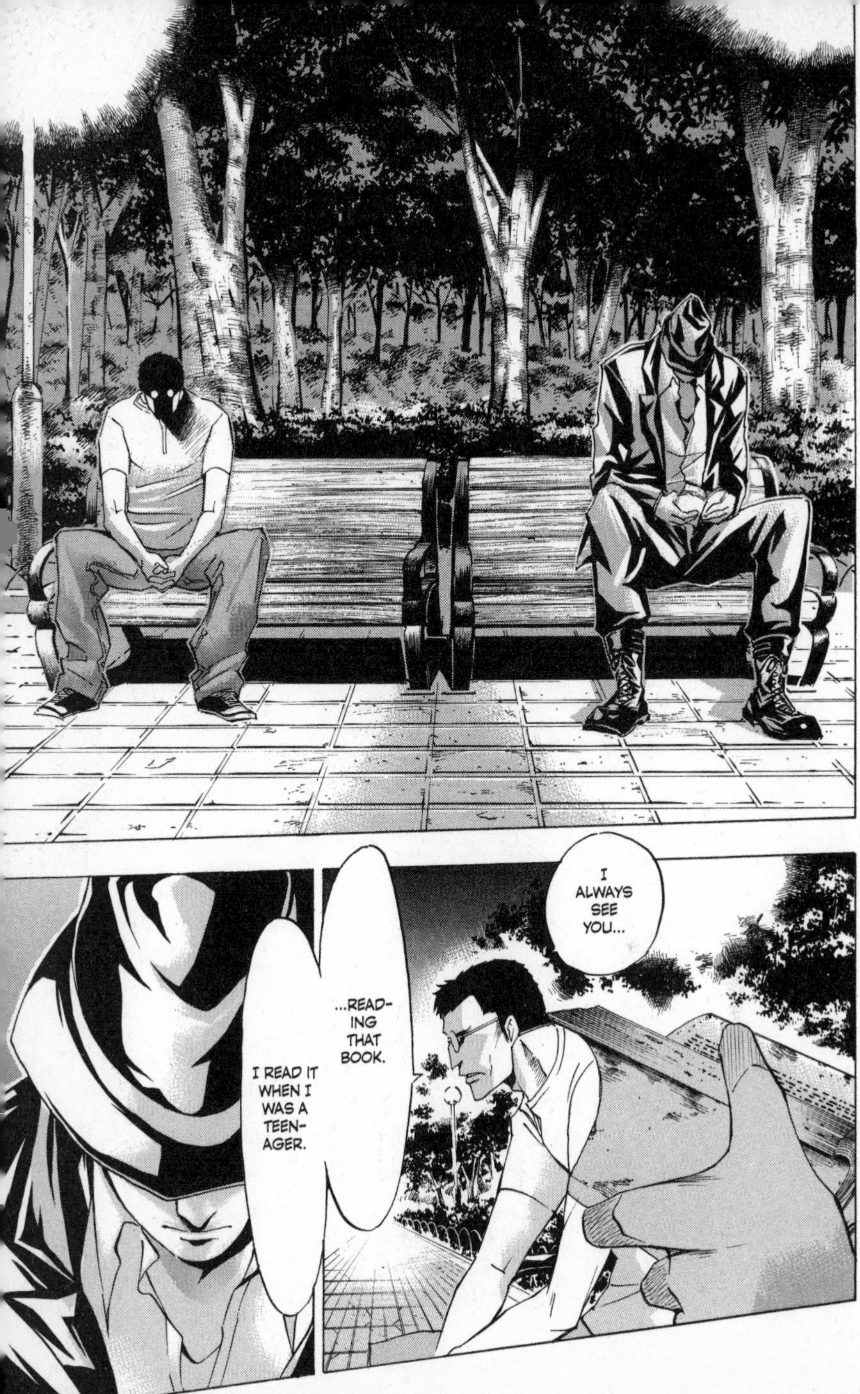
I ALWAYS SEE YOU...
...READING-ING THAT BOOK.
I READ IT WHEN I WAS A TEEN-AGER.

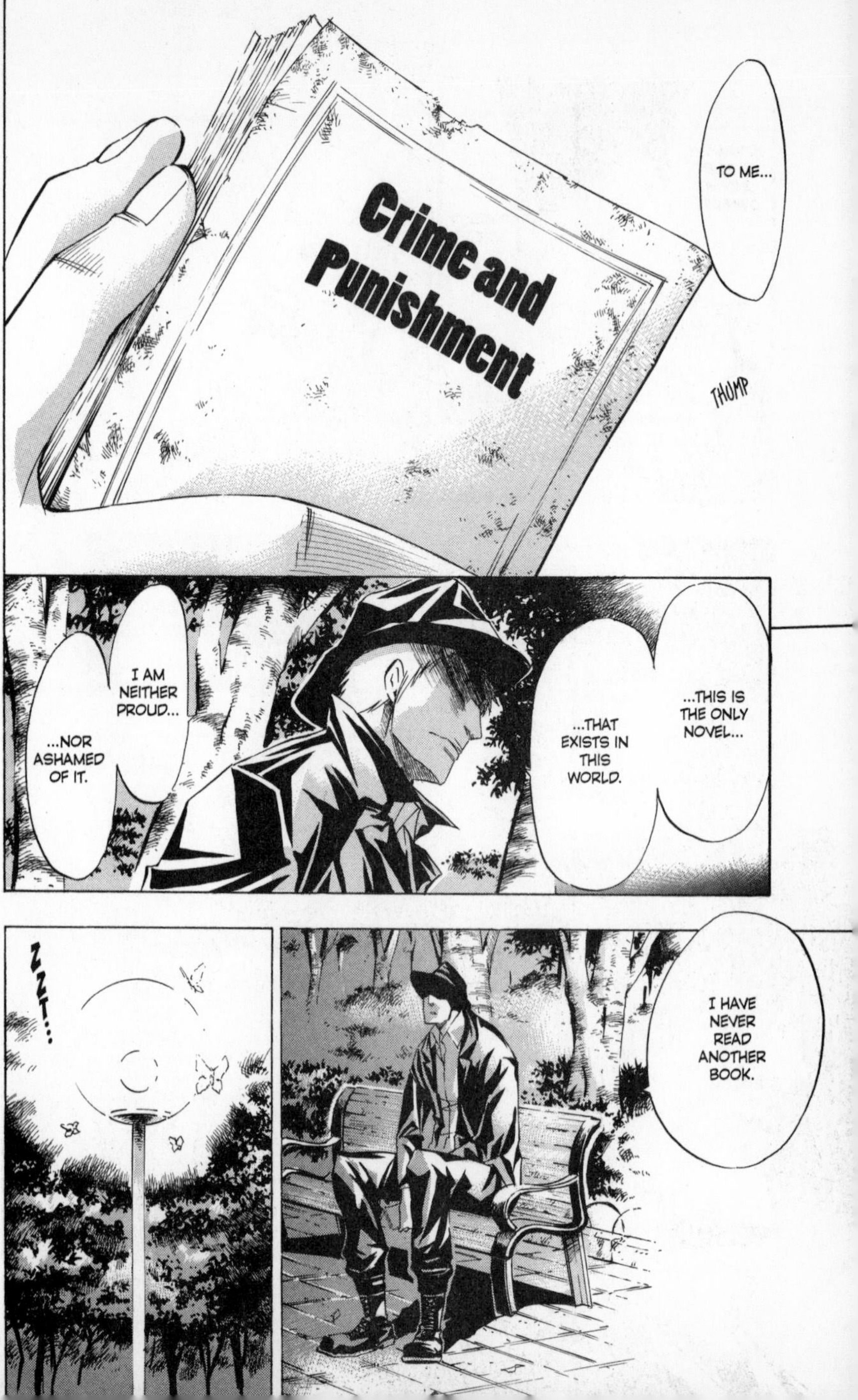
TO ME...
Crime and Punishment
THUMP
...THIS IS THE ONLY NOVEL...
...THAT EXISTS IN THIS WORLD.
I AM NEITHER PROUD...
...NOR ASHAMED OF IT.
I HAVE NEVER READ ANOTHER BOOK.
ZZZT...

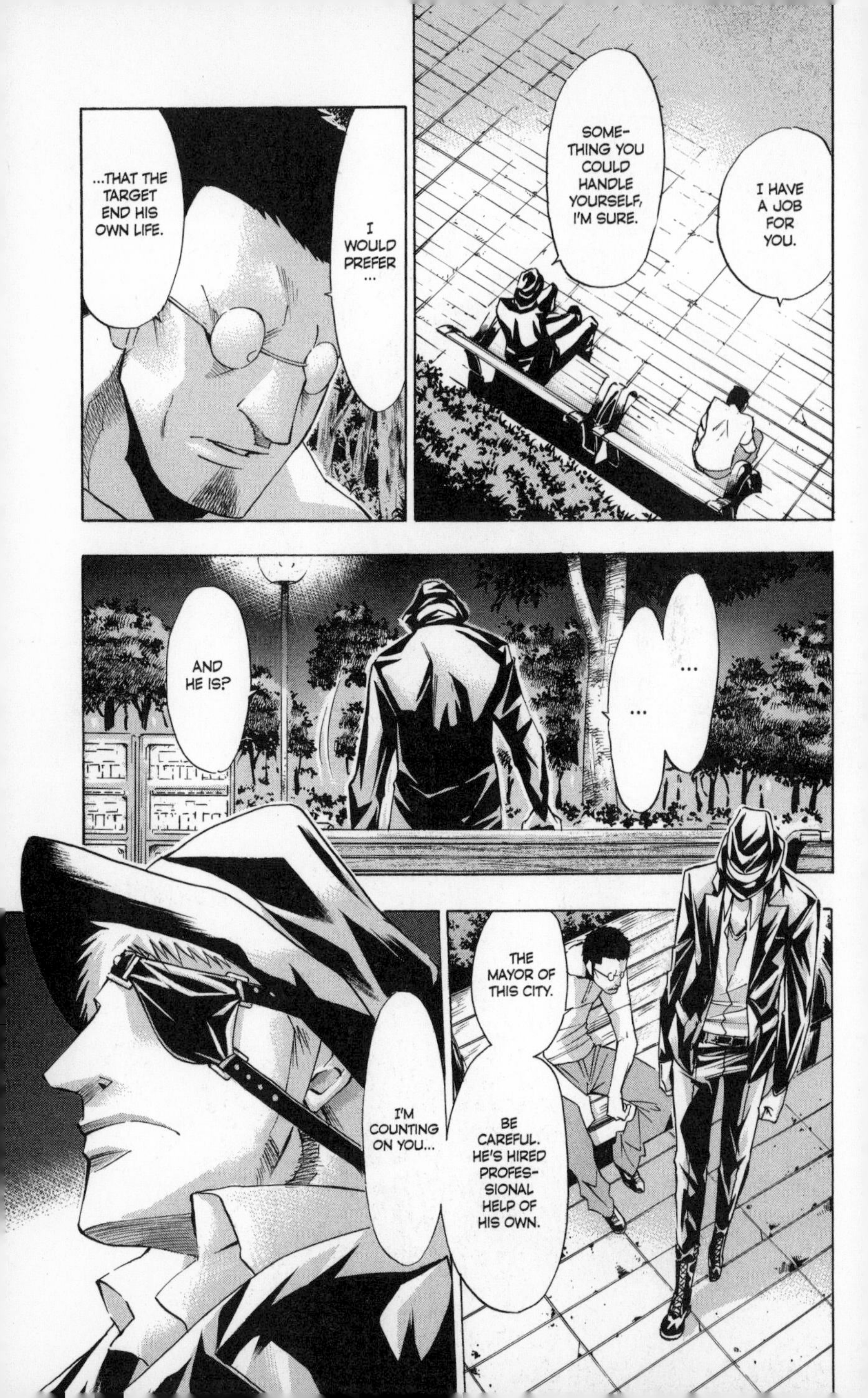
I HAVE A JOB FOR YOU.
SOME-THING YOU COULD HANDLE YOURSELF, I'M SURE.
I WOULD PREFER ...
...THAT THE TARGET END HIS OWN LIFE.
...
...
AND HE IS?
THE MAYOR OF THIS CITY.
BE CAREFUL. HE'S HIRED PROFES-SIONAL HELP OF HIS OWN.
I'M COUNTING ON YOU...

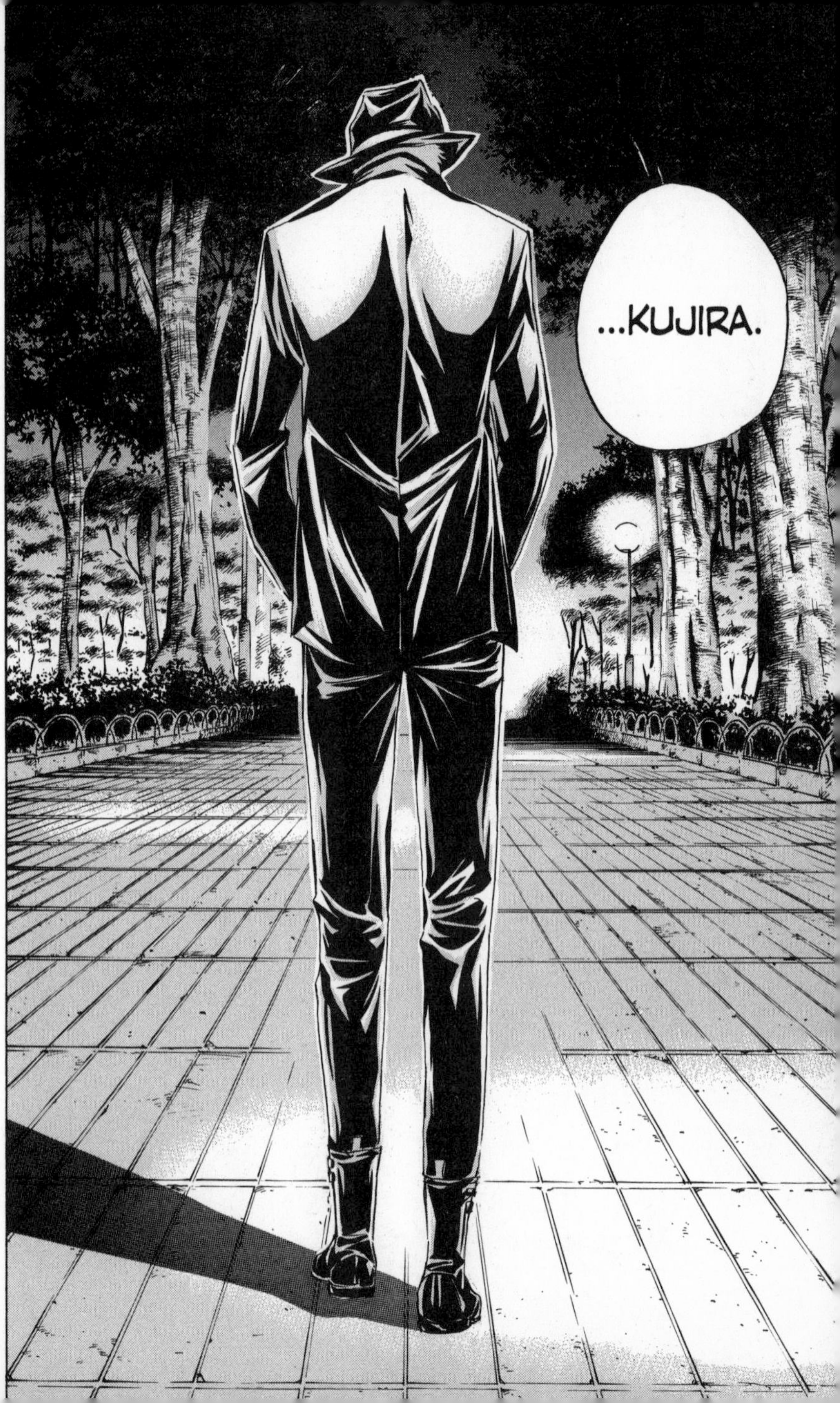
...KUJIRA.

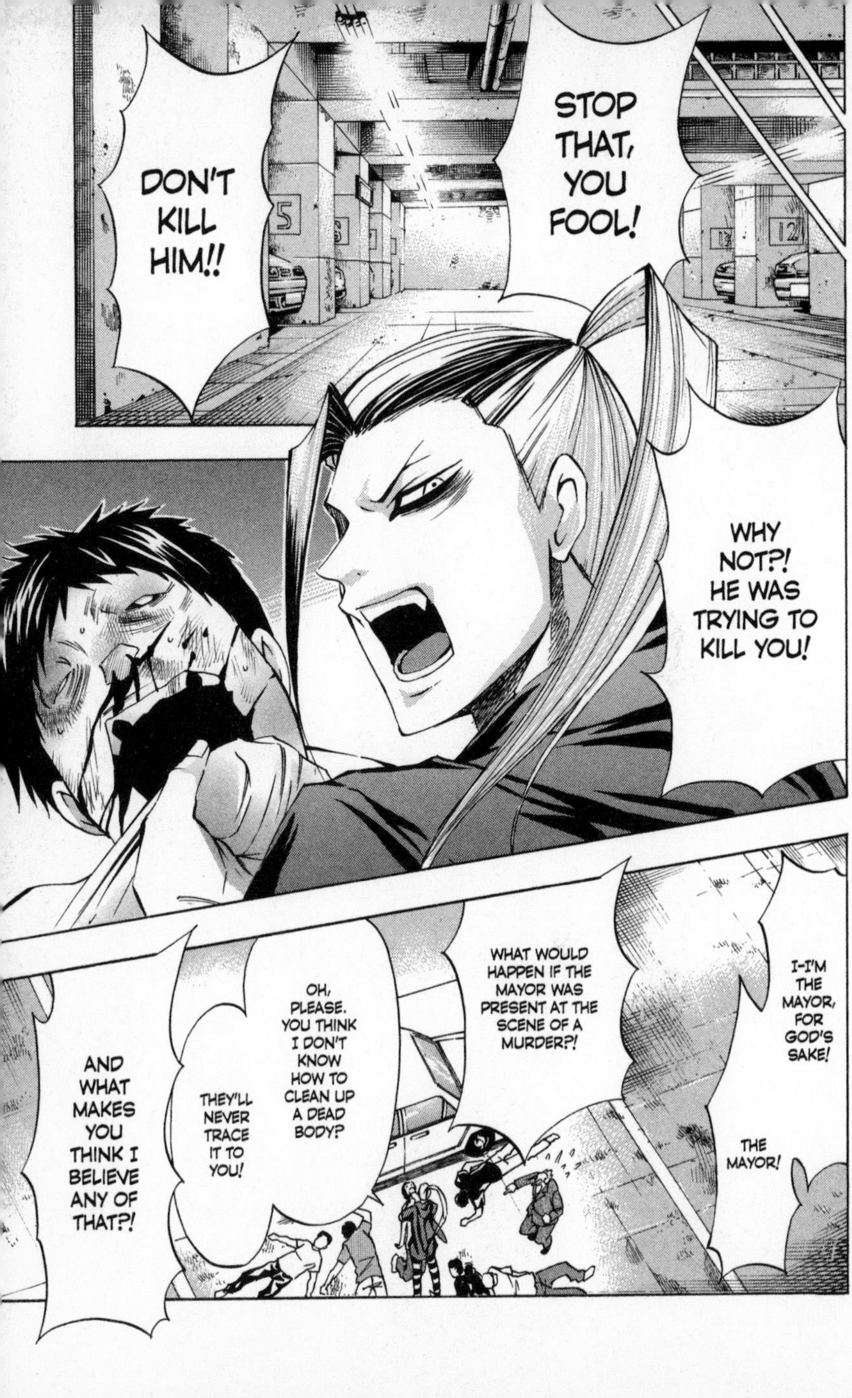
STOP THAT, YOU FOOL!
DON'T KILL HIM!!
WHY NOT?! HE WAS TRYING TO KILL YOU!
I-I'M THE MAYOR, FOR GOD'S SAKE!
THE MAYOR!
WHAT WOULD HAPPEN IF THE MAYOR WAS PRESENT AT THE SCENE OF A MURDER?!
OH, PLEASE. YOU THINK I DON'T KNOW HOW TO CLEAN UP A DEAD BODY?
THEY'LL NEVER TRACE IT TO YOU!
AND WHAT MAKES YOU THINK I BELIEVE ANY OF THAT?!

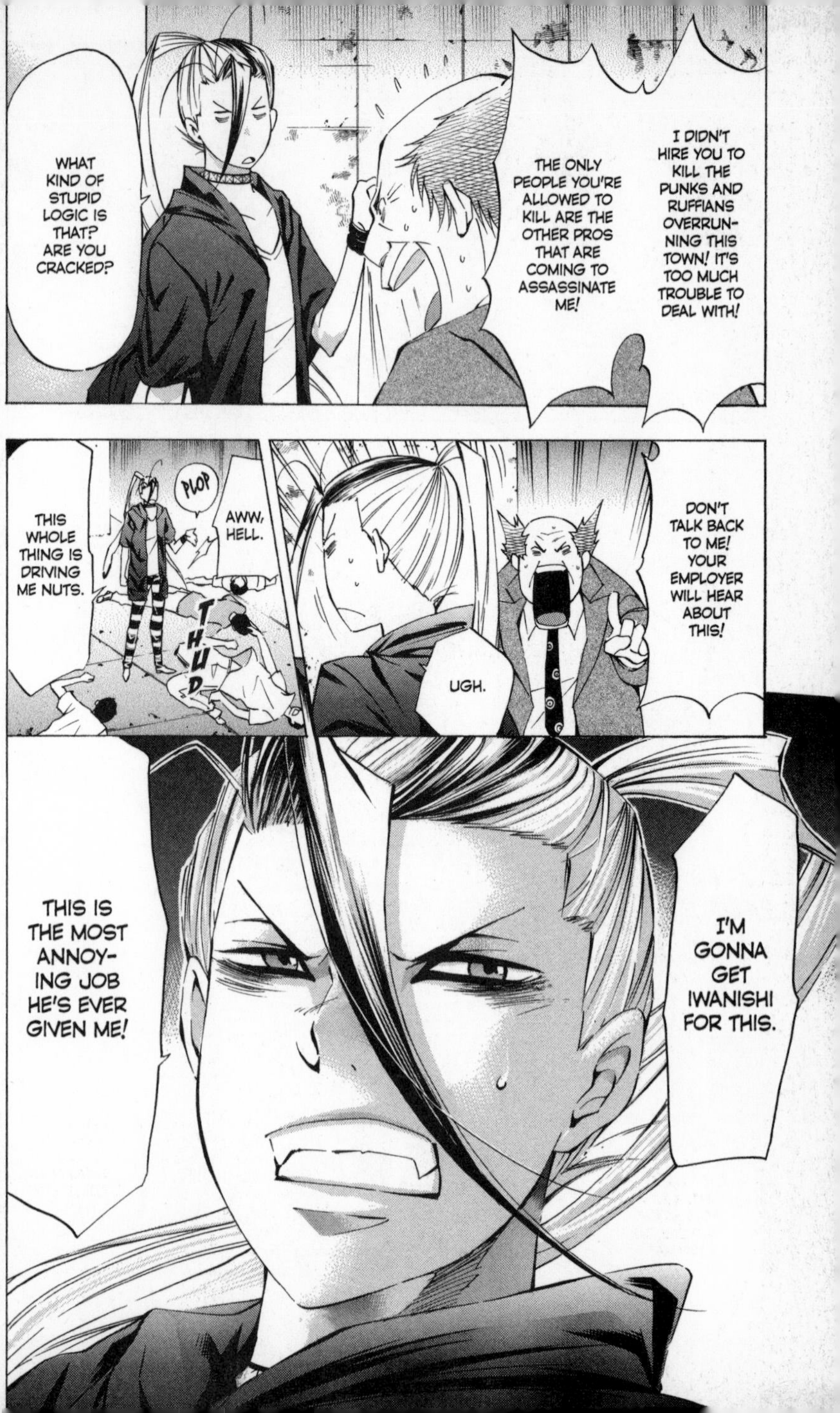
I DIDN'T HIRE YOU TO KILL THE PUNKS AND RUFFIANS OVERRUN-NING THIS TOWN! IT'S TOO MUCH TROUBLE TO DEAL WITH!
THE ONLY PEOPLE YOU'RE ALLOWED TO KILL ARE THE OTHER PROS THAT ARE COMING TO ASSASSINATE ME!
WHAT KIND OF STUPID LOGIC IS THAT? ARE YOU CRACKED?
DON'T TALK BACK TO ME! YOUR EMPLOYER WILL HEAR ABOUT THIS!
UGH.
AWW, HELL.
PLOP
THIS WHOLE THING IS DRIVING ME NUTS.
THUD
I'M GONNA GET IWANISHI FOR THIS.
THIS IS THE MOST ANNOY-ING JOB HE'S EVER GIVEN ME!

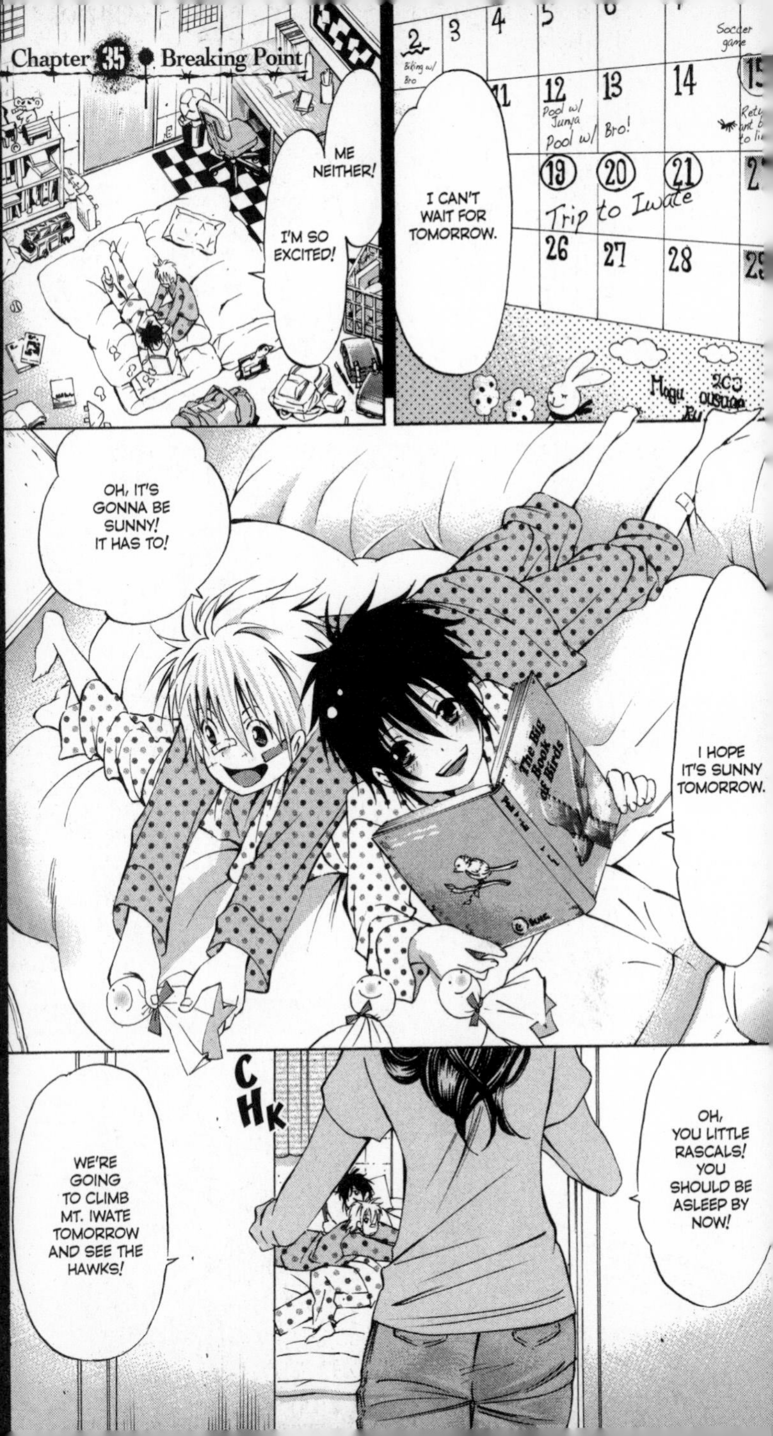
Chapter 35 Breaking Point
Soccer game
Biking w/ Bro
Pool w/ Junya
Pool w/ Bro!
Trip to Iwate
I CAN'T WAIT FOR TOMORROW.
ME NEITHER!
I'M SO EXCITED!
I HOPE IT'S SUNNY TOMORROW.
OH, IT'S GONNA BE SUNNY! IT HAS TO!
The Big Book of Birds
OH, YOU LITTLE RASCALS! YOU SHOULD BE ASLEEP BY NOW!
CHK
WE'RE GOING TO CLIMB MT. IWATE TOMORROW AND SEE THE HAWKS!

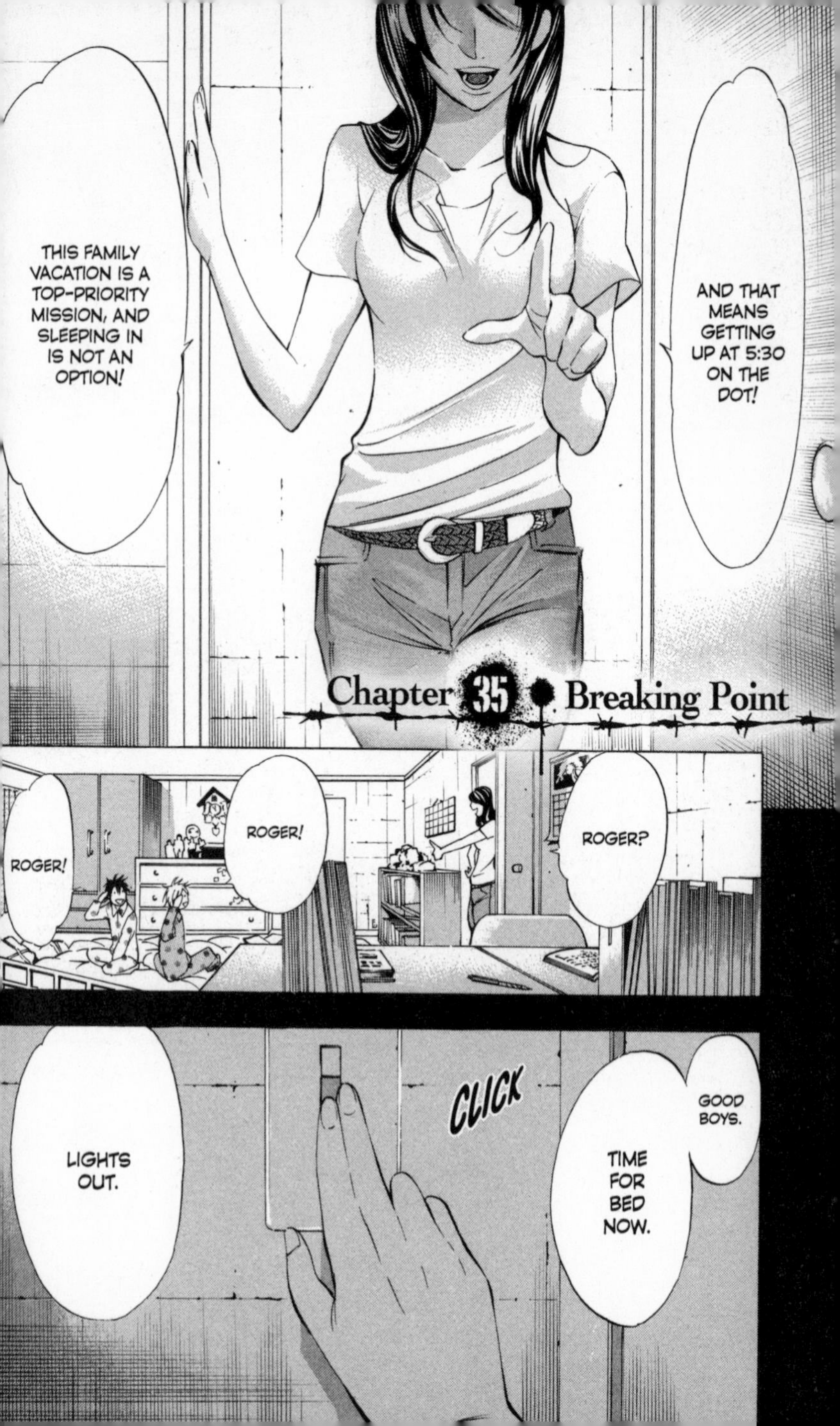
THIS FAMILY VACATION IS A TOP-PRIORITY MISSION, AND SLEEPING IN IS NOT AN OPTION!
AND THAT MEANS GETTING UP AT 5:30 ON THE DOT!
Chapter 35 Breaking Point
ROGER?
ROGER!
ROGER!
GOOD BOYS.
TIME FOR BED NOW.
CLICK
LIGHTS OUT.

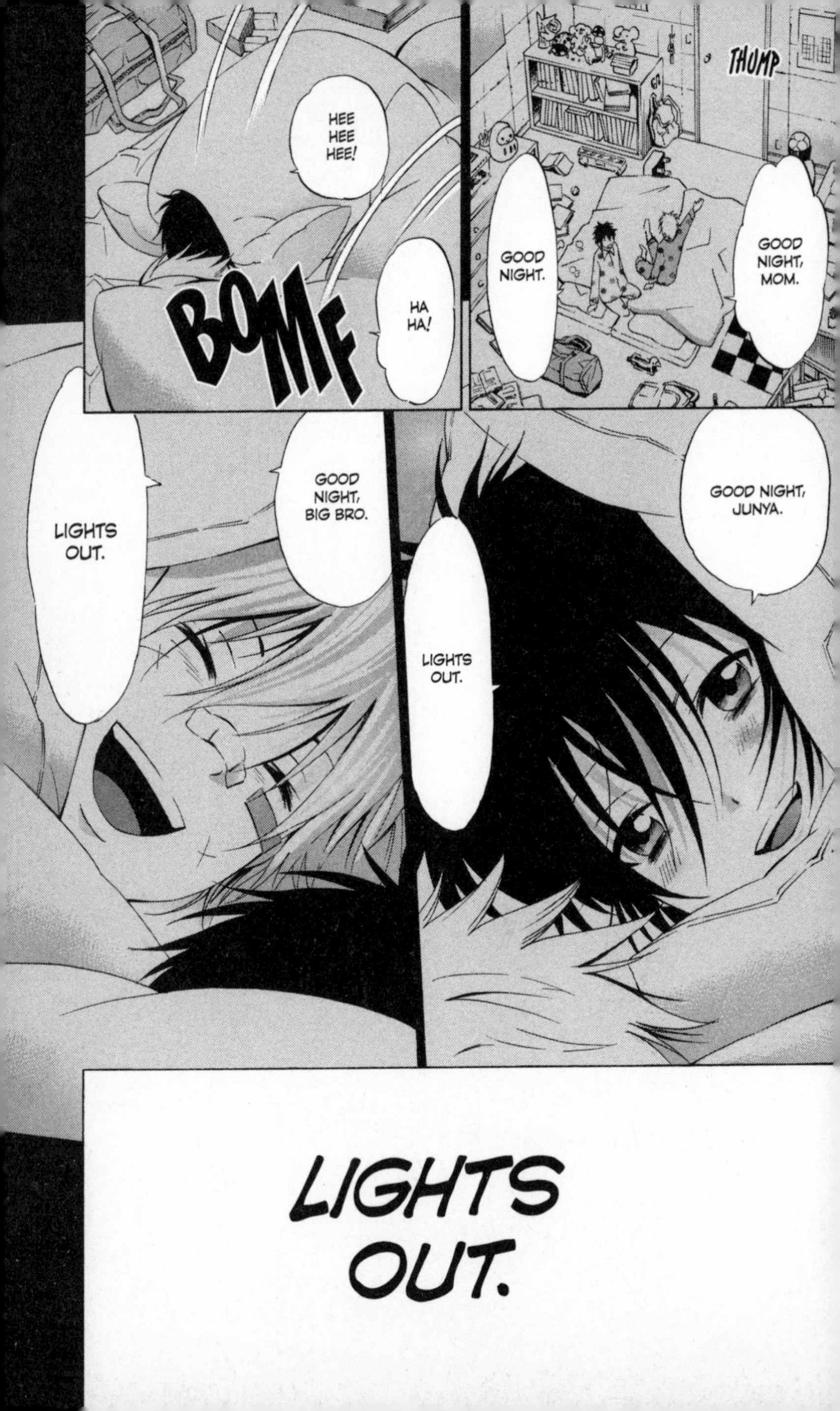
THUMP
GOOD NIGHT, MOM.
GOOD NIGHT.
HEE HEE HEE!
HA HA!
BOMF
GOOD NIGHT, JUNYA.
LIGHTS OUT.
GOOD NIGHT, BIG BRO.
LIGHTS OUT.
LIGHTS OUT.

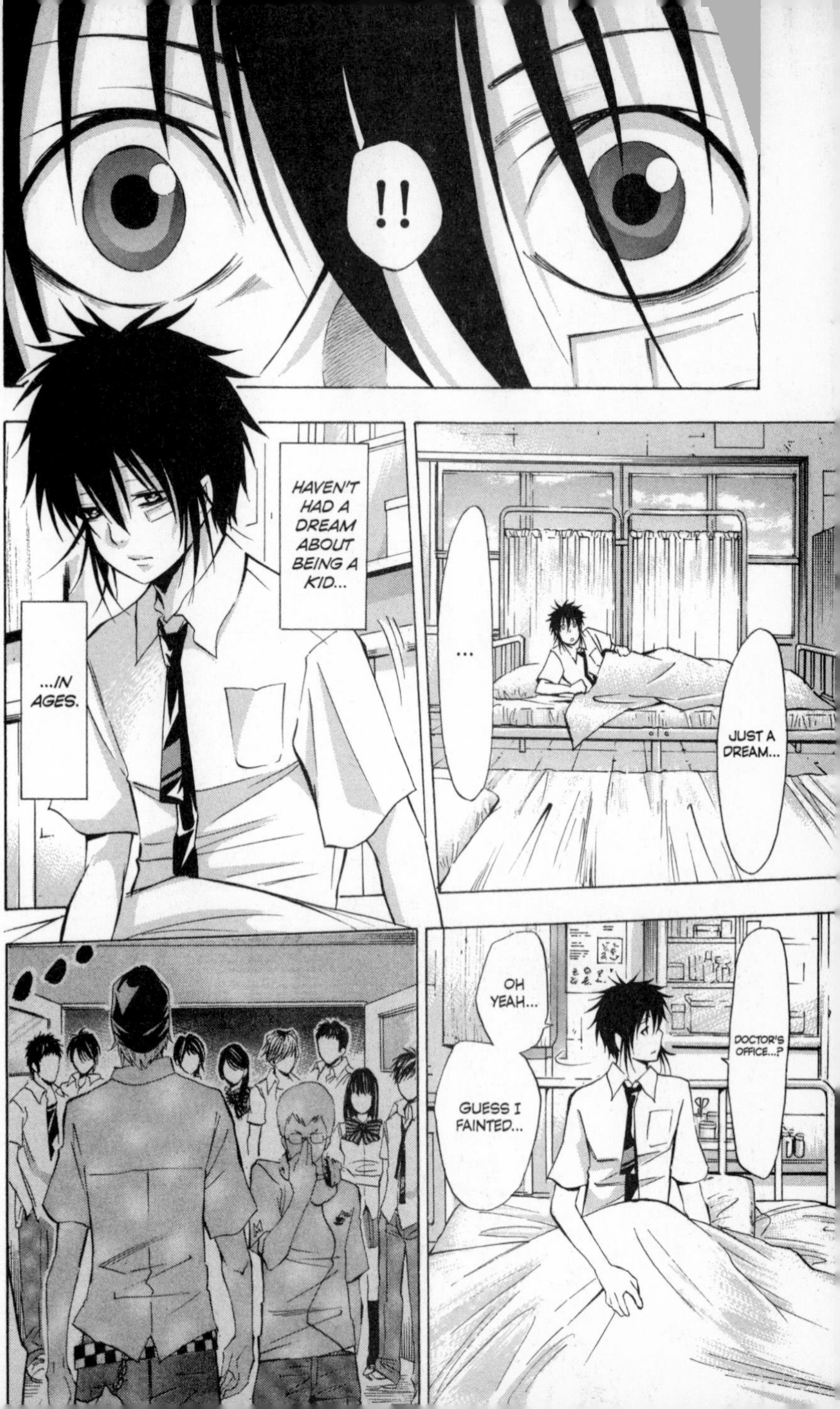
!!
JUST A DREAM...
...
HAVEN'T HAD A DREAM ABOUT BEING A KID...
...IN AGES.
DOCTOR'S OFFICE...?
OH YEAH...
GUESS I FAINTED...

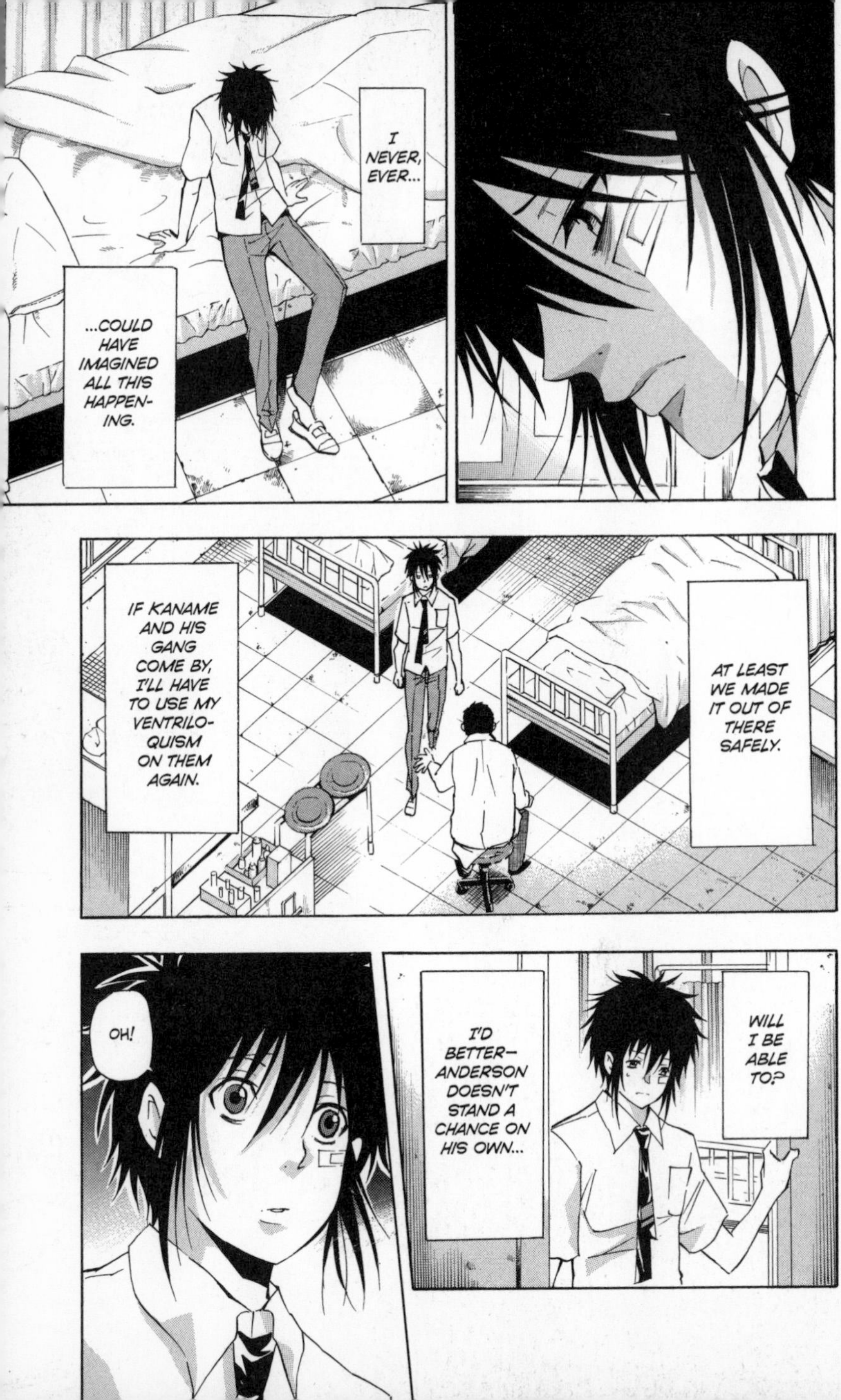
I NEVER, EVER...
...COULD HAVE IMAGINED ALL THIS HAPPENING.
AT LEAST WE MADE IT OUT OF THERE SAFELY.
IF KANAME AND HIS GANG COME BY, I'LL HAVE TO USE MY VENTRILOQUISM ON THEM AGAIN.
WILL I BE ABLE TO?
I'D BETTER—ANDERSON DOESN'T STAND A CHANCE ON HIS OWN...
OH!

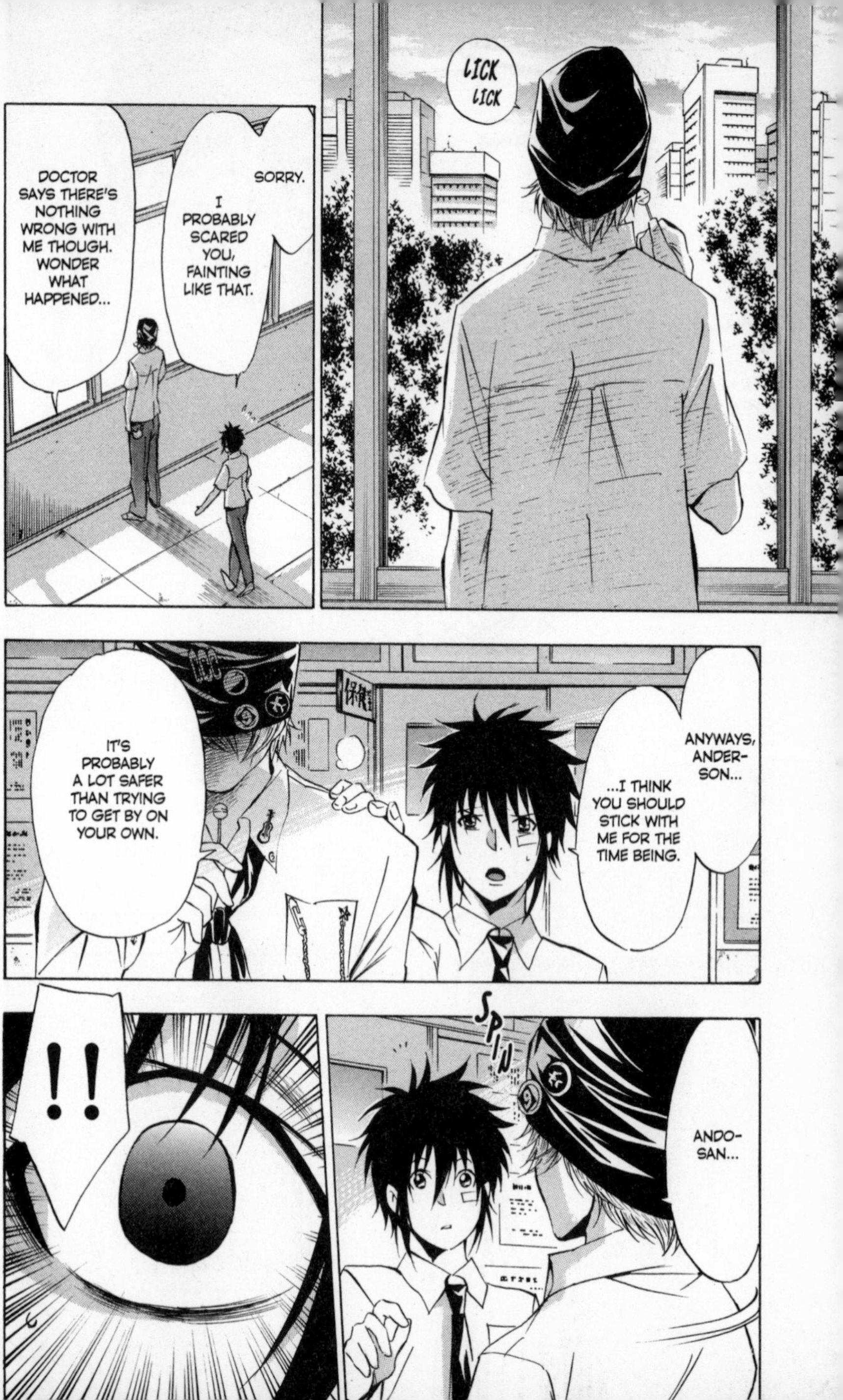
LICK LICK
SORRY.
I PROBABLY SCARED YOU, FAINTING LIKE THAT.
DOCTOR SAYS THERE'S NOTHING WRONG WITH ME THOUGH. WONDER WHAT HAPPENED...
ANYWAYS, ANDER-SON...
...I THINK YOU SHOULD STICK WITH ME FOR THE TIME BEING.
IT'S PROBABLY A LOT SAFER THAN TRYING TO GET BY ON YOUR OWN.
SPIN
ANDO-SAN...
!!

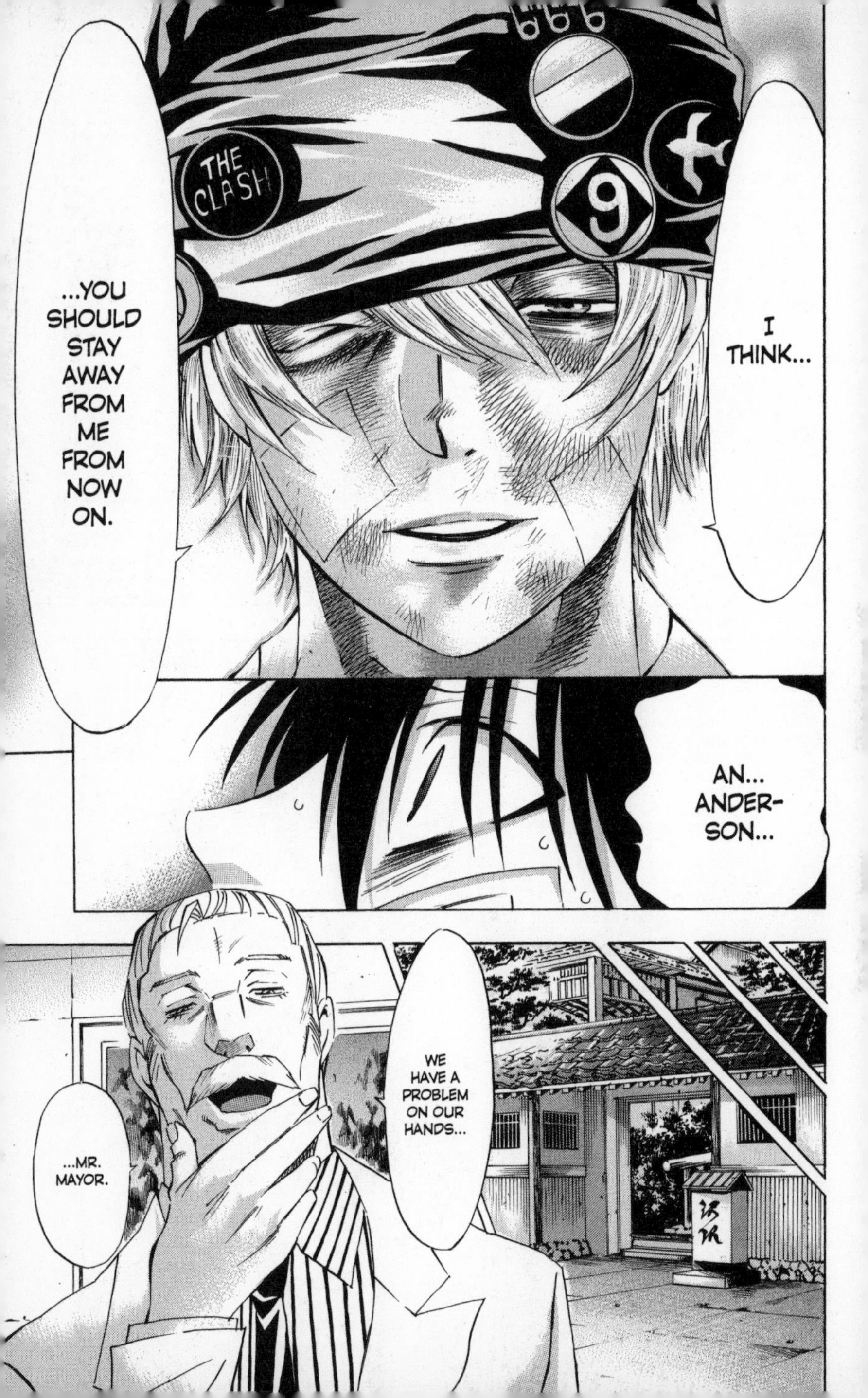
I THINK...
...YOU SHOULD STAY AWAY FROM ME FROM NOW ON.
THE CLASH
AN... ANDER-SON...
WE HAVE A PROBLEM ON OUR HANDS...
...MR. MAYOR.

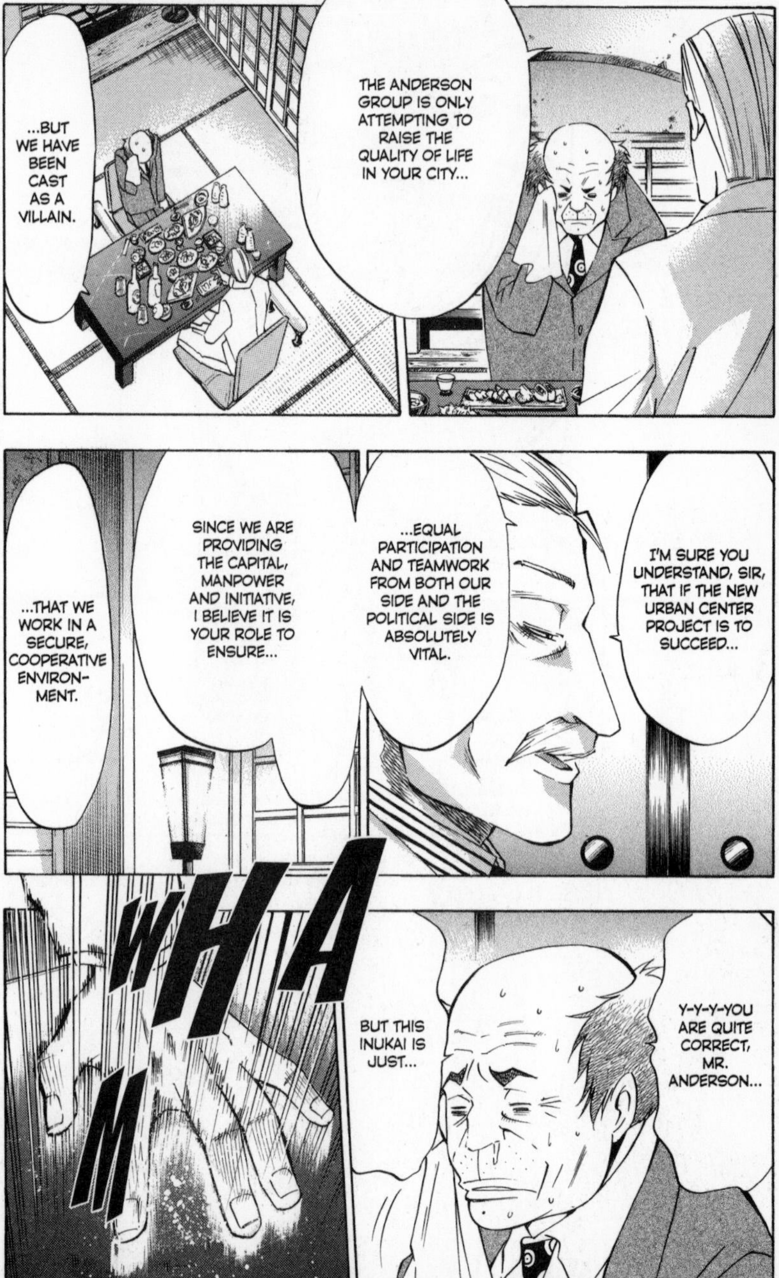
THE ANDERSON GROUP IS ONLY ATTEMPTING TO RAISE THE QUALITY OF LIFE IN YOUR CITY...
...BUT WE HAVE BEEN CAST AS A VILLAIN.
I'M SURE YOU UNDERSTAND, SIR, THAT IF THE NEW URBAN CENTER PROJECT IS TO SUCCEED...
...EQUAL PARTICIPATION AND TEAMWORK FROM BOTH OUR SIDE AND THE POLITICAL SIDE IS ABSOLUTELY VITAL.
SINCE WE ARE PROVIDING THE CAPITAL, MANPOWER AND INITIATIVE, I BELIEVE IT IS YOUR ROLE TO ENSURE...
...THAT WE WORK IN A SECURE, COOPERATIVE ENVIRON-MENT.
Y-Y-Y-YOU ARE QUITE CORRECT, MR. ANDERSON...
BUT THIS INUKAI IS JUST...
WHAM

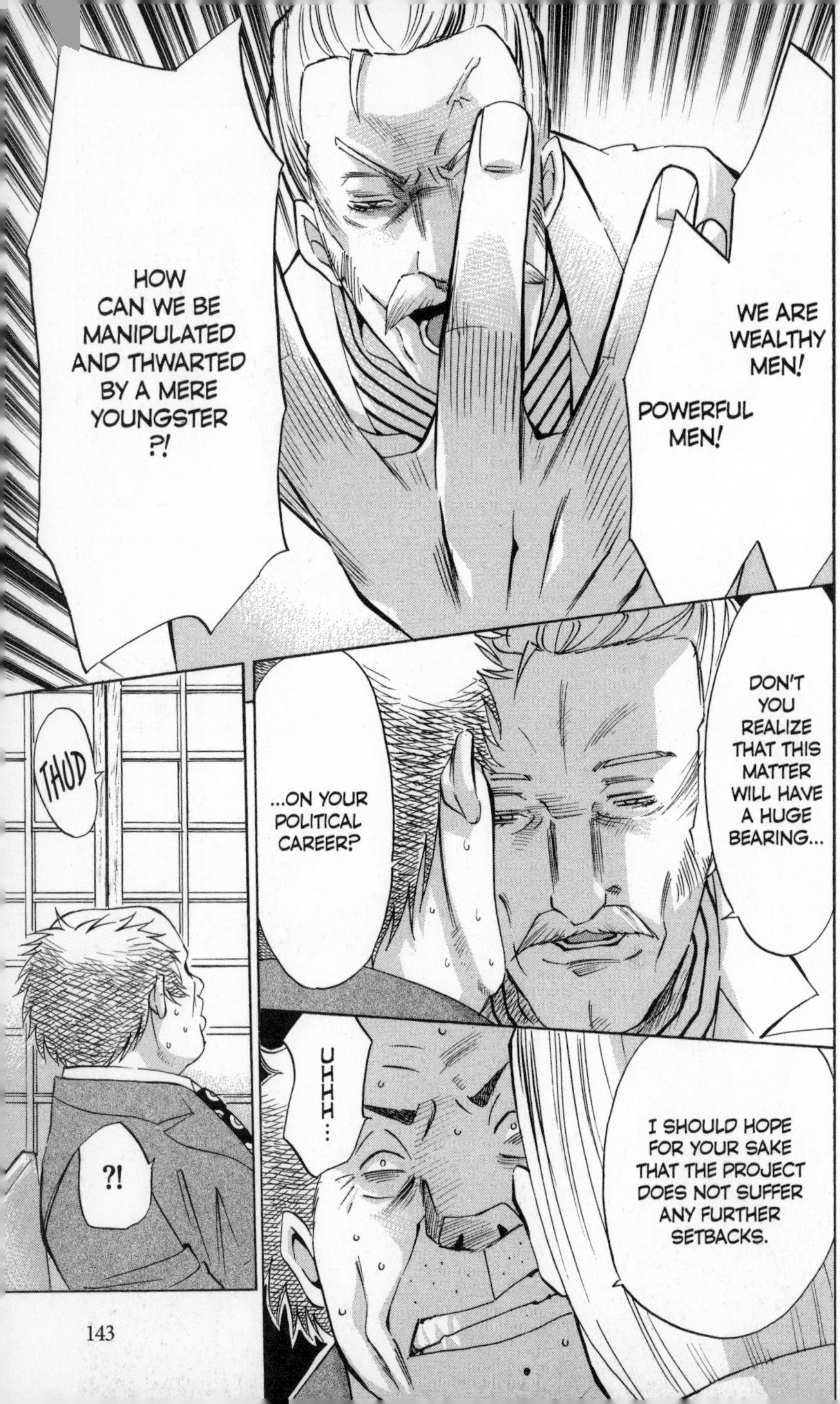
WE ARE WEALTHY MEN!
POWERFUL MEN!
HOW CAN WE BE MANIPULATED AND THWARTED BY A MERE YOUNGSTER ?!
DON'T YOU REALIZE THAT THIS MATTER WILL HAVE A HUGE BEARING...
...ON YOUR POLITICAL CAREER?
I SHOULD HOPE FOR YOUR SAKE THAT THE PROJECT DOES NOT SUFFER ANY FURTHER SETBACKS.
UHHH...
THUD
?!

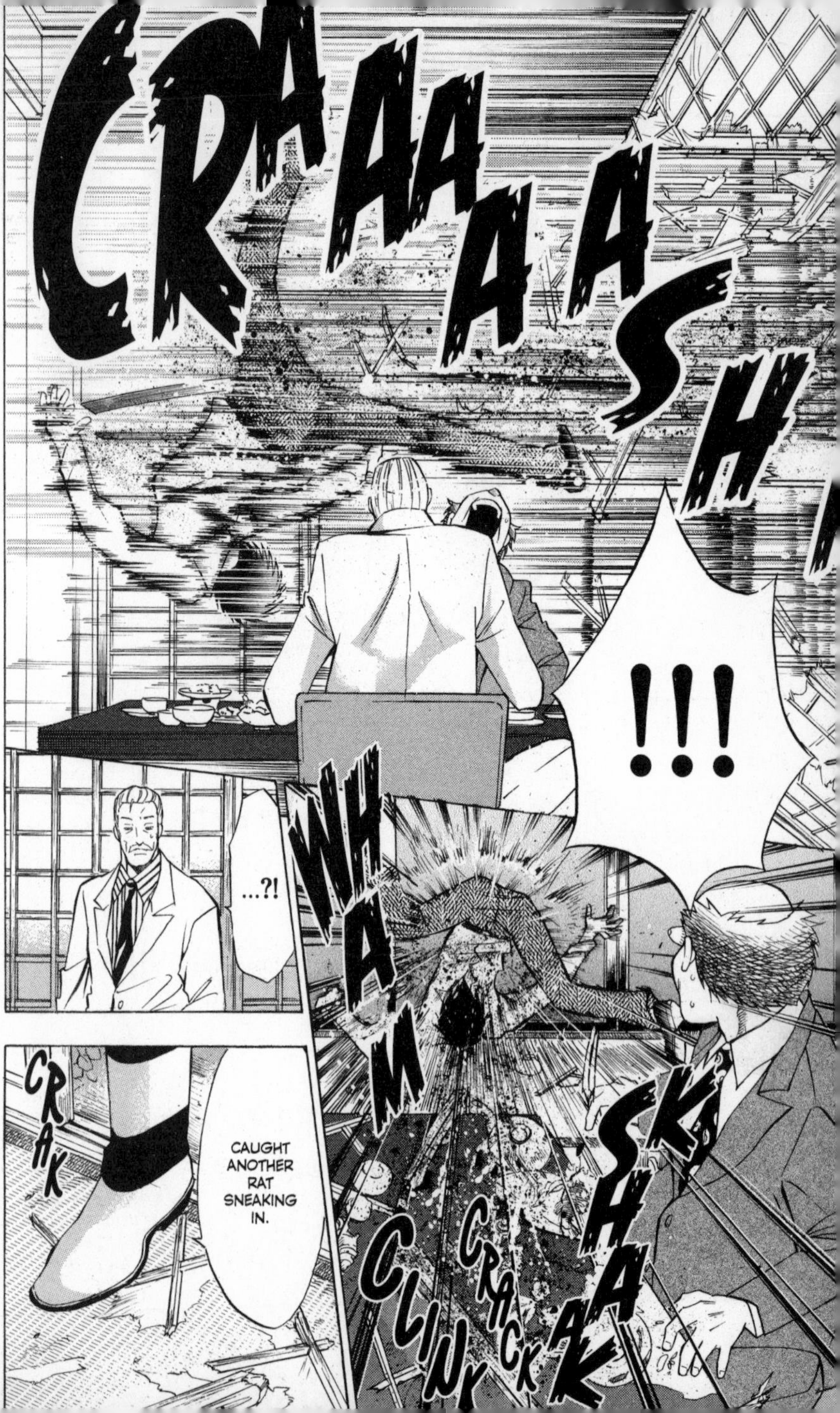
CRAAAASH
!!!
WHAM
SKSHAAK
CRACK
CLINK
...?!
CRAK
CAUGHT ANOTHER RAT SNEAKING IN.

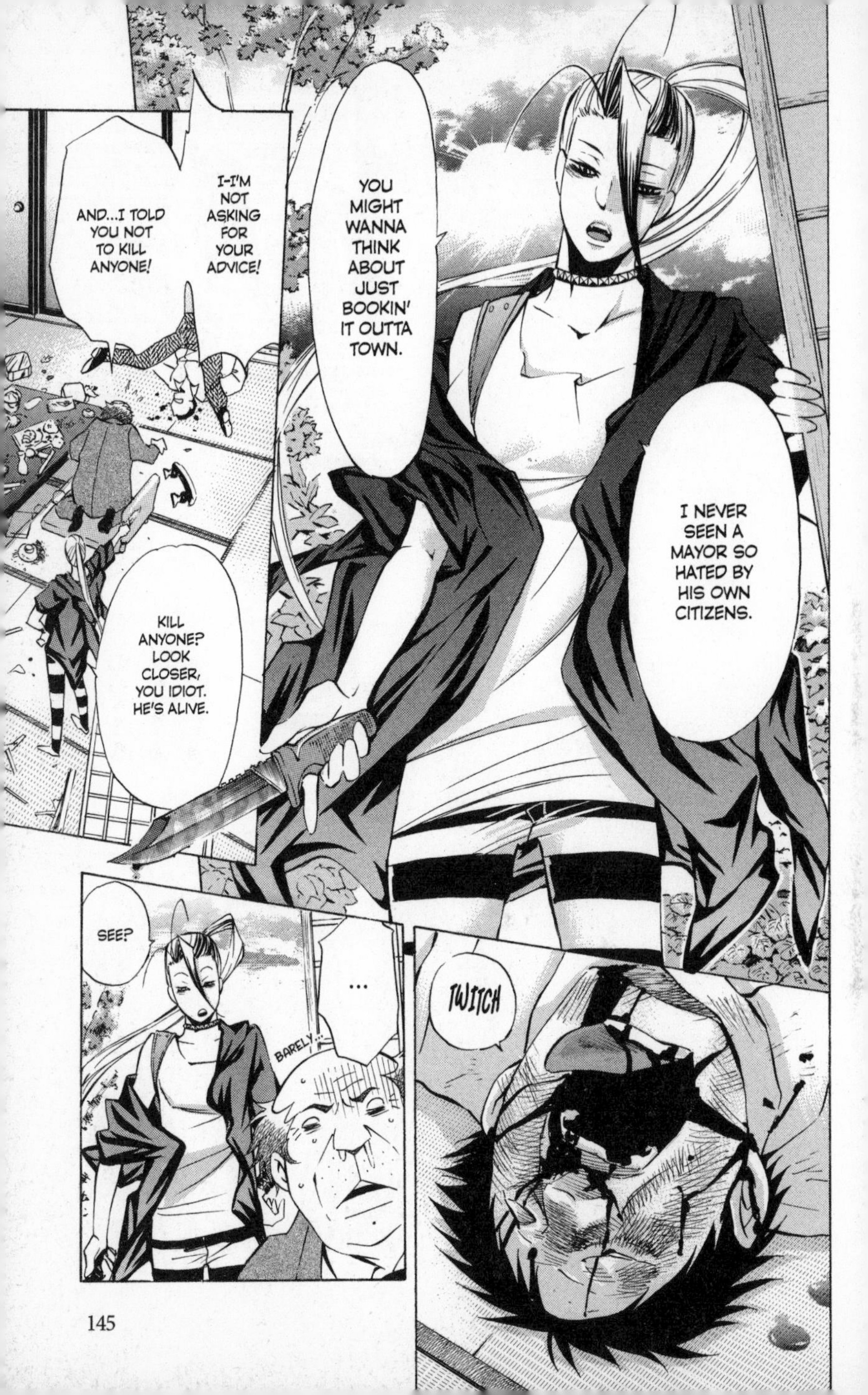

YOU MIGHT WANNA THINK ABOUT JUST BOOKIN' IT OUTTA TOWN.
I NEVER SEEN A MAYOR SO HATED BY HIS OWN CITIZENS.
I-I'M NOT ASKING FOR YOUR ADVICE!
AND...I TOLD YOU NOT TO KILL ANYONE!
KILL ANYONE? LOOK CLOSER, YOU IDIOT. HE'S ALIVE.
TWITCH
SEE?
...
BARELY...

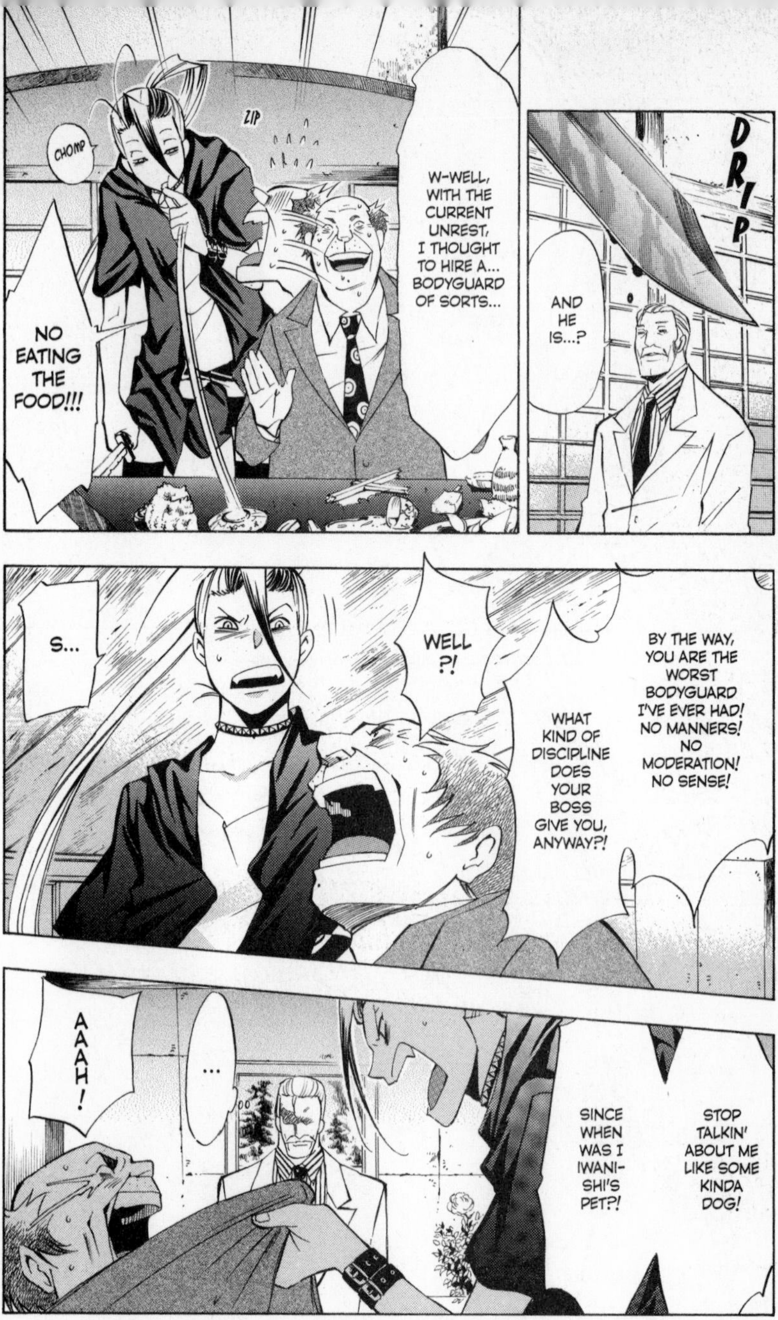
DRIP
AND HE IS...?
W-WELL, WITH THE CURRENT UNREST, I THOUGHT TO HIRE A... BODYGUARD OF SORTS...
ZIP
CHOMP
NO EATING THE FOOD!!!
BY THE WAY, YOU ARE THE WORST BODYGUARD I'VE EVER HAD! NO MANNERS! NO MODERATION! NO SENSE!
WHAT KIND OF DISCIPLINE DOES YOUR BOSS GIVE YOU, ANYWAY?!
WELL?!
S...
STOP TALKIN' ABOUT ME LIKE SOME KINDA DOG!
SINCE WHEN WAS I IWANI-SHI'S PET?!
...
AAAH!

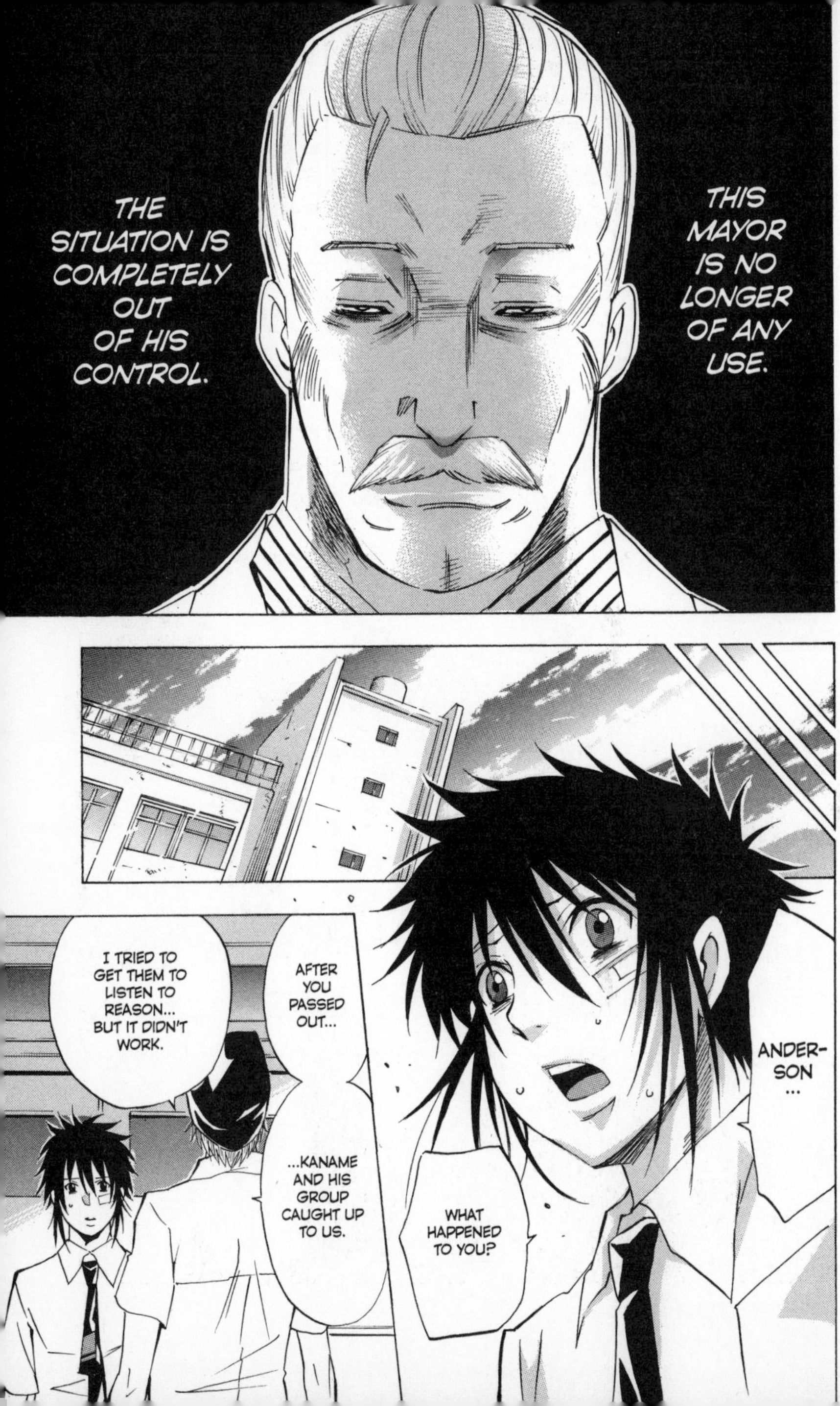
THIS MAYOR IS NO LONGER OF ANY USE.
THE SITUATION IS COMPLETELY OUT OF HIS CONTROL.
ANDER-SON...
WHAT HAPPENED TO YOU?
AFTER YOU PASSED OUT...
...KANAME AND HIS GROUP CAUGHT UP TO US.
I TRIED TO GET THEM TO LISTEN TO REASON... BUT IT DIDN'T WORK.

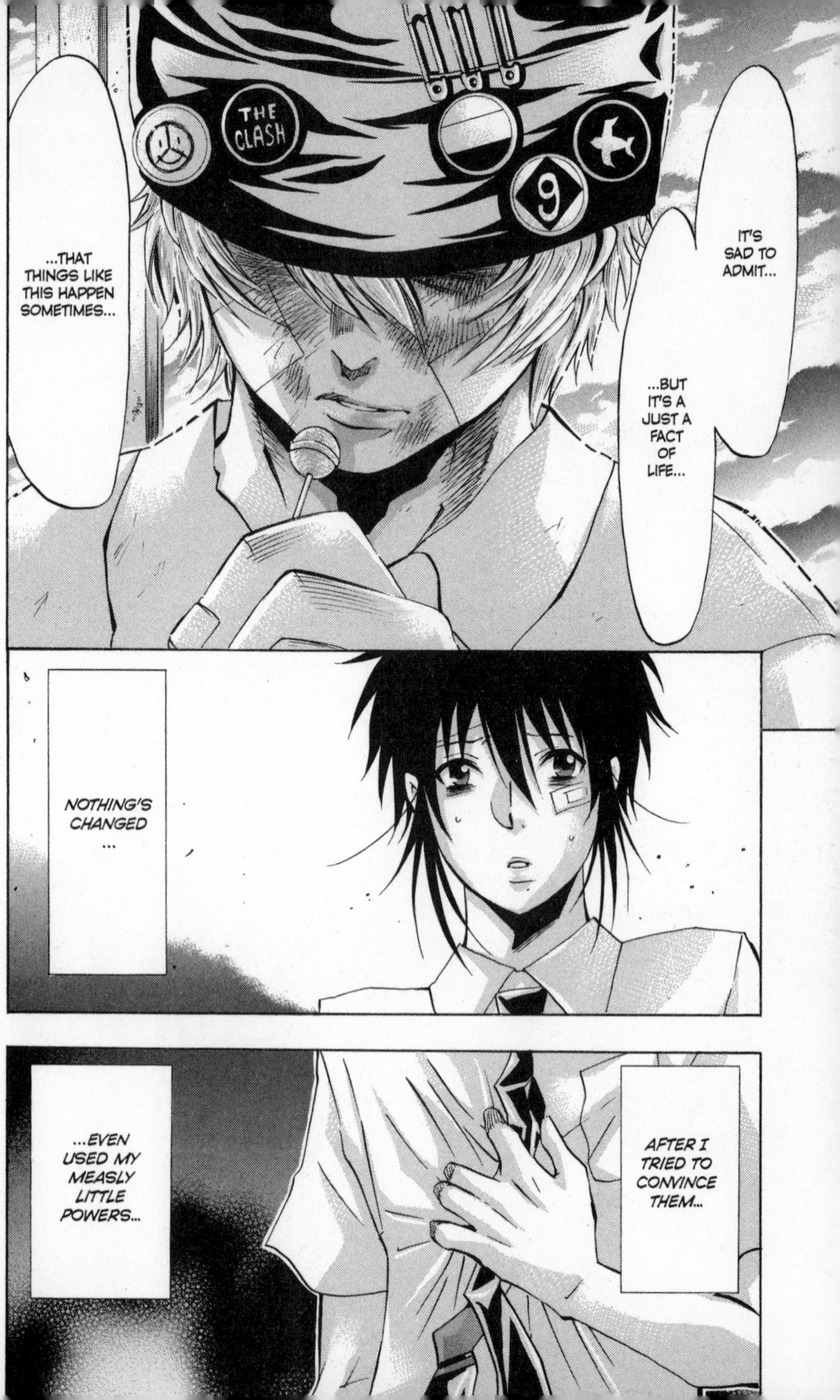
THE CLASH
IT'S SAD TO ADMIT...
...BUT IT'S A JUST A FACT OF LIFE...
...THAT THINGS LIKE THIS HAPPEN SOMETIMES...
NOTHING'S CHANGED ...
AFTER I TRIED TO CONVINCE THEM...
...EVEN USED MY MEASLY LITTLE POWERS...

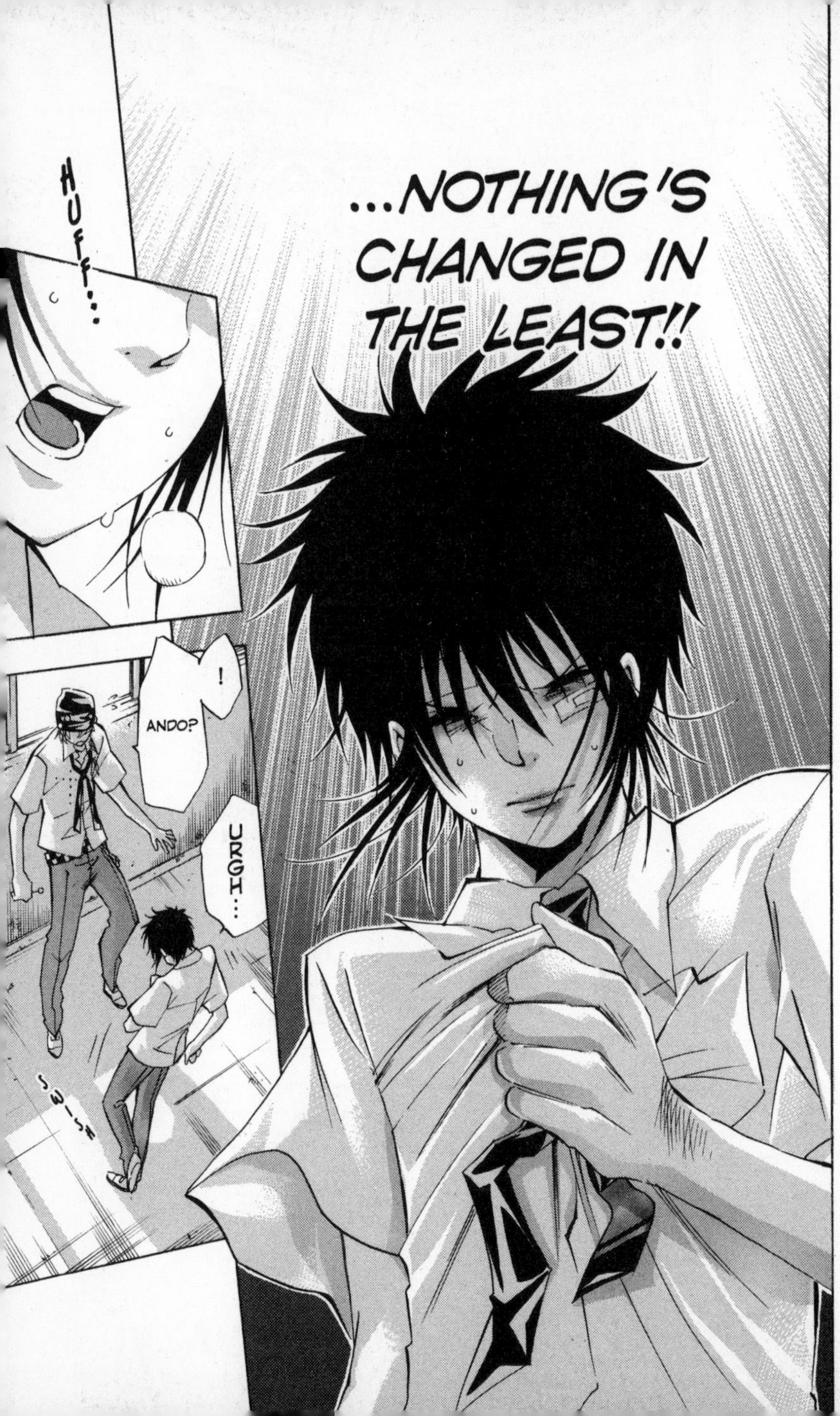
...NOTHING'S CHANGED IN THE LEAST!!
HUFF...
!
ANDO?
URGH...
SWISH

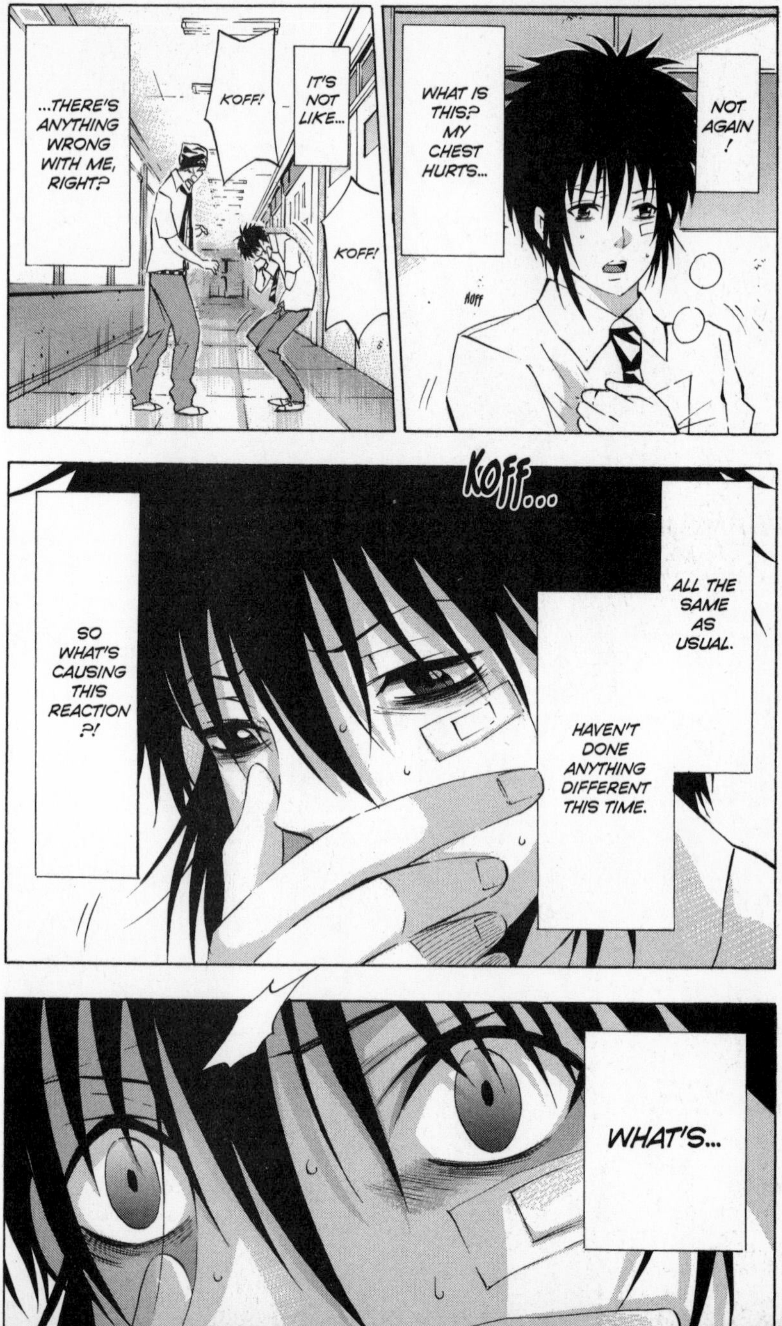
NOT AGAIN!
WHAT IS THIS? MY CHEST HURTS...
KOFF
IT'S NOT LIKE...
KOFF!
KOFF!
...THERE'S ANYTHING WRONG WITH ME, RIGHT?
KOFF...
ALL THE SAME AS USUAL.
HAVEN'T DONE ANYTHING DIFFERENT THIS TIME.
SO WHAT'S CAUSING THIS REACTION?!
WHAT'S...

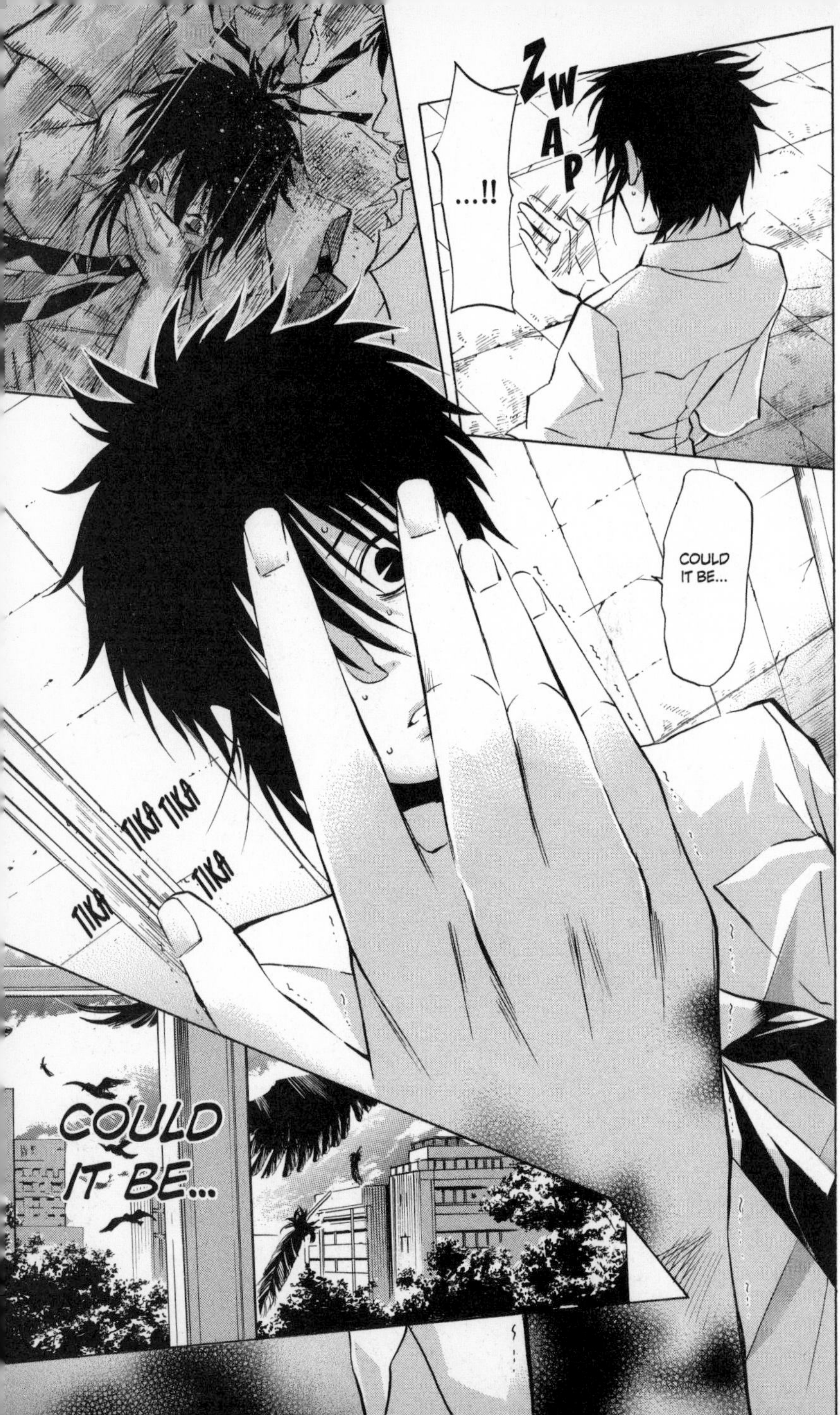
ZWAP
...!!
COULD IT BE...
TIKA TIKA
TIKA
TIKA
COULD IT BE...

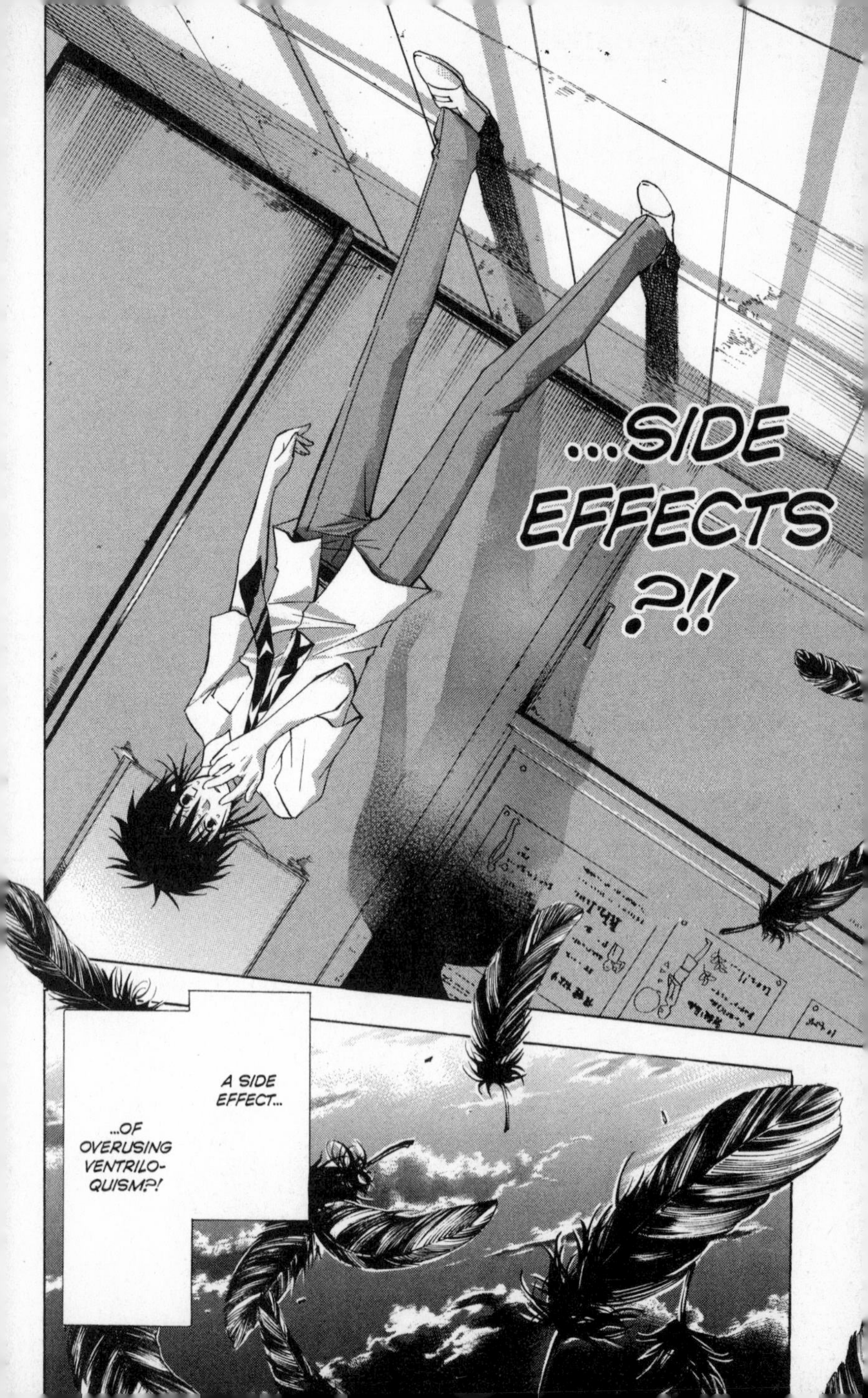
...SIDE EFFECTS ?!!
A SIDE EFFECT...
...OF OVERUSING VENTRILO-QUISM?!

Chapter 36 Dead End

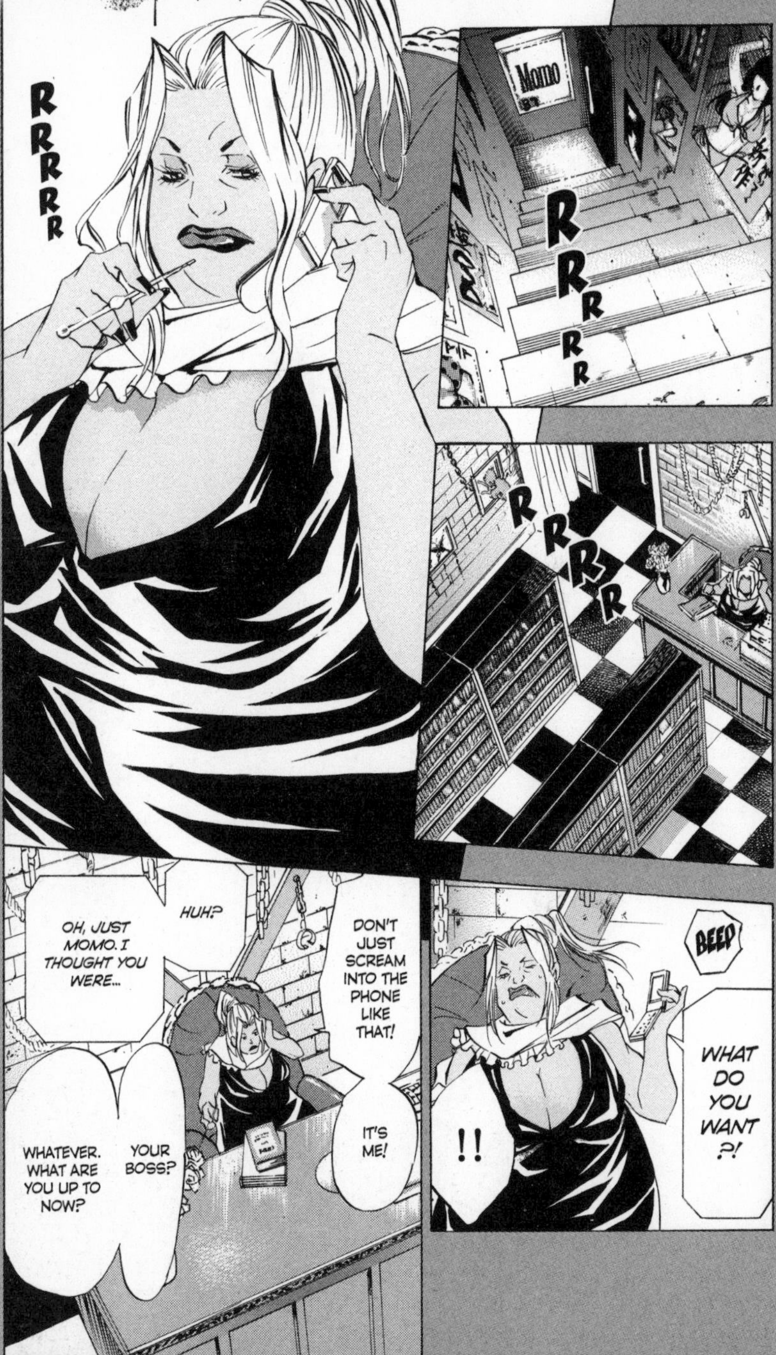
MOMO
RRRR
RRRRR
RRRRR
BEEP
WHAT DO YOU WANT?!
!!
DON'T JUST SCREAM INTO THE PHONE LIKE THAT!
HUH?
OH, JUST MOMO. I THOUGHT YOU WERE...
IT'S ME!
YOUR BOSS?
WHATEVER. WHAT ARE YOU UP TO NOW?

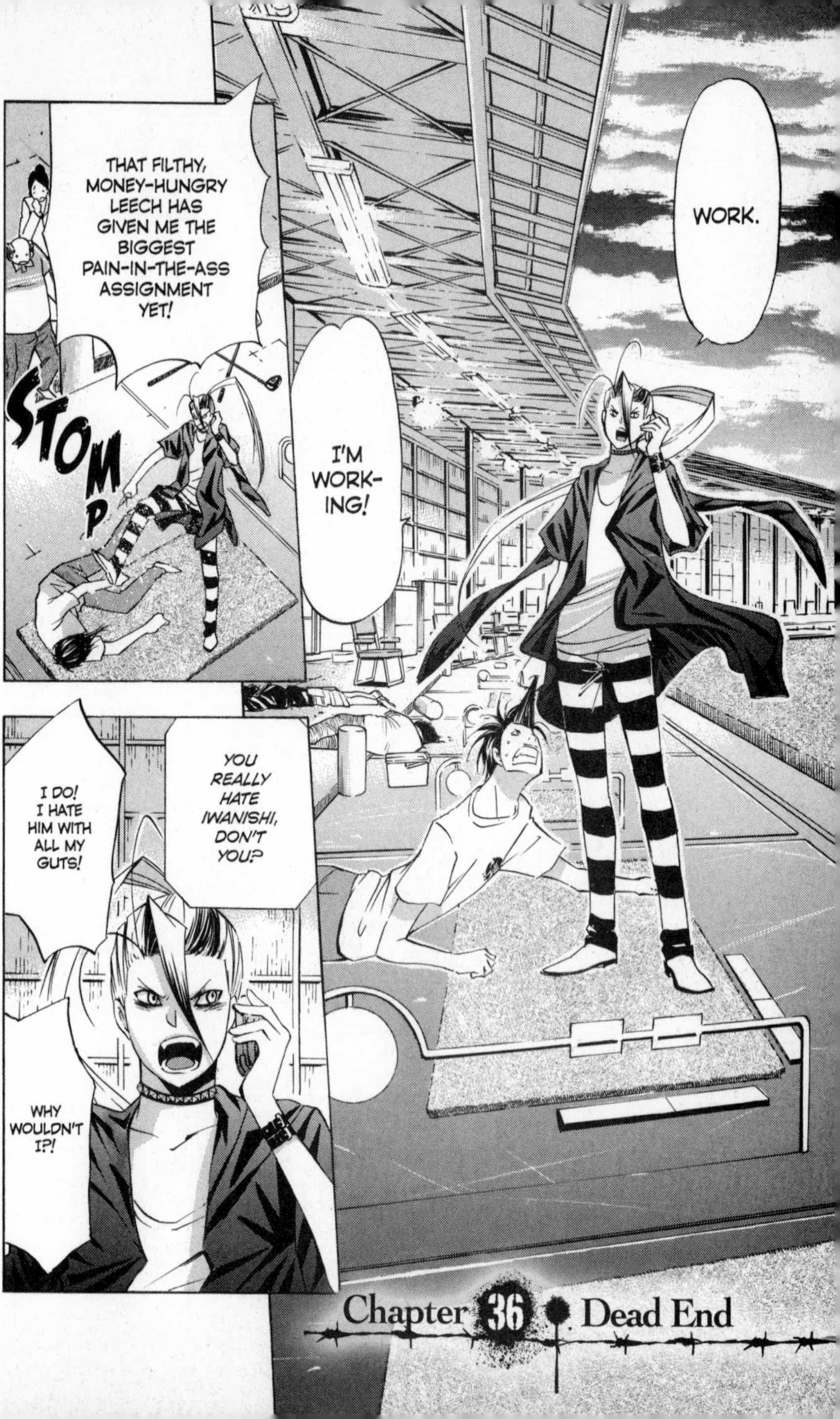
WORK.
I'M WORKING!
THAT FILTHY, MONEY-HUNGRY LEECH HAS GIVEN ME THE BIGGEST PAIN-IN-THE-ASS ASSIGNMENT YET!
STOMP
YOU REALLY HATE IWANISHI, DON'T YOU?
I DO! I HATE HIM WITH ALL MY GUTS!
WHY WOULDN'T I?!

Chapter 36 Dead End

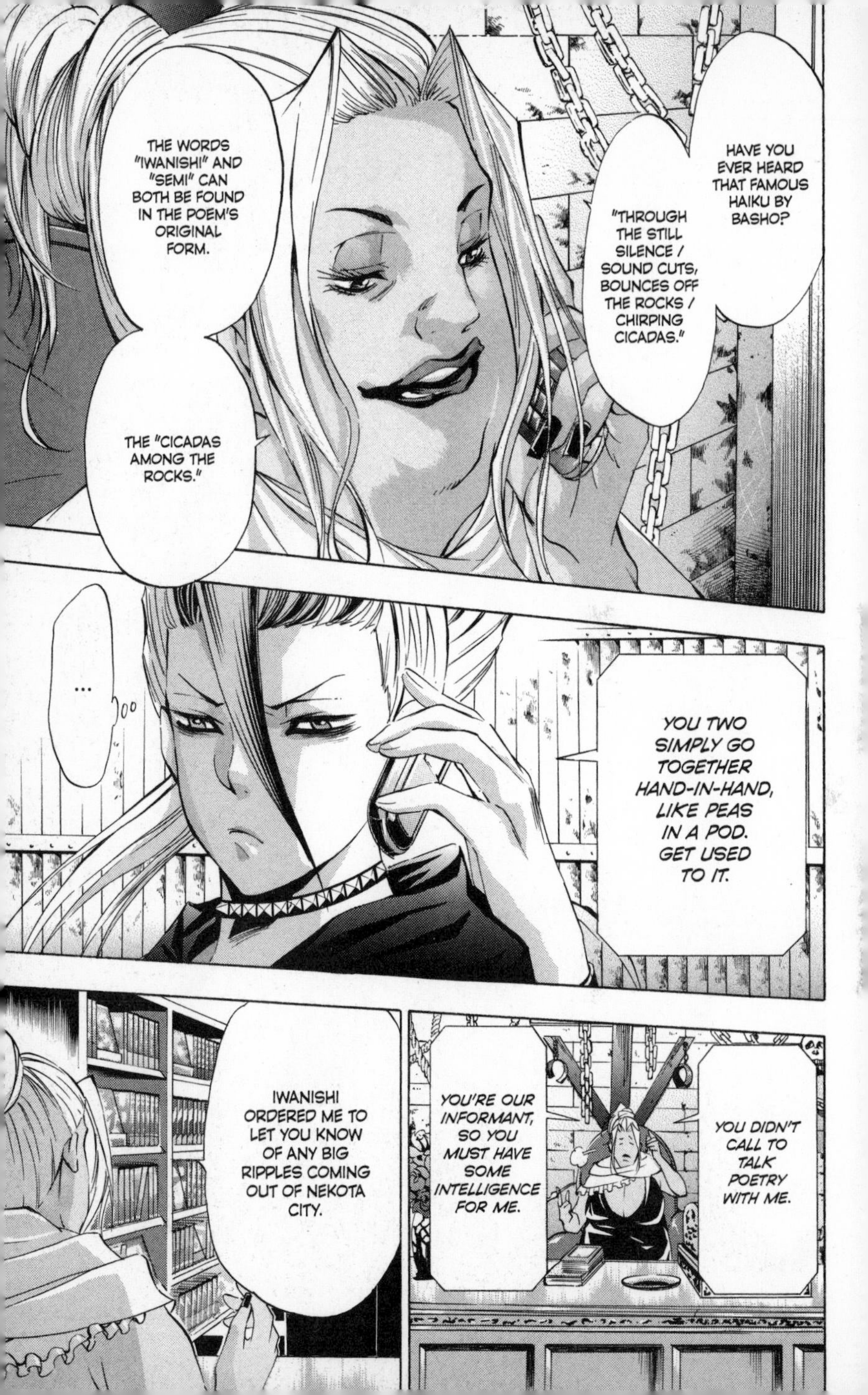
HAVE YOU EVER HEARD THAT FAMOUS HAIKU BY BASHO?
"THROUGH THE STILL SILENCE / SOUND CUTS, BOUNCES OFF THE ROCKS / CHIRPING CICADAS."
THE WORDS "IWANISHI" AND "SEMI" CAN BOTH BE FOUND IN THE POEM'S ORIGINAL FORM.
THE "CICADAS AMONG THE ROCKS."
YOU TWO SIMPLY GO TOGETHER HAND-IN-HAND, LIKE PEAS IN A POD. GET USED TO IT.
...
YOU DIDN'T CALL TO TALK POETRY WITH ME.
YOU'RE OUR INFORMANT, SO YOU MUST HAVE SOME INTELLIGENCE FOR ME.
IWANISHI ORDERED ME TO LET YOU KNOW OF ANY BIG RIPPLES COMING OUT OF NEKOTA CITY.

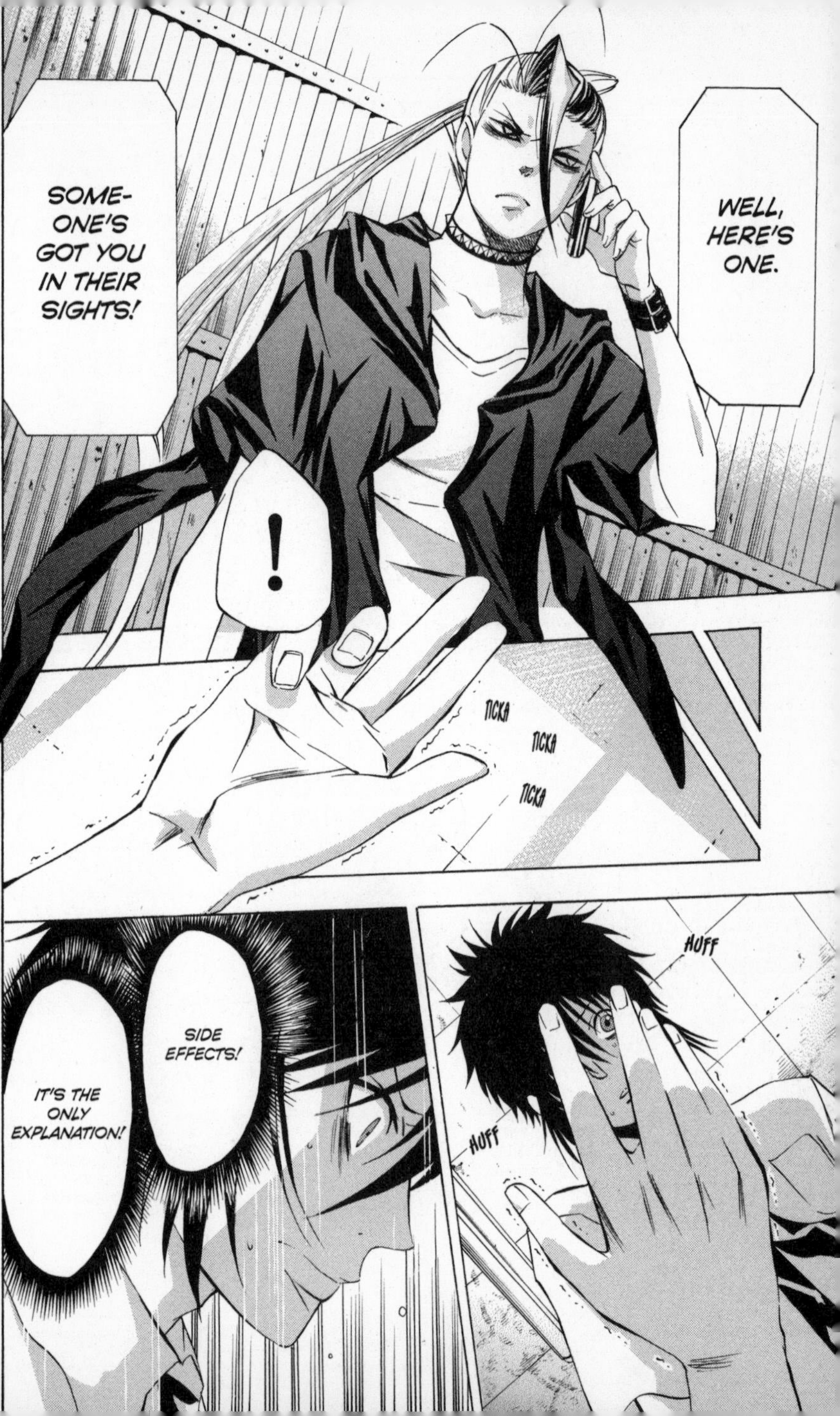
WELL, HERE'S ONE.
SOME-ONE'S GOT YOU IN THEIR SIGHTS!
!
TICKA
TICKA
TICKA
HUFF
HUFF
SIDE EFFECTS!
IT'S THE ONLY EXPLANATION!

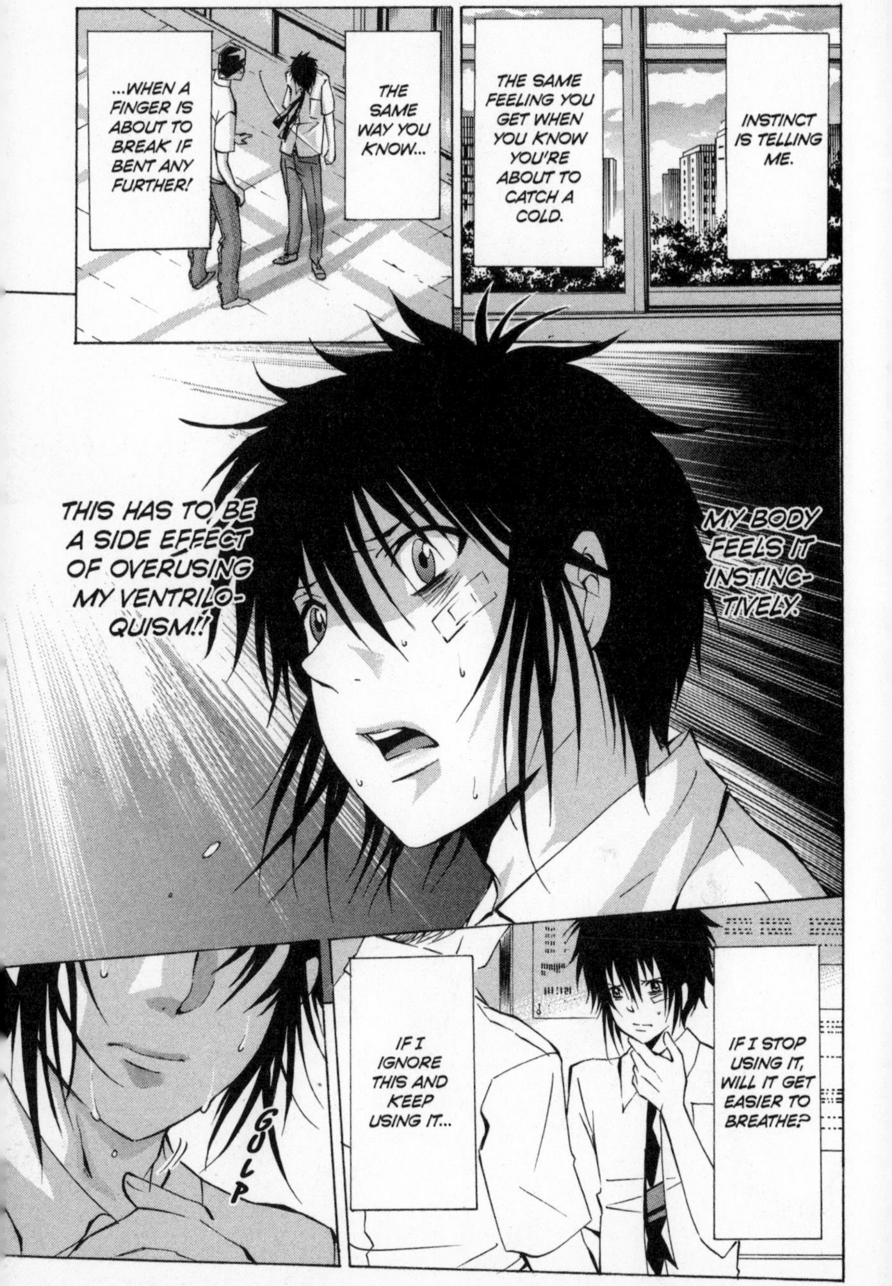
INSTINCT IS TELLING ME.
THE SAME FEELING YOU GET WHEN YOU KNOW YOU'RE ABOUT TO CATCH A COLD.
THE SAME WAY YOU KNOW...
...WHEN A FINGER IS ABOUT TO BREAK IF BENT ANY FURTHER!
MY BODY FEELS IT INSTINC-TIVELY.
THIS HAS TO BE A SIDE EFFECT OF OVERUSING MY VENTRILO-QUISM!!
IF I STOP USING IT, WILL IT GET EASIER TO BREATHE?
IF I IGNORE THIS AND KEEP USING IT...
GULP

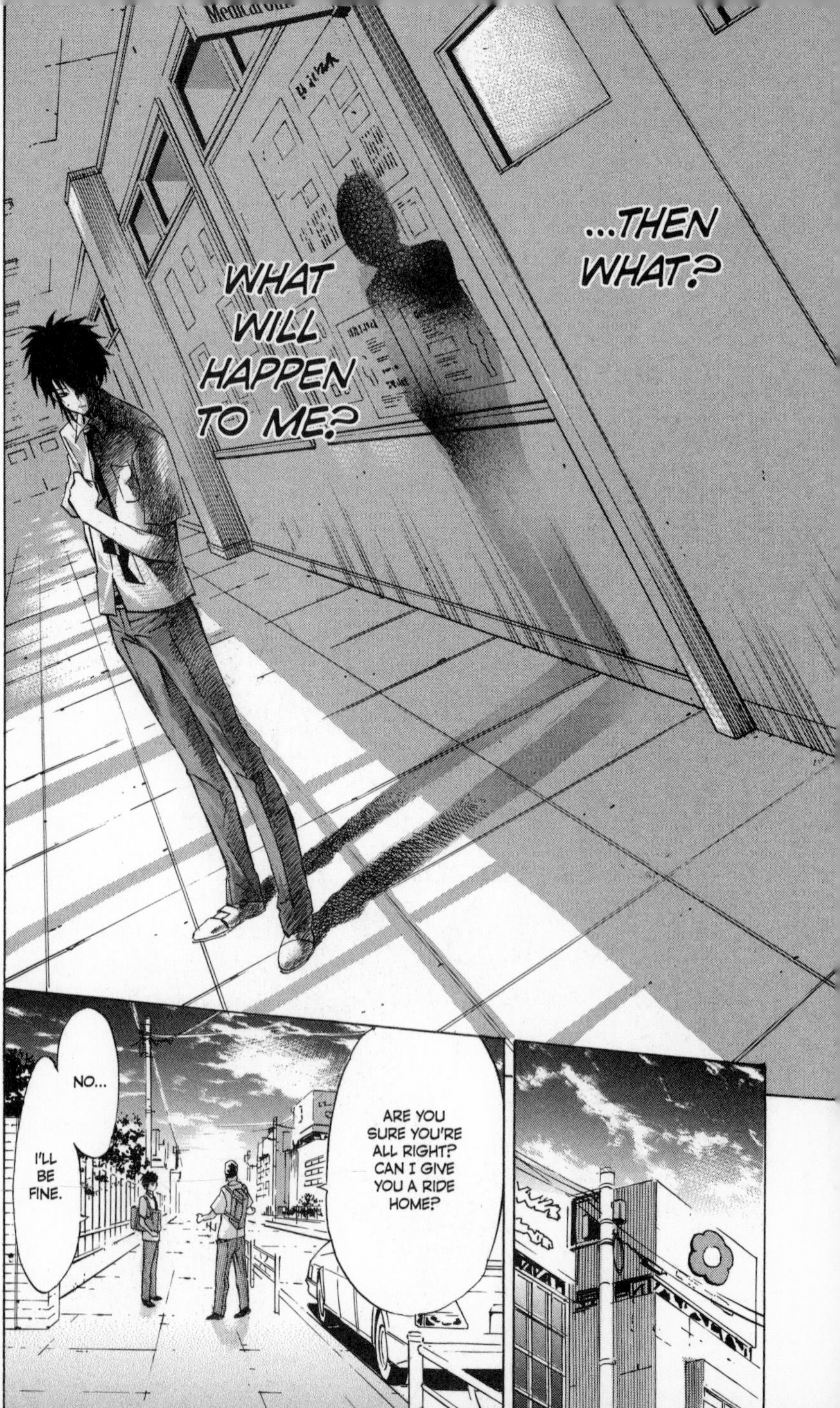
...THEN WHAT?
WHAT WILL HAPPEN TO ME?
ARE YOU SURE YOU'RE ALL RIGHT? CAN I GIVE YOU A RIDE HOME?
NO...
I'LL BE FINE.

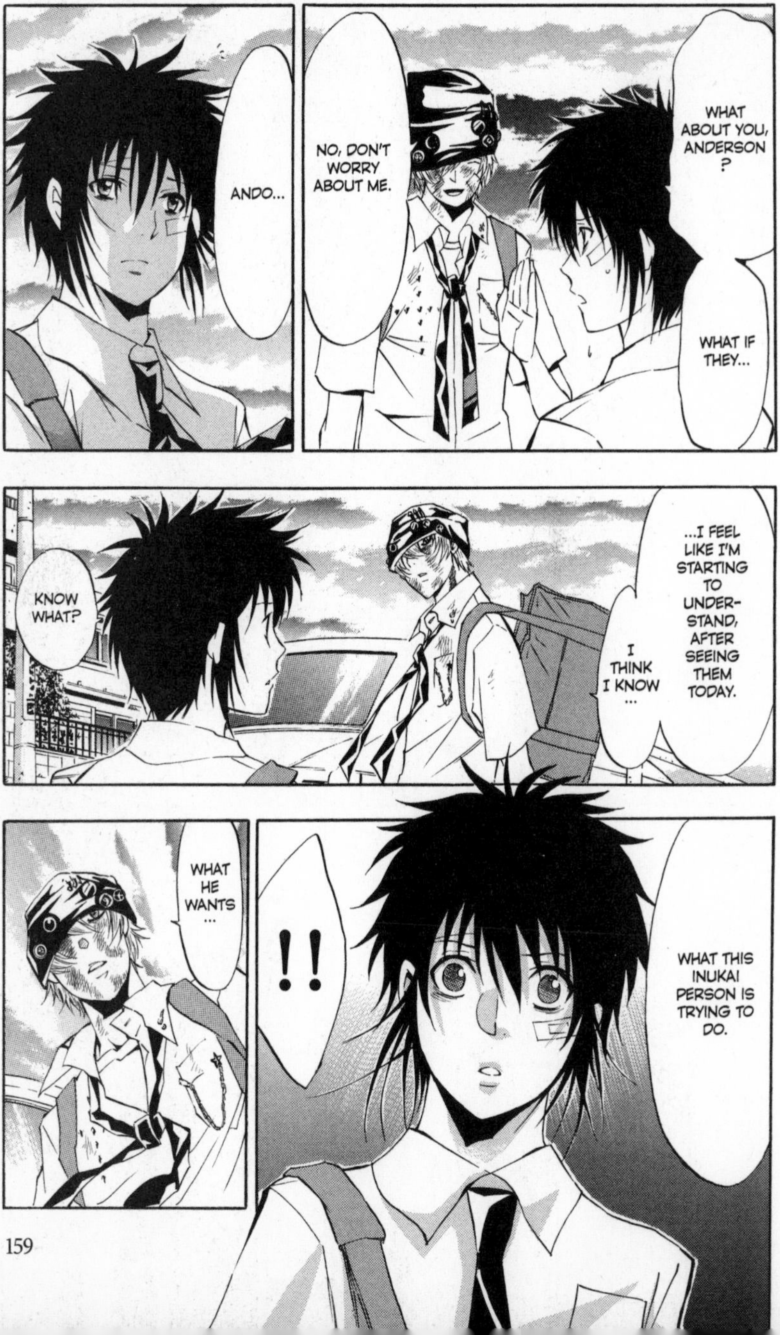
WHAT ABOUT YOU, ANDERSON?
WHAT IF THEY...
NO, DON'T WORRY ABOUT ME.
ANDO...
...I FEEL LIKE I'M STARTING TO UNDER-STAND, AFTER SEEING THEM TODAY.
I THINK I KNOW...
KNOW WHAT?
WHAT THIS INUKAI PERSON IS TRYING TO DO.
!!
WHAT HE WANTS...

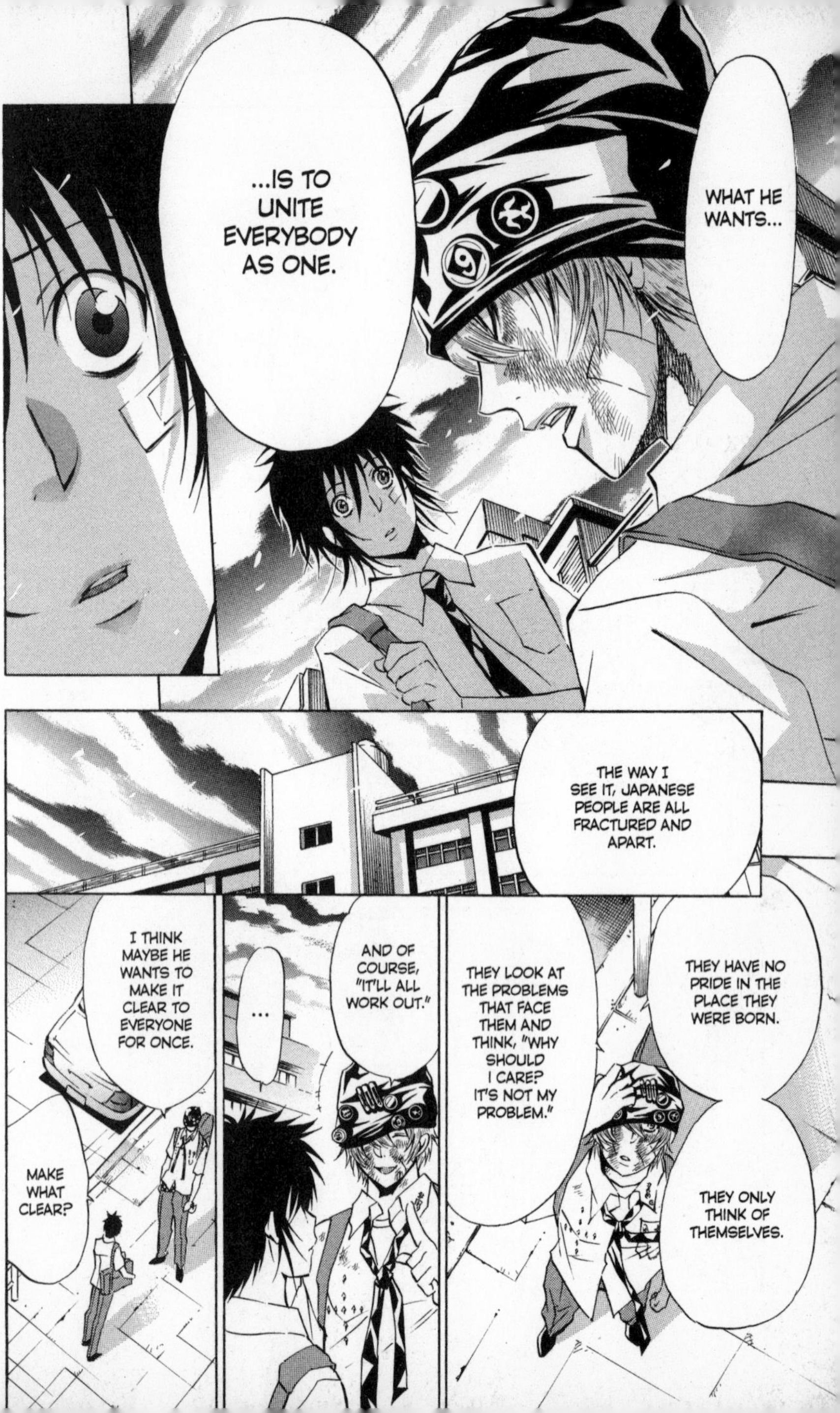
WHAT HE WANTS...
...IS TO UNITE EVERYBODY AS ONE.
THE WAY I SEE IT, JAPANESE PEOPLE ARE ALL FRACTURED AND APART.
THEY HAVE NO PRIDE IN THE PLACE THEY WERE BORN.
THEY LOOK AT THE PROBLEMS THAT FACE THEM AND THINK, "WHY SHOULD I CARE? IT'S NOT MY PROBLEM."
THEY ONLY THINK OF THEMSELVES.
AND OF COURSE, "IT'LL ALL WORK OUT."
...
I THINK MAYBE HE WANTS TO MAKE IT CLEAR TO EVERYONE FOR ONCE.
MAKE WHAT CLEAR?

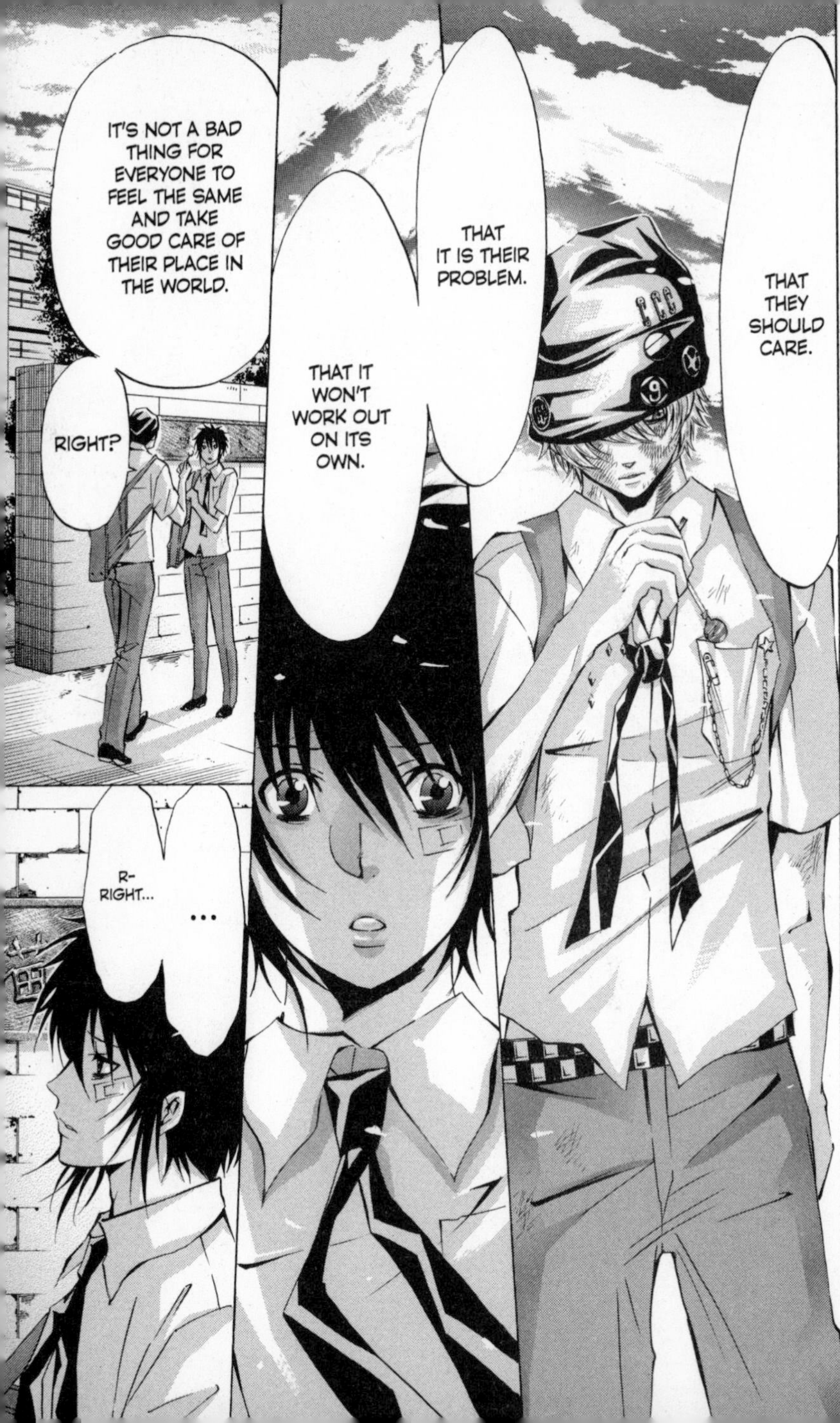
THAT THEY SHOULD CARE.
THAT IT IS THEIR PROBLEM.
THAT IT WON'T WORK OUT ON ITS OWN.
IT'S NOT A BAD THING FOR EVERYONE TO FEEL THE SAME AND TAKE GOOD CARE OF THEIR PLACE IN THE WORLD.
RIGHT?
R- RIGHT...
...

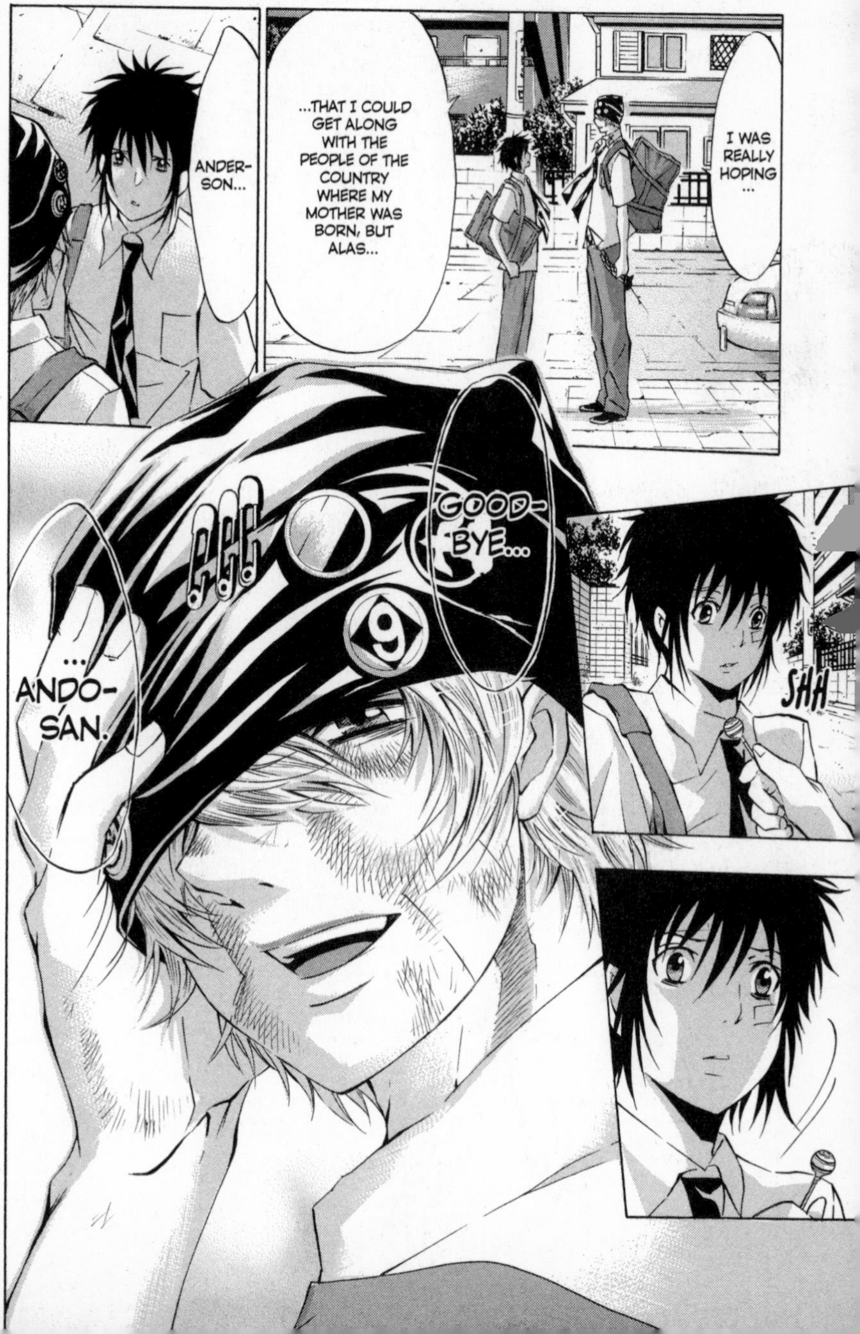
I WAS REALLY HOPING ...
...THAT I COULD GET ALONG WITH THE PEOPLE OF THE COUNTRY WHERE MY MOTHER WAS BORN, BUT ALAS...
ANDER-SON...
SHH
GOOD-BYE...
... ANDO-SAN.

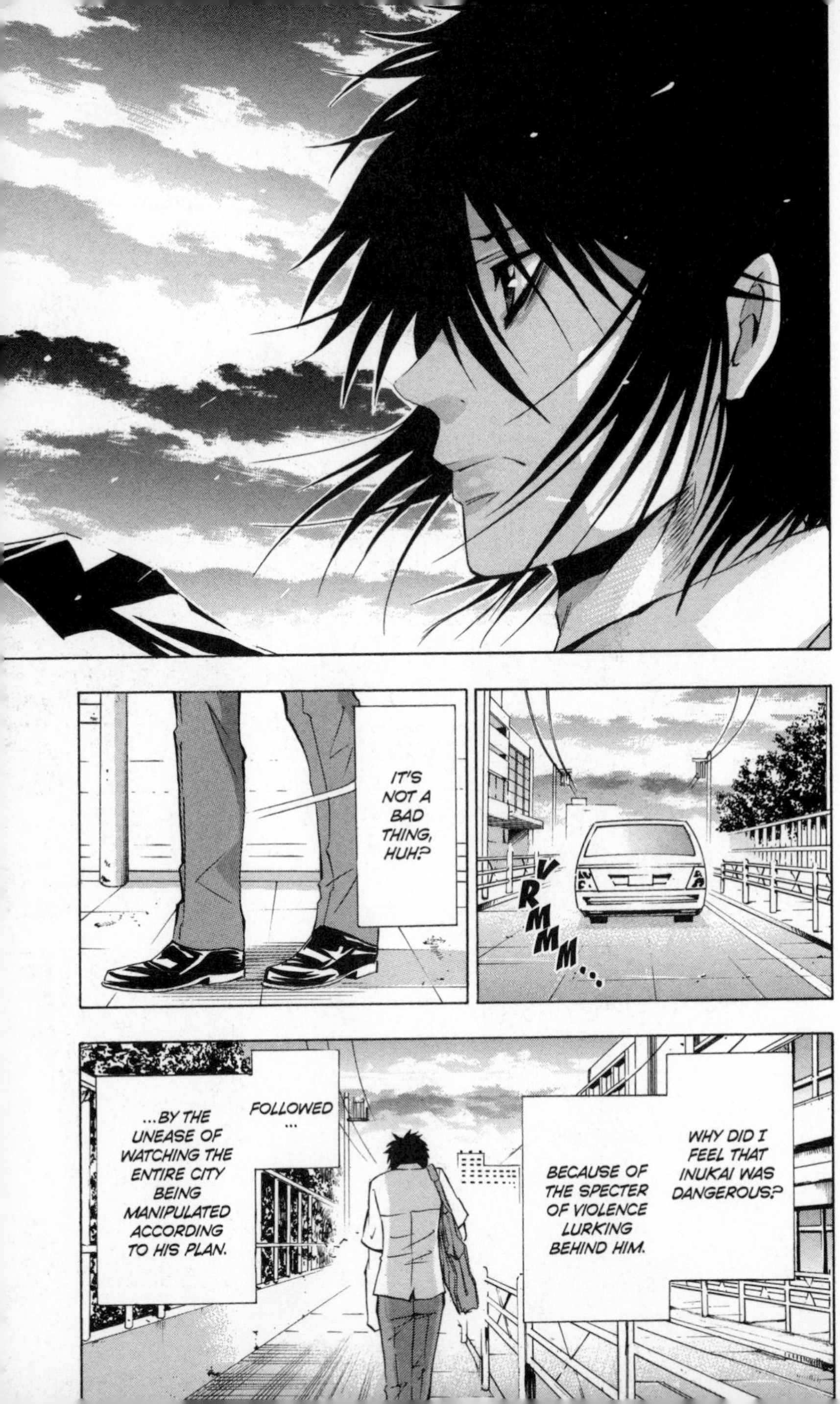
VRMMM...
IT'S NOT A BAD THING, HUH?
WHY DID I FEEL THAT INUKAI WAS DANGEROUS?
BECAUSE OF THE SPECTER OF VIOLENCE LURKING BEHIND HIM.
FOLLOWED ...
...BY THE UNEASE OF WATCHING THE ENTIRE CITY BEING MANIPULATED ACCORDING TO HIS PLAN.

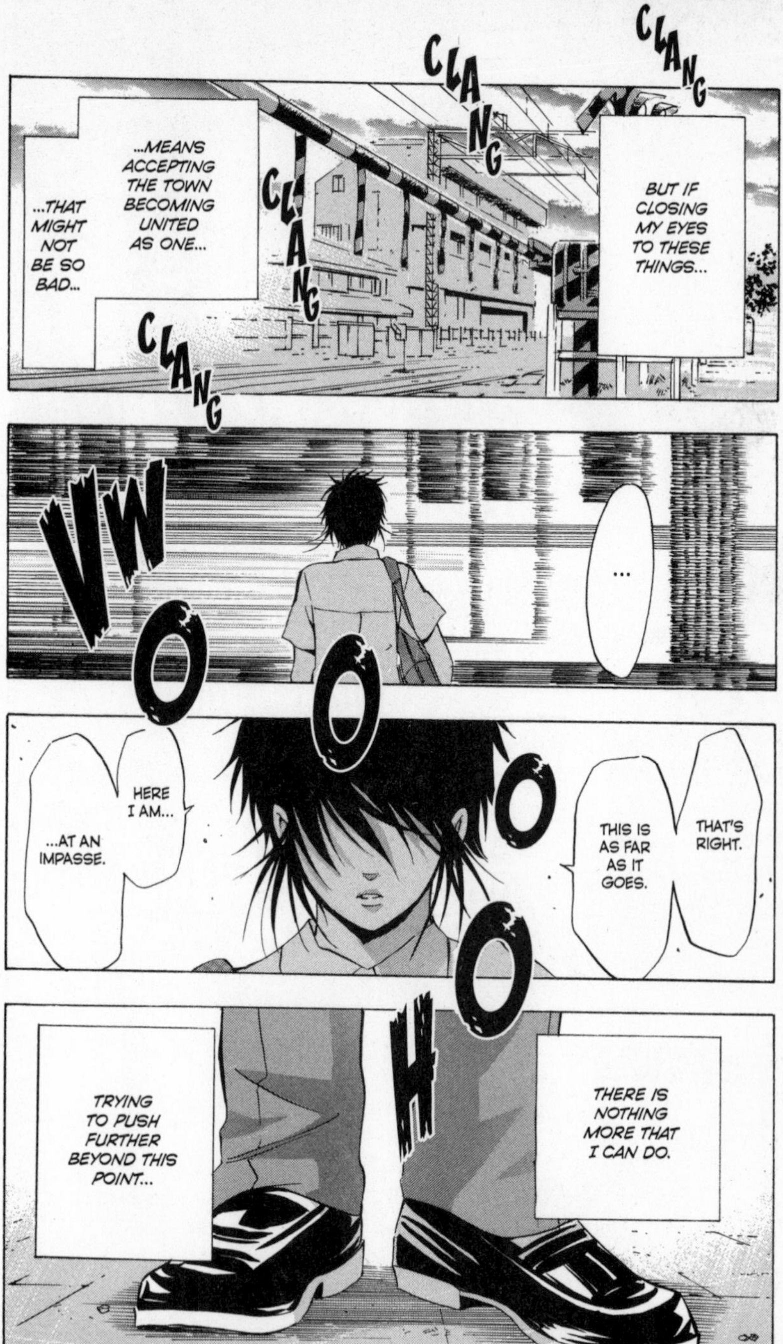
CLANG
CLANG
BUT IF CLOSING MY EYES TO THESE THINGS...
CLANG
...MEANS ACCEPTING THE TOWN BECOMING UNITED AS ONE...
...THAT MIGHT NOT BE SO BAD...
CLANG
...
VWOOOOOH
THAT'S RIGHT.
THIS IS AS FAR AS IT GOES.
HERE I AM...
...AT AN IMPASSE.
THERE IS NOTHING MORE THAT I CAN DO.
TRYING TO PUSH FURTHER BEYOND THIS POINT...

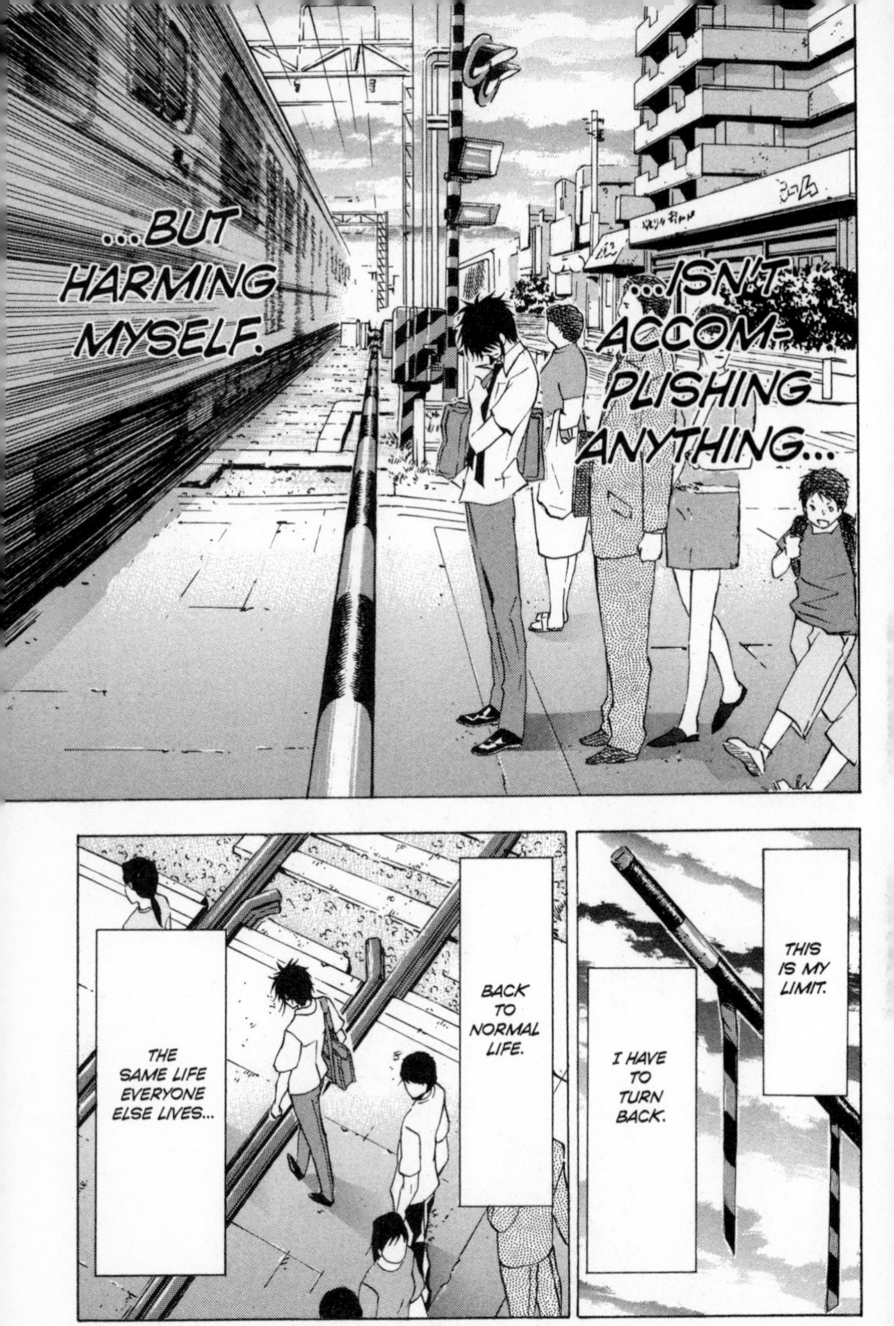
...BUT HARMING MYSELF.
...ISN'T ACCOM-PLISHING ANYTHING...
THIS IS MY LIMIT.
I HAVE TO TURN BACK.
BACK TO NORMAL LIFE.
THE SAME LIFE EVERYONE ELSE LIVES...

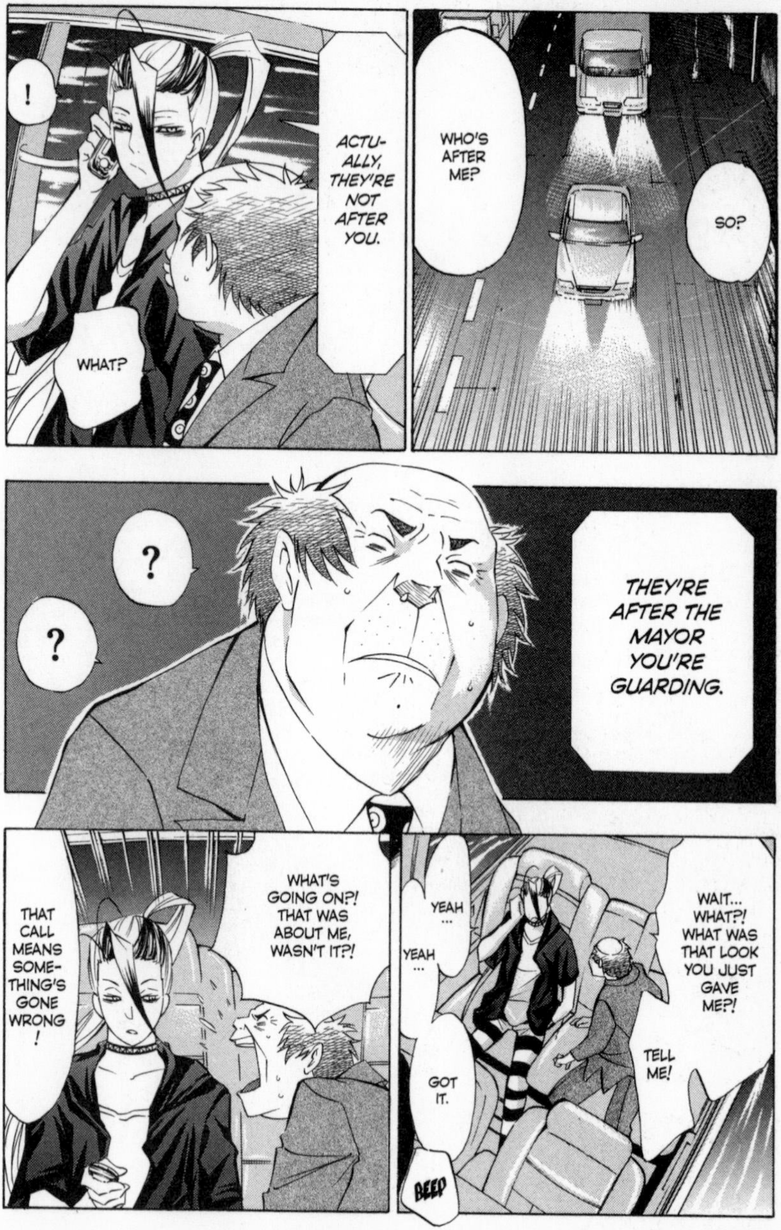
SO?
WHO'S AFTER ME?
ACTUALLY, THEY'RE NOT AFTER YOU.
!
WHAT?
THEY'RE AFTER THE MAYOR YOU'RE GUARDING.
?
?
WAIT... WHAT?! WHAT WAS THAT LOOK YOU JUST GAVE ME?!
TELL ME!
YEAH...
YEAH...
GOT IT.
BEEP
WHAT'S GOING ON?! THAT WAS ABOUT ME, WASN'T IT?!
THAT CALL MEANS SOMETHING'S GONE WRONG!

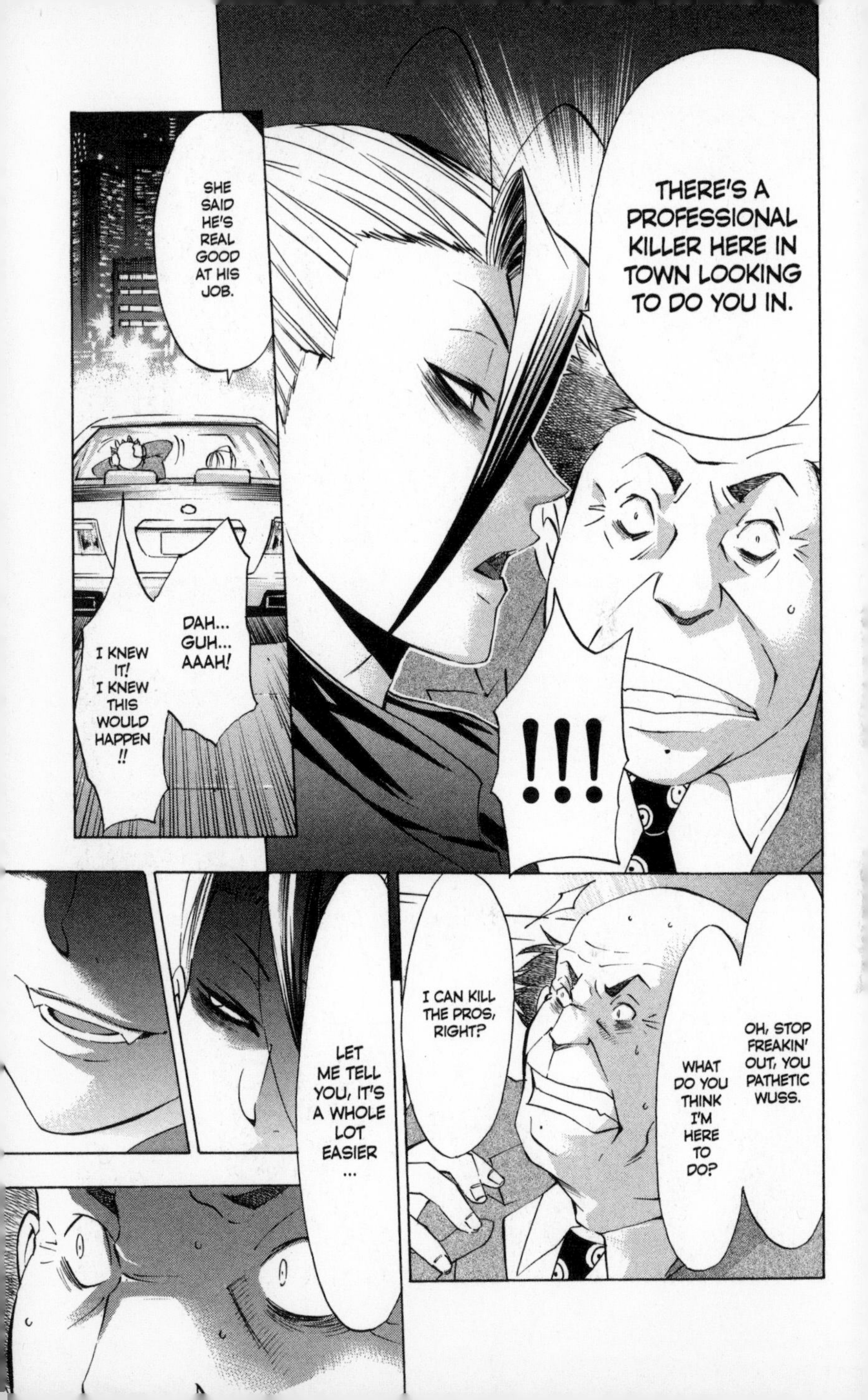
THERE'S A PROFESSIONAL KILLER HERE IN TOWN LOOKING TO DO YOU IN.
!!!
SHE SAID HE'S REAL GOOD AT HIS JOB.
DAH... GUH... AAAH!
I KNEW IT! I KNEW THIS WOULD HAPPEN!!
OH, STOP FREAKIN' OUT, YOU PATHETIC WUSS.
WHAT DO YOU THINK I'M HERE TO DO?
I CAN KILL THE PROS, RIGHT?
LET ME TELL YOU, IT'S A WHOLE LOT EASIER...

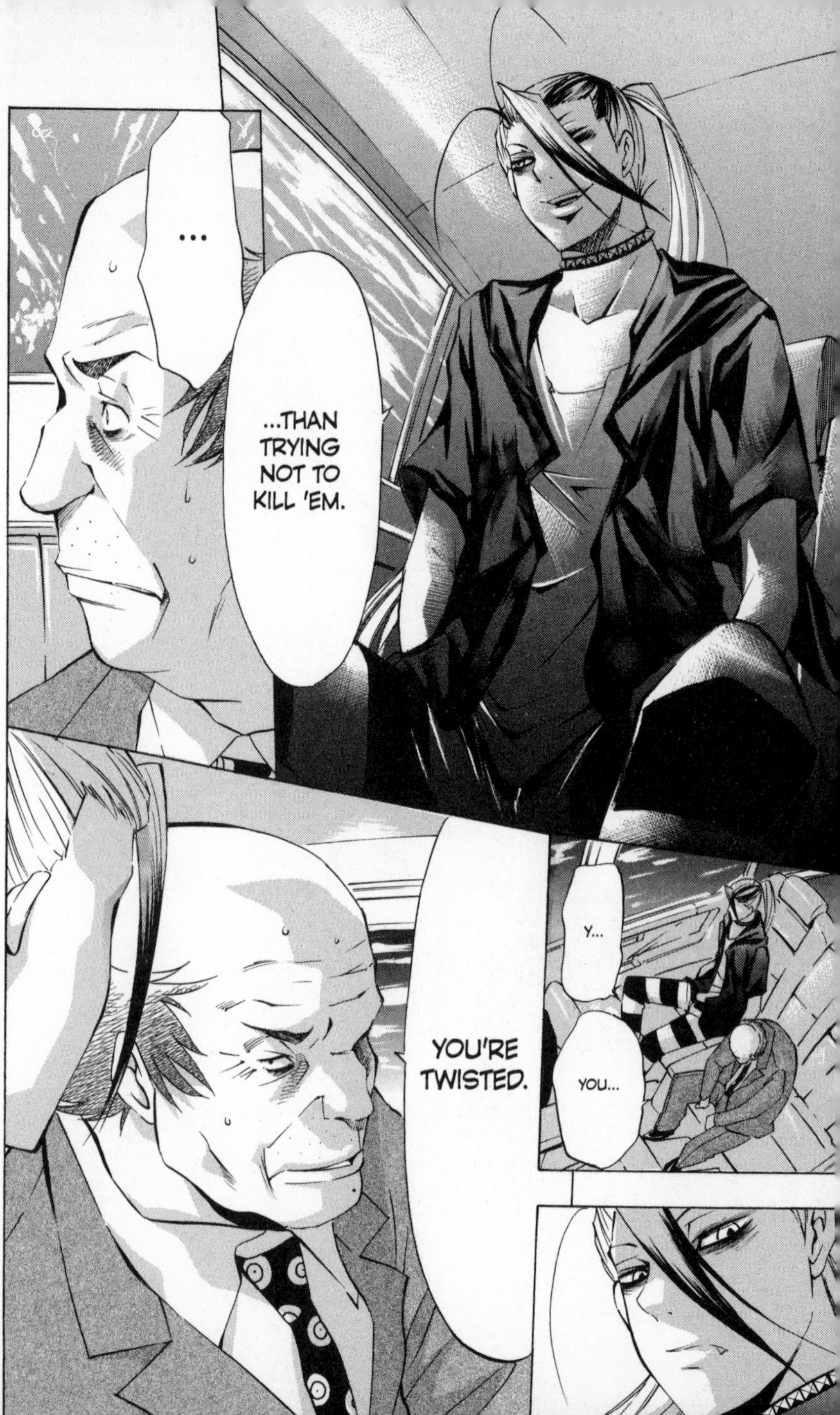
...THAN TRYING NOT TO KILL 'EM.
...
Y...
YOU...
YOU'RE TWISTED.

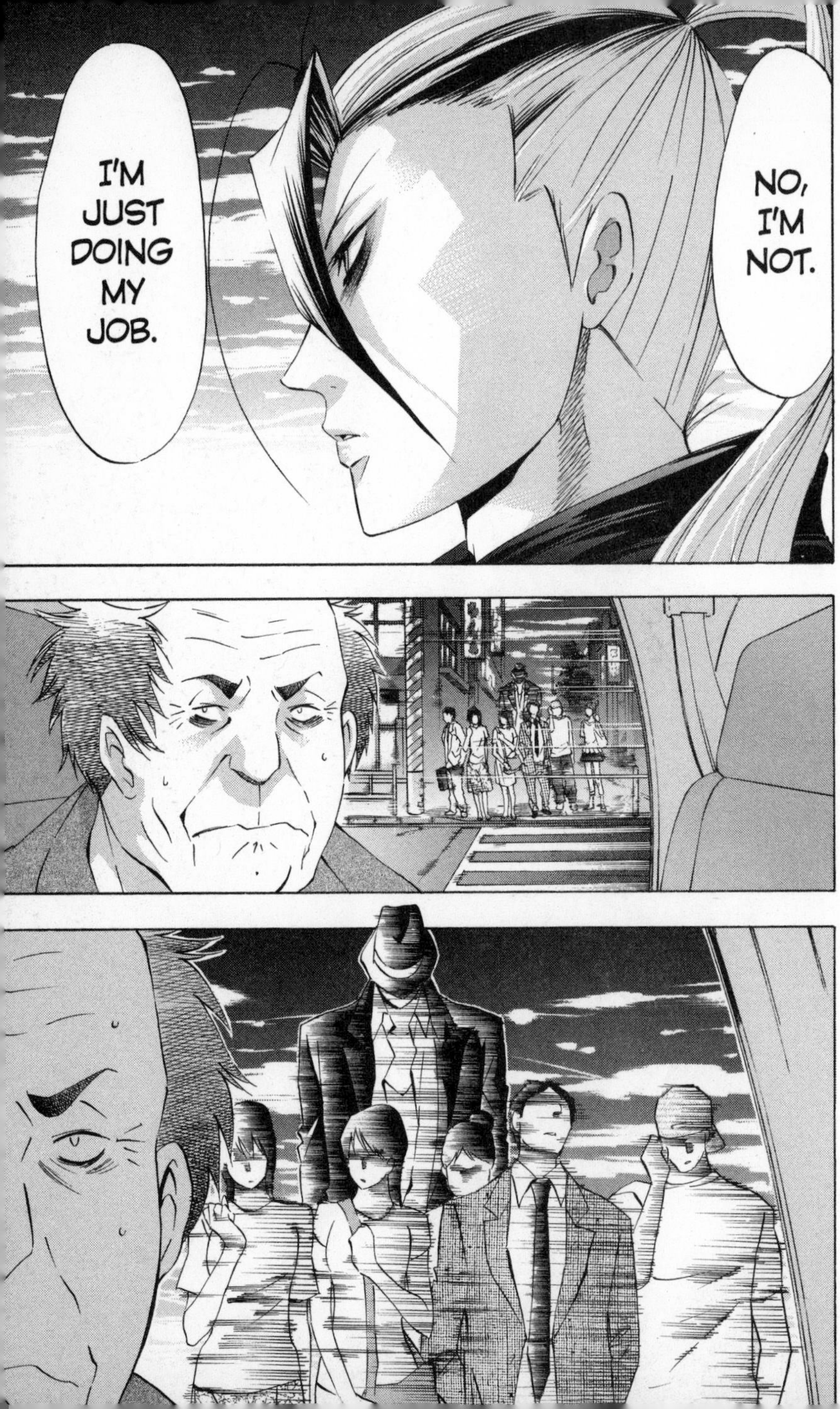
NO, I'M NOT.
I'M JUST DOING MY JOB.

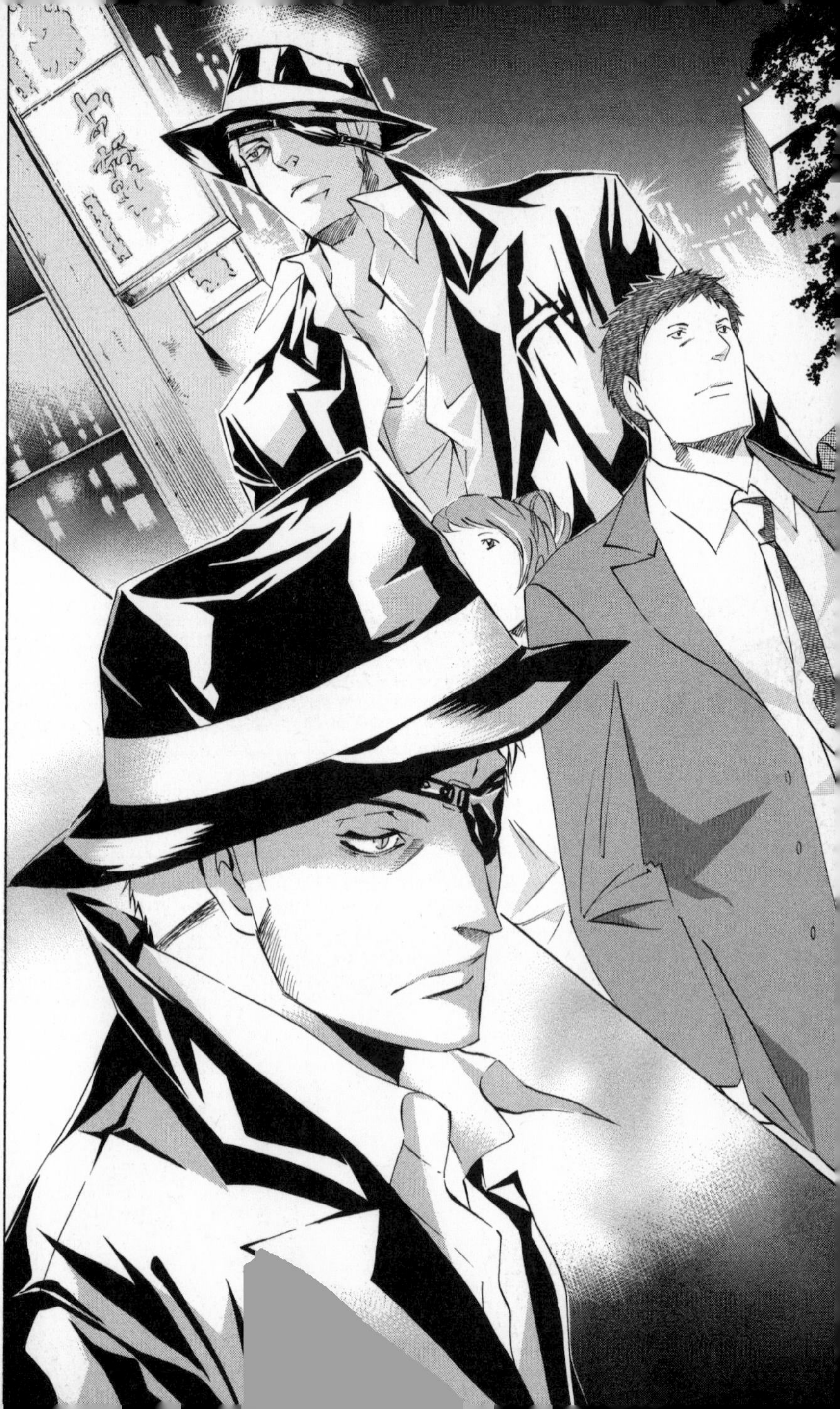

Chapter 37 The Future Before My Eyes

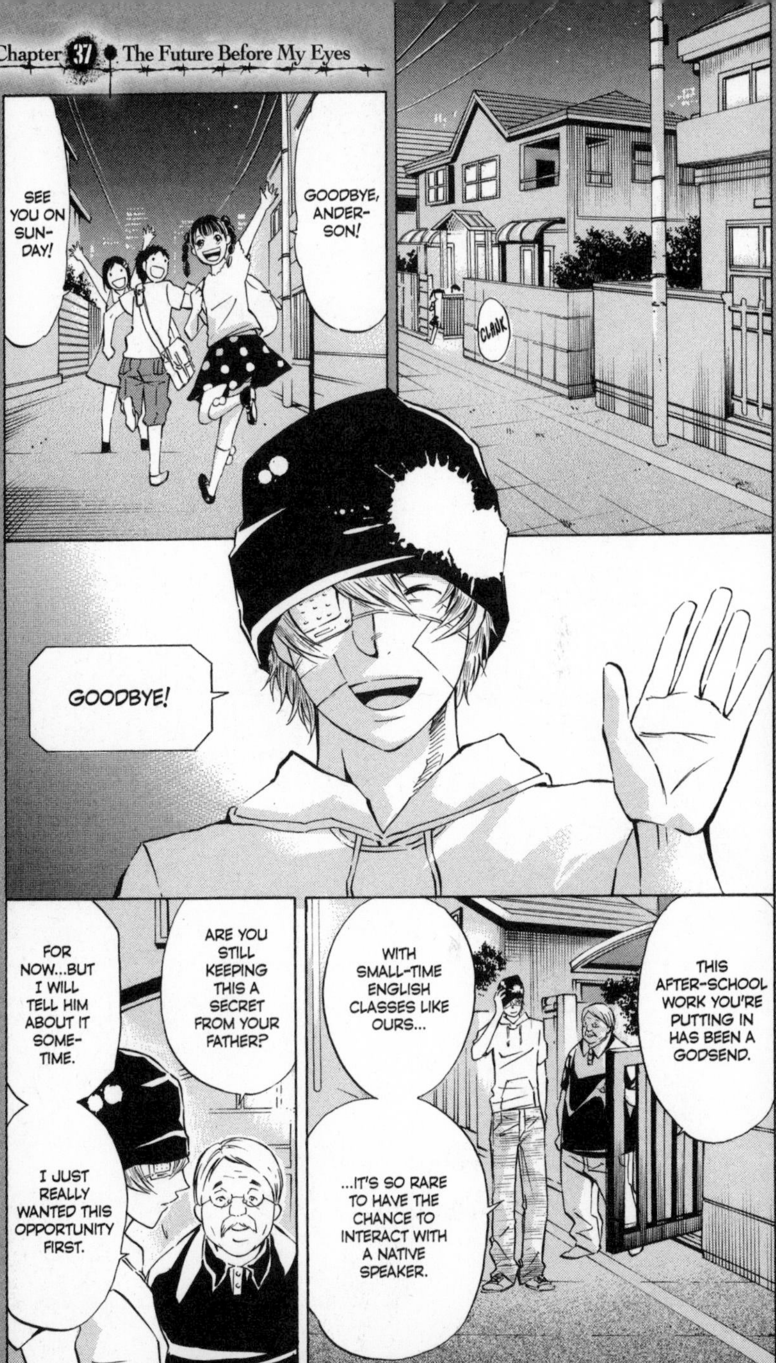
CLANK
GOODBYE, ANDER-SON!
SEE YOU ON SUN-DAY!
GOODBYE!
THIS AFTER-SCHOOL WORK YOU'RE PUTTING IN HAS BEEN A GODSEND.
WITH SMALL-TIME ENGLISH CLASSES LIKE OURS...
...IT'S SO RARE TO HAVE THE CHANCE TO INTERACT WITH A NATIVE SPEAKER.
ARE YOU STILL KEEPING THIS A SECRET FROM YOUR FATHER?
FOR NOW...BUT I WILL TELL HIM ABOUT IT SOME-TIME.
I JUST REALLY WANTED THIS OPPORTUNITY FIRST.

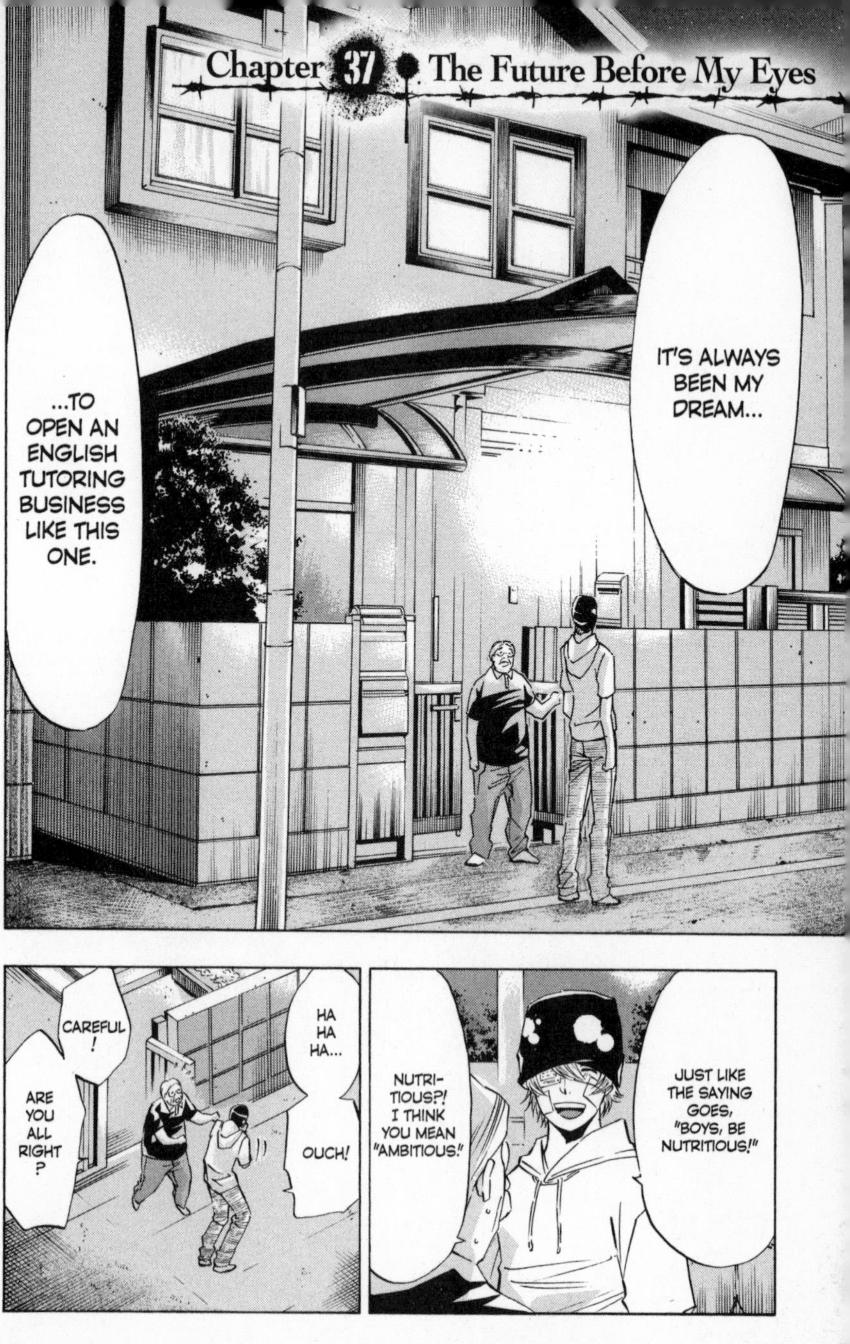
Chapter 37 The Future Before My Eyes
IT'S ALWAYS BEEN MY DREAM...
...TO OPEN AN ENGLISH TUTORING BUSINESS LIKE THIS ONE.
JUST LIKE THE SAYING GOES, "BOYS, BE NUTRITIOUS!"
NUTRI-TIOUS?! I THINK YOU MEAN "AMBITIOUS."
HA HA HA...
OUCH!
CAREFUL!
ARE YOU ALL RIGHT?

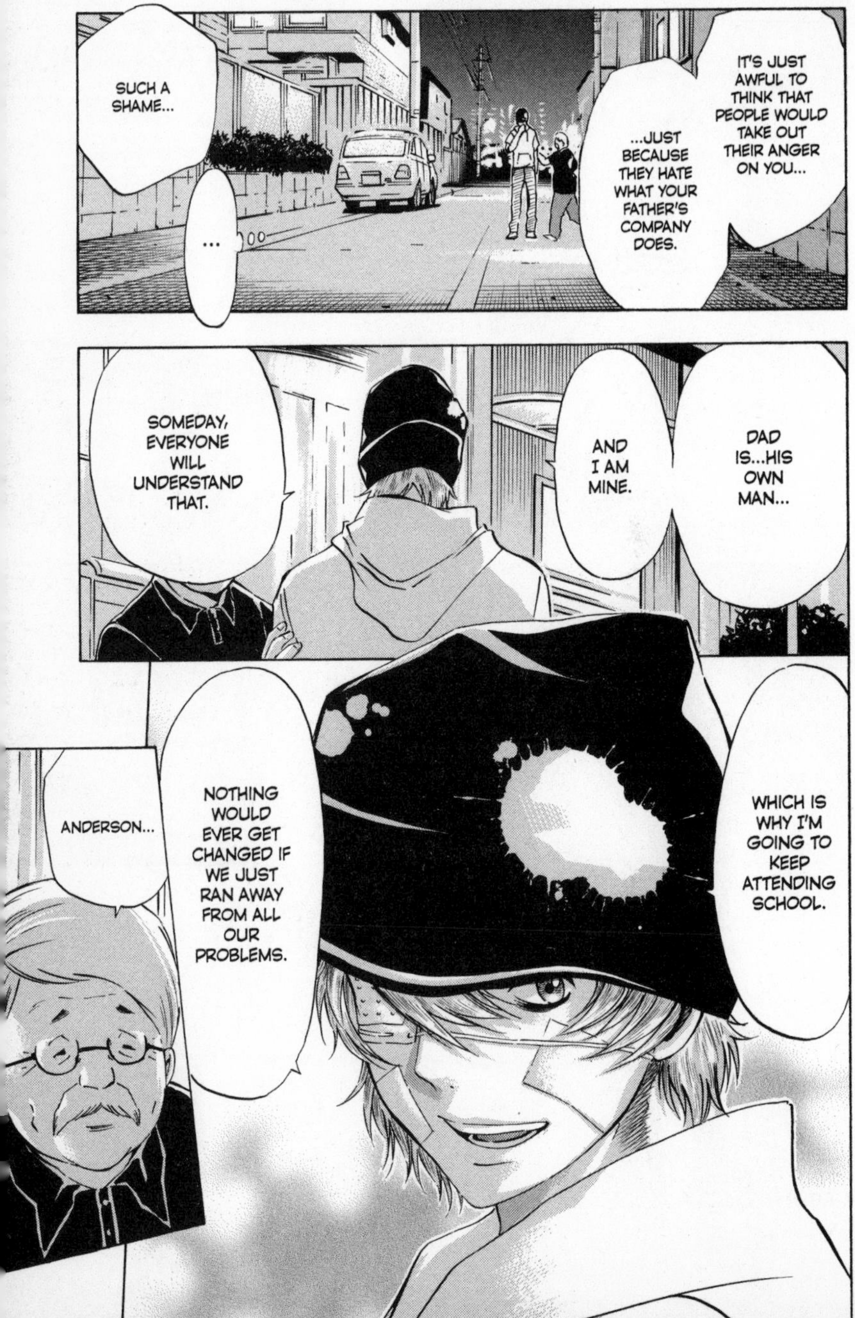
IT'S JUST AWFUL TO THINK THAT PEOPLE WOULD TAKE OUT THEIR ANGER ON YOU...
...JUST BECAUSE THEY HATE WHAT YOUR FATHER'S COMPANY DOES.
SUCH A SHAME...
...
DAD IS...HIS OWN MAN...
AND I AM MINE.
SOMEDAY, EVERYONE WILL UNDERSTAND THAT.
WHICH IS WHY I'M GOING TO KEEP ATTENDING SCHOOL.
NOTHING WOULD EVER GET CHANGED IF WE JUST RAN AWAY FROM ALL OUR PROBLEMS.
ANDERSON...

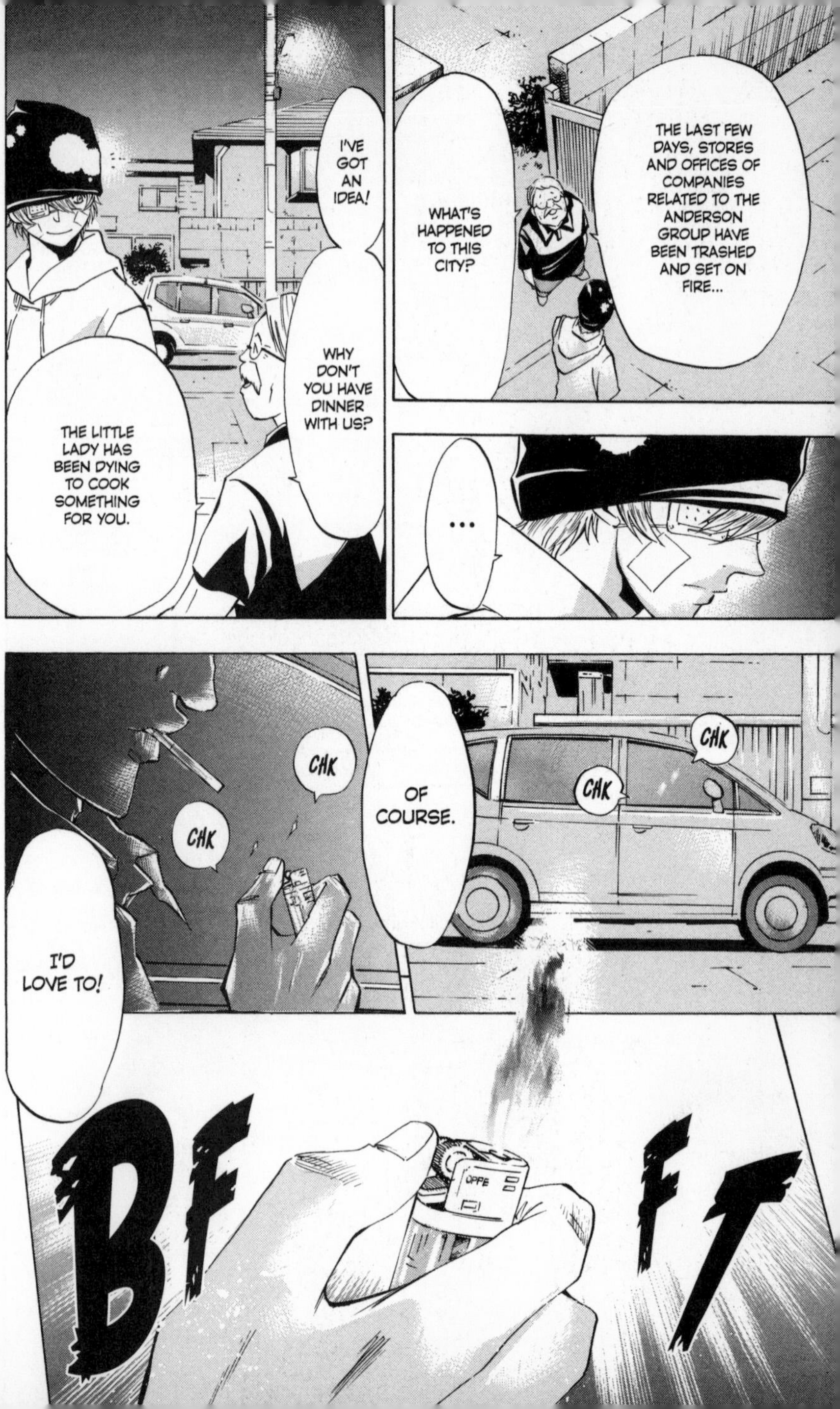
THE LAST FEW DAYS, STORES AND OFFICES OF COMPANIES RELATED TO THE ANDERSON GROUP HAVE BEEN TRASHED AND SET ON FIRE...
WHAT'S HAPPENED TO THIS CITY?
...
I'VE GOT AN IDEA!
WHY DON'T YOU HAVE DINNER WITH US?
THE LITTLE LADY HAS BEEN DYING TO COOK SOMETHING FOR YOU.
CHK
CHK
OF COURSE.
CHK
CHK
I'D LOVE TO!
BFFT

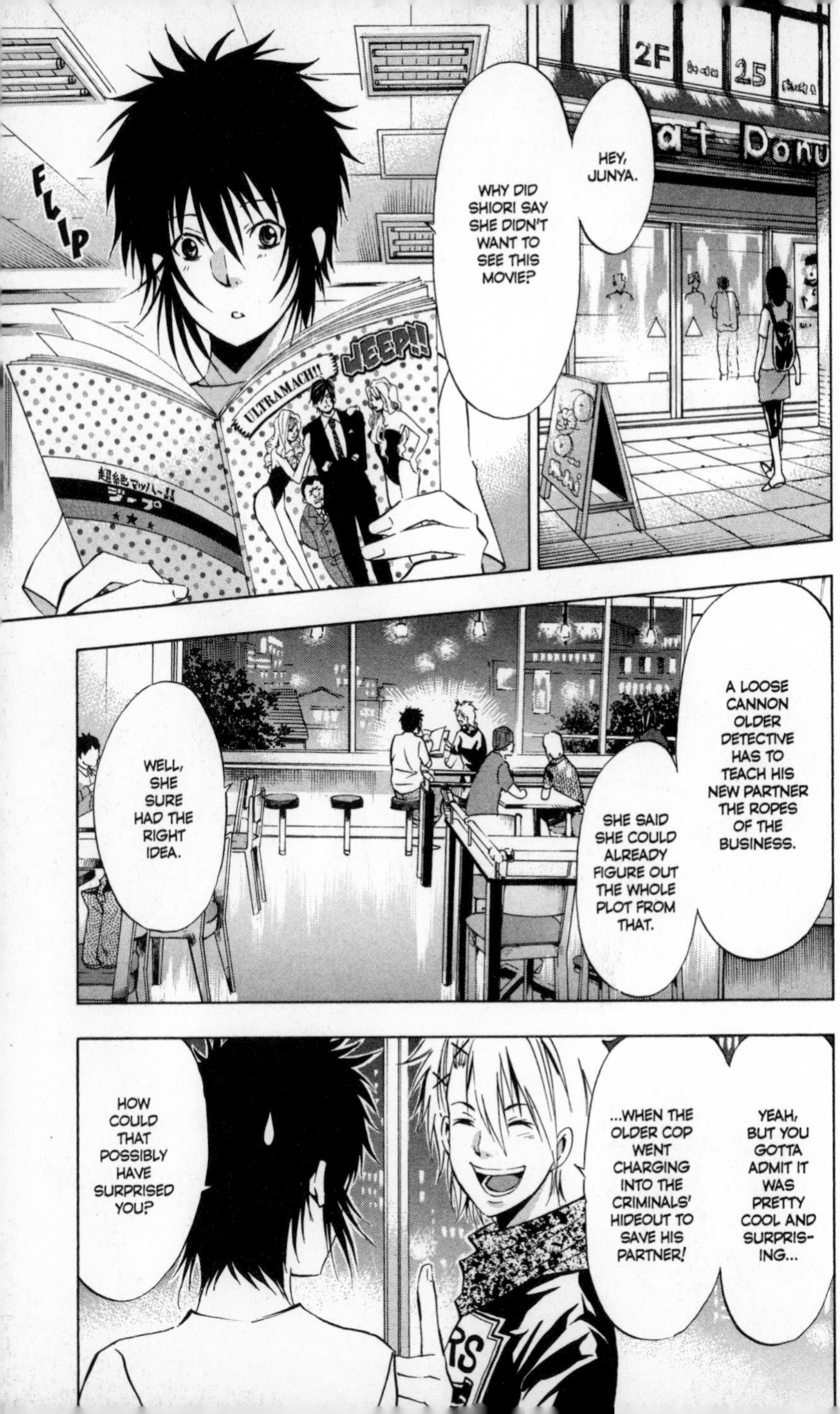
2F
25
HEY, JUNYA.
WHY DID SHIORI SAY SHE DIDN'T WANT TO SEE THIS MOVIE?
FLIP
JEEP!!
ULTRAMACH!!
超絶マッハ‼ ジープ
A LOOSE CANNON OLDER DETECTIVE HAS TO TEACH HIS NEW PARTNER THE ROPES OF THE BUSINESS.
SHE SAID SHE COULD ALREADY FIGURE OUT THE WHOLE PLOT FROM THAT.
WELL, SHE SURE HAD THE RIGHT IDEA.
YEAH, BUT YOU GOTTA ADMIT IT WAS PRETTY COOL AND SURPRIS-ING...
...WHEN THE OLDER COP WENT CHARGING INTO THE CRIMINALS' HIDEOUT TO SAVE HIS PARTNER!
HOW COULD THAT POSSIBLY HAVE SURPRISED YOU?

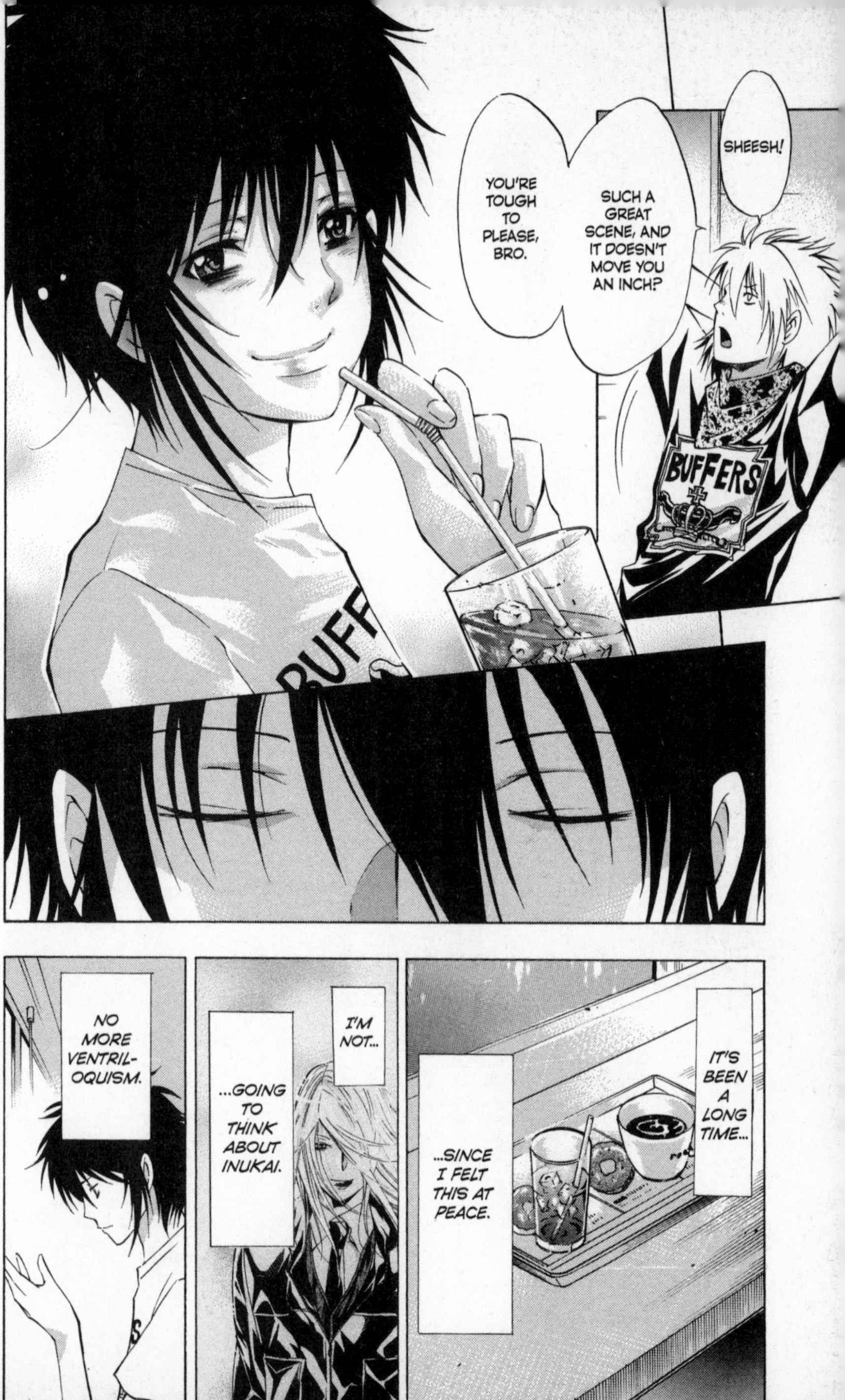
SHEESH!
SUCH A GREAT SCENE, AND IT DOESN'T MOVE YOU AN INCH?
YOU'RE TOUGH TO PLEASE, BRO.
IT'S BEEN A LONG TIME...
...SINCE I FELT THIS AT PEACE.
I'M NOT...
...GOING TO THINK ABOUT INUKAI.
NO MORE VENTRIL-OQUISM.

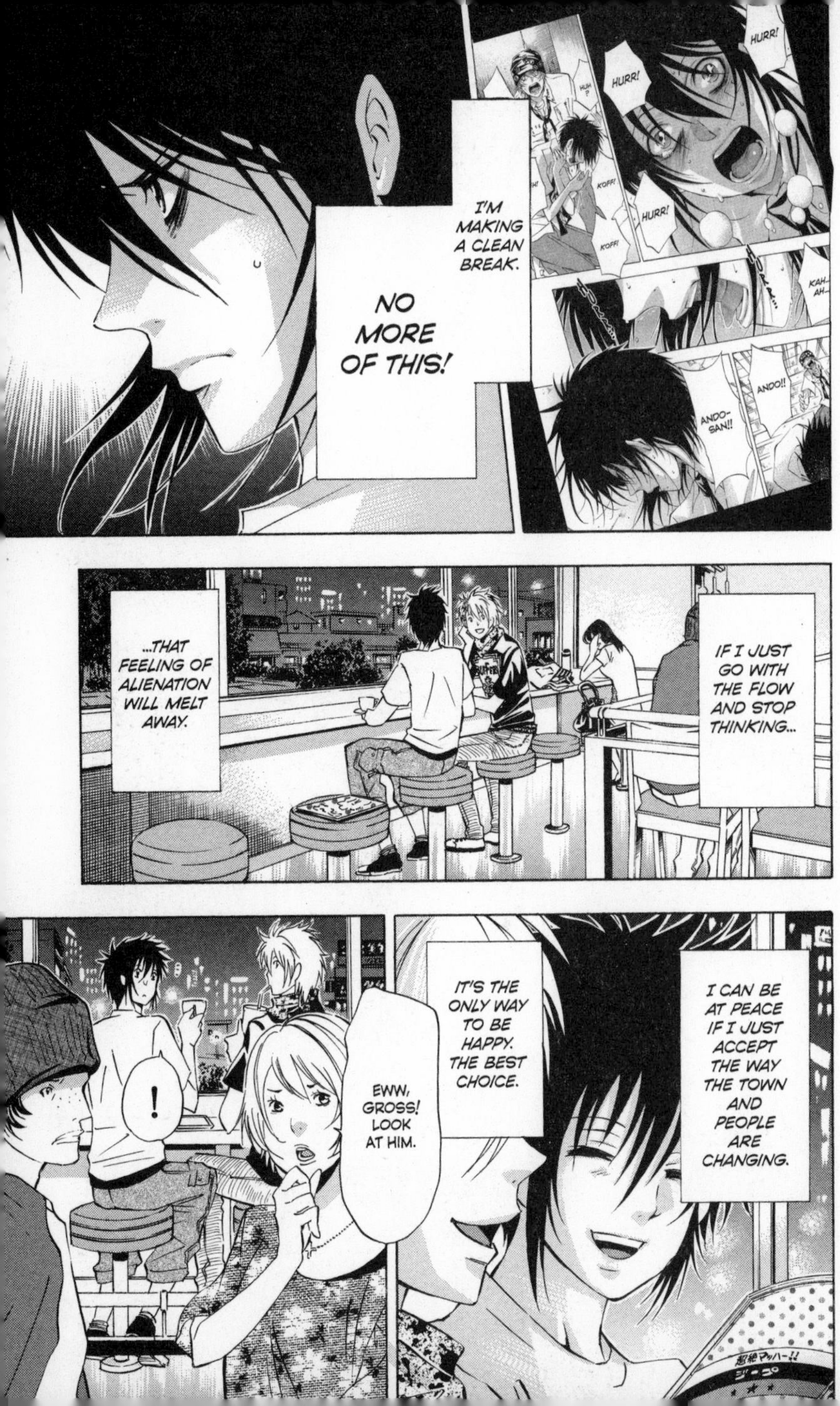
HURR!
HURR!
HUH?
KOFF!
HURR!
KOFF!
KAH... AH...
ANDO!!
ANDO-SAN!!
I'M MAKING A CLEAN BREAK.
NO MORE OF THIS!
IF I JUST GO WITH THE FLOW AND STOP THINKING...
...THAT FEELING OF ALIENATION WILL MELT AWAY.
I CAN BE AT PEACE IF I JUST ACCEPT THE WAY THE TOWN AND PEOPLE ARE CHANGING.
IT'S THE ONLY WAY TO BE HAPPY. THE BEST CHOICE.
超絶マッハー!!
EWW, GROSS! LOOK AT HIM.
!

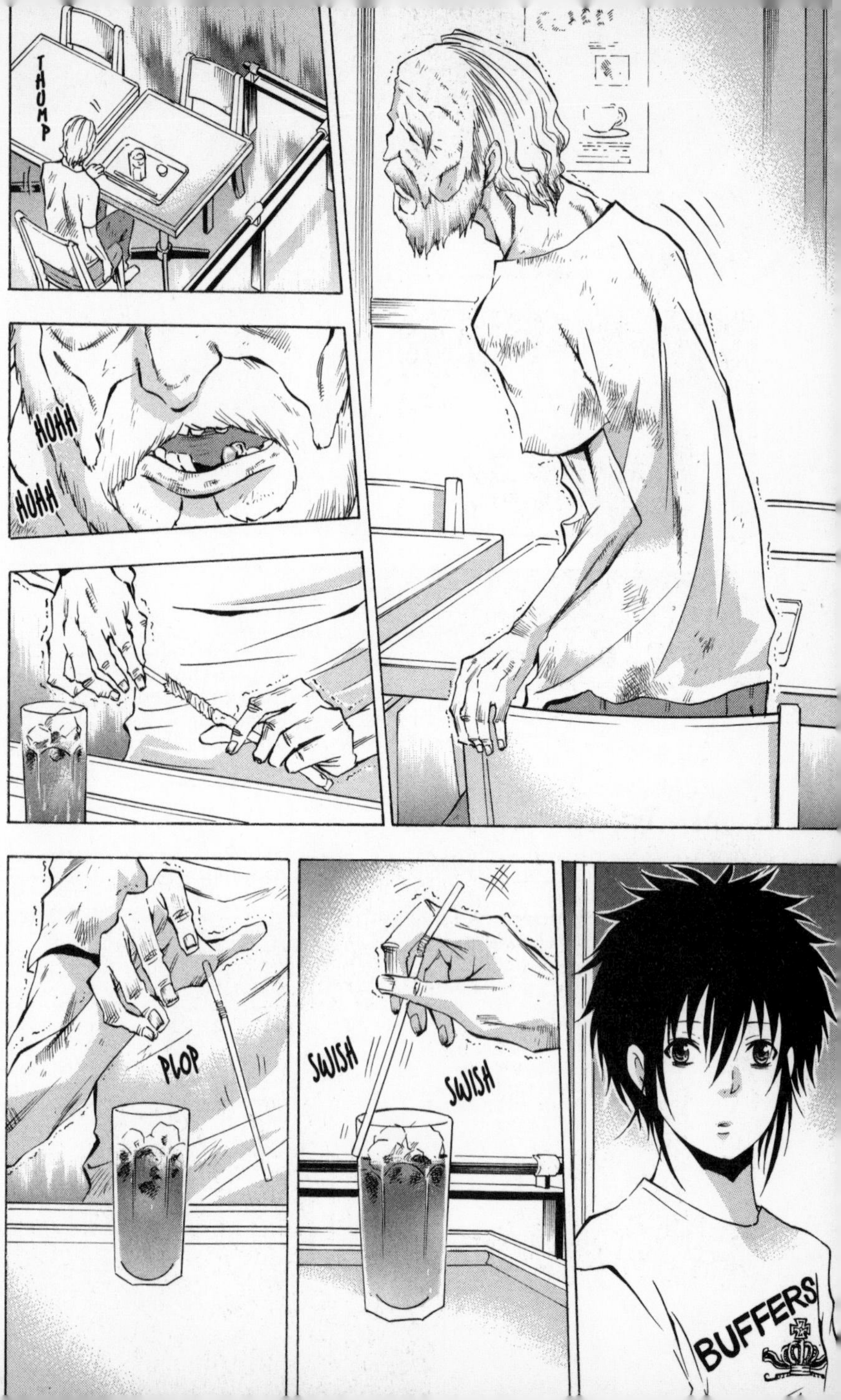
THUMP
HUHH
HUHH
BUFFERS
SWISH
SWISH
PLOP

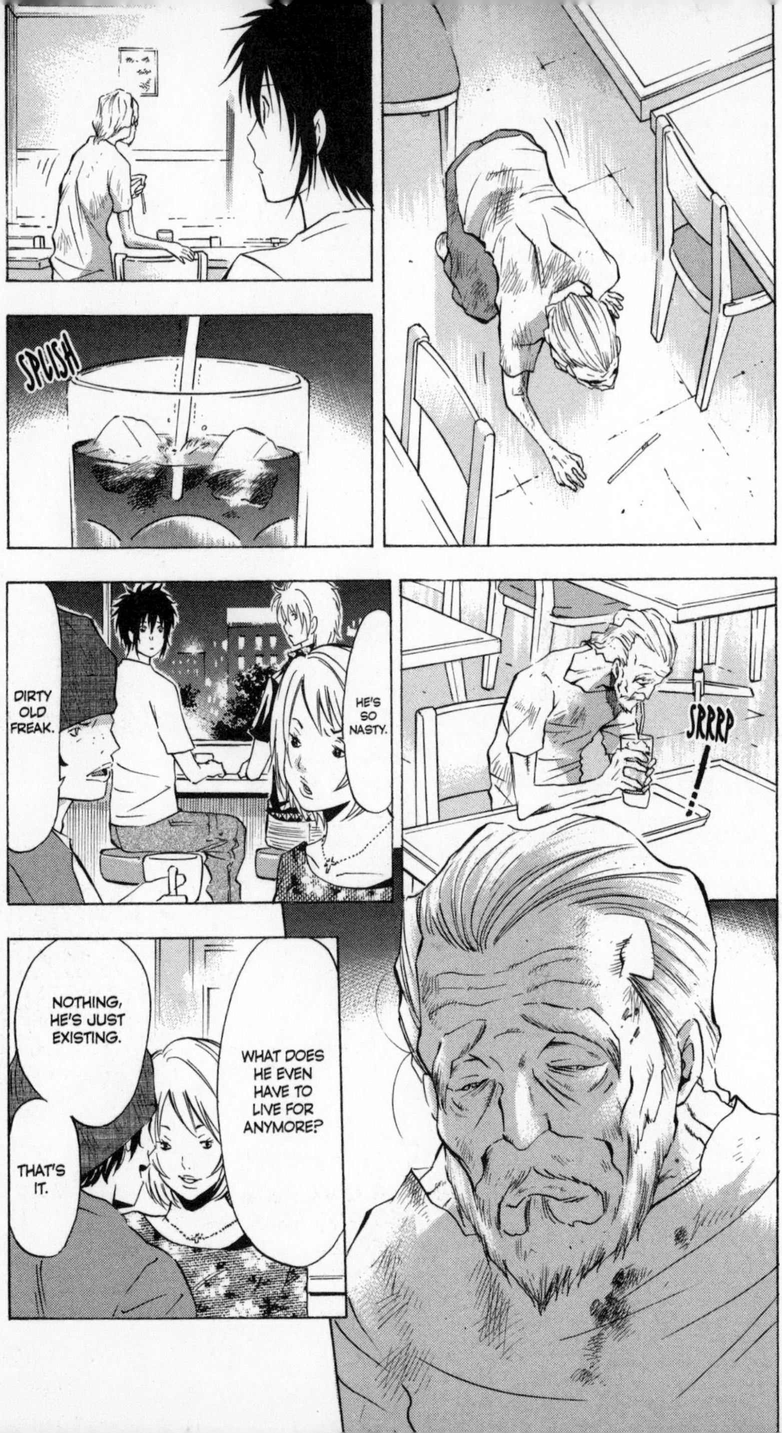
SPLISH
SRRRP
HE'S SO NASTY.
DIRTY OLD FREAK.
WHAT DOES HE EVEN HAVE TO LIVE FOR ANYMORE?
NOTHING, HE'S JUST EXISTING.
THAT'S IT.

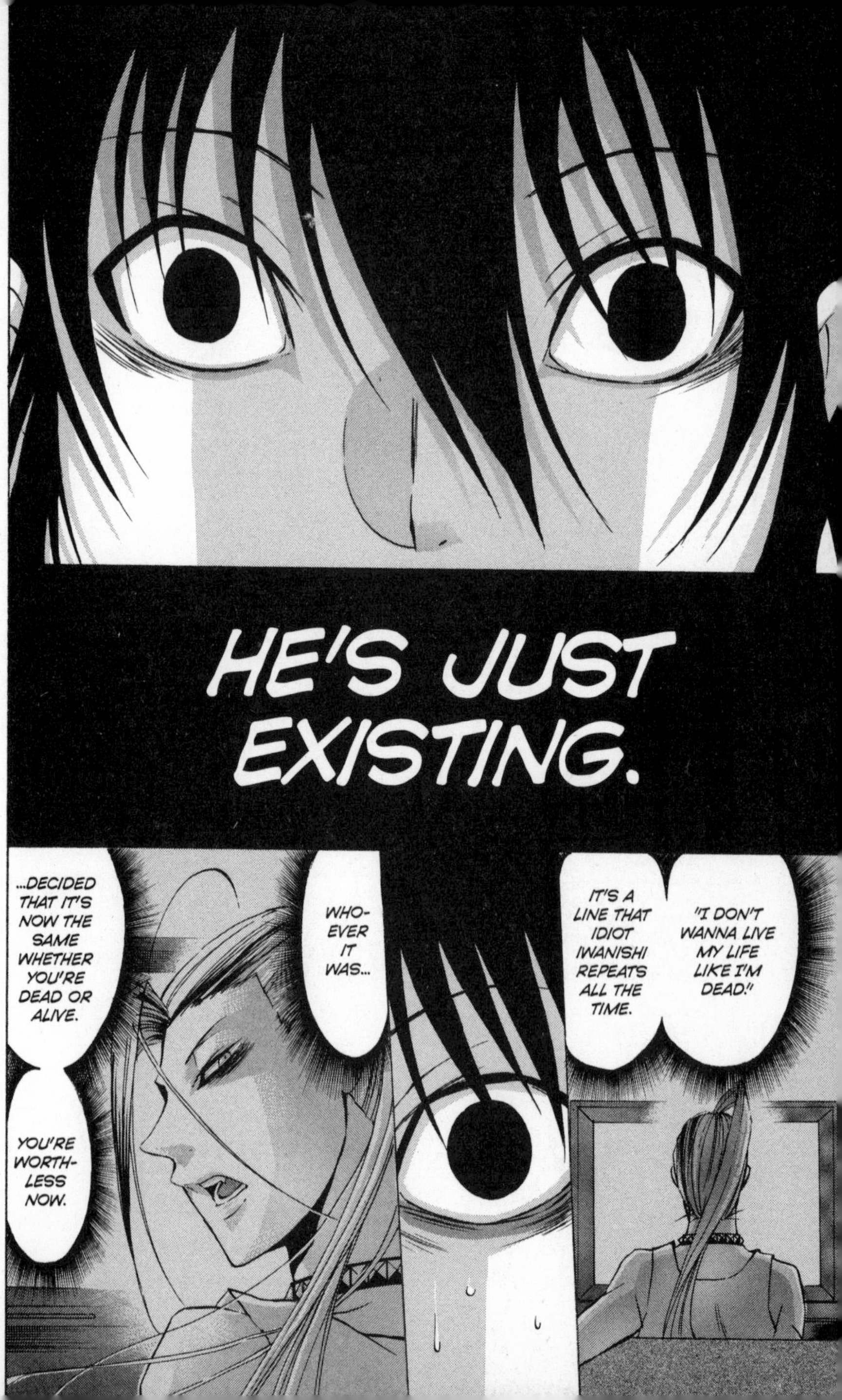
HE'S JUST EXISTING.
"I DON'T WANNA LIVE MY LIFE LIKE I'M DEAD."
IT'S A LINE THAT IDIOT IWANISHI REPEATS ALL THE TIME.
WHO-EVER IT WAS...
...DECIDED THAT IT'S NOW THE SAME WHETHER YOU'RE DEAD OR ALIVE.
YOU'RE WORTH-LESS NOW.

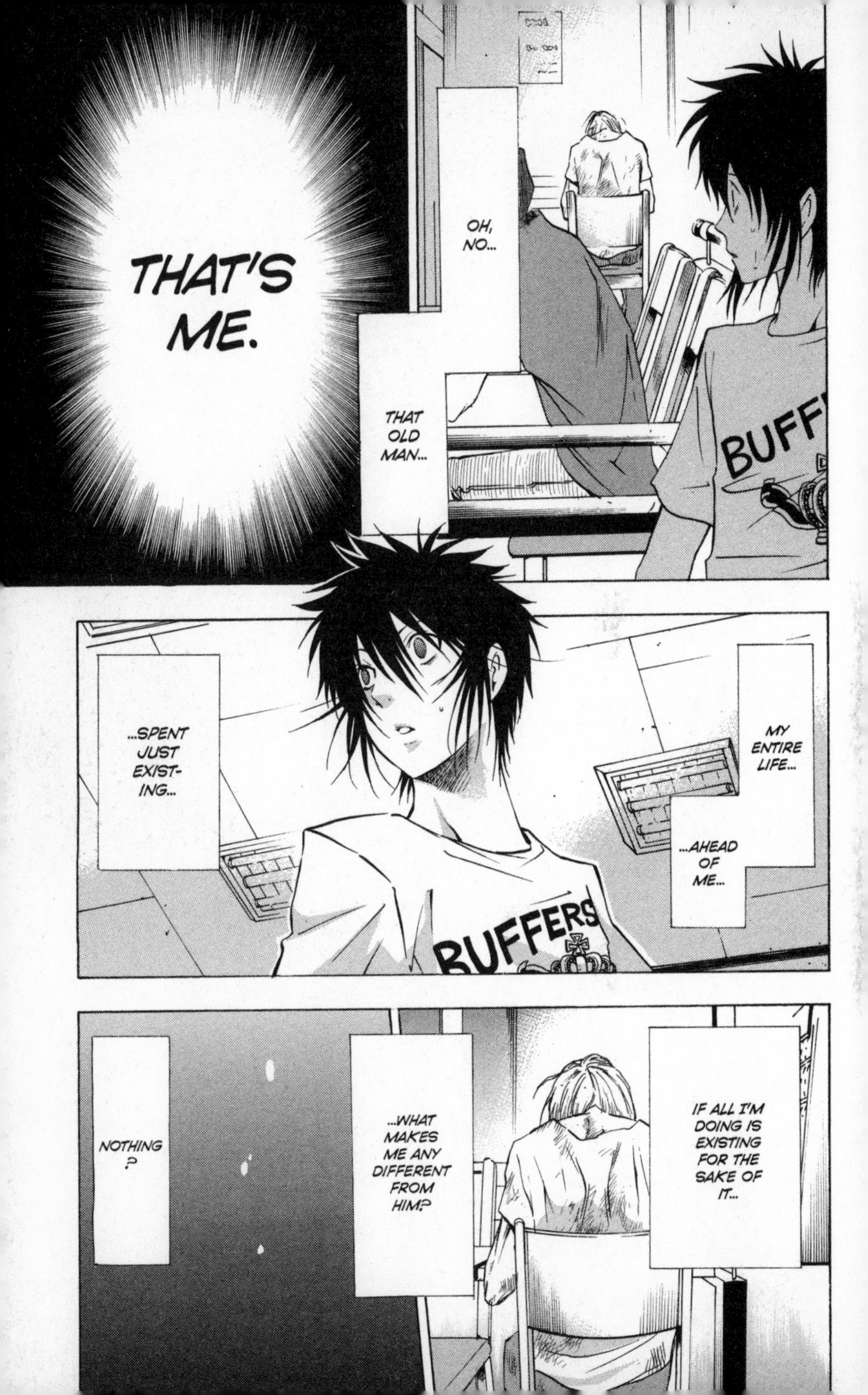
OH, NO...
THAT OLD MAN...
THAT'S ME.
MY ENTIRE LIFE...
...AHEAD OF ME...
...SPENT JUST EXIST-ING...
BUFFERS
IF ALL I'M DOING IS EXISTING FOR THE SAKE OF IT...
...WHAT MAKES ME ANY DIFFERENT FROM HIM?
NOTHING?

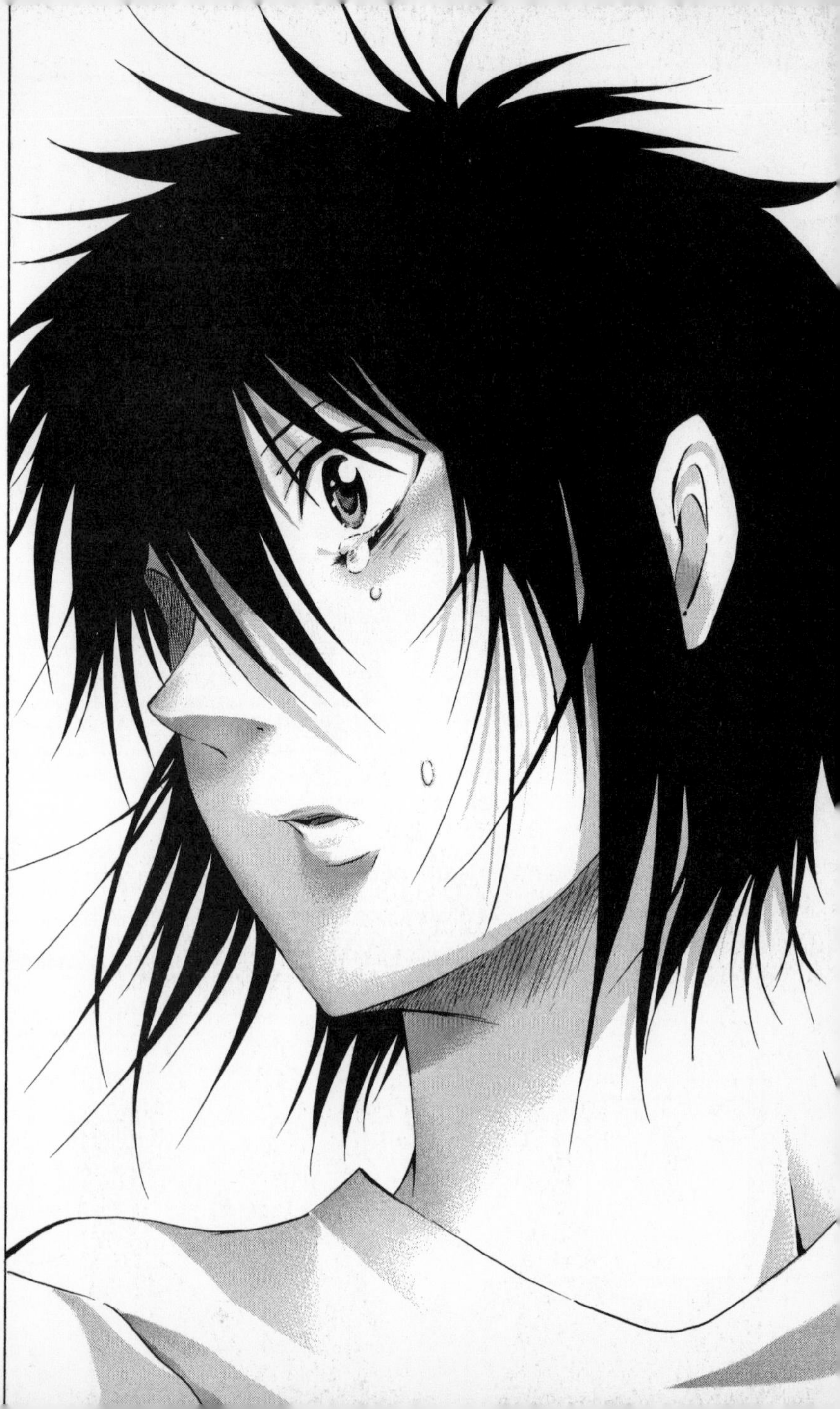

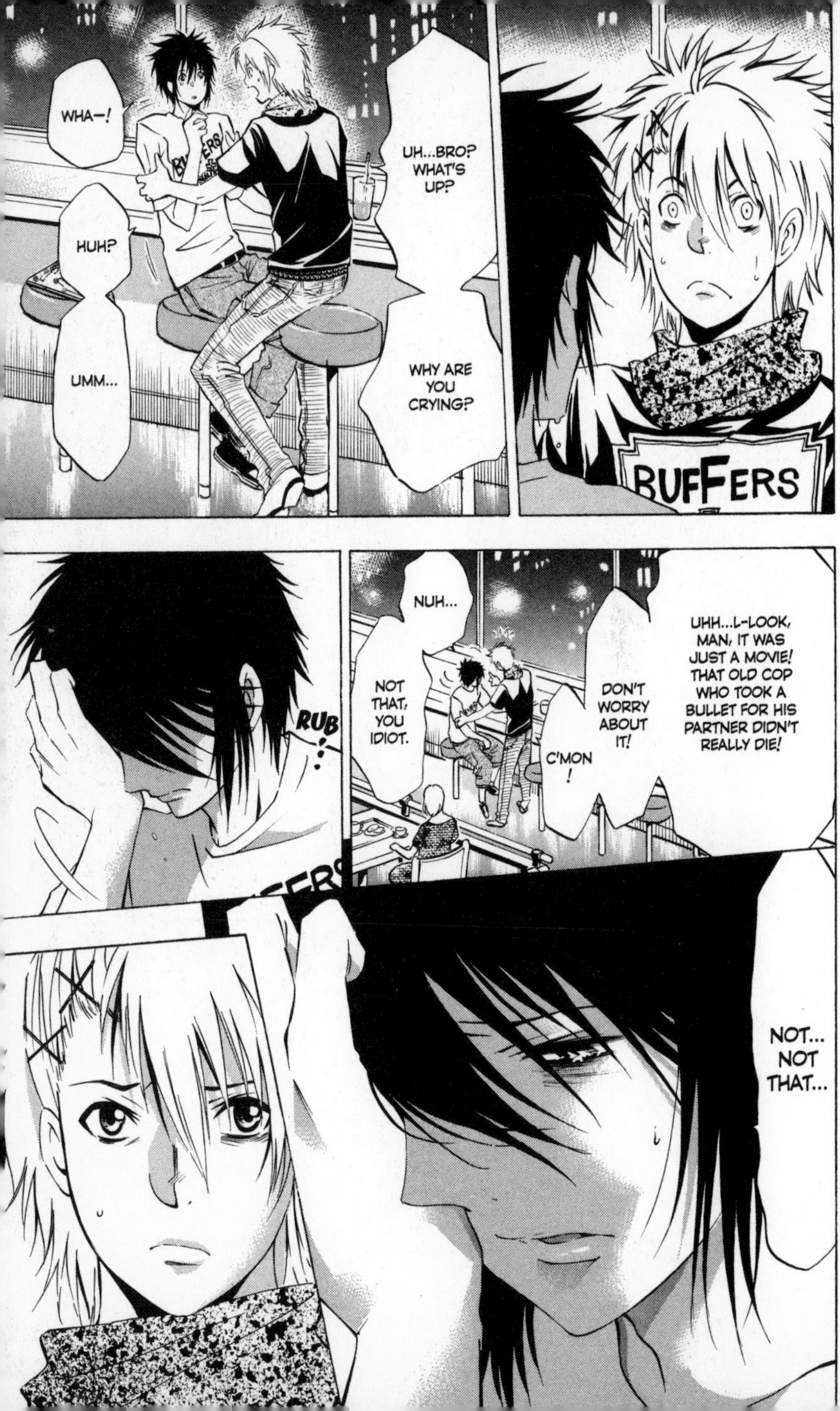
UH...BRO? WHAT'S UP?
WHY ARE YOU CRYING?
WHA–!
HUH?
UMM...
UHH...L-LOOK, MAN, IT WAS JUST A MOVIE! THAT OLD COP WHO TOOK A BULLET FOR HIS PARTNER DIDN'T REALLY DIE!
DON'T WORRY ABOUT IT!
C'MON!
NUH...
NOT THAT, YOU IDIOT.
RUB
NOT... NOT THAT...

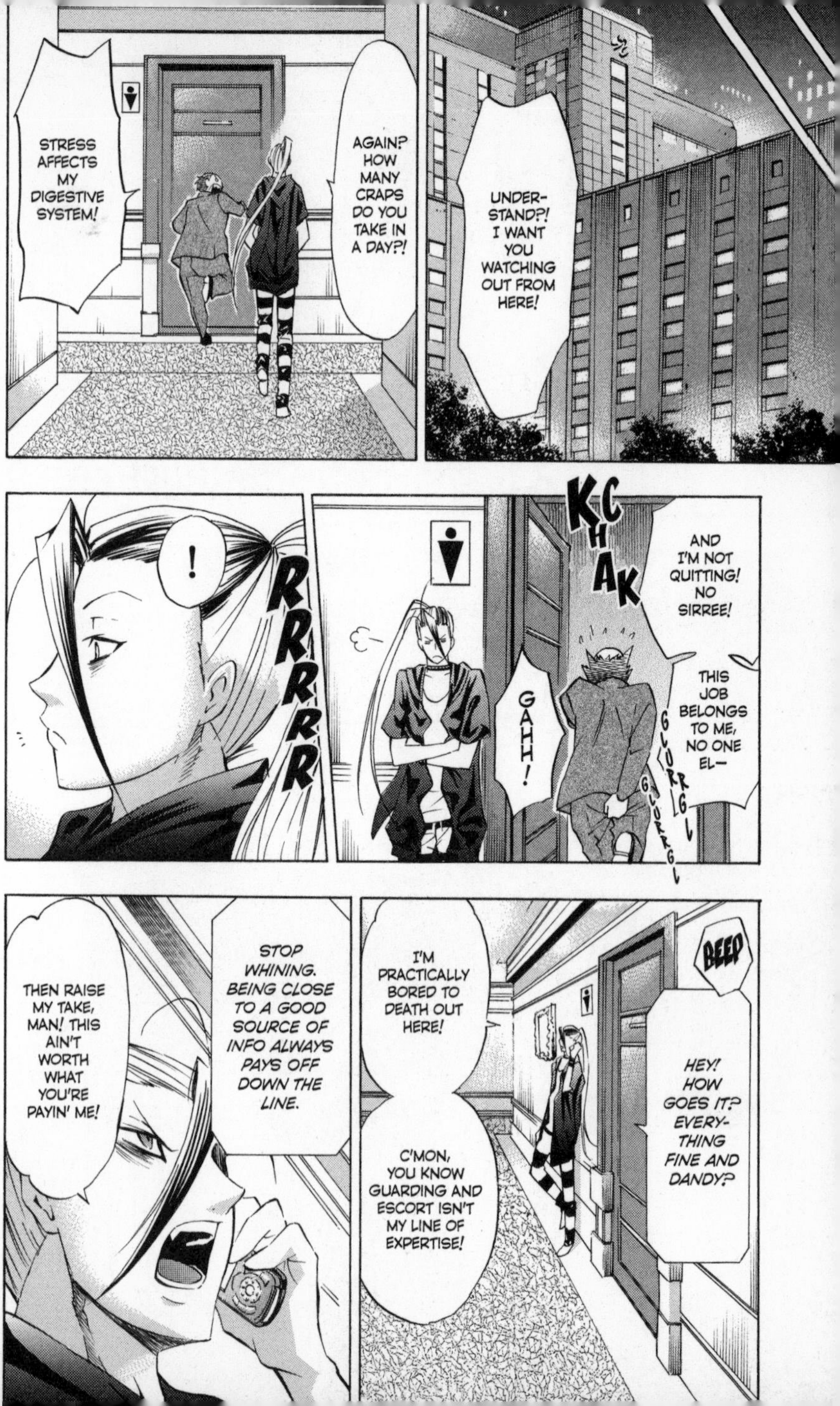
UNDER-STAND?! I WANT YOU WATCHING OUT FROM HERE!
AGAIN? HOW MANY CRAPS DO YOU TAKE IN A DAY?!
STRESS AFFECTS MY DIGESTIVE SYSTEM!
KCHAK
AND I'M NOT QUITTING! NO SIRREE!
THIS JOB BELONGS TO ME, NO ONE EL—
GLURRGL
GLURRGL
GAHH!
!
RRRRRR
BEEP
HEY! HOW GOES IT? EVERY-THING FINE AND DANDY?
I'M PRACTICALLY BORED TO DEATH OUT HERE!
C'MON, YOU KNOW GUARDING AND ESCORT ISN'T MY LINE OF EXPERTISE!
STOP WHINING. BEING CLOSE TO A GOOD SOURCE OF INFO ALWAYS PAYS OFF DOWN THE LINE.
THEN RAISE MY TAKE, MAN! THIS AIN'T WORTH WHAT YOU'RE PAYIN' ME!

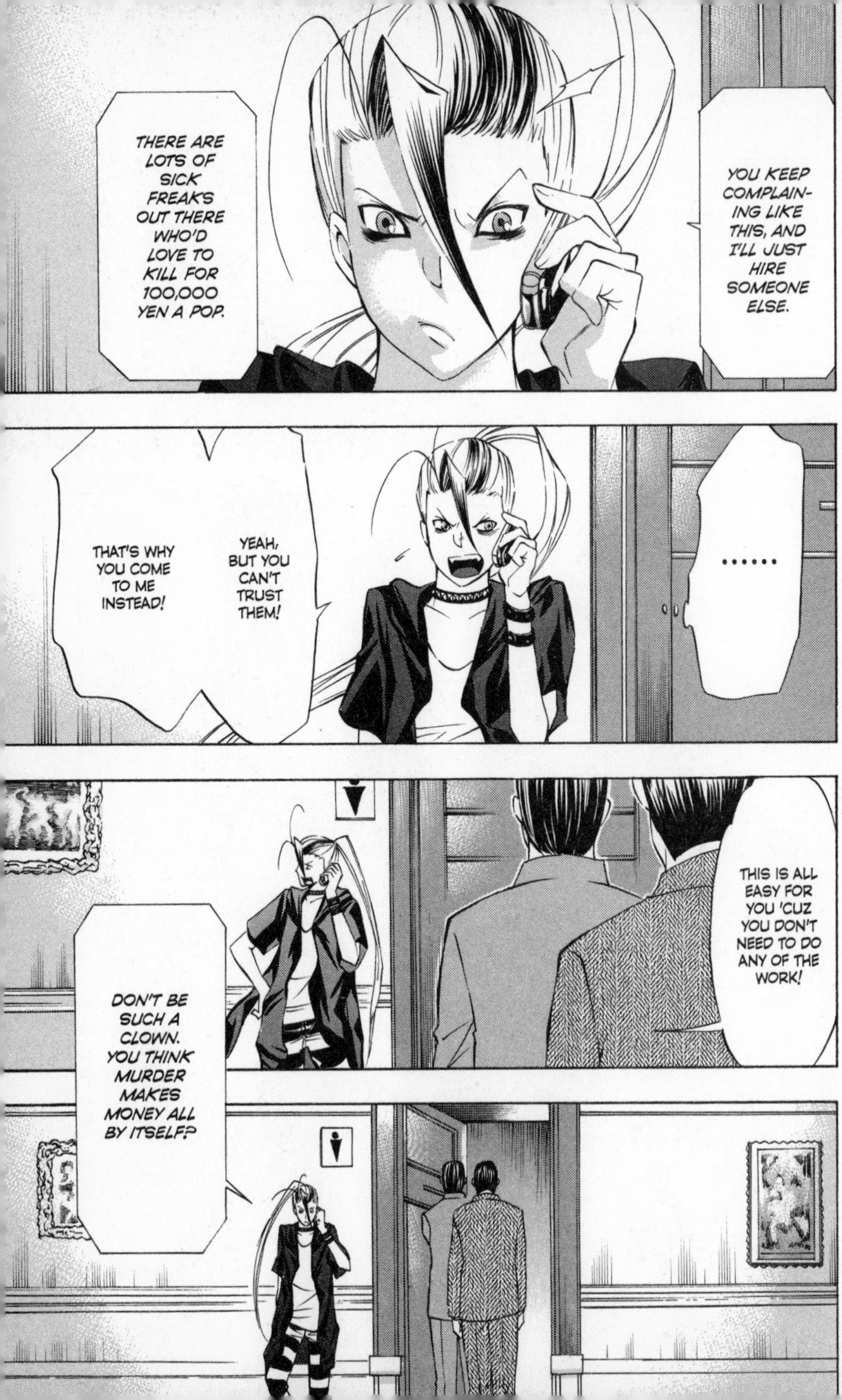
YOU KEEP COMPLAINING LIKE THIS, AND I'LL JUST HIRE SOMEONE ELSE.
THERE ARE LOTS OF SICK FREAKS OUT THERE WHO'D LOVE TO KILL FOR 100,000 YEN A POP.
......
YEAH, BUT YOU CAN'T TRUST THEM!
THAT'S WHY YOU COME TO ME INSTEAD!
THIS IS ALL EASY FOR YOU 'CUZ YOU DON'T NEED TO DO ANY OF THE WORK!
DON'T BE SUCH A CLOWN. YOU THINK MURDER MAKES MONEY ALL BY ITSELF?

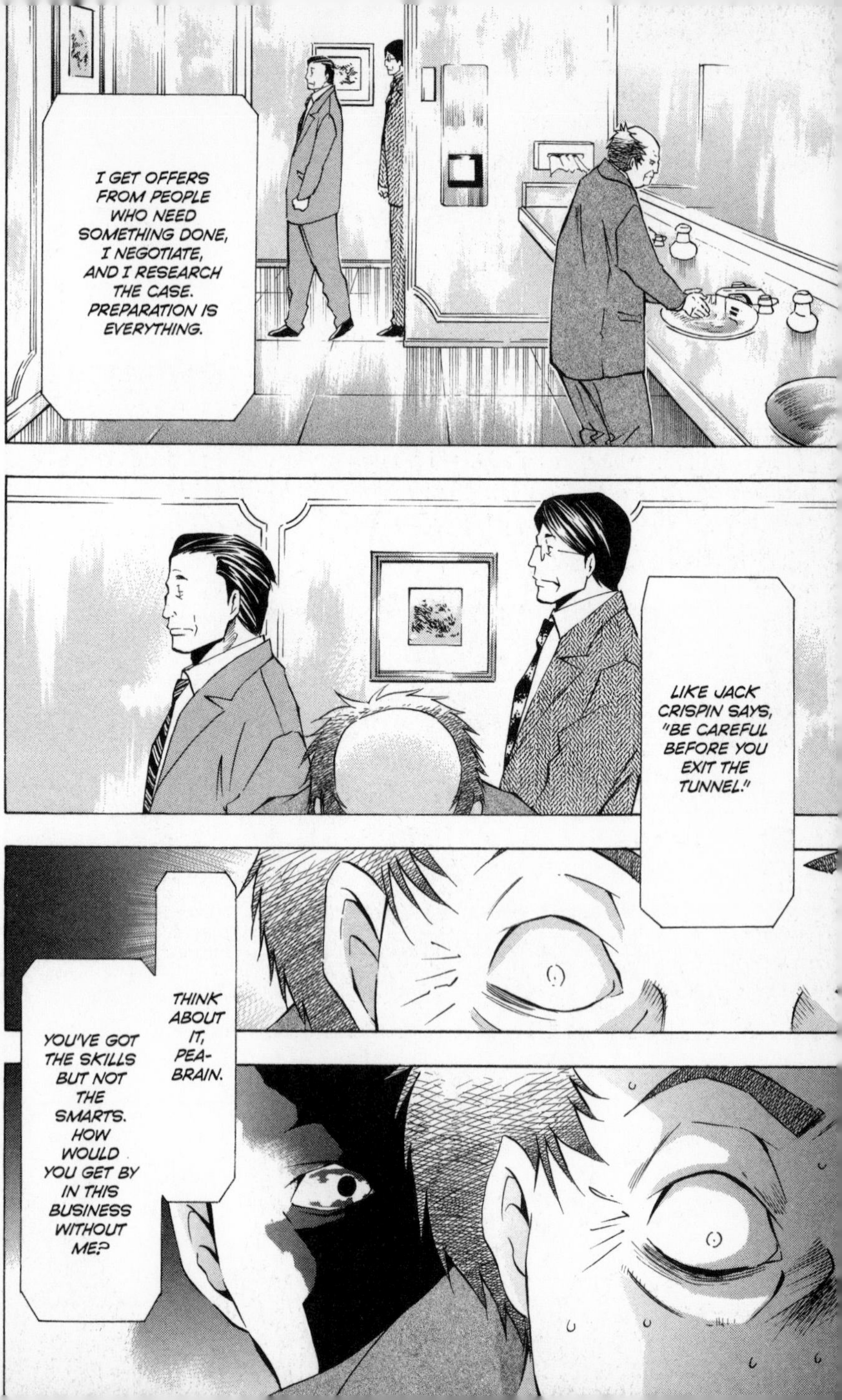
I GET OFFERS FROM PEOPLE WHO NEED SOMETHING DONE, I NEGOTIATE, AND I RESEARCH THE CASE. PREPARATION IS EVERYTHING.
LIKE JACK CRISPIN SAYS, "BE CAREFUL BEFORE YOU EXIT THE TUNNEL."
THINK ABOUT IT, PEA-BRAIN.
YOU'VE GOT THE SKILLS BUT NOT THE SMARTS. HOW WOULD YOU GET BY IN THIS BUSINESS WITHOUT ME?

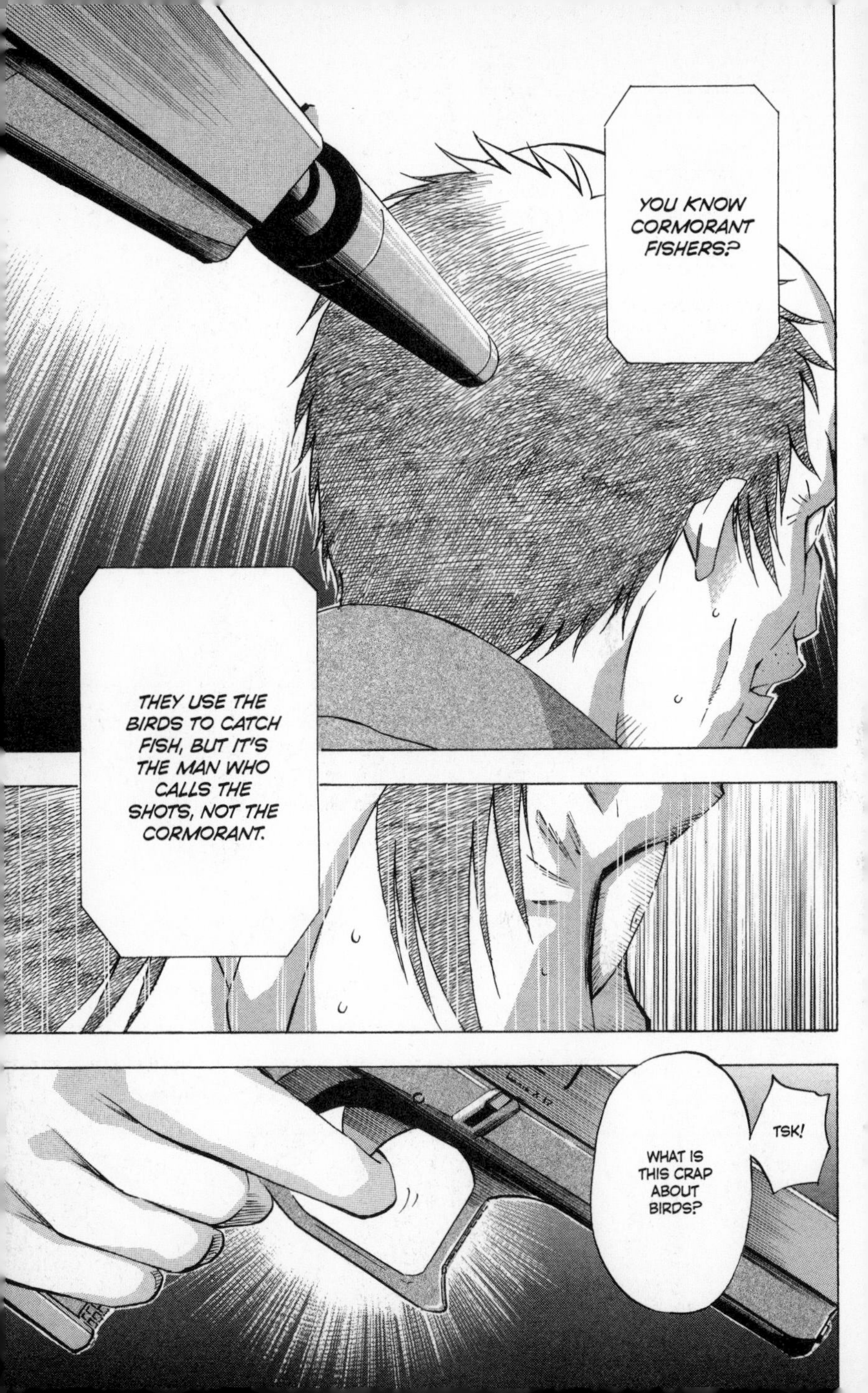
YOU KNOW CORMORANT FISHERS?
THEY USE THE BIRDS TO CATCH FISH, BUT IT'S THE MAN WHO CALLS THE SHOTS, NOT THE CORMORANT.
TSK!
WHAT IS THIS CRAP ABOUT BIRDS?

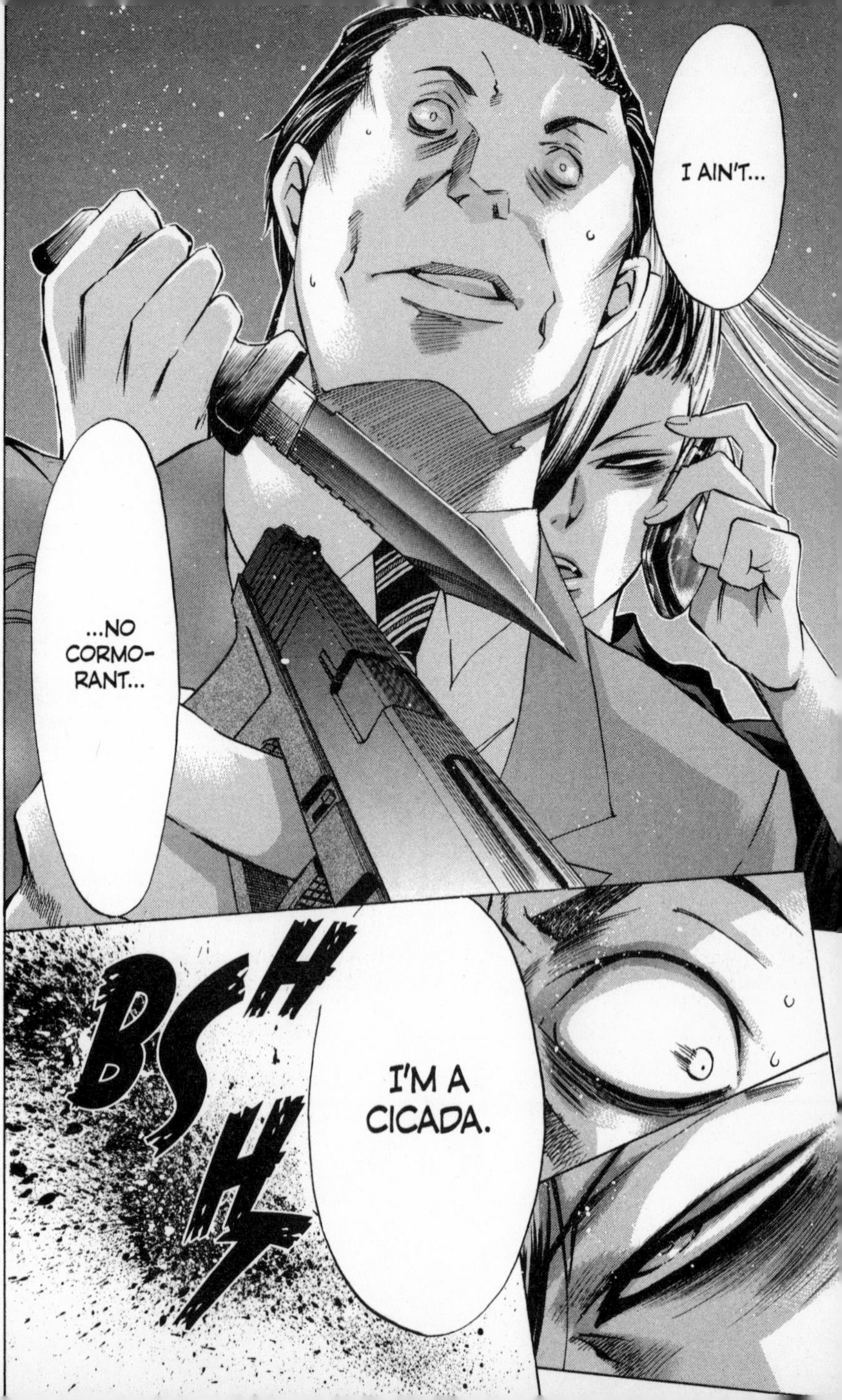
I AIN'T...
...NO CORMORANT...
I'M A CICADA.
BSHH

IT CONTINUES IN Vol.05